Practice and Problem Solving Workbook

PEARSON

Boston, Massachusetts Chandler, Arizona Glenview, Illinois Upper Saddle River, New Jersey

PEARSON

ISBN-13: 978-0-13-318614-7
ISBN-10: 0-13-318614-8

12 13 14 V001 18 17 16

Contents

Chapter 1

Chapter 2

Chapter 5

Chapter 7

Chapter 8

Chapter 9

Chapter 10

Chapter 11

Chapter 12

Name ______________________ Class ____________ Date ____________

1-1 Think About a Plan

Patterns and Expressions

Use the graph shown.

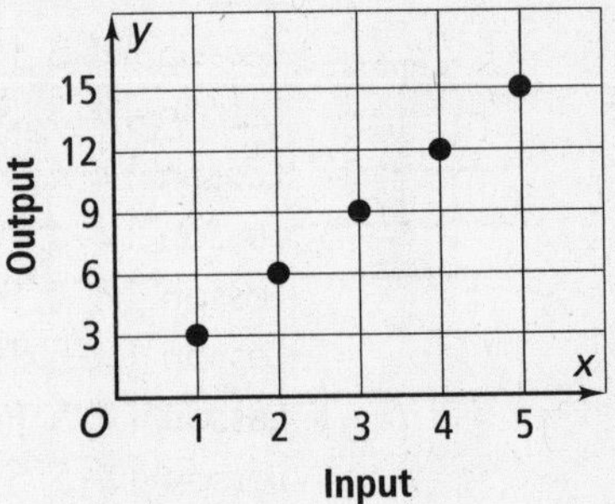

a. Identify a pattern of the graph by making a table of the inputs and outputs.

b. What are the outputs for inputs 6, 7, and 8?

1. What are the ordered pairs of the points in the graph?

____

2. Complete the table of the input and output values shown in the ordered pairs.

Input	Output
1	
2	
3	
4	
5	

3. Complete the process column with the process that takes each input value and gives the corresponding output value.

Input	Process Column	Output
1	1( )	
2	2( )	
3	3( )	
4	4( )	
5	5( )	

4. output = ____________________

5. Complete the process column for inputs 6, 7, and 8. Then find the outputs for inputs 6, 7, and 8.

Input	Process Column	Output
6	6( )	
7	7( )	
8	8( )	

6. The outputs for inputs 6, 7, and 8 are ______________________________

Name ______________________ Class ______________ Date ____________

1-1 Practice

Form G

Patterns and Expressions

Describe each pattern using words. Draw the next figure in each pattern.

1. 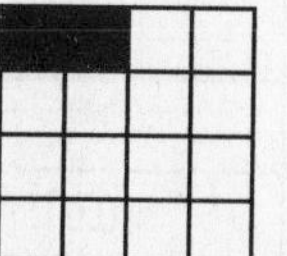 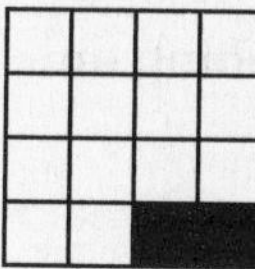

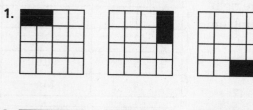

2. 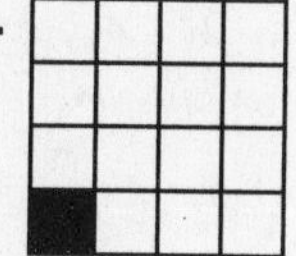 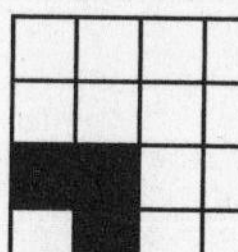 

3.  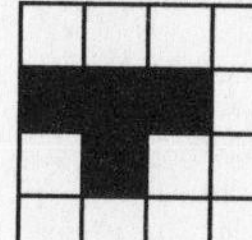 

Copy and complete each table. Include a process column.

4.

Input	Output
1	4
2	9
3	14
4	19
5	
6	
⋮	
n	

5.

Input	Output
1	−2
2	−4
3	−6
4	−8
5	
6	
⋮	
n	

6.

Input	Output
1	0.5
2	1.0
3	1.5
4	2.0
5	
6	
⋮	
n	

7. Describe the pattern using words.

 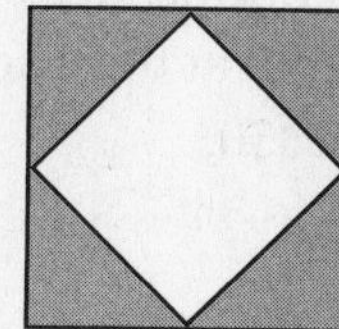 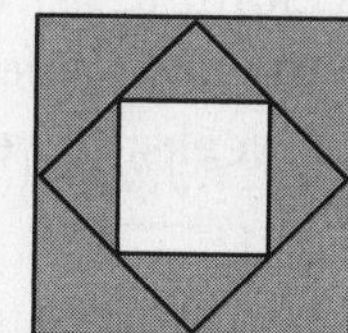 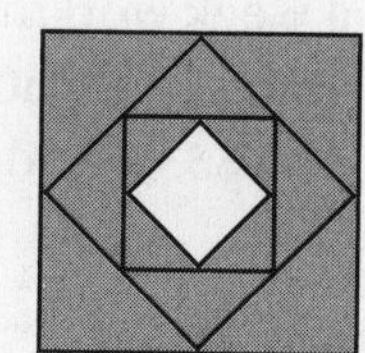

Name ______________________ Class ____________ Date ____________

1-1 Practice (continued)

Form G

Patterns and Expressions

A gardener plants a flower garden between his house and a brick pathway parallel to the house. The table at the right shows the area of the garden, in square feet, depending on the width of the garden, in feet.

Width	Area
1	3.5
2	7
3	10.5
4	14

8. What is the area of the garden if the width is 8 feet?

9. What is the area of the garden if the width is 15 feet?

Identify a pattern and find the next three numbers in the pattern.

10. $-5, -10, -20, -40, \ldots$

11. $5, 8, 11, 14, \ldots$

12. $3, 1, -1, -3, \ldots$

13. $1, 3, 6, 10, 15, \ldots$

14. $\frac{2}{3}, \frac{3}{4}, \frac{4}{5}, \frac{5}{6}, \ldots$

15. $10, 9, 6, 1, -6, \ldots$

The graph shows the cost depending on the number of DVDs that you purchase.

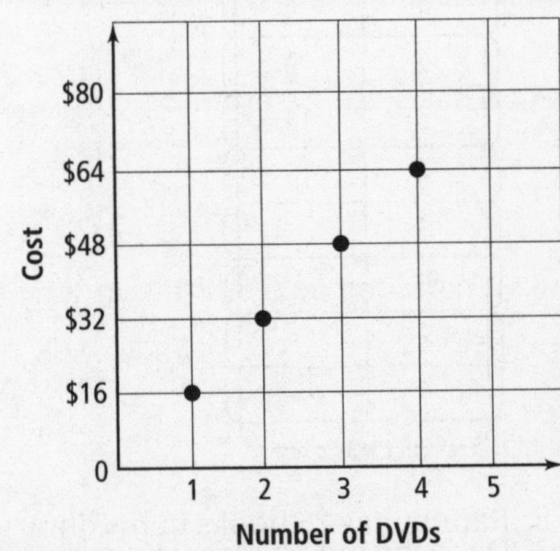

16. What is the cost of purchasing 5 DVDs?

17. What is the cost of purchasing 10 DVDs?

18. What is the cost of purchasing n DVDs?

Keesha earns $320 a week working in a clothing store. As a bonus, her employer pays her $15 more than she earned the previous week, so that at the end of the second week she earns $335, and after 3 weeks, she earns $350.

19. How much will Keesha earn at the end of the fifth week?

20. How much will Keesha earn at the end of the tenth week?

Name ______________________ Class ____________ Date ____________

1-1 Standardized Test Prep

Patterns and Expressions

Multiple Choice

For Exercises 1–5, choose the correct letter.

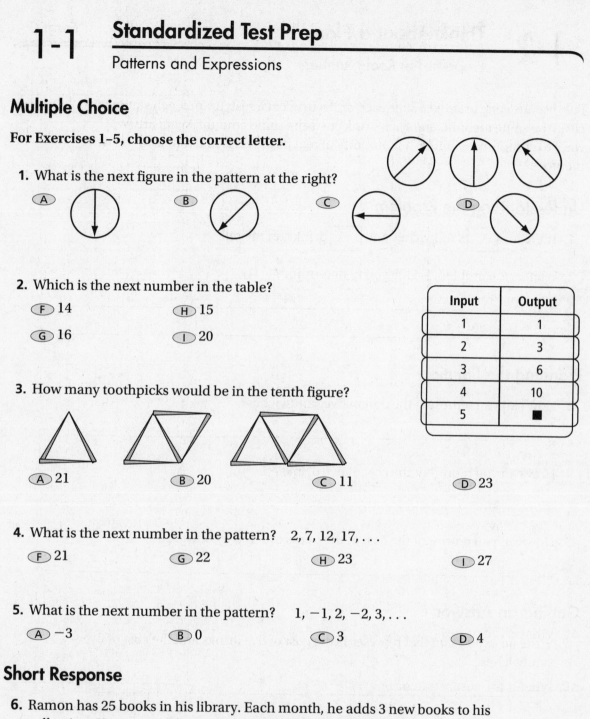

1. What is the next figure in the pattern at the right?

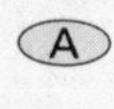 

Ⓑ 

Ⓒ 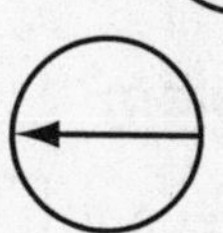

Ⓓ 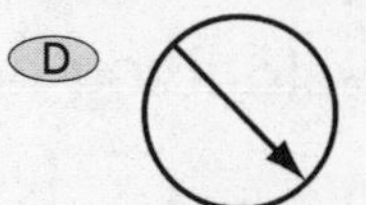

2. Which is the next number in the table?

Input	Output
1	1
2	3
3	6
4	10
5	■

Ⓕ 14 Ⓗ 15

Ⓖ 16 Ⓘ 20

3. How many toothpicks would be in the tenth figure?

 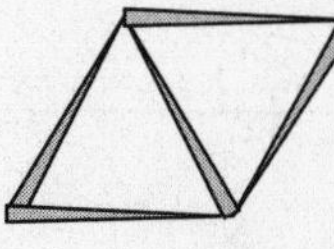 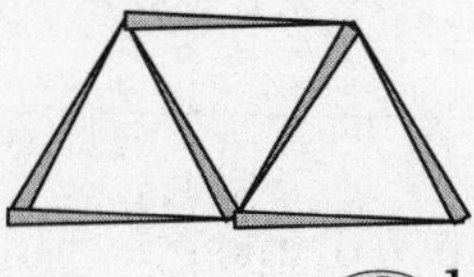

Ⓐ 21 Ⓑ 20 Ⓒ 11 Ⓓ 23

4. What is the next number in the pattern? 2, 7, 12, 17, . . .

Ⓕ 21 Ⓖ 22 Ⓗ 23 Ⓘ 27

5. What is the next number in the pattern? 1, −1, 2, −2, 3, . . .

Ⓐ −3 Ⓑ 0 Ⓒ 3 Ⓓ 4

Short Response

6. Ramon has 25 books in his library. Each month, he adds 3 new books to his collection. How many books will Ramon have after 12 months?

Name ______________________ Class ____________ Date ____________

1-2 Think About a Plan

Properties of Real Numbers

Five friends each ordered a sandwich and a drink at a restaurant. Each sandwich costs the same amount, and each drink costs the same amount. What are two ways to compute the bill? What property of real numbers is illustrated by the two methods?

Understanding the Problem

1. There are ☐ sandwiches and ☐ drinks on the bill.

2. What is the problem asking you to determine?

____

____

Planning the Solution

3. How can you represent the cost of five sandwiches?

____

4. How can you represent the cost of five drinks?

____

5. How can you represent the cost of the items ordered by one friend?

____

Getting an Answer

6. Write an expression that represents the cost of five drinks and the cost of five sandwiches.

____

7. Write an expression that represents the cost of the items ordered by five friends.

____

8. What property of real numbers tells you that these two expressions are equal? Explain.

____

Name ______________________ Class ____________ Date ____________

1-2 Practice

Form G

Properties of Real Numbers

Classify each variable according to the set of numbers that best describes its values.

1. the area of the circle A found by using the formula πr^2

2. the number n of equal slices in a pizza; the portion p of the pizza in one slice

3. the air temperature t in Saint Paul, MN, measured to the nearest degree Fahrenheit

4. the last four digits s of a Social Security number

Graph each number on a number line.

5. -1 **6.** $\sqrt{3}$ **7.** 2.8 **8.** $-2\frac{1}{2}$

Compare the two numbers. Use > or <.

9. $-\sqrt{2}, -2$

10. $4, \sqrt{17}$

11. $\sqrt{29}, 5$

12. $\sqrt{50}, 6.8$

13. $11, \sqrt{130}$

14. $-6, -\sqrt{30}$

15. $7\frac{1}{2}, \sqrt{67}$

16. $-\sqrt{10}, -\sqrt{12}$

Name the property of real numbers illustrated by each equation.

17. $2(3 + \sqrt{5}) = 2 \cdot 3 + 2 \cdot \sqrt{5}$

18. $16 + (-13) = -13 + 16$

19. $-7 \cdot \frac{1}{-7} = 1$

20. $5(0.2 \cdot 7) = (5 \cdot 0.2) \cdot 7$

Name ______________________ Class ____________ Date ____________

1-2 Practice (continued)

Form G

Properties of Real Numbers

Estimate the numbers graphed at the labeled points.

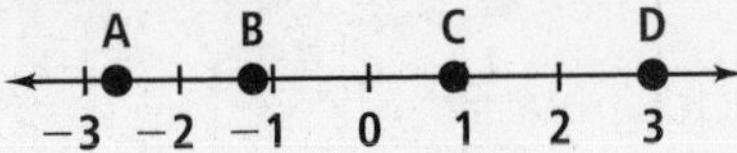

21. point A

22. point B

23. point C

24. point D

Geometry **To find the length of side b of a rectangular prism with a square base, use the formula $b = \sqrt{\frac{V}{h}}$, where V is the volume of the prism and h is the height. Which set of numbers best describes the value of b for the given values of V and h?**

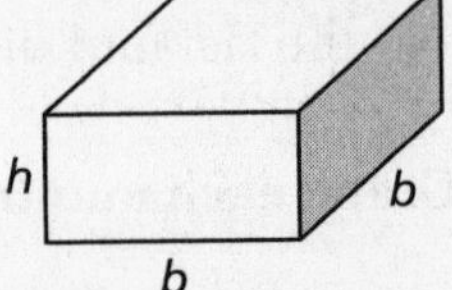

25. $V = 100, h = 5$

26. $V = 100, h = 25$

27. $V = 100, h = 20$

28. $V = 5, h = 20$

Write the numbers in increasing order.

29. $2\sqrt{2}, \frac{4}{5}, -\frac{5}{4}, 0.9, -1$

30. $\frac{5}{8}, -6, \frac{2}{3}, -\pi, -0.5$

Justify the equation by stating one of the properties of real numbers.

31. $(x + 37) + (-37) = x + (37 + (-37))$

32. $x \cdot 1 = x$

33. $x + (37 + (-37)) = x + 0$

34. $x + 0 = x$

Name ______________________ Class ____________ Date ____________

1-2 Standardized Test Prep

Properties of Real Numbers

Multiple Choice

For Exercises 1–5, choose the correct letter.

1. Which letter on the graph corresponds to $\sqrt{5}$?

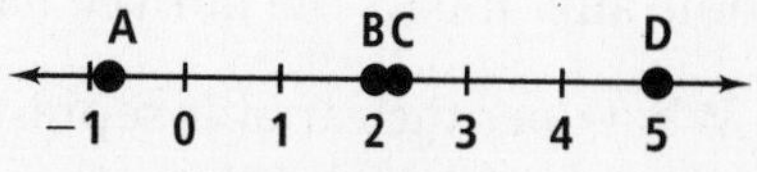

2. Which letter on the graph corresponds to -1.5?

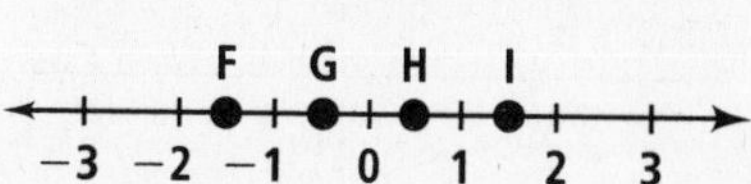

What property of real numbers is illustrated by the equation?

3. $-6 + (6 + 5) = (-6 + 6) + 5$

Ⓐ Identity Property of Addition

Ⓑ Inverse Property of Addition

Ⓒ Commutative Property of Addition

Ⓓ Associative Property of Addition

4. $2(-4 + x) = 2(-4) + 2 \cdot x$

Ⓕ Associative Property of Multiplication

Ⓖ Distributive Property

Ⓗ Associative Property of Addition

Ⓘ Closure Property of Multiplication

5. Which of the following shows the numbers 13, 1.3, $1\frac{2}{7}$, −4, and $-\sqrt{10}$ in order from greatest to least?

Ⓐ 13, 1.3, $1\frac{2}{7}$, −4, $-\sqrt{10}$

Ⓑ 13, 1.3, $1\frac{2}{7}$, $-\sqrt{10}$, −4

Ⓒ 13, $1\frac{2}{7}$, 1.3, $-\sqrt{10}$, −4

Ⓓ −4, $-\sqrt{10}$, $1\frac{2}{7}$, 1.3, 13

Short Response

Geometry The length c of the hypotenuse of a right triangle with legs having lengths a and b is found by using the formula $c = \sqrt{a^2 + b^2}$. Which set of numbers best describes the value of c for the given values of a and b?

6. $a = 3, b = 4$

7. $a = \frac{1}{3}, b = \frac{1}{4}$

8. $a = \sqrt{3}, b = \sqrt{4}$

Name _______________ Class _______ Date _______

1-3 Think About a Plan

Algebraic Expressions

Write an algebraic expression to model the situation.

The freshman class will be selling carnations as a class project. What is the class's income after it pays the florist a flat fee of \$200 and sells x carnations for \$2 each?

1. What does the variable represent?

____

2. How will the class's income change for each carnation sold?

____

3. Will paying the florist increase or decrease their income? By how much?

____

4. Will the expression include both the income for each carnation and the florist's fee? Explain.

____

____

5. Write the expression in words.

The income is [ ] and [ ] times [ ].

6. Write the expression using symbols.

income = [ ] [ ] [ ] [ ] [ ]

7. Check your expression by substituting 300 for the number of carnations. Does your answer make sense? Explain.

____

____

8. The algebraic expression [ ] models the freshman class income.

Name ______________________ Class ____________ Date ____________

1-3 Practice

Form G

Algebraic Expressions

Write an algebraic expression that models each word phrase.

1. seven less than the number t

2. the sum of 11 and the product of 2 and a number r

Write an algebraic expression that models each situation.

3. Arin has \$520 and is earning \$75 each week babysitting.

4. You have 50 boxes of raisins and are eating 12 boxes each month.

Evaluate each expression for the given values of the variables.

5. $-4v + 3(w + 2v) - 5w;\ v = -2$ and $w = 4$

6. $c(3 - a) - c^2;\ a = 4$ and $c = -1$

7. $2(3e - 5f) + 3(e^2 + 4f);\ e = 3$ and $f = -5$

Surface Area The expression $6s^2$ represents the surface area of a cube with edges of length s. What is the surface area of a cube with each edge length?

8. 3 inches

9. 1.5 meters

The expression $4.95 + 0.07x$ models a household's monthly long-distance charges, where x represents the number of minutes of long-distance calls during the month. What are the monthly charges for each number of long-distance minutes?

10. 73 minutes

11. 29 minutes

Simplify by combining like terms.

12. $5x - 3x^2 + 16x^2$

13. $\frac{3(a - b)}{9} + \frac{4}{9}b$

14. $t + \frac{t^2}{2} + t^2 + t$

15. $4a - 5(a + 1)$

16. $-2(j^2 - k) - 6(j^2 + 3k)$

17. $x(x - y) + y(y - x)$

1-3 Practice (continued)

Form G

Algebraic Expressions

18. In a soccer tournament, teams receive 6 points for winning a game, 3 points for tying a game, and 1 point for each goal they score. What algebraic expression models the total number of points that a soccer team receives in a tournament? Suppose one team wins two games and ties one game, scoring a total of five goals. How many points does the team receive?

Evaluate each expression for the given value of the variable.

19. $-t^2 - (3t + 2); t = 5$

20. $i^2 - 5(i^3 - i^2); i = 4$

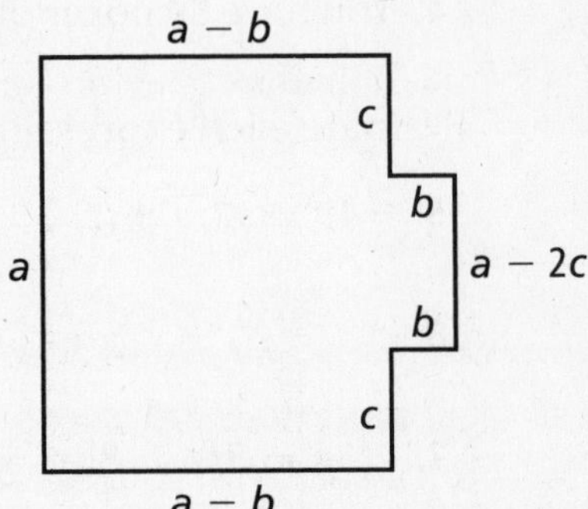

21. Perimeter Write an expression for the perimeter of the figure at the right as the sum of the lengths of its sides. What is the simplified form of this expression?

22. Simplify $-(2x - 5y) + 3(4x + 2y)$ and justify each step in your simplification.

23. Error Analysis Alana simplified the expression as shown. Do you agree with her work? Explain.

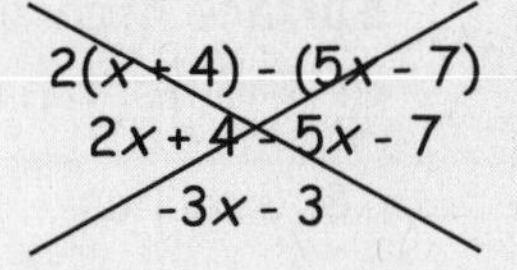

24. Open-Ended Write an example of an algebraic expression that always has the same value regardless of the value of the variable.

Match the property name with the appropriate equation.

25. Opposite of a Difference

A. $-[(-r) + 2p] = -(-r) - 2p$

26. Opposite of a Sum

B. $16d - (3d + 2)(0) = 16d - 0$

27. Opposite of an Opposite

C. $5(2 - x) = 10 - 5x$

28. Multiplication by 0

D. $-(4r + 3s) + t = (-1)(4r + 3s) + t$

29. Multiplication by -1

E. $-(8 - 3m) = 3m - 8$

30. Distributive Property

F. $-[-(9 - 2w)] = 9 - 2w$

Name ____________________ Class ____________ Date ____________

1-3 Standardized Test Prep

Algebraic Expressions

Multiple Choice

For Exercises 1–3, choose the correct letter.

1. The expression $2\pi(rh + r^2)$ represents the total surface area of a cylinder with height h and radius r. What is the surface area of a cylinder with height 6 centimeters and radius 2 centimeters?

(A) 16π cm^2 (C) 32π cm^2

(B) 28π cm^2 (D) 96π cm^2

2. Which expression best represents the simplified form of $3(m - 3) + m(5 - m) - m^2$?

(F) $-2m^2 + 8m - 9$ (H) $-2m^2 - 2m - 9$

(G) $8m - 9$ (I) $-2m - 9$

3. The price of a discount airline ticket starts at \$150 and increases by \$30 each week. Which algebraic expression models this situation?

(A) $30 + 150w$ (C) $30 - 150w$

(B) $150 - 30w$ (D) $150 + 30w$

Extended Response

4. Members of a club are selling calendars as a fundraiser. The club pays \$100 for a box of wall and desk calendars. They sell wall calendars for \$12 and desk calendars for \$8.

a. Write an algebraic expression to model the club's profit from selling w wall calendars and d desk calendars. Explain in words or show work for how you determined the expression

b. What is the club's profit from selling 9 wall calendars and 7 desk calendars? Show your work.

Name ______________________ Class ____________ Date ____________

1-4 Think About a Plan

Solving Equations

Geometry The measure of the supplement of an angle is 20° more than three times the measure of the original angle. Find the measures of the angles.

Know

1. The sum of the measures of the two angles is ☐.

2. What do you know about the supplemental angle?

____

Need

3. To solve the problem, I need to define:

____

____

Plan

4. What equation can you use to find the measure of the original angle?

5. Solve the equation.

6. What are the measures of the angles?

7. Are the solutions reasonable? Explain.

____

____

Name ______________________ Class ____________ Date ____________

1-4 Practice

Form G

Solving Equations

Solve each equation.

1. $7.2 + c = 19$

2. $8.5 = 5p$

3. $\frac{d}{4} = -31$

4. $s - 31 = 20.6$

Solve each equation. Check your answer.

5. $9(z - 3) = 12z$

6. $7y + 5 = 6y + 11$

7. $5w + 8 - 12w = 16 - 15w$

8. $3(x + 1) = 2(x + 11)$

Write an equation to solve each problem.

9. Two brothers are saving money to buy tickets to a concert. Their combined savings is $55. One brother has $15 more than the other. How much has each saved?

10. Geometry The sides of a triangle are in the ratio 5 : 12 : 13. What is the length of each side of the triangle if the perimeter of the triangle is 15 inches?

11. What three consecutive numbers have a sum of 126?

Determine whether the equation is *always, sometimes,* or *never* true.

12. $6(x + 1) = 2(5 + 3x)$

13. $3(y + 3) + 5y = 4(2y + 1) + 5$

Solve each formula for the indicated variable.

14. $S = L(1 - r)$, for r

15. $A = lw + wh + lh$, for w

Solve each equation for *y*.

16. $\frac{4}{9}(y + 3) = g$

17. $a(y + c) = b(y - c)$

18. $\frac{y + 3}{t} = t^2$

19. $3y - yz = 2z$

Name ______________________ Class ____________ Date ____________

1-4 Practice (continued)

Form G

Solving Equations

Solve each equation.

20. $0.5(x - 3) + (1.5 - x) = 5x$

21. $1.2(x + 5) = 1.6(2x + 5)$

22. $0.5(c + 2.8) - c = 0.6c + 0.3$

23. $\frac{u}{5} + \frac{u}{10} - \frac{u}{6} = 1$

Solve each formula for the indicated variable.

24. $V = \frac{\pi}{3}r^2h$, for h

25. $D = kA\left[\frac{T_2 - T_1}{L}\right]$ for T_1

Write an equation to solve each problem.

26. Two trains left a station at the same time. One traveled north at a certain speed and the other traveled south at twice that speed. After 4 hours, the trains were 600 miles apart. How fast was each train traveling?

27. Geometry The sides of one cube are twice as long as the sides of a second cube. What is the side length of each cube if the total volume of the cubes is 72 cm^3?

28. Error Analysis Brenna solved an equation for m. Do you agree with her? Explain your answer.

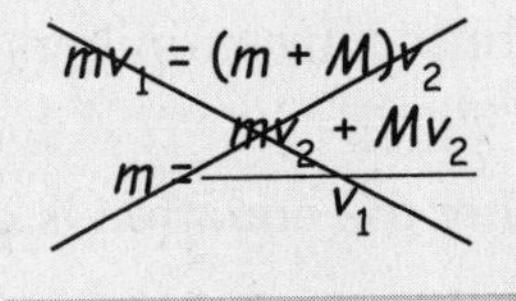

Solve each problem.

29. You and your friend left a bus terminal at the same time and traveled in opposite directions. Your bus was in heavy traffic and had to travel 20 miles per hour slower than your friend's bus. After 3 hours, the buses were 270 miles apart. How fast was each bus going?

30. Geometry The length of a rectangle is 5 centimeters greater than its width. The perimeter is 58 centimeters. What are the dimensions of the rectangle?

31. What four consecutive odd integers have a sum of 336?

Name ______________________ Class ____________ Date ____________

1-4 Standardized Test Prep

Solving Equations

Gridded Response

Solve each exercise and enter your answer in the grid provided.

1. A bookstore owner estimates that her weekly profits p can be described by the equation $p = 8b - 560$, where b is the number of books sold that week. Last week the store's profit was \$720. What is the number of books sold?

2. What is the value of m in the equation $0.6m - 0.2 = 3.7$?

3. Three consecutive even integers have a sum of 168. What is the value of the largest integer?

4. If $6(x - 3) - 2(x - 2) = 11$, what is the value of x?

5. Your long distance service provider charges you \$.06 per minute plus a monthly access fee of \$4.95. For referring a friend, you receive a \$10 service credit this month. If your long-distance bill is \$7.85, how many long-distance minutes did you use?

Answers

1. 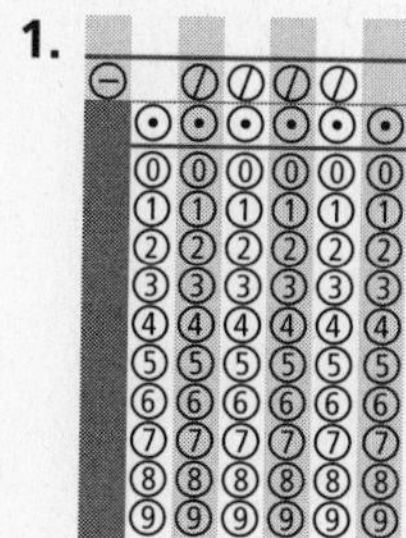

2. 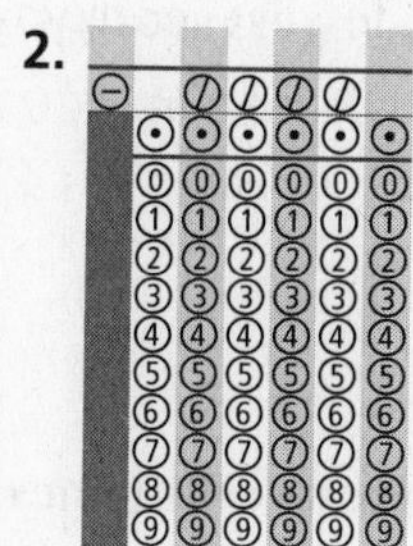

3. 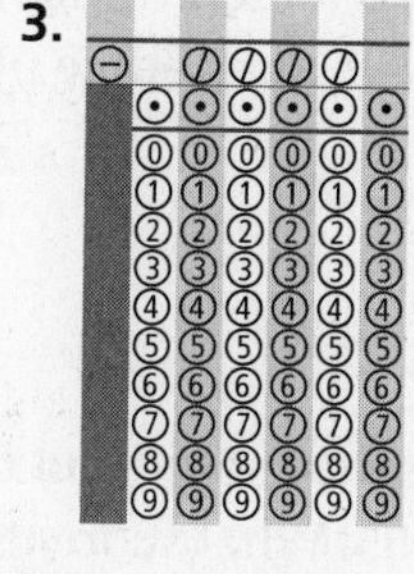

4. 

5. 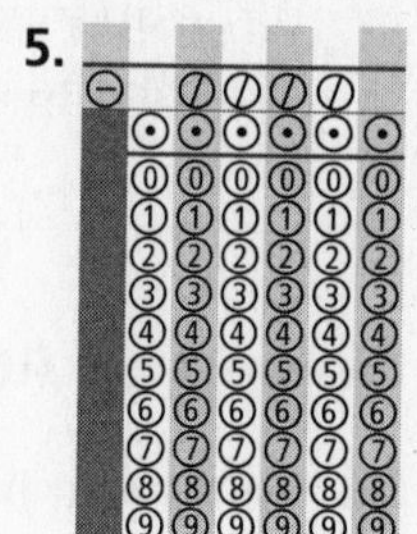

Name ____________________ Class ____________ Date ____________

1-5 Think About a Plan

Solving Inequalities

Your math test scores are 68, 78, 90, and 91. What is the lowest score you can earn on the next test and still achieve an average of at least 85?

Understanding the Problem

1. What information do you need to find an average of scores? How do you find an average?

____

____

2. How many scores should you include in the average? ____________

3. You want to achieve an average that is [ ] or [ ] what score?

____

Planning the Solution

4. Assign a variable, *x*.

____

5. Write an expression for the sum of all of the scores, including the next test.

____

6. Write an expression for the average of all of the scores.

____

7. Write an inequality that can be used to determine the lowest score you can earn on the next test and still achieve an average of at least 85.

____

Getting an Answer

8. Solve your inequality to find the lowest score you can earn on the next test and still achieve an average of at least 85. What score do you need to earn?

Name ______________________ Class ____________ Date ____________

1-5 Practice

Solving Inequalities

Form G

Write the inequality that represents the sentence.

1. Four less than a number is greater than -28.

2. Twice a number is at least 15.

3. A number increased by 7 is less than 5.

4. The quotient of a number and 8 is at most -6.

Solve each inequality. Graph the solution.

5. $3(x + 1) + 2 < 11$

6. $5t - 2(t + 2) \geq 8$

7. $2[(2y - 1) + y] \leq 5(y + 3)$

8. $\frac{1}{3}(7a - 1) \leq 2a + 7$

9. $5 - 2(n + 2) \leq 4 + n$

10. $-2(w - 7) + 3 > w - 1$

Solve each problem by writing an inequality.

11. Geometry The length of a rectangular yard is 30 meters. The perimeter is at most 90 meters. Describe the width of the yard.

12. Geometry A piece of rope 20 feet long is cut from a longer piece that is at least 32 feet long. The remainder is cut into four pieces of equal length. Describe the length of each of the four pieces.

13. A school principal estimates that no more than 6% of this year's senior class will graduate with honors. If 350 students graduate this year, how many will graduate with honors?

14. Two sisters drove 144 miles on a camping trip. They averaged at least 32 miles per gallon on the trip. Describe the number of gallons of gas they used.

Name ______________________ Class __________ Date __________

1-5 Practice (continued)

Form G

Solving Inequalities

Is the inequality *always, sometimes,* or *never* true?

15. $3(2x + 1) > 5x - (2 - x)$

16. $2(x - 1) \geq x + 7$

17. $7x + 2 \leq 2(2x - 4) + 3x$

18. $5(x - 3) < 2(x - 9)$

Solve each compound inequality. Graph the solution.

19. $3x > -6$ and $2x < 6$

20. $4x \geq -12$ and $7x \leq 7$

21. $5x > -20$ and $8x \leq 32$

22. $6x < -12$ or $5x > 5$

23. $6x \leq -18$ or $2x > 18$

24. $2x > 3 - x$ or $2x < x - 3$

Solve each problem by writing and solving a compound inequality.

25. A student believes she can earn between $5200 and $6250 from her summer job. She knows that she will have to buy four new tires for her car at $90 each. She estimates her other expenses while she is working at $660. How much can the student save from her summer wages?

26. Before a chemist can combine a solution with other liquids in a laboratory, the temperature of the solution must be between 39°C and 52°C. The chemist places the solution in a warmer that raises the temperature 6.5°C per hour. If the temperature is originally 0°C, how long will it take to raise the temperature to the necessary range of values?

27. The Science Club advisor expects that between 42 and 49 students will attend the next Science Club field trip. The school allows $5.50 per student for sandwiches and drinks. What is the advisor's budget for food for the trip?

Name ______________________ Class ____________ Date ____________

1-5 Standardized Test Prep

Solving Inequalities

Multiple Choice

For Exercises 1–5, choose the correct letter.

1. What is the solution of $4t - (3 + t) \leq t + 7$?

(A) $t \leq \frac{5}{2}$ (B) $t \leq 5$ (C) $t \leq 2$ (D) $t \leq 1$

2. What is the solution of $-17 - 2r < 3(r + 1)$?

(F) $r > 4$ (G) $r > -20$ (H) $r < -4$ (I) $r > -4$

3. Which graph best represents the solution of $\frac{3}{4}(m + 4) > m + 3$?

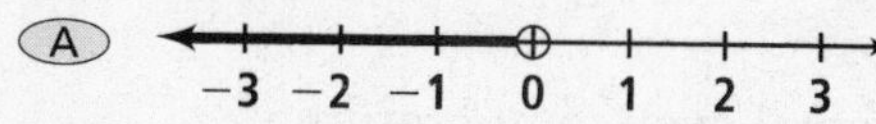

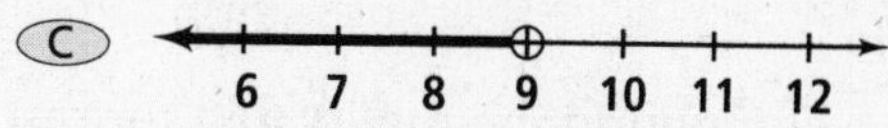

(A)
−3 −2 −1 0 1 2 3

(C)
6 7 8 9 10 11 12

(B)
−3 −2 −1 0 1 2 3

(D)
−3 −2 −1 0 1 2 3

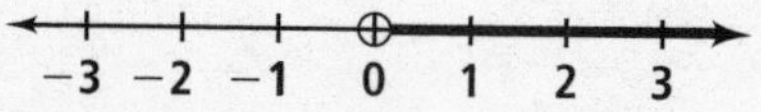

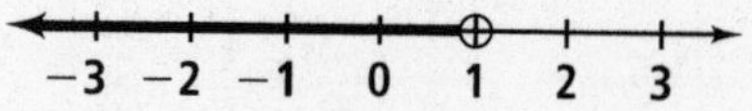

4. What is the solution of the compound inequality $4x < -8$ or $9x > 18$?

(F) $x < 2$ or $x > -2$

(H) $x > 2$

(G) $x < -2$

(I) $x < -2$ or $x > 2$

5. What is the solution of the compound inequality $-2x \leq 6$ and $-3x > -27$?

(A) $x \leq -3$ and $x > 9$

(C) $x \geq -3$ and $x < 9$

(B) $x \geq 3$ and $x < -9$

(D) $x \leq 3$ and $x > -9$

Short Response

6. Geometry The lengths of the sides of a triangle are in the ratio 3 : 4 : 5. Describe the length of the longest side if the perimeter is not more than 72 in.

7. Between 8.5% and 9.4% of the city's population uses the municipal transit system daily. According to the latest census, the city's population is 785,000. How many people use the transit system daily?

Name ______________________ Class ____________ Date ____________

1-6 Think About a Plan

Absolute Value Equations and Inequalities

Write an absolute value inequality to represent the situation.

Cooking Suppose you used an oven thermometer while baking and discovered that the oven temperature varied between +5 and −5 degrees from the setting. If your oven is set to 350°, let *t* be the actual temperature.

1. How do you have to think to solve this problem?

____

____

____

2. Write a compound inequality that represents the actual oven temperature *t*.

3. It often helps to draw a picture. Graph this compound inequality on a number line.

4. What is the definition of tolerance?

____

____

____

5. What is the tolerance of the oven? ________

6. Use the tolerance to write an inequality without absolute values.

7. Rewrite the inequality as an absolute value inequality.

Name ______________________ Class ____________ Date ____________

1-6 Practice

Form G

Absolute Value Equations and Inequalities

Solve each equation. Check your answers.

1. $|-3x| = 18$

2. $|5y| = 35$

3. $|t + 5| = 8$

4. $3|z + 7| = 12$

5. $|2x - 1| = 5$

6. $|4 - 2y| + 5 = 9$

Solve each equation. Check for extraneous solutions.

7. $|x + 5| = 3x - 7$

8. $|2t - 3| = 3t - 2$

9. $|4w + 3| - 2 = 5$

10. $2|z + 1| - 3 = z - 2$

Solve each inequality. Graph the solution.

11. $5|y + 3| < 15$

12. $|2t - 3| \leq 5$

13. $|4b| - 3 > 9$

14. $\frac{1}{2}|2w - 1| - 3 \geq 1$

15. $2|4x + 1| - 5 \leq 1$

16. $|3z - 2| + 5 > 9$

Write each compound inequality as an absolute value inequality.

17. $-7.3 \leq a \leq 7.3$

18. $11 \leq m \leq 19$

19. $28.6 \leq F \leq 29.2$

20. $0.0015 \leq t \leq 0.0018$

Write an absolute value equation or inequality to describe each graph.

21. 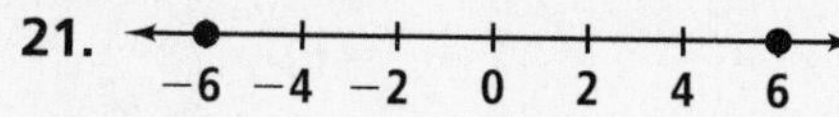

22. −3 −2 −1 0 1 2 3

1-6 Practice (continued)

Form G

Absolute Value Equations and Inequalities

Solve each equation.

23. $3|2x + 5| = 9x - 6$

24. $|4 - 3m| = m + 10$

25. $2|4w - 5| = 12w - 18$

26. $\frac{3}{4}|8t - 12| = 6(t - 1)$

27. $|5p + 3| - 4 = 2p$

28. $|7y - 3| + 1 = 0$

Solve each inequality. Graph the solution.

29. $-3|2t + 1| < 9$

30. $|-2x + 4| \geq 4$

31. $\left|\frac{y + 2}{3}\right| - 1 < 2$

32. $\frac{1}{7}|4z + 5| + 2 > 5$

Write an absolute value inequality to represent each situation.

33. To become a potential volunteer donor listed on the National Marrow Donor Program registry, a person must be between the ages of 18 and 60. Let *a* represent the age of a person on the registry.

34. Two friends are hiking in Death Valley National Park. Their elevation ranges from 228 ft below sea level at Badwater to 690 ft above sea level at Zabriskie Point. Let *x* represent their elevation.

35. The outdoor temperature ranged between 37°F and 62°F in a 24-hour period. Let *t* represent the temperature during this time period.

The diameter of a ball bearing in a wheel assembly must be between 1.758 cm and 1.764 cm.

36. What is the tolerance?

37. What absolute value inequality represents the diameter of the ball bearing? Let *d* represent the diameter in cm.

Name ______________________ Class ____________ Date ____________

1-6 Standardized Test Prep

Absolute Value Equations and Inequalities

Multiple Choice

For Exercises 1–5, choose the correct letter.

1. What is the solution of $|5t - 3| = 8$?

(A) $t = 8$ or $t = -8$

(B) $t = 1$ or $t = -\frac{11}{5}$

(C) $t = \frac{11}{5}$ or $t = -1$

(D) $t = \frac{8}{5}$ or $t = -\frac{8}{3}$

2. What is the solution of $|3z - 2| \leq 8$?

(F) $-2 \leq z \leq \frac{10}{3}$

(G) $-\frac{10}{3} \leq z \leq 2$

(H) $z \leq -2$ or $z \geq \frac{10}{3}$

(I) $z \leq -\frac{10}{3}$ or $z \geq 2$

3. What is the solution of $\frac{1}{2}|2x + 3| - 1 > 1$?

(A) $-\frac{7}{2} < x < \frac{1}{2}$

(B) $x < -\frac{7}{2}$ or $x > \frac{1}{2}$

(C) $x > \frac{7}{2}$ or $x < -\frac{1}{2}$

(D) $x < \frac{1}{2}$ or $x > -\frac{7}{2}$

4. Which absolute value inequality is equivalent to the compound inequality $23 \leq T \leq 45$?

(F) $|T - 11| \leq 34$ (G) $|T - 45| \leq 22$ (H) $|T - 24| \leq 1$ (I) $|T - 34| \leq 11$

5. Which is the correct graph for the solution of $|2b + 1| - 3 \leq 2$?

(A) 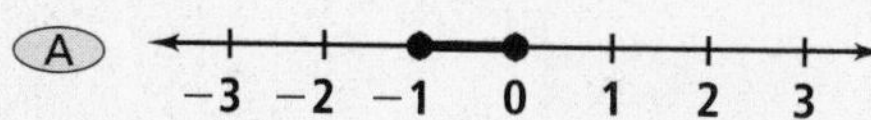

(B) 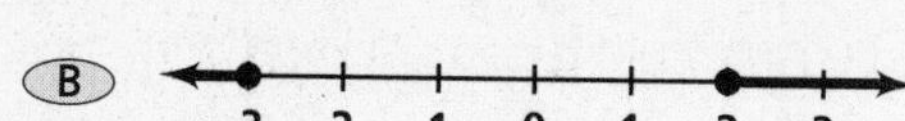

(C) 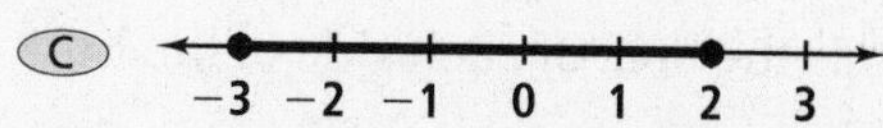

(D) 

Short Response

6. An employee's monthly earnings at an electronics store are based on a salary plus commissions on her sales. Her earnings can range from \$2500 to \$3200, depending on her commission. Write a compound inequality to describe *E*, the amount of her monthly earnings. Then rewrite your inequality as an absolute value inequality.

Name ______________________ Class ____________ Date ____________

2-1 Think About a Plan

Relations and Functions

Geometry Suppose you have a box with a 4×4-in. square base and variable height h. The surface area of this box is a function of its height. Write a function to represent the surface area. Evaluate the function for $h = 6.5$ in.

Understanding the Problem

1. The width of the box is ☐ inches. The length of the box is ☐ inches.
   The height of the box is ☐ inches.

2. What is the problem asking you to determine?

   ____

   ____

Planning the Solution

3. What is the area of the top of the box? What is the area of the bottom of the box?

4. What is the total area of the top and the bottom of the box?

5. What is the area of each side of the box?

6. What is the total area of the sides of the box?

Getting an Answer

7. Write a function to represent the surface area of the box.

8. Evaluate your function for $h = 6.5$ inches.

Name ______________________ Class ____________ Date ____________

2-1 Practice

Form G

Relations and Functions

The table shows the number of gold medals won by United States athletes during the Summer Olympics.

U.S. Gold Medals in Summer Olympics

Year	1988	1992	1996	2000	2004	2008
Gold Medals	36	37	44	40	35	36

1. Represent the data using each of the following:
   a. a mapping diagram
   b. ordered pairs
   c. a graph on the coordinate plane

2. What is the domain and range of this data set?

Determine whether each relation is a function.

3. 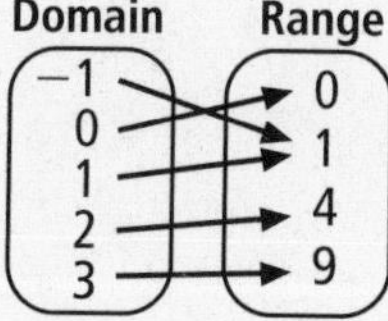

4. 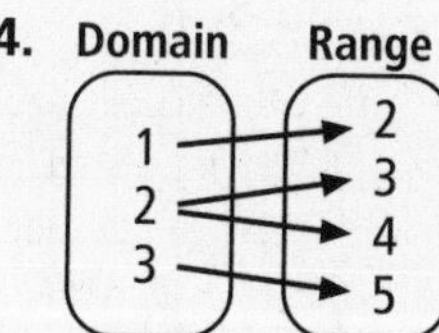

5. 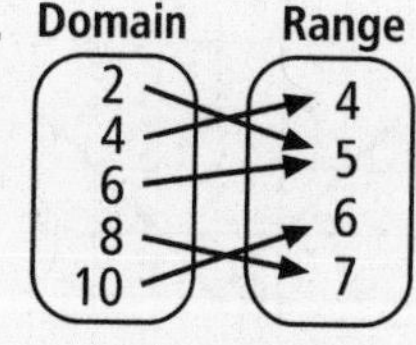

Use the vertical line test to determine whether each graph represents a function.

6. 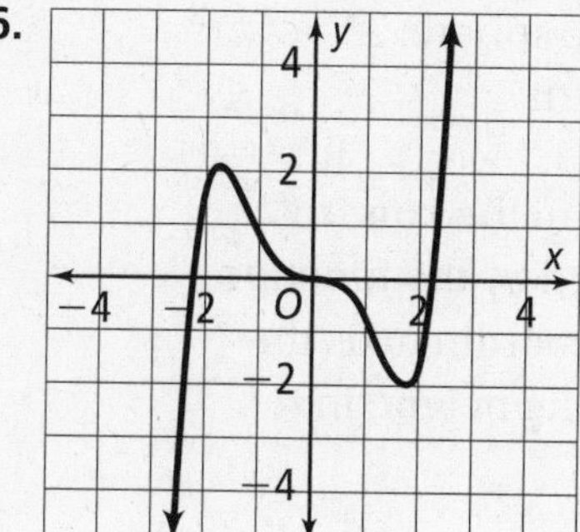

7. 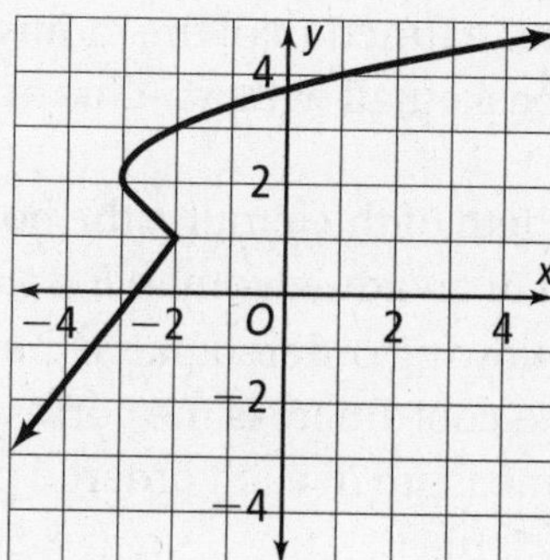

8. 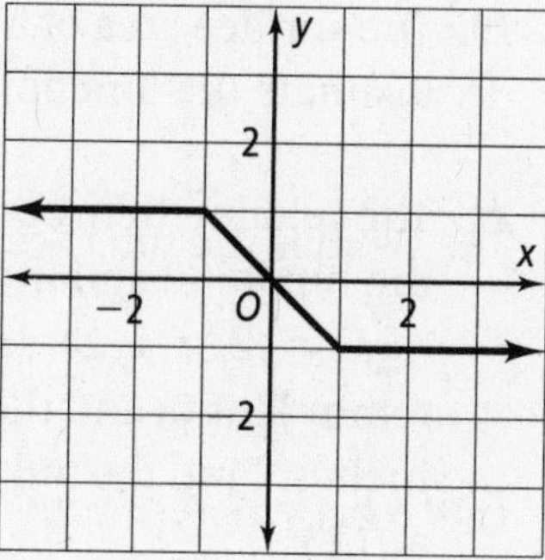

Name ______________________ Class ____________ Date ____________

2-1 Practice (continued) Form G

Relations and Functions

Evaluate each function for the given value of x, and write the input x and the output $f(x)$ as an ordered pair.

9. $f(x) = -3x + 2$ for $x = 3$

10. $f(x) = \frac{1}{2}x - 1$ for $x = -2$

11. $f(x) = 5x - 22$ for $x = 12$

12. $f(x) = -5x - 3$ for $x = -7$

13. $f(x) = \frac{9}{4}x - 15$ for $x = 4$

14. $f(x) = \frac{5}{3}x - \frac{3}{5}$ for $x = 3$

Write a function rule to model the cost of renting a truck for one day. Then evaluate the function for the given number of miles.

15. Daily rental: \$19.95
Rate per mile: \$.50 per mile
Miles traveled: 73 miles

16. Daily rental: \$39.95
Rate per mile: \$.60 per mile
Miles traveled: 48 miles

Find the domain and range of each relation, and determine whether it is a function.

17.

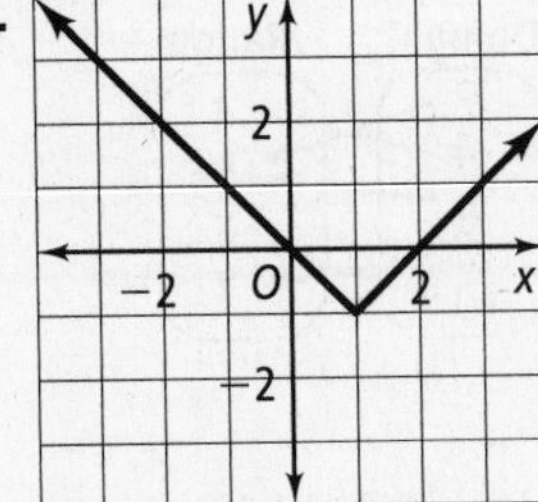

18.

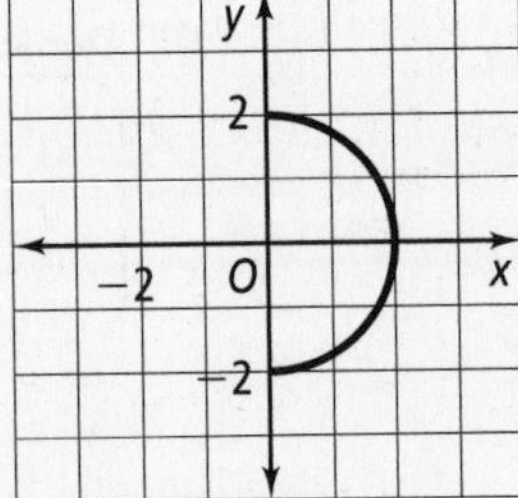

19. The surface area of a sphere is a function of the radius of the sphere: $A = 4\pi r^2$. Evaluate the function for a basketball with a radius of 11.5 cm.

20. The relation between the length of the femur f, the bone from the knee to the hip joint, and the height of an adult woman h is modeled by the function $h(f) = 2.3f + 24$. In the following ordered pairs, the first coordinate is the femur length and the second coordinate is the corresponding height, in inches. Find the unknown measure in each ordered pair.

a. $(13, t)$ **b.** $(14.5, p)$ **c.** $(m, 56.2)$ **d.** $(n, 72.3)$

Name ______________________ Class ____________ Date ____________

2-1 Standardized Test Prep

Relations and Functions

Multiple Choice

For Exercises 1–4, choose the correct letter.

1. Which relations are functions?

I.

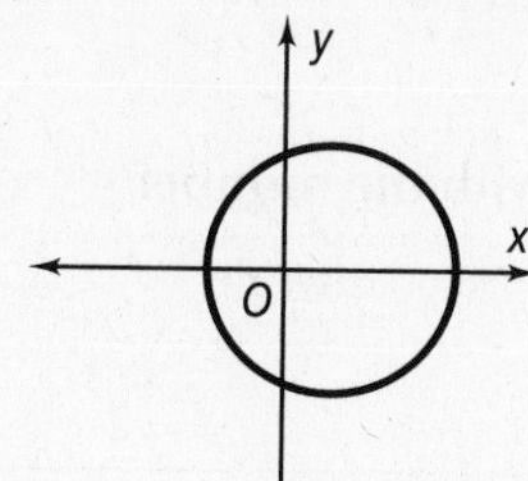

III.

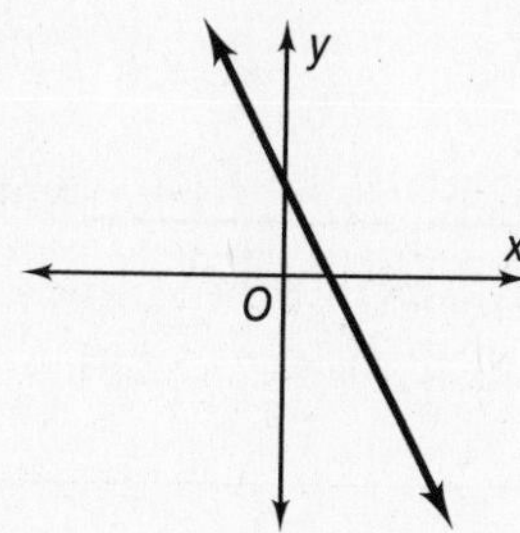

II.

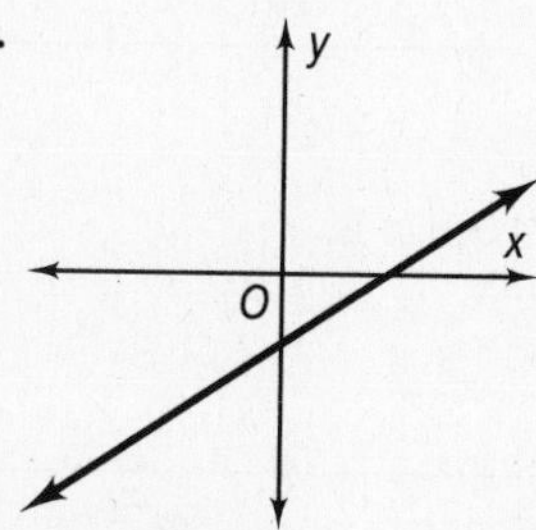

IV.

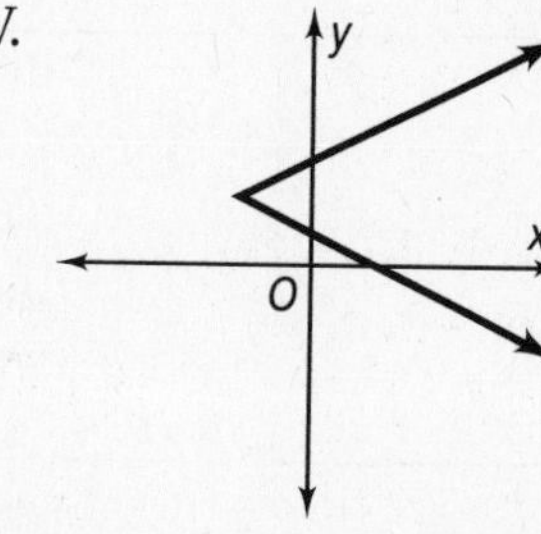

Ⓐ II and III Ⓑ I and II Ⓒ III and IV Ⓓ I and IV

2. Which point could not be part of a function that includes $(3, -1)$, $(4, 2)$, $(5, 4)$, $(-2, 0)$, and $(8, -3)$?

Ⓕ $(6, -7)$ Ⓖ $(3, -2)$ Ⓗ $(7, 4)$ Ⓘ $(2, 2)$

3. For the function $f(x) = -4x - 3$, which of the following is $f(-2)$?

Ⓐ -11 Ⓑ -2 Ⓒ 5 Ⓓ 11

4. What is the domain of the relation given by the ordered pairs?

$$(2, -1), (-4, 1), (-2, -1), (3, -3), (2, 3)$$

Ⓕ $\{-3, -2, 1, 3\}$ Ⓖ $\{-4, -2, 2, 3\}$ Ⓗ $\{-3, -1, 1, 3\}$ Ⓘ $\{-4, -1, 1, 3\}$

Short Response

5. A phone store employee earns a salary of $450 per week plus 10% commission on her weekly sales.

a. What function rule models the employee's weekly earnings?

b. If the employee earned $570 in a week, what was the amount of her sales for that week?

Name ______________________ Class ____________ Date ____________

2-2 Think About a Plan

Direct Variation

Sports The number of rotations of a bicycle wheel varies directly with the number of pedal strokes. Suppose that in the bicycle's lowest gear, 6 pedal strokes move the cyclist about 357 in. In the same gear, how many pedal strokes are needed to move 100 ft?

Know

1. The number of ______________________ varies directly with the number of ______________.

2. ____

____

Need

3. To solve the problem I need to:

____

____

____

Plan

4. Write an equation of direct variation to model the situation. Find the constant of variation.

5. Substitute for one variable and the constant of variation in the equation of direct variation.

6. What does the solution mean?

____

7. Is the solution reasonable? Explain.

____

____

Name ______________________ Class ____________ Date ____________

2-2 Practice

Direct Variation

Form G

For each function, determine whether *y* varies directly with *x*. If so, find the constant of variation and write the function rule.

1.

x	y
−6	−2
9	3
21	7

2.

x	y
2	8
3	12
5	20

3.

x	y
7	56
11	22
16	32

Determine whether *y* varies directly with *x*. If so, find the constant of variation.

4. $y = \frac{4}{9}x$

5. $y = -1.2x$

6. $y + 4x = 0$

7. $y - 3x = 1$

8. $y = 3x$

9. $y + 2 = x$

For Exercises 10–13, *y* varies directly with *x*.

10. If $y = 3$ when $x = -9$, find x when $y = 5$.

11. If $y = -14$ when $x = -7$, find x when $y = 22$.

12. If $y = 5$ when $x = 8$, find x when $y = 2$.

13. If $y = 4$ when $x = 14$, find y when $x = -5$.

14. The distance a spring stretches varies directly with the amount of weight that is hanging on it. A weight of 2.5 pounds stretches a spring 18 inches. What is the stretch of the spring when a weight of 6.4 pounds is hanging on it?

15. The amount of lemon juice in a lemonade recipe varies directly with the amount of water. The recipe calls for 8 oz of lemon juice and 32 oz of water. How much lemon juice should you use if you start with 28 oz of water?

Name ______________________ Class ____________ Date ____________

2-2 Practice (continued)

Form G

Direct Variation

Make a table of *x*- and *y*-values and use it to graph the direct variation equation.

16. $y = \frac{1}{5}x$

17. $y = 2^3x$

Write and graph a direct variation equation that passes through each point.

18. $(6, 2)$

19. $(-1.5, 9)$

20. $(-5, 90)$

21. $(7, 3)$

22. $\left(-1, -\frac{2}{3}\right)$

23. $\left(\frac{3}{5}, -\frac{7}{2}\right)$

24. $(10, 25)$

25. $(3, 165)$

For Exercises 26–28, *y* varies directly with *x*.

26. If $y = 3$ when $x = 2$, find x when $y = 5$.

27. If $y = \frac{5}{17}$ when $x = 10$, find y when $x = 5$.

28. If $y = -4$ when $x = \frac{1}{2}$, find y when $x = \frac{2}{3}$.

29. A new hybrid car has a 12-gallon gas tank. On one tank of gas, the owner can drive 540 miles. The number of miles traveled varies directly with the number of gallons of gas the car uses.

a. Write an equation that relates the number of miles traveled with the number of gallons of gas used.

b. How many miles can the owner travel on 9 gallons of gas?

30. On a certain calling plan, a 15-minute long-distance phone call costs \$.90. The cost varies directly with the length of the call. Write an equation that relates the cost to the length of the call. How long is a call that costs \$1.32?

Name ______________________ Class ____________ Date ____________

2-2 Standardized Test Prep

Direct Variation

Multiple Choice

For Exercises 1–5, choose the correct letter.

1. If y varies directly with x and y is 18 when x is 6, which of the following represents this situation?

(A) $y = 24x$ (B) $y = 3x$ (C) $y = 12x$ (D) $y = \frac{1}{3}x$

2. Which function best represents the relationship between the quantities in the table?

x	y
6	4
12	8
21	14
30	20

(F) $x = \frac{2}{3}y - 2$ (G) $x = \frac{2}{3}y + 2$ (H) $y = \frac{2}{3}x$ (I) $y = \frac{3}{2}x$

3. If y varies directly with x and y is 9 when x is 5, what is x when y is -1?

(A) -1 (B) $-\frac{5}{9}$ (C) 1 (D) $\frac{5}{9}$

4. Which equation of direct variation has $(24, -8)$ as a solution?

(F) $y = \frac{1}{3}x$ (G) $y = -3x$ (H) $y = 3x$ (I) $y = -\frac{1}{3}x$

5. Which equation does NOT represent a direct variation?

(A) $y - 4x = 0$ (B) $\frac{y}{x} = \frac{3}{4}$ (C) $y - 4 = \frac{1}{4}x$ (D) $4y = -\frac{1}{4}x$

Short Response

6. You can download a 5 MB file in 2 seconds. The time t it takes to download a file varies directly with the size s of the file. Write an equation of direct variation to represent the situation. How long will it take you to download a 3 MB file?

Name ____________________ Class ____________ Date ____________

2-3 Think About a Plan

Linear Functions and Slope-Intercept Form

The equation $d = 4 - \frac{1}{15}t$ represents your distance (in miles) from home d for each minute of your walk t.

a. If you graphed this equation, what would the slope represent? Explain.

b. Are you walking towards or away from your home? Explain.

1. What does d represent?

____

2. What does t represent?

____

3. Is the equation in slope-intercept form? If not, write the equation in slope-intercept form.

____

4. What units make sense for the slope? Explain.

____

____

____

5. What does the slope represent? Explain.

____

____

____

6. Is your distance from home increasing or decreasing?

____

Name ______________________ Class ____________ Date ____________

2-3 Practice

Form G

Linear Functions and Slope-Intercept Form

Find the slope of the line through each pair of points.

1. (0, 1) and (3, 0)

2. $\left(\frac{1}{2}, \frac{2}{3}\right)$ and $\left(-\frac{3}{2}, \frac{5}{3}\right)$

3. (−3, −2) and (1, 6)

4. (4, −1) and (−2, −3)

5. (3, −5) and (1, 2)

6. (8, 9) and (8, 3)

7. (−3, −3) and (−1, −3)

8. $\left(\frac{1}{2}, \frac{1}{2}\right)$ and (−2, −4)

Write an equation for each line.

9. $m = -4$ and the y-intercept is 3.

10. $m = \frac{2}{5}$ and the y-intercept is $\frac{17}{5}$.

11. $m = 0$ and the y-intercept is −4.

12. $m = -1$ and the y-intercept is 2.

Find the slope and y-intercept of each line.

13.

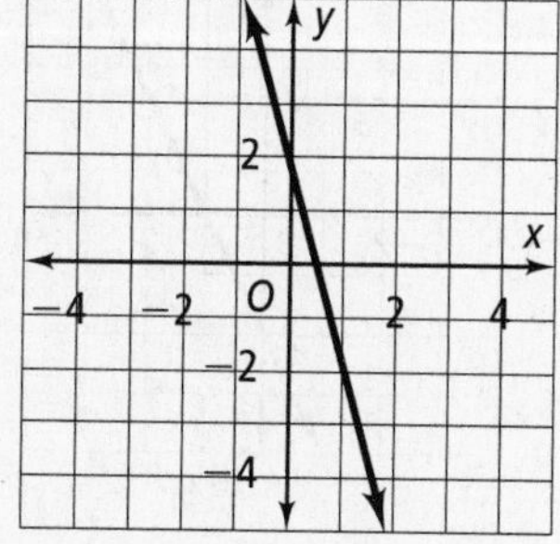

14.

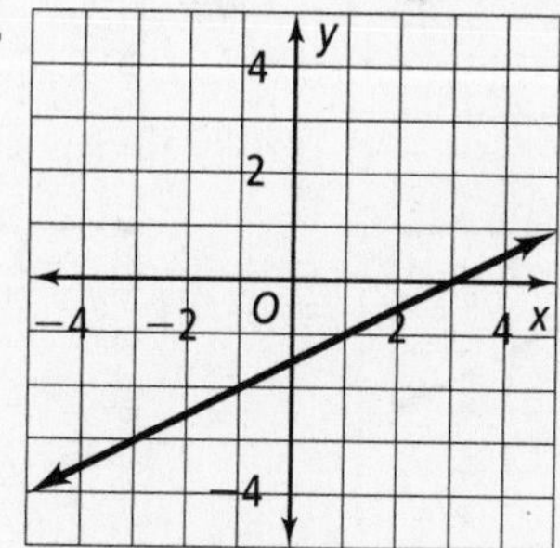

Name ______________________ Class ____________ Date ____________

2-3 Practice (continued) Form G

Linear Functions and Slope-Intercept Form

Find the slope and *y*-intercept of each line.

15. $3x - 4y = 12$

16. $y = -2$

17. $f(x) = \frac{5}{4}x + 7$

18. $x = 5$

19. $4x - 3y = -6$

20. $g(x) = -3x - 17.5$

Graph each equation.

21. $4x + 3y = 12$

22. $\frac{x}{3} - \frac{y}{6} = 1$

23. $y = -\frac{3}{2}x + \frac{1}{2}$

Find the slope and *y*-intercept of each line.

24.

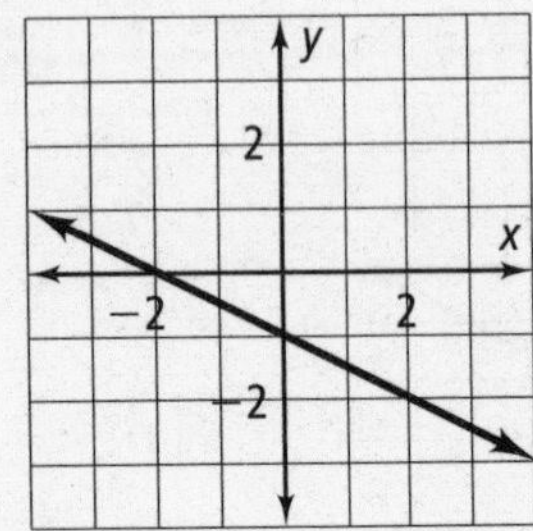

25.

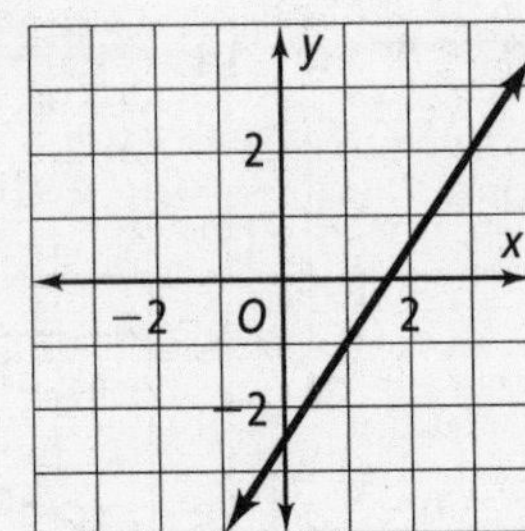

26.

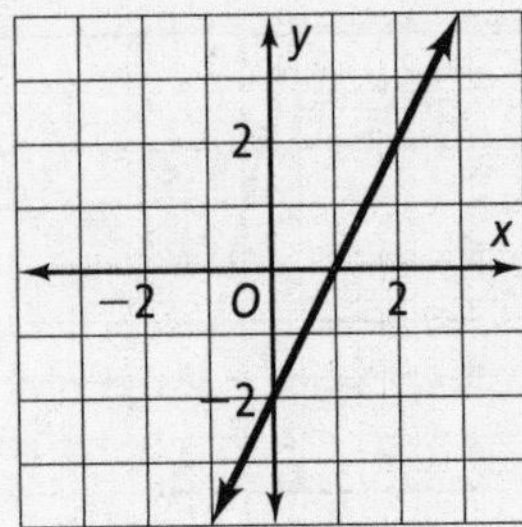

27. The equation $e = 1200 + 11t$ represents your elevation e in feet for each minute t you hike from a trailhead.

a. If you graphed this equation, what would the slope represent? Explain.

b. Are you hiking uphill or downhill? Explain.

Name ______________________ Class ____________ Date ____________

2-3 Standardized Test Prep

Linear Functions and Slope-Intercept Form

Multiple Choice

For Exercises 1–5, choose the correct letter.

1. For the linear equation $5x - y = 2$, which of the following has a value of 5?

(A) the slope (B) the x-intercept (C) the y-intercept (D) the origin

2. What is true about the line that passes through the points $(3, -7)$ and $(3, 2)$?

(F) It is horizontal.
(H) It is vertical.
(G) It rises from left to right.
(I) It falls from left to right.

3. What is the slope-intercept form of $3x + 2y = 1$?

(A) $y = \frac{3}{2}x - \frac{1}{2}$ (B) $y = -\frac{3}{2}x + \frac{1}{2}$ (C) $y = -\frac{2}{3}x + \frac{1}{2}$ (D) $y = \frac{2}{3}x - \frac{1}{2}$

4. What is the y-intercept of the graph of $5x - 9y = 45$?

(F) -9 (G) 9 (H) -5 (I) 5

5. Which of the following is a graph of $4x = -\frac{1}{2}y - 1$?

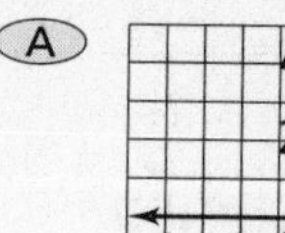
(A)
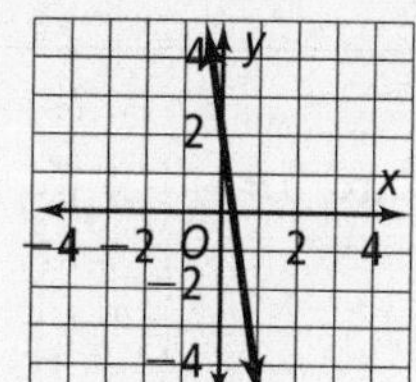

(B)
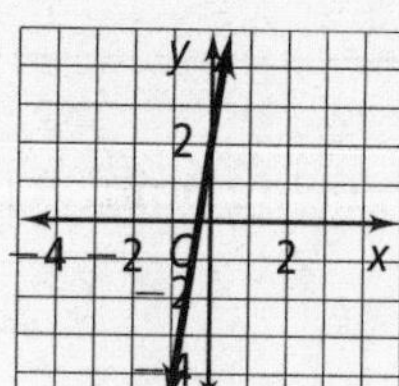

(C)
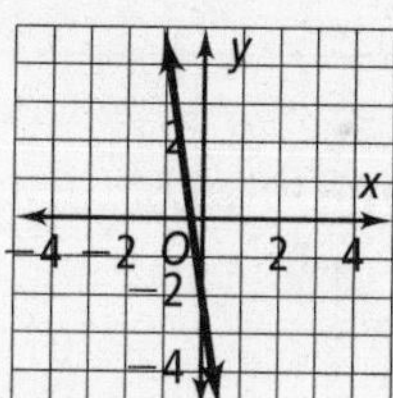

(D)
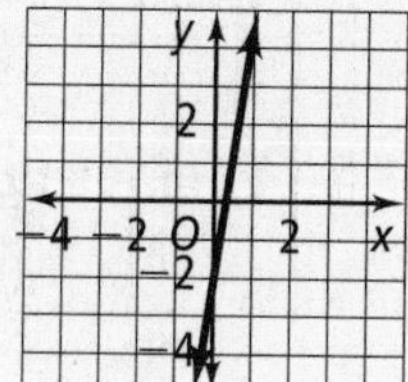

Short Response

Write the equation in slope-intercept form. What are the slope and the y-intercept?

6. $\frac{1}{2}x + \frac{3}{2}y - 1 = 0$

Name ______________________ Class ____________ Date ____________

2-4 Think About a Plan

More About Linear Equations

a. Write the point-slope form of the line that passes through $A(-3, 12)$ and $B(9, -4)$. Use point A in the equation.

b. Write the point-slope form of the same line using point B in the equation.

c. Rewrite each equation in standard form. What do you notice?

1. What is the point-slope form of an equation of a line?

____

2. What is the standard form of an equation of a line?

____

3. What is the slope formula? Use the slope formula to find m.

____

4. Use point A to write the point-slope form. $x_1 = \square$ $y_1 = \square$

____

5. Write the point-slope form of the equation using point A in standard form.

____

6. Use point B to write the point-slope form. $x_1 = \square$ $y_1 = \square$

____

7. Write the point-slope form of the equation using point B in standard form.

____

8. Compare the standard form of the equation using point A with the standard form of the equation using point B.

____

Name ______________________ Class ____________ Date ____________

2-4 Practice

Form G

More About Linear Equations

Write an equation of each line.

1. slope = 2; (2, 1)
2. slope = −1; (2, 0)
3. slope = 0; (−2, 3)
4. slope = $\frac{3}{4}$; (−3, 5)
5. slope = $\frac{5}{9}$; (10, 4)
6. slope = $-\frac{1}{4}$; (0, −1)

Write in point-slope form an equation of the line through each pair of points.

7. (−2, 3) and (2, 9)
8. (0, 7) and (3, 5)
9. (−2, −3) and (2, −1)
10. (−5, −2) and (−3, 8)
11. (−12, 20) and (−21, 29)
12. (11, 8) and (−2, −3)

Write an equation of each line in standard form with integer coefficients.

13. $y = \frac{3}{2}x - \frac{1}{2}$
14. $y = -\frac{3}{2}x - \frac{1}{4}$
15. $y = 4.2x + 1.8$
16. $y = -\frac{4}{5}x + 5$

Find the intercepts and graph each line.

17. $x + 3y = -4$
18. $-5x - 2y = -6$

Name ______________________ Class ____________ Date ____________

2-4 Practice (continued) — Form G

More About Linear Equations

Write and graph an equation to represent each situation.

19. You have a $30 gift card to an online music store. The gift card will allow you to purchase 5 albums.

20. You park your car in a parking garage for 6 hours. Your fee upon exiting the garage is $42.

Write the equation of the line through each point. Use slope-intercept form.

21. through (7, 1) and perpendicular to $y = -x + 3$

22. through (2, 9) and parallel to $y = 3x - 2$

23. through (3, 1) and perpendicular to $-4x + y - 1 = 0$

24. through (−6, 2) and perpendicular to $x = -2$

Graph each equation.

25. $3x + y = 4$

26. $2x + 5y = 8$

27. $-35x - 7y = 56$

28. **a.** Graph $y = 3x + 2$.

b. Write an equation of the line parallel to the line in part (a) passing through the point (2, 0). Graph the line on the same set of axes.

c. Write an equation of the line perpendicular to the line in part (a) passing through the point (0, −4). Graph the line on the same set of axes.

d. What is the relationship between the lines from part (b) and part (c)?

Name ______________________ Class __________ Date __________

2-4 Standardized Test Prep

More About Linear Equations

Multiple Choice

For Exercises 1–5, choose the correct letter.

1. For the linear equation $x - 2y = 10$, which of the following has value 10?

   (A) the slope (B) the x-intercept (C) the y-intercept (D) the origin

2. Which represents the slope of a line that is parallel to a line with a slope of -2?

   (F) $-\frac{1}{2}$ (G) $\frac{1}{2}$ (H) -2 (I) 2

3. Which equation represents a line through $(-2, 1)$ that is perpendicular to $y = -5x + 2$?

   (A) $y = \frac{1}{5}x + \frac{7}{5}$ (B) $y = -5x - 9$ (C) $y = -\frac{1}{5}x - \frac{7}{5}$ (D) $y = 5x + 9$

4. Which equation represents a line through $(-1, 1)$ with a slope of $\frac{2}{3}$?

   (F) $y - 1 = \frac{2}{3}(x + 1)$ (H) $y - 1 = \frac{2}{3}(x - 1)$

   (G) $y + 1 = \frac{2}{3}(x - 1)$ (I) $y + 1 = \frac{2}{3}(x + 1)$

5. Which of the following equations is shown in the graph?

   (A) $y + 2 = -\frac{1}{2}(x + 2)$ (C) $y - 3 = -\frac{1}{2}(x - 6)$

   (B) $y + 3 = -\frac{1}{2}(x + 6)$ (D) $y - 2 = -\frac{1}{2}(x - 2)$

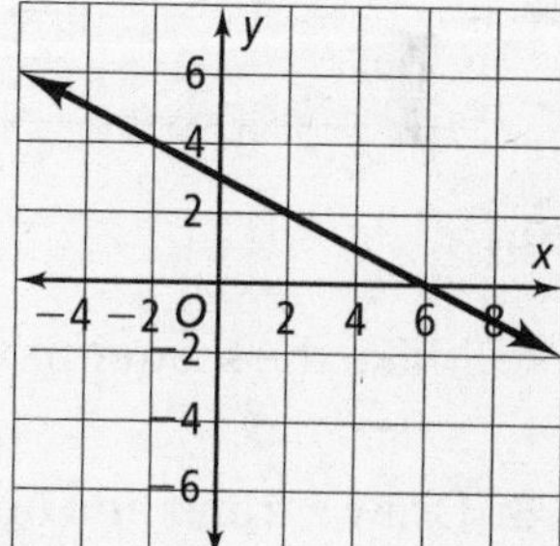

Short Response

6. The line $y = \frac{5}{9}x + 6$ is graphed on a coordinate plane. A second line is drawn on the same plane with a slope of $-\frac{5}{9}$ and y-intercept $(0, -6)$. Write the equation of the second line. Describe the relationship between these two graphs.

Name ______________________ Class ____________ Date ____________

2-5 Think About a Plan

Using Linear Models

Data Analysis The table shows population and licensed driver statistics from a recent year.

a. Make a scatter plot.

b. Draw a trend line.

c. The population of Michigan was approximately 10 million that year. About how many licensed drivers lived in Michigan that year?

d. Writing Is the correlation between population and number of licensed drivers strong or weak? Explain.

Licensed Drivers

State	Population (millions)	Number of Drivers (millions)
Arkansas	2.7	1.9
Illinois	12.4	7.7
Kansas	2.7	1.8
Massachusetts	6.4	4.4
Pennsylvania	12.3	8.3
Texas	20.9	12.8

Know

1. The independent variable should be ______________________.

2. Points to plot: ______________________

Need

3. To solve the problems, I need to ______________________

____

____

Plan

4. Make the scatter plot.

5. Draw a trend line on the scatter plot.

6. How do you find the equation of the trend line? Write the equation.

____

____

7. About how many licensed drivers lived in Michigan that year? ______________

8. What is correlation? Is the correlation between population and licensed drivers strong or weak? Explain.

____

____

Name ______________________ Class ____________ Date ____________

2-5 Practice

Form G

Using Linear Models

Make a scatter plot and describe the correlation.

1. $\{(1, 7), (2, 11), (3, 16), (4, 20), (5, 22)\}$

2. The table shows the percent of people of voting age who reported they voted in presidential election years.

Voting in Presidential Election Years

Year	1988	1992	1996	2000	2004
% of People Who Voted	57	61	54	55	58

SOURCE: http://www.census.gov/population/www/socdemo/voting.html#hist

Write the equation of a trend line, if possible.

3. $\{(1, 2.1), (3, 3.1), (5, 4.0), (7, 5.2), (9, 5.9)\}$

4. $\{(-2, 3.9), (-1, 1.8), (0, 0.1), (1, -1.9), (2, -3.8)\}$

5. The table shows the number of misdirected bags and the number of late flight arrivals by week, for one airline.

Incidents per Week for January

Number of Misdirected Bags	37	42	25	9
Number of Late Arrivals	12	8	28	36

6. The table shows the value of rice produced in Texas from 2001 to 2007.

Value of Rice Produced in Texas

Year	2001	2002	2003	2004	2005	2006	2007
Price per lb	\$.461	\$.416	\$.735	\$.796	\$.777	\$1.00	\$1.13

SOURCE: http://www.nass.usda.gov/Statistics_by_State/Texas/index.asp#.html

a. Use a calculator to find the line of best fit. Let $x =$ the number of years since 2000.

b. Using your linear model, predict the value of rice in Texas in 2015.

c. Using your linear model, predict when the price is likely to reach \$2.60 per pound.

Name ______________________ Class ____________ Date ____________

2-5 Practice (continued)

Form G

Using Linear Models

7. The table shows the percent of the population not covered by health insurance in selected states for the years 1997 and 2006.

Percent of Population Not Covered by Health Insurance

State	Idaho	Illinois	Michigan	Montana	New York
1997	17.7	12.4	11.6	19.5	17.5
2006	15.4	14	10.5	17.1	14

SOURCE: www.census.gov

a. Which variable should be the independent variable?
b. Make a scatter plot. Use a calculator to find the line of best fit.
c. In Wyoming, 15.5% of the population was not covered by health insurance in 1997. Use the equation from part (c) to predict the percent of the population that was not covered in 2006.
d. **Writing** The actual percent for Wyoming in 2006 was 14.6%. Is the line of best fit accurate? Explain.

8. The table shows the numbers of countries that participated in the Winter Olympics from 1984 to 2006.

Winter Olympic Participation

Year	1984	1988	1992	1994	1998	2002	2006
Number of Countries	49	57	64	67	72	77	80

SOURCE: www.infoplease.com

a. Make a scatter plot. Let $x =$ the number of years since 1980.
b. Use a calculator to find the line of best fit and write the equation for the line.
c. Predict the number of participating countries in 2022.

9. The table shows the price per box of fresh Florida oranges from 2001 to 2006.

Florida Oranges

Year	2001	2002	2003	2004	2005	2006
Price per Box	$6.39	$6.99	$7.78	$6.07	$9.27	$8.40

SOURCE: http://www.nass.usda.gov/Data_and_Statistics/Quick_Stats/

a. Make a scatter plot and find the trend line. Let $x =$ the number of years since 2000.
b. In 2007, the price per box of fresh oranges was $16. Does this information follow the trend? Explain.
c. **Reasoning** Is a model invalid if new data does not fit its predictions? Explain.

Name ______________________ Class ____________ Date ____________

2-5 Standardized Test Prep

Using Linear Models

Gridded Response

Solve each exercise and enter your answer in the grid provided.

Use the table and the scatter plot for Exercises 1–4.

U.S. Health Expenditures Drug and Other Medical Nondurables

Year	Expenditures (billions of dollars)
1995	8.9
1996	9.4
1997	10.0
1998	10.6

SOURCE: *The World Almanac and Book of Facts, 2001*

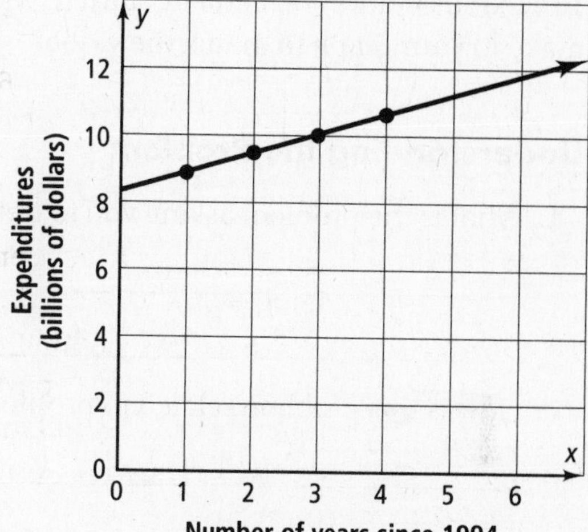

1. What is the y-intercept of the trend line if the trend line using a slope of 0.6 and the point (1, 8.9)?

2. During what year did the U.S. spend $10 billion in health expenditures?

3. Using the points for 1995 and 1997, what is the slope of the trend line? Round to the nearest hundredth.

4. Use the equation $y = 0.6x + 8.3$, where $x = 0$ is 1994. About how many billion dollars would the U.S. have spent on health expenditures in the year 2001, rounded to the nearest tenth?

Answers

1. 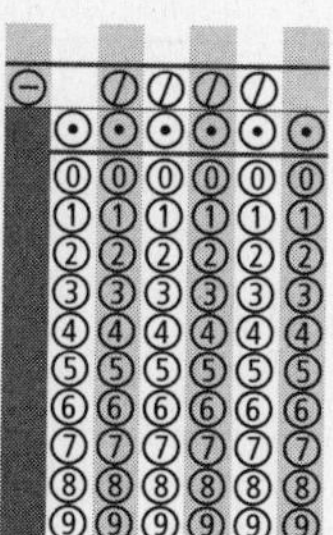

2. 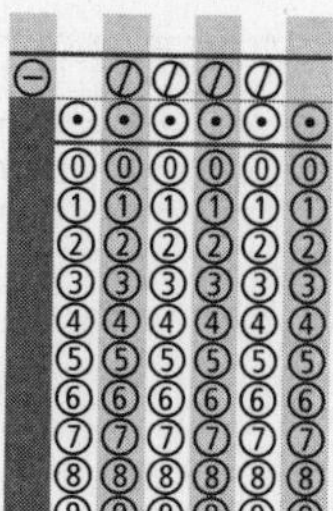

3. 

4. 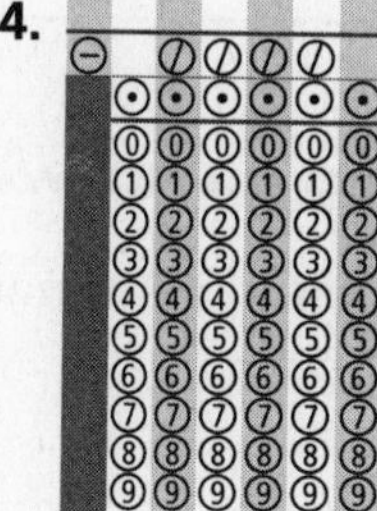

Name ______________________ Class ____________ Date ____________

2-6 Think About a Plan

Families of Functions

Suppose you are playing with a yo-yo during a school talent show. You make a graph of the yo-yo's distance from the auditorium floor during the show. If someone started to take a video of your yo-yo routine when you were introduced, 10 seconds before you actually started, what transformation would you have to make to your graph to match the video?

Understanding the Problem

1. What is the problem asking you to determine?

____

____

2. How is this problem related to problems about parent functions?

____

____

Planning the Solution

3. What quantity is represented by the independent axis in your graph? __________

4. What quantity is represented by the dependent axis in your graph?

____

5. If you graph the routine that you perform, what is represented on the independent axis in your graph? The dependent axis?

____

6. If you graph the routine that you see on the video, what is represented on the independent axis in your graph? The dependent axis?

____

Getting an Answer

7. What transformation would you make to your graph to match a graph of the video?

____

Name ______________________ Class ____________ Date ____________

2-6 Practice

Form G

Families of Functions

How is each function related to $y = x$? Graph the function by translating the parent function.

1. $y = x + 2$

2. $y = x - 1.2$

Make a table of values for $f(x)$ after the given translation.

3. 2 units down

x	f(x)
−2	−7
0	−5
3	−2
5	0
6	1

4. 3 units up

x	f(x)
−2	2
−1	3
0	4
1	5
3	7

5. 1 unit down

x	f(x)
−1	1
1	3
3	5
5	7
7	9

Write an equation for each vertical translation of $y = f(x)$.

6. $\frac{1}{4}$ unit down

7. 5 units up

For each function, identify the horizontal translation of the parent function $f(x) = x^2$. Then graph the function.

8. $y = (x - 5)^2$

9. $y = (x + 1.8)^2$

10. The graph of the function $f(x)$ is shown at the right.
    a. Make a table of values for $f(x)$ and $f(x) - 2$.
    b. Graph $f(x)$ and $f(x) - 2$ on the same coordinate grid.

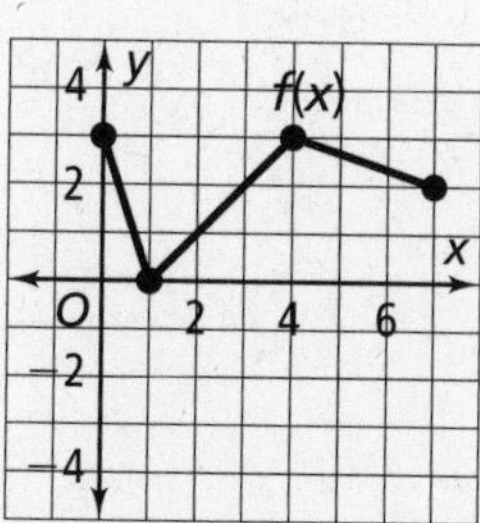

2-6 Practice (continued) Form G

Families of Functions

Write an equation for each transformation of $y = x$.

11. vertical stretch by a factor of 3

12. vertical compression by a factor of $\frac{1}{5}$

Describe the transformations of $f(x)$ that produce $g(x)$.

13. $f(x) = 4x;\ g(x) = \frac{x}{2} - 1$

14. $f(x) = 5x;\ g(x) = -2(5x - 1)$

Write the equations for $f(x)$ and $g(x)$. Then identify the reflection that transforms the graph of $f(x)$ to the graph of $g(x)$.

15. 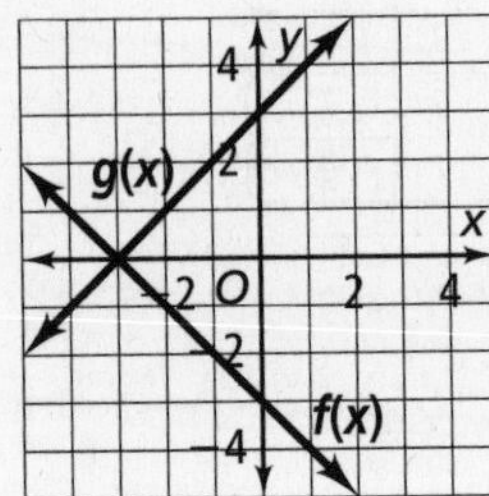

16. 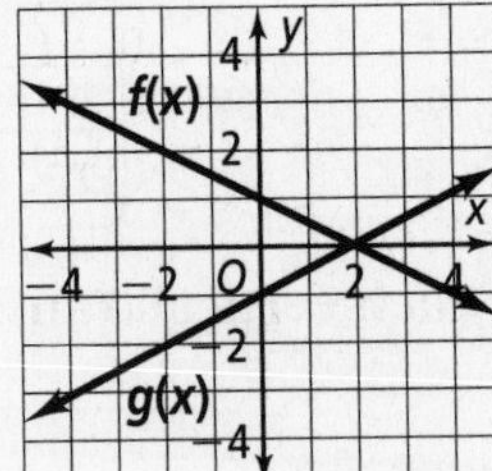

Graph each pair of functions on the same coordinate plane. Describe a transformation that changes $f(x)$ to $g(x)$.

17. $f(x) = x + 3$
$g(x) = x - 2$

18. $f(x) = -x - 4$
$g(x) = x + 1$

Name ______________________ Class ____________ Date ____________

2-6 Standardized Test Prep

Families of Functions

Multiple Choice

For Exercises 1–5, choose the correct letter.

1. Which of the following is the graph of $y = -3x - 6$ reflected in the y-axis and vertically compressed by a factor of $\frac{1}{3}$?

Ⓐ 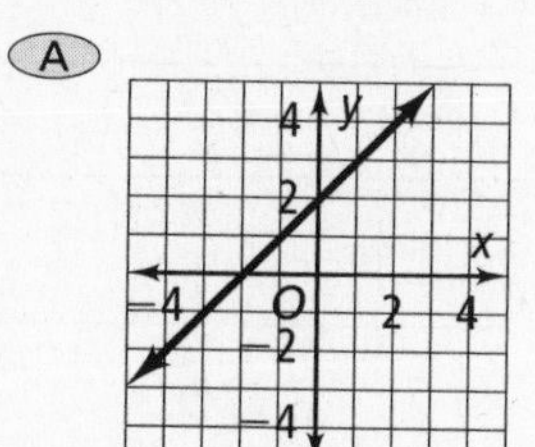

Ⓑ 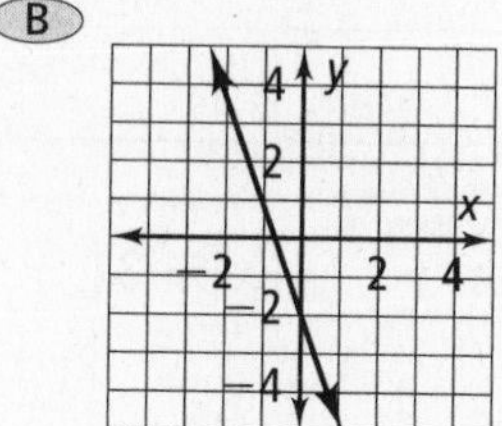

Ⓒ 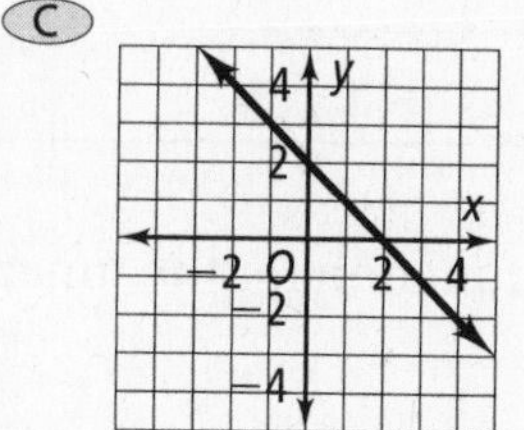

Ⓓ 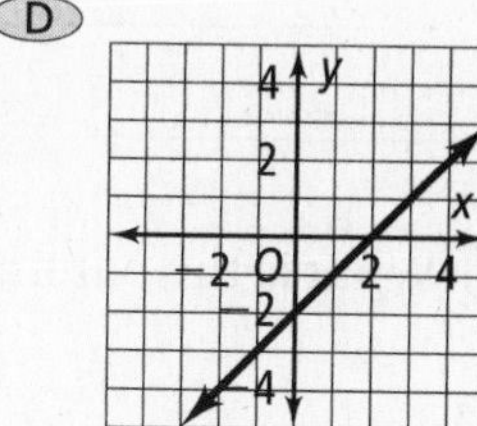

2. The graph of $y = x + 4$ is translated 3 units down. Which point is on the new graph?

Ⓕ $(-2, 5)$ Ⓖ $(0, 8)$ Ⓗ $(1, 5)$ Ⓘ $(-1, 0)$

3. The graph of $y = f(x)$ is reflected in the x-axis and translated 3 units right. Which is the equation of the new graph?

Ⓐ $y = -f(x + 3)$ Ⓑ $y = f(-x + 3)$ Ⓒ $y = -f(x - 3)$ Ⓓ $y = f(-x - 3)$

4. Which equation represents the vertical translation of $y = f(x)$ up 5 units?

Ⓕ $y = f(x) - 5$ Ⓖ $y = f(x - 5)$ Ⓗ $y = f(x) + 5$ Ⓘ $y = f(x + 5)$

5. Which equation represents the horizontal translation of $y = 3x - 2$ to the left $\frac{2}{3}$ units?

Ⓐ $y = 3x$ Ⓑ $y = 3x + \frac{8}{3}$ Ⓒ $y = 3x + \frac{4}{3}$ Ⓓ $y = 3x - \frac{8}{3}$

Short Response

6. How will a vertical compression of the parent function $y = x$ change the graph of the function? Write a new equation that represents this transformation.

Name ____________________ Class ____________ Date ____________

2-7 Think About a Plan

Absolute Value Functions and Graphs

Graph $y = 4|x - 3| + 1$. List the vertex and the x- and y-intercepts, if any.

Understanding the Problem

1. What is the problem asking you to determine?

____

____

2. What is the parent function for the function $y = 4|x - 3| + 1$? ____________

Planning the Solution

3. What do you know about the function $y = 4|x - 3| + 1$?

____

____

4. Graph the parent function.

5. What transformations do you need to apply to the parent function to graph this function?

____

____

Getting an Answer

6. What is the vertex of the function? ____________

7. What are the x- and y-intercepts of the function?

____

8. Graph the function.

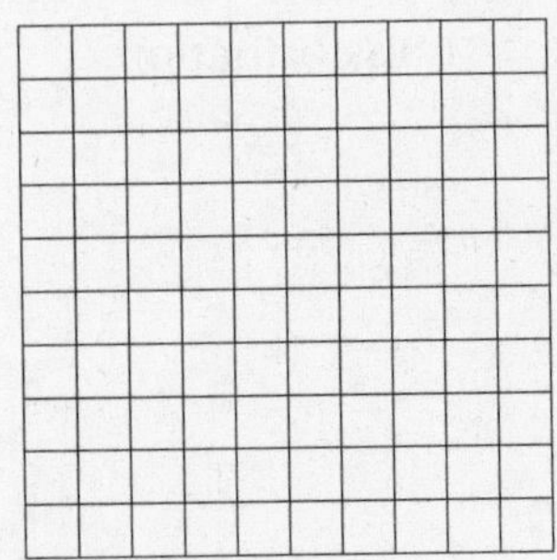

Name ______________________ Class ____________ Date ____________

2-7 Practice

Form G

Absolute Value Functions and Graphs

Graph each equation.

1. $y = |x| - 2$

2. $y = |x| + 3$

3. $y = |x| - 5$

4. $y = |x| - 4$

5. $y = |x - 3| + 1$

6. $y = |x + 1| - 4$

Graph each equation. Then describe the transformation from the parent function $f(x) = |x|$.

7. $y = 2|x|$

8. $y = \frac{1}{4}|x|$

9. $y = -3|x|$

Without graphing, identify the vertex, axis of symmetry, and transformations from the parent function $f(x) = |x|$.

10. $y = |x - 4|$

11. $y = -3|x| - 2$

12. $y = -|3x| + 4$

13. $y = 5 - |x - 1|$

2-7 Practice (continued)

Form G

Absolute Value Functions and Graphs

14. Graph $y = -|x - 4| + 5$. List the vertex and the x- and y-intercepts, if any.

Graph each absolute value equation.

15. $y = |3 - x|$

16. $y = 3 - |x + 1|$

17. $y = -|-x - 2|$

18. $y = -|x| + 2$

19. $y = |3x - 1| - 2$

20. $y = \left|\frac{3}{4}x + 1\right|$

21. $y = \frac{1}{3}|2x - 9|$

22. $y = |x + 1| - 3$

23. $y = -\frac{1}{2}|2x - 4|$

24. a. Graph the equations $y = 2|x + 4| - 1$ and $y = \frac{1}{2}|x - 4| + 1$ on the same set of axes.

b. Writing Describe the similarities and differences in the graphs.

Name ______________________ Class ____________ Date ____________

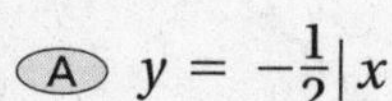

2-7 Standardized Test Prep

Absolute Value Functions and Graphs

Multiple Choice

For Exercises 1–3, choose the correct letter.

1. Which equation has the graph shown at the right?

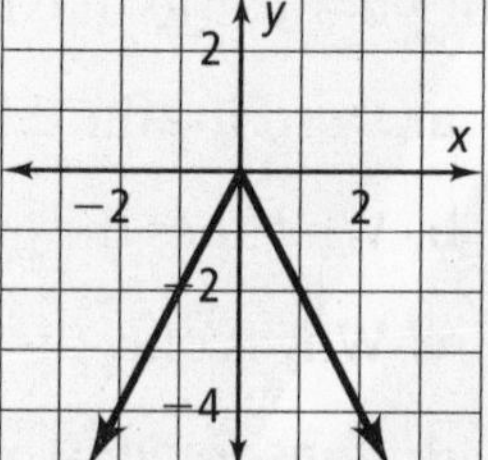

Ⓐ $y = -\frac{1}{2}|x|$

Ⓑ $y = 2|x|$

Ⓒ $y = \frac{1}{2}|x|$

Ⓓ $y = -2|x|$

2. Which statement about the graph of the function $y = -\frac{1}{3}|x + 2| - 5$ is true?

Ⓕ the vertex is at $(2, -5)$

Ⓖ the vertex is at $(2, 5)$

Ⓗ the vertex is at $(-2, 5)$

Ⓘ the vertex is at $(-2, -5)$

3. The graph of which equation is the graph of $f(x) = |x|$ reflected in the x-axis, translated 2 units left, vertically compressed by a factor of $\frac{1}{3}$, and translated up 4 units?

Ⓐ $y = 3|x - 2| + 4$

Ⓑ $y = -\frac{1}{3}|x + 2| + 4$

Ⓒ $y = -3|x + 2| + 4$

Ⓓ $y = -\frac{1}{3}|x - 2| + 4$

Extended Response

4. Determine the parent function of $y = -|x + 4| - 1$. Describe the graph of $y = -|x + 4| - 1$ as three transformations of the parent function. Then graph the parent function and each translation.

Name ______________ Class ______________ Date ______________

2-8 Think About a Plan

Two-Variable Inequalities

The graph at the right relates the amount of gas in the tank of your car to the distance you can drive.

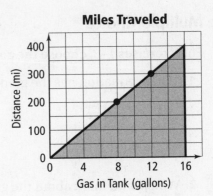

Miles Traveled

Distance (mi): 0, 100, 200, 300, 400

Gas in Tank (gallons): 0, 4, 8, 12, 16

Describe the domain for this situation.

Why does the graph stop?

c. y is only the first quadrant shown?

d. Re oning Would every point in the solution region be a lution?

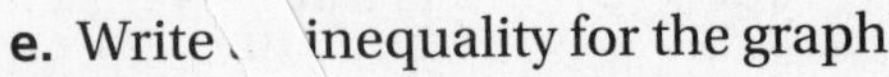

e. Write inequality for the graph.

f. What do the coefficient of x represent?

1. What is the main of a function? ______________

2. What is the do in for this situation?

____

3. What is the upper bo d of the domain in this situation? ______________

4. Why does the graph sto

____

5. What do you know about the and y-values of points in the first quadrant?

____

6. Why is only the first quadrant shown?

____

7. Would every point in the solution region be a solution? Explain.

____

____

8. Write an equation for the boundary line in the graph. ______________

9. Write an inequality for the graph. ______________

10. What does the coefficient of x represent? ______________

Name ______________________ Class ____________ Date ____________

2-8 Practice

Form G

Two-Variable Inequalities

Graph each inequality.

1. $y < x$

2. $y \geq x$

3. $y > 2$

4. $y < 2$

5. $x \leq 2$

6. $-2y \leq -x - 2$

7. $-2x - y < -1$

8. $y \geq 3x - 4$

9. You have a \$25 calling card. Calls made using the card within the United States cost \$.10 per minute while calls made from the US to France cost \$.25 per minute.

a. Write an inequality that relates the number of minutes x you can use for calls within the U.S. and the number of minutes y you can use for calls from the U.S. to France.

b. Graph the inequality.

Graph each absolute value inequality.

10. $y \geq |x|$

11. $y > |x + 2|$

12. $y \leq |x - 2|$

13. $y > |x| + 2$

Write an inequality for each graph. The equation for the boundary line is given.

14. $y - 2x = 4$

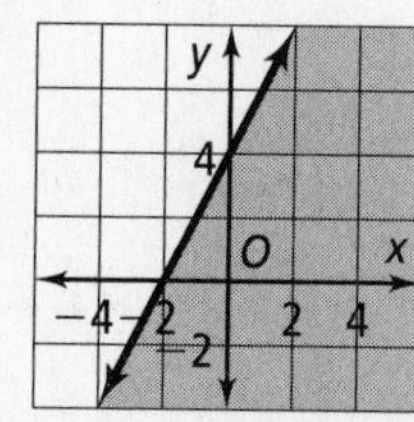

15. $-2x - 3y = 6$

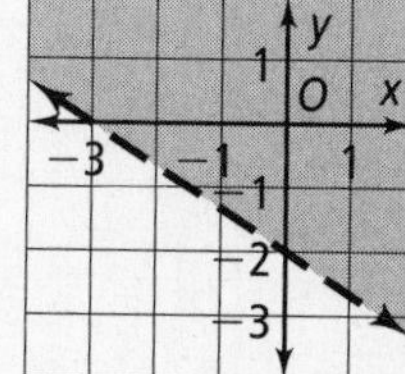

16. $3y = |x - 3|$

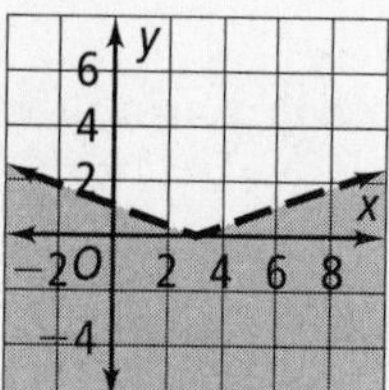

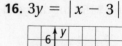

Name ________________________ Class ______________ Date ______________

2-8 Practice (continued)

Form G

Two-Variable Inequalities

Graph each inequality on a coordinate plane.

17. $4x + 2y \leq 8$ **18.** $3x \leq 5y$ **19.** $y > -\frac{1}{6}x - 1$ **20.** $y \geq \left|\frac{1}{6}x\right| - 3$

Write an inequality for each graph.

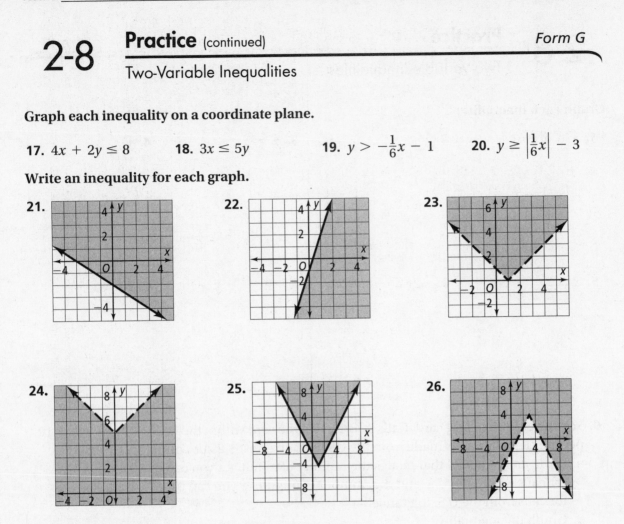

21.

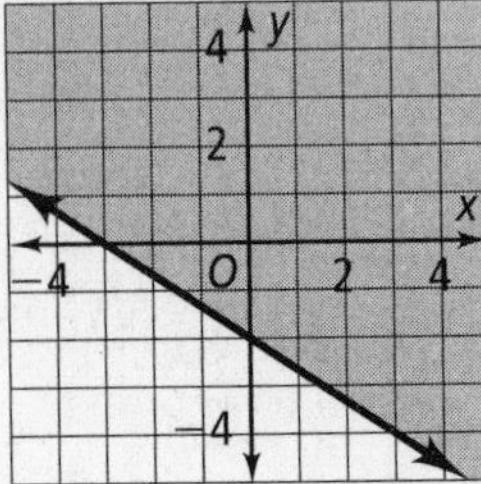

22.

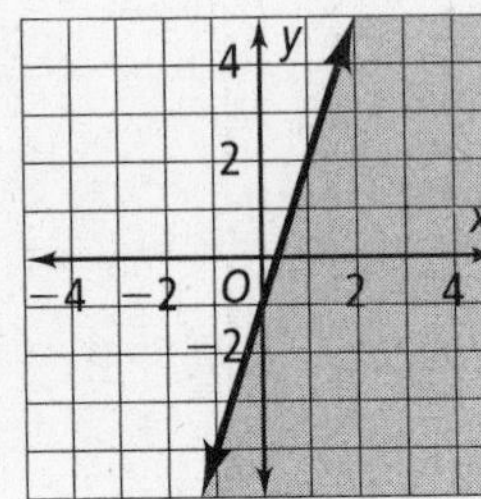

23.

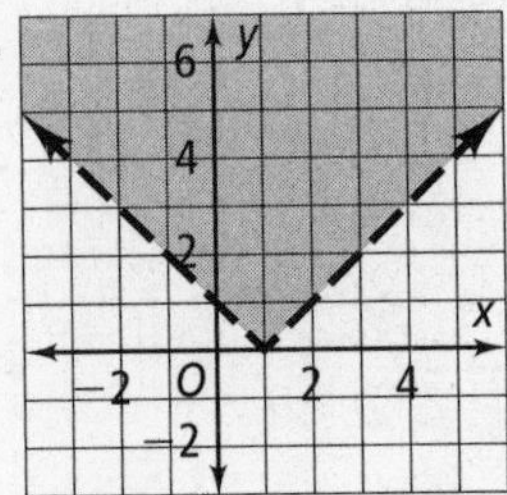

24.

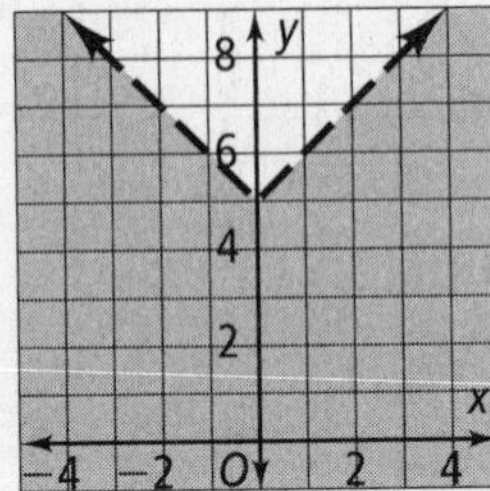

25.

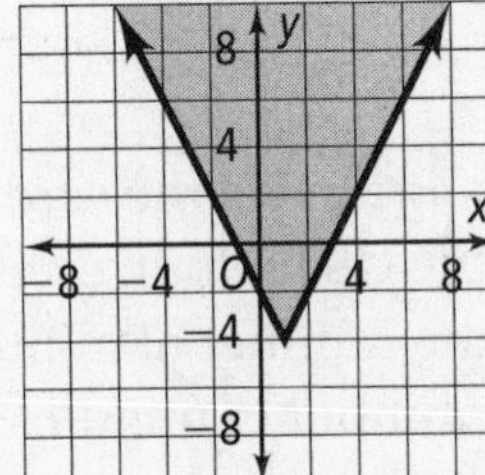

26.

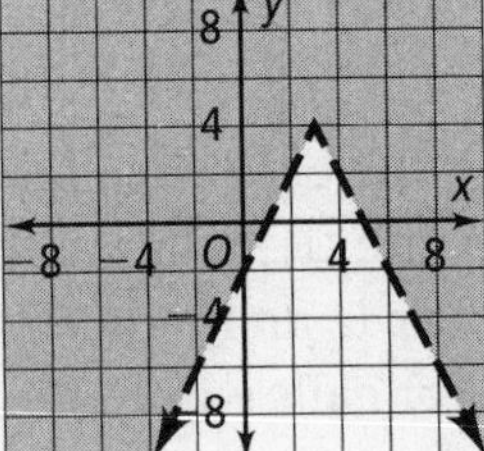

27. Open-Ended Write an inequality that includes (0, 9), (−10, 10), (10, −20), and (−20, 15) as solutions.

28. A salesperson sells two models of vacuum cleaners. One brand sells for \$150 each and the other sells for \$200 each. The salesperson has a weekly sales goal of at least \$1800.

a. Write an inequality relating the revenue from the vacuum cleaners to the sales goal.

b. Graph the inequality.

c. If the salesperson sold exactly six \$200 models last week, how many \$150 models did she have to sell to make her sales goal?

Name ______________________ Class ____________ Date ____________

2-8 Standardized Test Prep

Two-Variable Inequalities

Multiple Choice

For Exercises 1–4, choose the correct letter.

1. Which graph best represents the solution of the inequality $-6x - 2y \leq 4$?

A 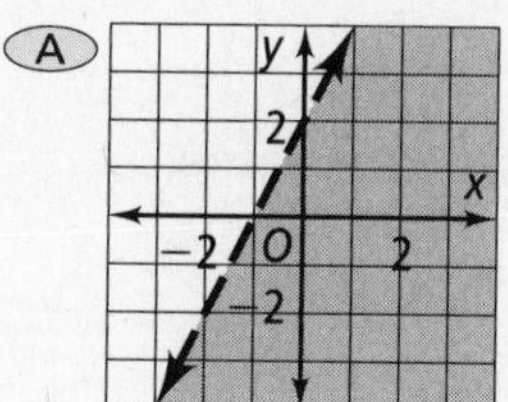

B 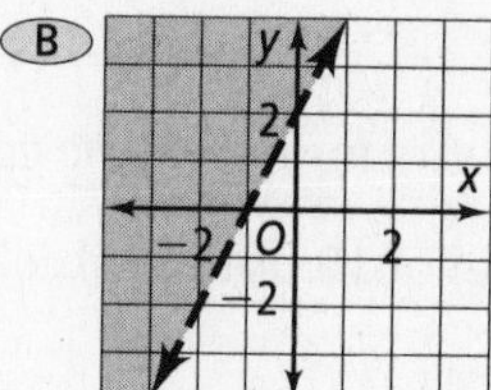

C 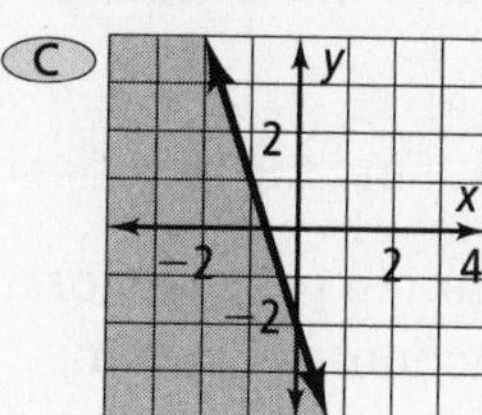

D 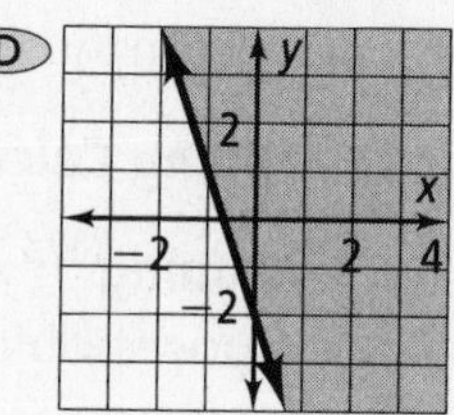

2. Which ordered pair is a solution of $2x - 2y > 8$?

F $(-2, 0)$ G $(2, -4)$ H $(0, -4)$ I $(4, 1)$

3. Which ordered pair is not a solution of $y \geq \frac{1}{2}|x + 2|$?

A $(-2, 0)$ B $(-1, -2)$ C $(0, 2)$ D $(2, 2)$

4. The graph of which absolute value inequality has its vertex at $(1, 5)$?

F $y > |x - 1| + 5$

H $y > -|x + 1| - 5$

G $y > |x + 1| - 5$

I $y > -5|x - 1|$

Short Response

5. Transportation The high school band is expecting to take at least 120 students to a regional band competition. The school rents some passenger vans that can transport 8 students. Other students, in groups of 4, will need to ride in personal vehicles driven by parents.

a. Write an inequality that shows all the possible combinations of vans and cars that could be used to drive students to the competition.

b. Explain in words or show work for how you determined the inequality.

Name ______________________ Class ____________ Date ____________

3-1 Think About a Plan

Solving Systems Using Tables and Graphs

Sports You can choose between two tennis courts at two university campuses to learn how to play tennis. One campus charges $25 per hour. The other campus charges $20 per hour plus a one-time registration fee of $10.

a. Write a system of equations to represent the cost c for h hours of court use at each campus.

b. Graphing Calculator Find the number of hours for which the costs are the same.

c. Reasoning If you want to practice for a total of 10 hours, which university campus should you choose? Explain.

1. What is an equation that represents the cost c for h hours of court use for the first campus?

____

2. What is an equation that represents the cost c for h hours of court use for the second campus?

____

3. What is one method you can use to find the number of hours for which the costs are the same?

____

4. What is another method you can use to find the number of hours for which the costs are the same?

____

____

5. Use one of your methods to find the number of hours for which the costs are the same.

____

6. What happens to the cost at the two campuses after you have practiced for the number of hours you found in Exercise 5?

____

____

7. If you want to practice for a total of 10 hours, which university campus should you choose? Explain.

____

____

____

Name ______________________ Class ____________ Date ____________

3-1 Practice

Form G

Solving Systems Using Tables and Graphs

Solve each system by graphing or using a table. Check your answers.

1. $\begin{cases} y = x - 2 \\ x + y = 10 \end{cases}$

2. $\begin{cases} y = 7 - x \\ x + 3y = 11 \end{cases}$

3. $\begin{cases} x - 2y = 10 \\ y = x - 11 \end{cases}$

4. $\begin{cases} 5x + y = 11 \\ x - y = 1 \end{cases}$

5. $\begin{cases} x + y = -1 \\ x - y = 3 \end{cases}$

6. $\begin{cases} x - y = -1 \\ 2x + 2y = 10 \end{cases}$

7. $\begin{cases} 4x + 3y = -16 \\ -x + y = 4 \end{cases}$

8. $\begin{cases} y = -3x \\ x + y = 2 \end{cases}$

9. $\begin{cases} y = \frac{2}{3}x - 5 \\ y = -\frac{2}{3}x - 3 \end{cases}$

10. $\begin{cases} y = \frac{1}{2}x + 3 \\ y = -\frac{1}{4}x - 3 \end{cases}$

11. $\begin{cases} 2x - 4y = -4 \\ 3x - y = 4 \end{cases}$

12. $\begin{cases} x + y = 6 \\ x - y = 4 \end{cases}$

Write and solve a system of equations for each situation. Check your answers.

13. Your school sells tickets for its winter concert. Student tickets are $5 and adult tickets are $10. If your school sells 85 tickets and makes $600, how many of each ticket did they sell?

14. A grocery store has small bags of apples for $5 and large bags of apples for $8. If you buy 6 bags and spend $45, how many of each size bag did you buy?

15. The spreadsheet below shows the monthly income and expenses for a new business.

a. Use your graphing calculator to find linear models for income and expenses as functions of the number of the month.

b. In what month will income equal expenses?

	A	B	C
	Month	Income	Expenses
1	May	$1500	$21,400
2	June	$3500	$18,800
3	July	$5500	$16,200
4	August	$7500	$13,600

Name ______________________ Class ____________ Date ____________

3-1 Practice (continued) — Form G

Solving Systems Using Tables and Graphs

Without graphing, classify each system as *independent, dependent,* or *inconsistent.*

16. $\begin{cases} x + y = 3 \\ y = 2x - 3 \end{cases}$

17. $\begin{cases} 2x + y = 3 \\ y = -2x - 1 \end{cases}$

18. $\begin{cases} x + 3y = 9 \\ -2x - 6y = -18 \end{cases}$

19. $\begin{cases} x + y = 4 \\ y = 2x + 1 \end{cases}$

20. $\begin{cases} x + 3y = 9 \\ 9y + 3x = 27 \end{cases}$

21. $\begin{cases} x + 2y = 5 \\ 2x + 3y = 9 \end{cases}$

22. $\begin{cases} 3x + 2y = 7 \\ 3x - 15 = -6y \end{cases}$

23. $\begin{cases} x + y = 6 \\ 3x + 3y = 3 \end{cases}$

24. $\begin{cases} x + y = 11 \\ y = x - 5 \end{cases}$

25. $\begin{cases} x + 2y = 13 \\ 2y = 7 - x \end{cases}$

26. $\begin{cases} y = 12 - 5x \\ x - 4y = -6 \end{cases}$

27. $\begin{cases} 25x - 10y = 0 \\ 2y = 5x \end{cases}$

28. You and your business partner are mailing advertising flyers to your customers. You address 6 flyers each minute and have already done 80. Your partner addresses 4 flyers each minute and has already done 100. Graph and solve a system of equations to find when the two of you will have addressed equal numbers of flyers.

29. You are going on vacation and leaving your dog in a kennel. Kennel A charges \$25 per day which includes a one-time grooming treatment. Kennel B charges \$20 per day and a one-time fee of \$30 for grooming.

a. Write a system of equations to represent the cost *c* for *d* days that your dog will stay at the kennel.

b. If your vacation is 7 days long, which kennel should you choose? Explain.

Open-Ended Write a second equation for each system so that the system will have the indicated number of solutions.

30. one
$\begin{cases} y = 5x - 3 \\ ? \end{cases}$

31. none
$\begin{cases} y = -x + 3 \\ ? \end{cases}$

32. an infinite number
$\begin{cases} y = 3x - 2 \\ ? \end{cases}$

33. Multiple Choice Which ordered pair of numbers is the solution of the system?

$\begin{cases} x + y = -3 \\ x - 2y = 0 \end{cases}$

Ⓐ $(-6, -3)$ Ⓑ $(-2, -1)$ Ⓒ $(6, -3)$ Ⓓ $(2, 1)$

Name ______________________ Class ____________ Date ____________

3-1 Standardized Test Prep

Solving Systems Using Tables and Graphs

Multiple Choice

For Exercises 1–4, choose the correct letter.

1. Which system of equations is inconsistent?

(A) $\begin{cases} x + y = 4 \\ x - y = 3 \end{cases}$ (C) $\begin{cases} 6x + 3y = 12 \\ 2y = -4x + 4 \end{cases}$

(B) $\begin{cases} 2y - x = 5 \\ 4y = 2x + 10 \end{cases}$ (D) $\begin{cases} -3x + y = 4 \\ 2y = -6x + 8 \end{cases}$

2. Which ordered pair of numbers is the solution of the system? $\begin{cases} 2x + 3y = 12 \\ 2x - y = 4 \end{cases}$

(F) (2, 3) (G) (3, 2) (H) (1, −2) (I) (−3, 6)

3. Which of the following graphs shows the solution of the system?

$\begin{cases} x + y = -4 \\ 2x - 2y = -8 \end{cases}$

(A) 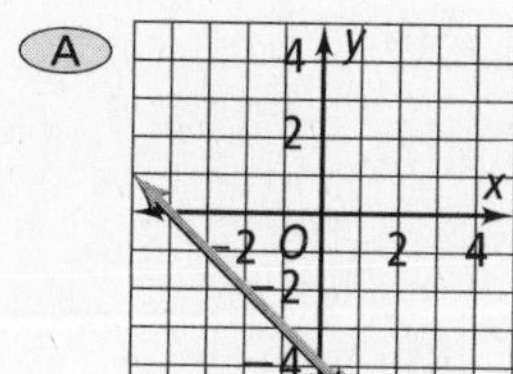

(B) 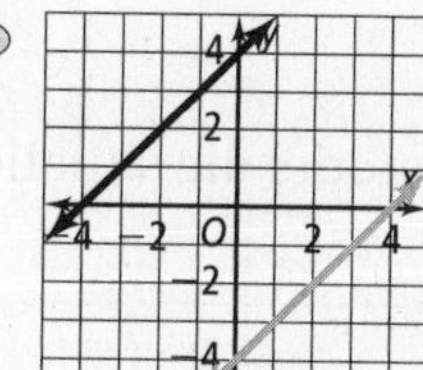

(C) 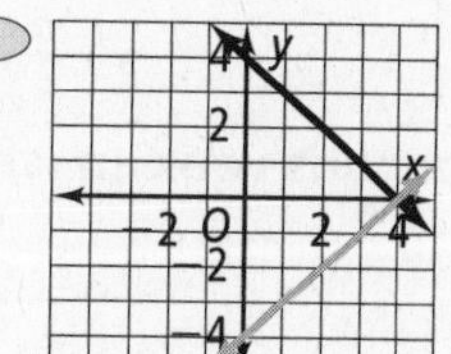

(D) 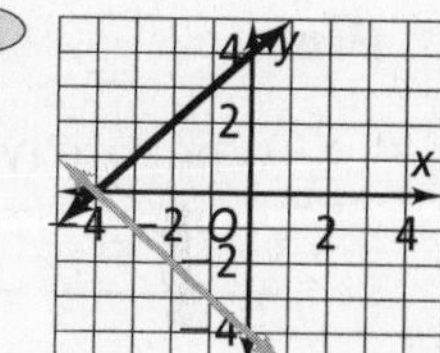

4. You and your friend are both knitting scarves for charity. You knit 8 rows each minute and already have knitted 10 rows. Your friend knits 5 rows each minute and has already knitted 19 rows. When will you both have knitted the same number of rows?

(F) 2.6 minutes (G) 3 minutes (H) 9.7 minutes (I) 34 minutes

Short Response

5. The sides of an angle are two lines whose equations are $4x + y = 12$ and $y = 3x - 2$. An angle has its vertex at the point where the lines meet. Use a graph to determine the coordinates of the vertex. What are the coordinates of the vertex?

Name ______________________ Class ____________ Date ____________

3-2 Think About a Plan

Solving Systems Algebraically

Chemistry A scientist wants to make 6 milliliters of a 30% sulfuric acid solution. The solution is to be made from a combination of a 20% sulfuric acid solution and a 50% sulfuric acid solution. How many milliliters of each solution must be combined to make the 30% solution?

Know

1. The scientist will begin with ☐ % and ☐ % solutions.

2. The scientist wants to make ☐ ml of 30% solution.

Need

3. To solve the problem you need to define:

____

____

Plan

4. What are two equations you can write to model the situation?

____

5. Which method should you use to solve the system of equations? Explain.

____

____

6. Solve the system of equations.

____

7. How can you interpret the solutions in the context of the problem?

____

8. Do your solutions check? Explain.

____

____

Name ______________________ Class ____________ Date ____________

3-2 Practice

Form G

Solving Systems Algebraically

Solve each system by substitution. Check your answers.

1. $\begin{cases} y = x + 1 \\ 2x + y = 7 \end{cases}$

2. $\begin{cases} x = y - 2 \\ 3x - y = 6 \end{cases}$

3. $\begin{cases} y = 2x + 3 \\ 5x - y = -3 \end{cases}$

4. $\begin{cases} 6x - 3y = -33 \\ 2x + y = -1 \end{cases}$

5. $\begin{cases} 2x - y = 7 \\ 3x - 2y = 10 \end{cases}$

6. $\begin{cases} 4x = 8y \\ 2x + 5y = 27 \end{cases}$

7. $\begin{cases} x + 3y = -4 \\ y + x = 0 \end{cases}$

8. $\begin{cases} 3x + 2y = 9 \\ x + y = 3 \end{cases}$

9. $\begin{cases} 2y - 3x = 4 \\ x = -4 \end{cases}$

10. Suppose you bought eight oranges and one grapefruit for a total of \$4.60. Later that day, you bought six oranges and three grapefruits for a total of \$4.80. What is the price of each type of fruit?

Solve each system by elimination.

11. $\begin{cases} x + y = 10 \\ x - y = 2 \end{cases}$

12. $\begin{cases} -x + 3y = -1 \\ x - 2y = 2 \end{cases}$

13. $\begin{cases} x + y = 7 \\ x + 3y = 11 \end{cases}$

14. $\begin{cases} 4x - 3y = -2 \\ 4x + 5y = 14 \end{cases}$

15. $\begin{cases} x + 2y = 10 \\ 3x - y = 9 \end{cases}$

16. $\begin{cases} 2x - 5y = 11 \\ 4x + 10y = 18 \end{cases}$

17. $\begin{cases} x - y = 0 \\ x + y = 2 \end{cases}$

18. $\begin{cases} x + 3y = -4 \\ x + y = 0 \end{cases}$

19. $\begin{cases} 3x - y = 17 \\ 2x + y = 8 \end{cases}$

20. There are a total of 15 apartments in two buildings. The difference of two times the number of apartments in the first building and three times the number of apartments in the second building is 5.
    a. Write a system of equations to model the relationship between the number of apartments in the first building f and the number of apartments in the second building s.
    b. How many apartments are in each building?

Solve each system by elimination.

21. $\begin{cases} -x + y = 3 \\ 5x + y = 9 \end{cases}$

22. $\begin{cases} 5x + 4y = 2 \\ -5x - 2y = 4 \end{cases}$

23. $\begin{cases} -2x + y = 3 \\ 5x - y = -3 \end{cases}$

24. $\begin{cases} 14x + 2y = 10 \\ x - 5y = 11 \end{cases}$

25. $\begin{cases} x + 5y = 1 \\ 2x + 10y = 2 \end{cases}$

26. $\begin{cases} 0.3x + 0.4y = 0.8 \\ 0.7x - 0.8y = -6.8 \end{cases}$

27. $\begin{cases} 4x + 3y = -6 \\ 5x - 6y = -27 \end{cases}$

28. $\begin{cases} 2x + y = 0 \\ 4x + 2y = -11 \end{cases}$

29. $\begin{cases} 1.2x + 1.4y = 2.7 \\ 0.4x - 0.3y = 0.9 \end{cases}$

Name ______________________ Class ____________ Date ____________

3-2 Practice (continued) Form G

Solving Systems Algebraically

30. Writing Explain what it means when elimination results in an equation that is always true.

For each system, choose the solution method that seems easier to use. Explain why you made each choice. Solve each system.

31. $\begin{cases} b = 2a - 5 \\ b = 3 + a \end{cases}$

32. $\begin{cases} 4x - 2y = 11 \\ 4x + 3y = 6 \end{cases}$

33. $\begin{cases} 5p + 2q = 10 \\ 4p + q = 4 \end{cases}$

34. $\begin{cases} j - 3k = 3 \\ j = -k + 15 \end{cases}$

35. Error Analysis You and your friend are solving the system $4x - y = 5$ and $4x + y = 3$. Your friend says there is no solution, and you say the solution is $(1, -1)$. Who is correct? Explain.

36. You can buy DVDs at a local store for $15.49 each. You can buy them at an online store for $13.99 each plus $6 for shipping. How many DVDs can you buy for the same amount at the two stores?

37. Last year, a baseball team paid $20 per bat and $12 per glove, spending a total of $1040. This year, the prices went up to $25 per bat and $16 per glove. The team spent $1350 to purchase the same amount of equipment as last year. How many bats and gloves did the team purchase each year?

38. If the perimeter of the square at the right is 72 units, what are the values of x and y?

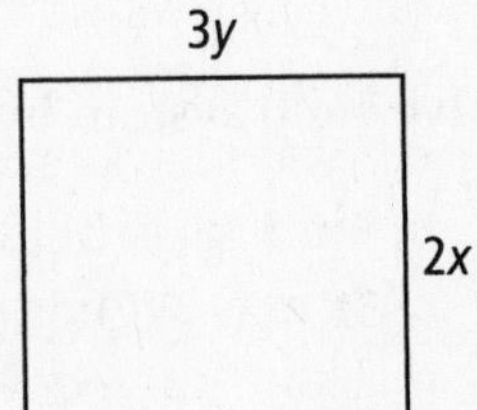

Name ______________________ Class ____________ Date ____________

3-2 Standardized Test Prep

Solving Systems Algebraically

Multiple Choice

For Exercises 1–4, choose the correct letter.

Use the system of equations for Exercises 1 and 2. $\begin{cases} 4x - 10y = -3 \\ 12x + 5y = 12 \end{cases}$

1. What is the value of x in the solution?

(A) $-\frac{9}{7}$ (B) $-\frac{15}{28}$ (C) $\frac{3}{5}$ (D) $\frac{3}{4}$

2. What is the value of y in the solution?

(F) $\frac{3}{35}$ (G) $\frac{3}{5}$ (H) $\frac{3}{4}$ (I) $\frac{24}{35}$

3. Which of the following systems of equations has the solution $(4, -1)$?

(A) $\begin{cases} 3x - 2y = 14 \\ 2x + 2y = 6 \end{cases}$

(B) $\begin{cases} 3x - y = 0 \\ 4x + 3y = 26 \end{cases}$

(C) $\begin{cases} -2x + 4y = 6 \\ -3x + 6y = 8 \end{cases}$

(D) $\begin{cases} 4x + 9y = 1 \\ 4x + 6y = -2 \end{cases}$

4. At a bookstore, used hardcover books sell for \$8 each and used softcover books sell for \$2 each. You purchase 36 used books and spend \$144. How many softcover books do you buy?

(F) 9 (G) 12 (H) 18 (I) 24

Extended Response

5. A local cell phone company offers two different calling plans. In the first plan, you pay a monthly fee of \$30 and \$.35 per minute. In the second plan you pay a monthly fee of \$99 and \$.05 per minute.

a. Write a system of equations showing the two calling plans.
b. When is it better to use the first calling plan?
c. When is it better to use the second calling plan?
d. How much does it cost when the calling plans are equal?

Name ______________________ Class ____________ Date ____________

3-3 Think About a Plan

Systems of Inequalities

College Admissions An entrance exam has two sections, a verbal section and a mathematics section. You can score a maximum of 1600 points. For admission, the school of your choice requires a math score of at least 600. Write a system of inequalities to model scores that meet the school's requirements. Then solve the system by graphing.

Know

1. The sum of the verbal score and the mathematics score must be

____

2. Each of the scores must be _______________________

3. ____

Need

4. To solve the problem, you need to find _______________________

____.

Plan

5. What system of inequalities models this situation?

____

____

6. Graph your system of inequalities on the grid at the right.

7. How do you know which region in your graph represents the solution?

____

____

____

Name ______________________ Class ____________ Date ____________

3-3 Practice

Systems of Inequalities

Form G

Find all whole number solutions of each system using a table.

1. $\begin{cases} -x + y = 1 \\ x + 2y \leq 20 \end{cases}$

2. $\begin{cases} x - y \geq 1 \\ 2x + 3y \leq 21 \end{cases}$

3. $\begin{cases} y < -2x + 4 \\ y \leq x + 2 \end{cases}$

4. $\begin{cases} x - y \leq 2 \\ 2x + y \leq 5 \end{cases}$

5. $\begin{cases} y > 4x + 2 \\ y - x \leq 3 \end{cases}$

6. $\begin{cases} y < -\frac{x}{3} + 3 \\ 2x + y \geq 4 \end{cases}$

7. The dry cleaner charges $4 to clean a pair of pants and $3 to clean a shirt. You want to get at least 8 items cleaned. You have $32 to spend on dry cleaning.
   a. Write a system of inequalities to model the situation.
   b. Solve the system by using a table.

Solve each system of inequalities by graphing.

8. $\begin{cases} y > x + 2 \\ y \leq -x + 1 \end{cases}$

9. $\begin{cases} y \leq x + 3 \\ y \geq x + 2 \end{cases}$

10. $\begin{cases} x + y < 5 \\ y < 3x - 2 \end{cases}$

11. $\begin{cases} x - 2y < 3 \\ 2x + y > 8 \end{cases}$

12. $\begin{cases} -3x + y < 3 \\ x + y > -1 \end{cases}$

13. $\begin{cases} x + 2y > 4 \\ 2x - y > 6 \end{cases}$

14. $\begin{cases} 2x \geq y + 3 \\ x < 3 - 2y \end{cases}$

15. $\begin{cases} 3 < 2x - y \\ x - 3y \leq 4 \end{cases}$

16. $\begin{cases} 2x + y > 2 \\ x - y \geq 3 \end{cases}$

Name ______________________ Class ____________ Date ____________

3-3 Practice (continued)

Form G

Systems of Inequalities

17. Suppose you are buying two kinds of notebooks for school. A spiral notebook costs \$2, and a three-ring notebook costs \$5. You must have at least 6 notebooks. The cost of the notebooks can be no more than \$20.
    a. Write a system of inequalities to model the situation.
    b. Graph and solve the system.

18. A camp counselor needs no more than 30 campers to sign up for two mountain hikes.The counselor needs at least 10 campers on the low trail and at least 5 campers on the high trail.
    a. Write a system of inequalities to model the situation.
    b. Graph and solve the system.

Solve each system of inequalities by graphing.

19. $\begin{cases} y < x - 3 \\ y \geq |x - 4| \end{cases}$

20. $\begin{cases} -2x + y > 1 \\ y > |x| \end{cases}$

21. $\begin{cases} y < -3 \\ y < -|x| \end{cases}$

22. $\begin{cases} y \geq -2 \\ y \leq -|x + 3| \end{cases}$

23. $\begin{cases} y < x + 3 \\ y > |x - 1| \end{cases}$

24. $\begin{cases} y > x \\ y < |x + 2| \end{cases}$

25. **Error Analysis** Your homework assignment is to solve the system $\begin{cases} y \geq 2 \\ y \geq |x| \end{cases}$ using a graph. You turn in the graph at the right. What did you do wrong? Draw a correct graph.

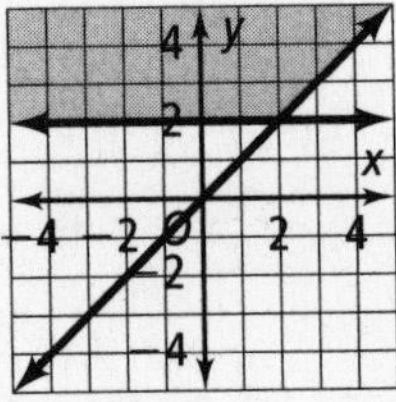

26. **Open-Ended** Write a system of inequalities that has no solution.

27. A doctor needs at least 60 adults for a medical study. He cannot use more than 40 men in the study. Write a system of inequalities to model the situation and solve the system by graphing.

Name ______________________ Class ____________ Date ____________

3-3 Standardized Test Prep

Systems of Inequalities

Multiple Choice

For Exercises 1–4, choose the correct letter.

1. Which system of inequalities is shown in the graph?

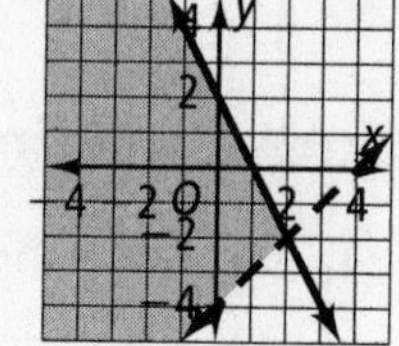

Ⓐ $\begin{cases} y \le -2x + 2 \\ y > x - 4 \end{cases}$

Ⓑ $\begin{cases} y > -2x + 2 \\ y \le x - 4 \end{cases}$

Ⓒ $\begin{cases} y \ge -2x + 2 \\ y < x - 4 \end{cases}$

Ⓓ $\begin{cases} y < -2x + 2 \\ y \ge x - 4 \end{cases}$

2. Which of the following graphs shows the solution of the system of inequalities? $\begin{cases} y \ge -2x + 2 \\ y \le |3x| \end{cases}$

Ⓕ 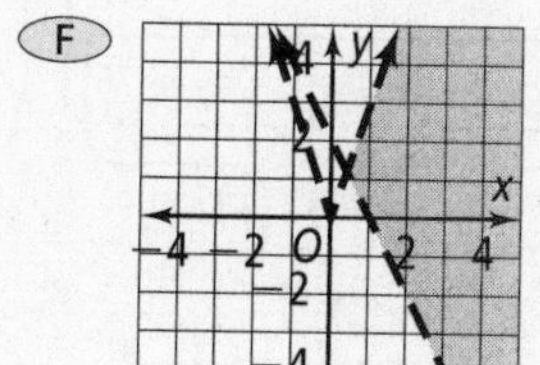

Ⓖ 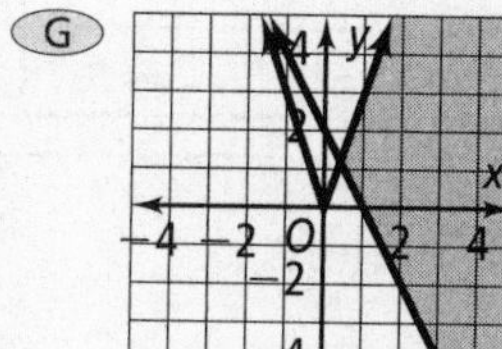

Ⓗ 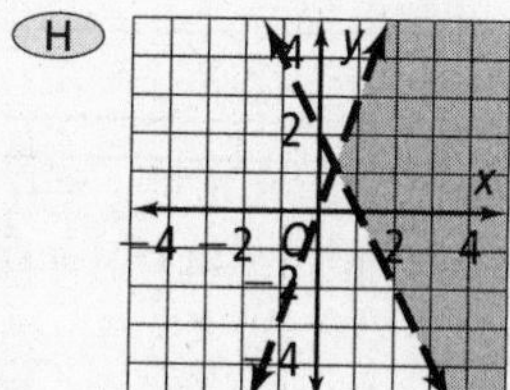

Ⓘ 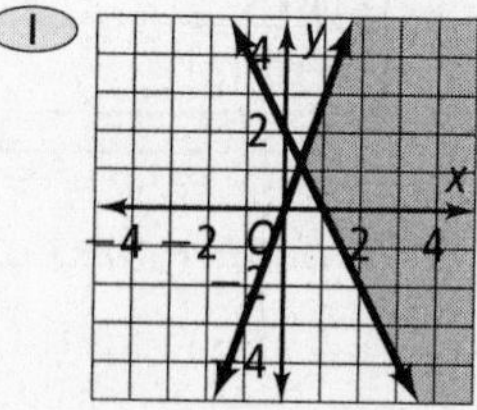

3. Which point lies in the solution set for the system? $\begin{cases} y < 5x - 1 \\ y \ge 7 - 3x \end{cases}$

Ⓐ $(-5, 1)$ Ⓑ $(2, -3)$ Ⓒ $(4, 4)$ Ⓓ $(1, 6)$

4. How many of the ordered pairs in the data table provided are solutions of the system? $\begin{cases} x + y \le 4 \\ x \ge 1 \end{cases}$

Ⓕ 6

Ⓖ 10

Ⓗ 9

Ⓘ 15

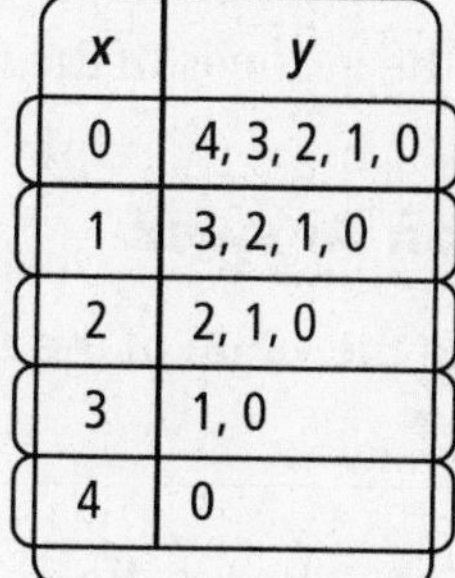

x	y
0	4, 3, 2, 1, 0
1	3, 2, 1, 0
2	2, 1, 0
3	1, 0
4	0

Short Response

5. Is $(4, -2)$ a solution of the system? $\begin{cases} x + y > 2 \\ 2x - y < 1 \end{cases}$

Explain how you made your determination.

Name ______________________ Class ____________ Date ____________

3-4 Think About a Plan

Linear Programming

Cooking Baking a tray of corn muffins takes 4 cups of milk and 3 cups of wheat flour. Baking a tray of bran muffins takes 2 cups of milk and 3 cups of wheat flour. A baker has 16 cups of milk and 15 cups of wheat flour. He makes $3 profit per tray of corn muffins and $2 profit per tray of bran muffins. How many trays of each type of muffin should the baker make to maximize his profit?

Understanding the Problem

1. Organize the information in a table.

	Corn Muffin Trays, x	Bran Muffin Trays, y	Total
Milk (cups)			
Flour (cups)			
Profit			

2. What are the constraints and the objective function?

Constraints: ____________
____
____
____

Objective Function: ____________

Planning the Solution

3. Graph the constraints on the grid at the right.

4. Label the vertices of the feasible region on your graph.

Getting an Answer

5. What is the value of the objective function at each vertex?

____

6. At which vertex is the objective function maximized?

____

7. How can you interpret the solution in the context of the problem?

____

____

Name _________________________ Class _____________ Date ___________

3-4 Practice

Form G

Linear Programming

Find the values of *x* and *y* that maximize or minimize the objective function for each graph.

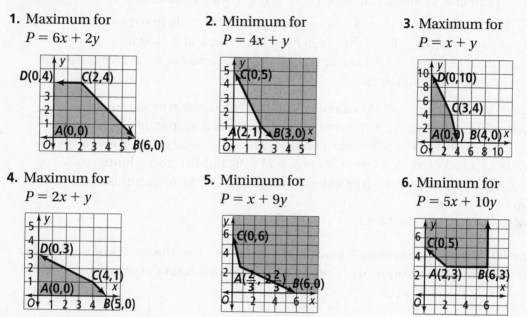

1. Maximum for
$P = 6x + 2y$

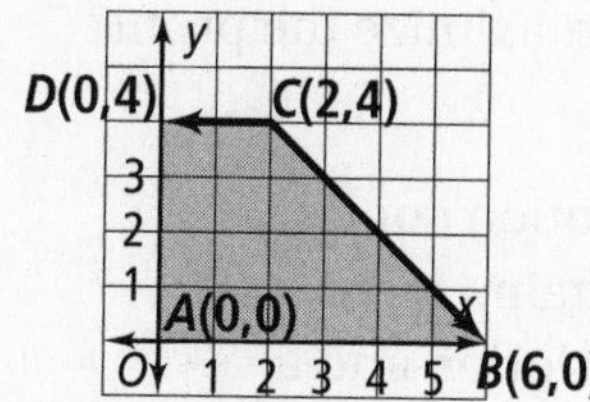

2. Minimum for
$P = 4x + y$

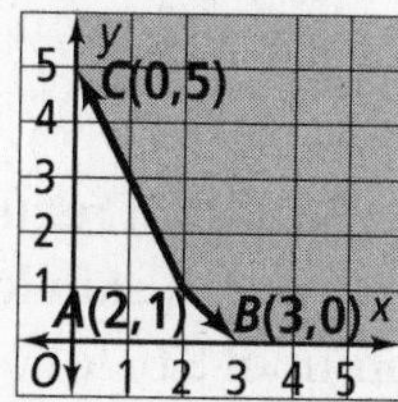

3. Maximum for
$P = x + y$

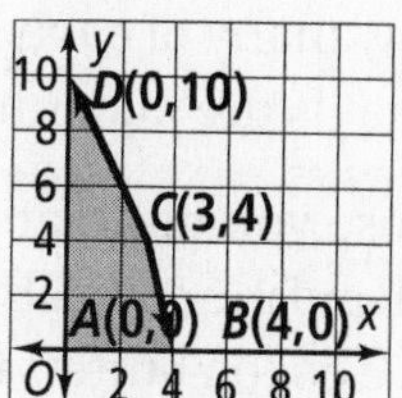

4. Maximum for
$P = 2x + y$

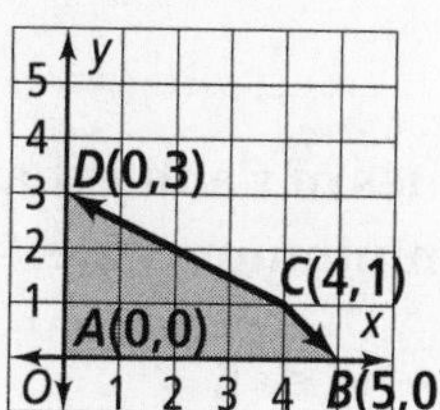

5. Minimum for
$P = x + 9y$

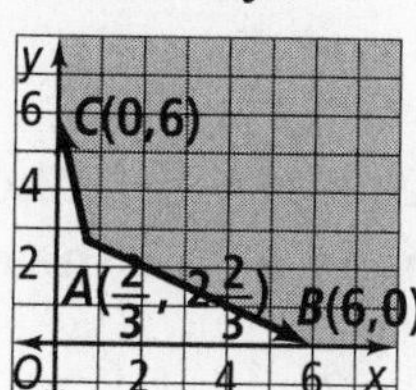

6. Minimum for
$P = 5x + 10y$

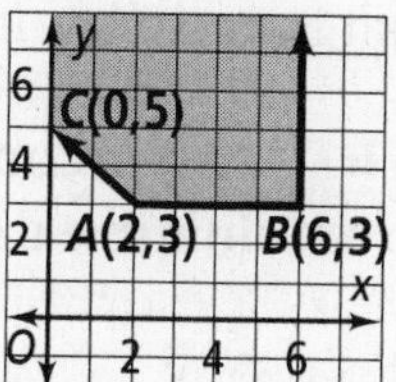

Graph each system of constraints. Name all vertices. Then find the values of *x* and *y* that maximize or minimize the objective function.

7. $\begin{cases} x + 2y \le 6 \\ x \ge 2 \\ y \ge 1 \end{cases}$

Minimum for
$C = 3x + 4y$

8. $\begin{cases} x + y \le 5 \\ x + 2y \le 8 \\ x \ge 0, y \ge 0 \end{cases}$

Maximum for
$P = x + 3y$

9. $\begin{cases} x + y \le 6 \\ 2x + y \le 10 \\ x \ge 0, y \ge 0 \end{cases}$

Maximum for
$P = 4x + y$

3-4 Practice (continued)

Form G

Linear Programming

10. You are going to make and sell baked goods. A loaf of Irish soda bread is made with 2 c flour and $\frac{1}{4}$ c sugar. Kugelhopf cake is made with 4 c flour and 1 c sugar. You will make a profit of \$1.50 on each loaf of Irish soda bread and a profit of \$4 on each Kugelhopf cake. You have 16 c flour and 3 c sugar.

a. How many of each kind of baked goods should you make to maximize the profit?

b. What is the maximum profit?

11. Suppose you make and sell skin lotion. A quart of regular skin lotion contains 2 c oil and 1 c cocoa butter. A quart of extra-rich skin lotion contains 1 c oil and 2 c cocoa butter. You will make a profit of \$10/qt on regular lotion and a profit of \$8/qt on extra-rich lotion. You have 24 c oil and 18 c cocoa butter.

a. How many quarts of each type of lotion should you make to maximize your profit?

b. What is the maximum profit?

Graph each system of constraints. Name all vertices. Then find the values of *x* and *y* that maximize or minimize the objective function. Find the maximum or minimum value.

12. $\begin{cases} 3x + 2y \leq 6 \\ 2x + 3y \leq 6 \\ x \geq 0, y \geq 0 \end{cases}$

Maximum for $P = 4x + y$

13. $\begin{cases} 4x + 2y \leq 4 \\ 2x + 4y \leq 4 \\ x \geq 0, y \geq 0 \end{cases}$

Maximum for $P = 3x + y$

14. $\begin{cases} x + y \leq 5 \\ 4x + y \leq 8 \\ x \geq 0, y \geq 0 \end{cases}$

Minimum for $C = x + 3y$

15. Writing Explain why solving a system of linear equations is a necessary skill for linear programming.

16. A doctor allots 15 minutes for routine office visits and 45 minutes for full physicals. The doctor cannot do more than 10 physicals per day. The doctor has 9 available hours for appointments each day. A routine office visit costs \$60 and a full physical costs \$100. How many routine office visits and full physicals should the doctor schedule to maximize her income for the day? What is the maximum income?

Name ______________________ Class ____________ Date ____________

3-4 Standardized Test Prep
Linear Programming

Multiple Choice

For Exercises 1–4, choose the correct letter.

1. The vertices of a feasible region are (0, 0), (0, 2), (5, 2), and (4, 0). For which objective function is the maximum cost C found at the vertex (4, 0)?

Ⓐ $C = -2x + 3y$ Ⓑ $C = 2x + 7y$ Ⓒ $C = 4x - 3y$ Ⓓ $C = 5x + 3y$

2. A feasible region has vertices at (0, 0), (3, 0), $\left(\frac{3}{2}, \frac{7}{2}\right)$, and (0, 3). What are the maximum and minimum values for the objective function $P = 6x + 8y$?

Ⓕ minimum (0, 0) = 0
maximum $\left(\frac{3}{2}, \frac{7}{2}\right) = 37$

Ⓖ minimum (0, 0) = 0
maximum (3, 0) = 24

Ⓗ minimum (0, 0) = 14
maximum $\left(\frac{3}{2}, \frac{7}{2}\right) = 17$

Ⓘ minimum (0, 0) = 0
maximum (0, 3) = 30

3. Which values of x and y minimize N for the objective function $N = 2x + y$?

Constraints $\begin{cases} x + y \geq 8 \\ x + 2y \geq 14 \\ x \geq 0, y \geq 0 \end{cases}$

Ⓐ (0, 0) Ⓑ (0, 7) Ⓒ (2, 6) Ⓓ (8, 0)

4. Which of the following systems has the vertices (0, 5), (1, 4), (3, 0), and (0, 0)?

Ⓕ $\begin{cases} x + y \geq 5 \\ 2x + y \geq 6 \\ x \geq 0, y \geq 0 \end{cases}$ Ⓖ $\begin{cases} x + y \leq 5 \\ 2x + y \leq 6 \\ x \geq 0, y \geq 0 \end{cases}$ Ⓗ $\begin{cases} x + y \leq 5 \\ x + 2y \leq 6 \\ x \geq 0, y \geq 0 \end{cases}$ Ⓘ $\begin{cases} x + y \leq 5 \\ 2x + 2y \leq 6 \\ x \geq 0, y \geq 0 \end{cases}$

Short Response

5. The figure at the right shows the feasible region for a system of constraints. This system includes $x \geq 0$ and $y \geq 0$. What are the remaining constraints? Show your work.

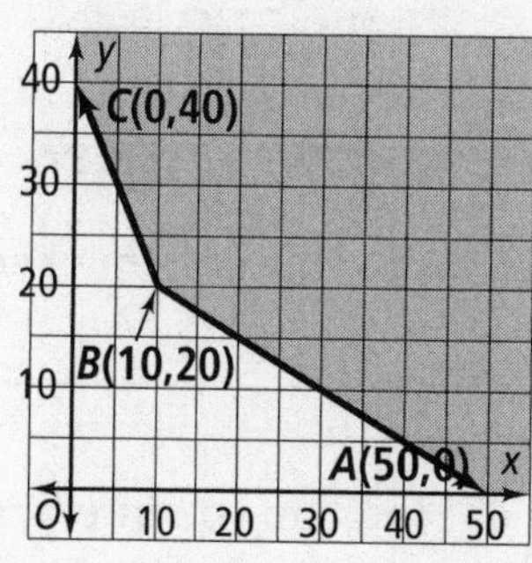

Name ________________ Class ________ Date ________

3-5 Think About a Plan

Systems With Three Variables

Sports A stadium has 49,000 seats. Seats sell for $25 in Section A, $20 in Section B, and $15 in Section C. The number of seats in Section A equals the total number of seats in Sections B and C. Suppose the stadium takes in $1,052,000 from each sold-out event. How many seats does each section hold?

Understanding the Problem

1. Define a variable for each unknown in this problem.

   Let $x =$ ________________

   Let $y =$ ________________

   Let $z =$ ________________

2. What system of equations represents this situation?

   ____

   ____

   ____

Planning the Solution

3. Can you write a simpler equivalent equation for one of the equations in your system? If so, write the equivalent equation.

   ____

4. What method of solving looks easier for this problem? Explain.

   ____

   ____

Getting an Answer

5. Solve the system of equations.

   ____

6. How can you interpret the solution in the context of the problem?

   ____

   ____

Name ______________________ Class ____________ Date ____________

3-5 Practice

Form G

Systems With Three Variables

Solve each system by elimination. Check your answers.

1. $\begin{cases} x + y + z = -1 \\ 2x - y + 2z = -5 \\ -x + 2y - z = 4 \end{cases}$

2. $\begin{cases} x + y + z = 3 \\ 2x - y + 2z = 6 \\ 3x + 2y - z = 13 \end{cases}$

3. $\begin{cases} 2x + y = 9 \\ x - 2z = -3 \\ 2y + 3z = 15 \end{cases}$

4. $\begin{cases} x - y + 2z = 10 \\ -x + y - 2z = 5 \\ 3x - 3y + 6z = -2 \end{cases}$

5. $\begin{cases} 2x - y + z = -4 \\ 3x + y - 2z = 0 \\ 3x - y = -4 \end{cases}$

6. $\begin{cases} 2x - y - z = 4 \\ -x + 2y + z = 1 \\ 3x + y + z = 16 \end{cases}$

7. $\begin{cases} x + 5y + 5z = -10 \\ x + y + z = 2 \\ x + 2y + 3z = -3 \end{cases}$

8. $\begin{cases} x - y - z = 0 \\ x - 2y - 2z = 3 \\ -2x + 2y - z = 3 \end{cases}$

9. $\begin{cases} 3x + y + z = 6 \\ 3x - 2y + 2z = 14 \\ 3x + 3y - 3z = -6 \end{cases}$

10. $\begin{cases} x + y + z = -2 \\ 2x + 2y - 3z = 11 \\ 3x - y + z = 4 \end{cases}$

11. $\begin{cases} x - 5y + z = 3 \\ x + 2y - 2z = -12 \\ 2x + 2z = 6 \end{cases}$

12. $\begin{cases} 2x + 3z = 2 \\ 3x + 6y = 6 \\ x - 2z = 8 \end{cases}$

Solve each system by substitution. Check your answers.

13. $\begin{cases} x + y - z = 0 \\ 3x - y + z = 4 \\ 5x + z = 7 \end{cases}$

14. $\begin{cases} x - 2y = 1 \\ x + 3y + z = 0 \\ 2x - 2z = 18 \end{cases}$

15. $\begin{cases} x + y + 4z = 5 \\ -2x + 2z = 3 \\ 3x + y - 2z = 0 \end{cases}$

16. $\begin{cases} 3x + 2y + 2z = 4 \\ -6x + 4y - 2z = -9 \\ 9x - 2y + 2z = 10 \end{cases}$

17. $\begin{cases} 2x - 3y + z = -3 \\ x - 5y + 7z = -11 \\ -10x + 4y - 6z = 28 \end{cases}$

18. $\begin{cases} x + y + z = -8 \\ x - y - z = 6 \\ 2x - 3y + 2z = -1 \end{cases}$

19. $\begin{cases} 14x - 3y + 5z = -15 \\ 3x + 2y - 6z = 10 \\ 7x - y + 4z = -5 \end{cases}$

20. $\begin{cases} 5x - 3y + 2z = 39 \\ 4x + 4y - 3z = 34 \\ 3x - 2y + 6z = 14 \end{cases}$

21. $\begin{cases} x + y + z = 6 \\ 2x - y + 2z = 6 \\ -x + y + 3z = 10 \end{cases}$

22. $\begin{cases} 2x + y - z = 3 \\ 3x - y + 3z = 3 \\ -x - 3y + 2z = 3 \end{cases}$

23. $\begin{cases} 2x - 3y + z = 4 \\ -2x + 3y - z = -4 \\ 6x - 9y + 3z = 12 \end{cases}$

24. $\begin{cases} x + y - z = 1 \\ x + 2z = 3 \\ 2x + 2y = 4 \end{cases}$

3-5 Practice (continued) Form G

Systems With Three Variables

Write and solve a system of equations for each problem.

25. The sum of three numbers is -2. The sum of three times the first number, twice the second number, and the third number is 9. The difference between the second number and half the third number is 10. Find the numbers.

26. Monica has \$1, \$5, and \$10 bills in her wallet that are worth \$96. If she had one more \$1 bill, she would have just as many \$1 bills as \$5 and \$10 bills combined. She has 23 bills total. How many of each denomination does she have?

27. Writing How do you decide whether substitution is the best method to solve a system in three variables?

28. Error Analysis A student solves the system of equations. $\begin{cases} 2x + y - z = 13 \\ x + 3y + 3z = 47 \\ 5x - y + z = 1 \end{cases}$

The student gets a solution of (2, 12, 3). Is the solution correct? How can you be sure? Show your work.

29. Reasoning Why is there no solution to the system? $\begin{cases} 2x - 3y + z = 5 \\ 2x - 3y + z = -2 \\ -4x + 6y - 2z = 10 \end{cases}$

30. The first number plus the third number is equal to the second number. The sum of the first number and the second number is six more than the third number. Three times the first number minus two times the second number is equal to the third number. What is the sum of the three numbers?

31. Which of the following is a system with the solution $(6, -2, -3)$?

(A) $\begin{cases} 2x + y - z = 5 \\ x + 4y + 2z = 16 \\ 15x + 6y - 2z = 12 \end{cases}$

(C) $\begin{cases} -2x - 2y + z = 16 \\ 3x - 3y + 2z = 9 \\ 4x + y - z = -20 \end{cases}$

(B) $\begin{cases} 4x - 3y + z = 31 \\ x - 2y + 2z = 8 \\ -3x + y - 4z = -13 \end{cases}$

(D) $\begin{cases} -x + 2y - z = -7 \\ 3x + 5y + 2z = 2 \\ -2x + 3y + 4z = -30 \end{cases}$

Name ______________________ Class ____________ Date ____________

3-5 Standardized Test Prep

Systems With Three Variables

Gridded Response

Solve each exercise and enter your answer in the grid provided.

1. A change machine contains nickels, dimes, and quarters. There are 75 coins in the machine, and the value of the coins is \$7.25. There are 5 times as many nickels as dimes. How many quarters are in the machine?

2. The sum of three numbers is 23. The first number is equal to twice the second number minus 7. The third number is equal to one more than the sum of the first and second numbers. What is the first number?

3. A fish's tail weighs 9 lb. Its head weighs as much as its tail plus half its body. Its body weighs as much as its head and tail. How many pounds does the fish weigh?

4. You are training for a triathlon. In your training routine each week, you bike 5 times as far as you run and you run 4 times as far as you swim. One week you trained a total of 200 miles. How many miles did you swim that week?

5. Three multiplied by the first number is equal to the second number plus 4. The second number is equal to one plus two multiplied by the third number. The third number is one less than the first number. What is the sum of all three numbers?

Answers

1. 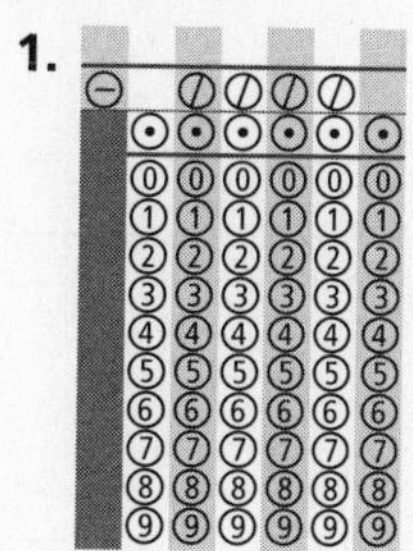

2. 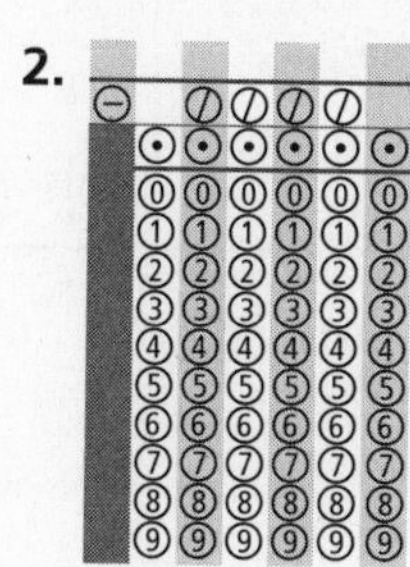

3. 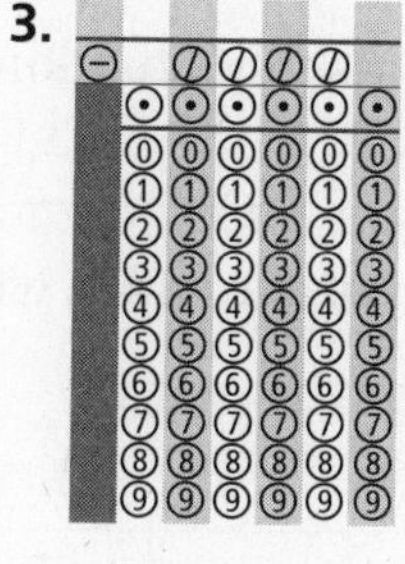

4. 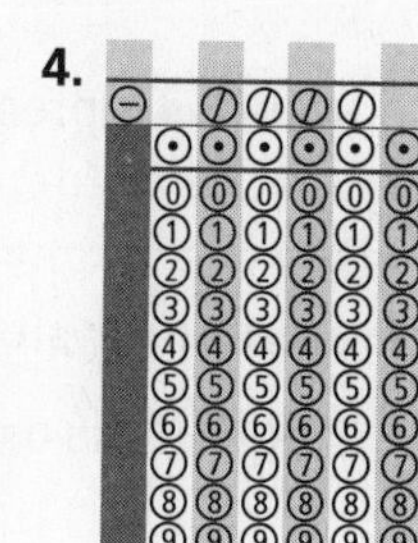

5. 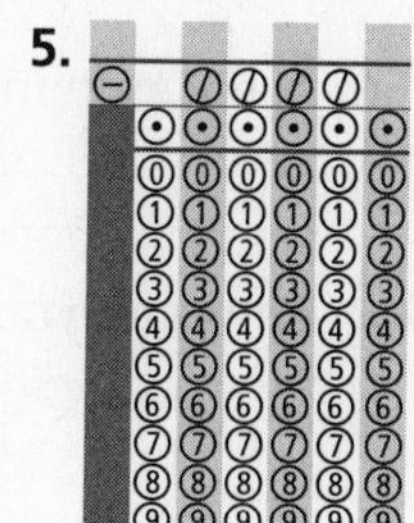

Name ______________________ Class ____________ Date ____________

3-6 Think About a Plan

Solving Systems Using Matrices

Paint A hardware store mixes paints in a ratio of two parts red to six parts yellow to make two gallons of pumpkin orange. A ratio of five parts red to three parts yellow makes two gallons of pepper red. A gallon of pumpkin orange sells for $25, and a gallon of pepper red sells for $28. Find the cost of 1 quart of red paint and the cost of 1 quart of yellow paint.

Know

1. There are ☐ quarts in 1 gallon.

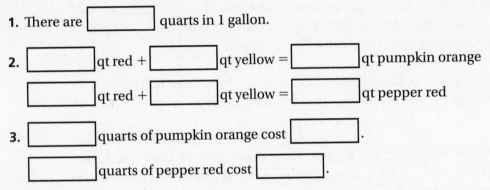

2. ☐ qt red + ☐ qt yellow = ☐ qt pumpkin orange

   ☐ qt red + ☐ qt yellow = ☐ qt pepper red

3. ☐ quarts of pumpkin orange cost ☐.

   ☐ quarts of pepper red cost ☐.

Need

4. To solve the problem you need to define:

   ____

5. To solve the problem you need to find:

   ____

Plan

6. What system of equations represents this situation?

   ____

7. How can you represent the system of equations with a matrix?

8. Solve the system of equations using the matrix.

   ____

9. How can you interpret the solutions in the context of the problem?

   ____

Name ______________________ Class ____________ Date ____________

3-6 Practice

Form G

Solving Systems Using Matrices

Identify the indicated element.

$A = \left[\begin{array}{cc|c} 3 & 5 & 8 \\ 4 & 1 & 6 \end{array}\right]$ $\quad B = \left[\begin{array}{ccc|c} 0 & 6 & 3 & 2 \\ 4 & 5 & 1 & 13 \\ 2 & 2 & 0 & -10 \end{array}\right]$

1. A_{13} **2.** B_{24} **3.** B_{12} **4.** A_{22}

5. B_{31} **6.** A_{21} **7.** B_{23} **8.** A_{11}

Write a matrix to represent each system.

9. $\begin{cases} 3x + y = -4 \\ -2x + 4y = 7 \end{cases}$ **10.** $\begin{cases} 6x = 11 \\ -3x + 4y = 2 \end{cases}$ **11.** $\begin{cases} 4x \quad\; y + 2z = 10 \\ 5x + 2y - 3z = 0 \\ x - 3y + z = 6 \end{cases}$

Write the system of equations represented by each matrix.

12. $\left[\begin{array}{ccc|c} 2 & 5 & 0 & 13 \\ -3 & 1 & 2 & 6 \\ 4 & 0 & -3 & 5 \end{array}\right]$ **13.** $\left[\begin{array}{cc|c} 2 & 1 & -7 \\ 0 & 4 & 9 \end{array}\right]$ **14.** $\left[\begin{array}{ccc|c} 6 & 4 & -2 & 17 \\ 1 & -5 & 2 & -10 \\ 0 & 3 & -1 & 0 \end{array}\right]$

Solve the system of equations using a matrix.

15. $\begin{cases} 4x - y = 10 \\ -2x + 5y = 4 \end{cases}$ **16.** $\begin{cases} x - 2y + 3z = 18 \\ 9x + 2y - z = -2 \\ -6x - y + 2z = 4 \end{cases}$ **17.** $\begin{cases} 3x - 4y + z = 15 \\ -2x - 6y + 3z = 4 \\ 2x + 2y - 2z = -1 \end{cases}$

Name ______________________ Class ____________ Date ____________

3-6 Practice (continued)

Form G

Solving Systems Using Matrices

Graphing Calculator **Solve each system.**

18. $\begin{cases} 4x + y - 2z = 3 \\ 2y + z = 4 \\ 3x - 3y - z = 9 \end{cases}$

19. $\begin{cases} 5x - 2y + z = -1 \\ -x - y - 2z = 5 \\ 3x + 2y + 2z = 2 \end{cases}$

20. $\begin{cases} 3x + 5z = -4 \\ -2x + y - 3z = 9 \\ -x - 2y + 9z = 0 \end{cases}$

21. Suppose the movie theater you work at sells popcorn in three different sizes. A small costs \$2, a medium costs \$5, and a large costs \$10. On your shift, you sold 250 total containers of popcorn and brought in \$1726. You sold twice as many large containers as small ones.

a. How many of each popcorn size did you sell?

b. How much money did you bring in from selling small size containers?

22. **Open Ended** Write a matrix for a system of equations that does not have a unique solution.

23. The following matrix shows the prices passengers on an airline flight paid for a recent ticket and how many passengers were on that flight. Some passengers paid full price for their tickets, and some bought their tickets during a half-price sale. How many passengers bought each price of ticket?

$$\left[\begin{array}{cc|c} 1 & 1 & 100 \\ 120 & 240 & 20{,}160 \end{array}\right]$$

24. **Error Analysis** Your friend says that the matrix below represents the system of equations. What error did your friend make? What is the correct system of equations?

$$\left[\begin{array}{ccc|c} 4 & 0 & -1 & 4 \\ -3 & 2 & -2 & -2 \\ 1 & -3 & -2 & -6 \end{array}\right] \qquad \begin{cases} 4x + y - z = 4 \\ -3x + 2y - 2z = -2 \\ x - 3y - 2z = -6 \end{cases}$$

Name ______________________ Class ____________ Date ____________

3-6 Standardized Test Prep

Solving Systems Using Matrices

Multiple Choice

For Exercises 1–3, choose the correct letter.

1. Which system of equations is equivalent to $\left[\begin{array}{ccc|c} 4 & -1 & 2 & 6 \\ 3 & 0 & 4 & 2 \\ 1 & 5 & 3 & 7 \end{array}\right]$?

(A) $\begin{cases} 4x + y + 2z = 6 \\ 3x + 4z = 2 \\ x + 5y + 3z = 7 \end{cases}$

(C) $\begin{cases} 4x + y + 2z = 6 \\ 3x + y + 4z = 2 \\ x + 5y + 3z = 7 \end{cases}$

(B) $\begin{cases} 4x - y + 2z = 6 \\ 3x + 4z = 2 \\ x + 5y + 3z = 7 \end{cases}$

(D) $\begin{cases} 4x - y + 2z = 6 \\ 3x + y + 4z = 2 \\ x + 5y + 3z = 7 \end{cases}$

2. What is the solution of the system represented by the matrix $\left[\begin{array}{ccc|c} 2 & 3 & -1 & 2 \\ -3 & -4 & 2 & -2 \\ 1 & 2 & -1 & 3 \end{array}\right]$?

(F) (1, 3, 4) (G) (4, −3, 1) (H) (−4, 3, −1) (I) (3, −4, −1)

3. How many elements are in a 2 × 3 matrix?

(A) 2 (B) 4 (C) 5 (D) 6

Short Response

4. A clothing store is having a sale. A pair of jeans costs \$15 and a shirt costs \$8. You spend \$131 and buy a total of 12 items. Using a matrix, how many pairs of jeans and shirts do you buy? Show your work.

Name ____________________ Class ____________ Date ____________

4-1 Think About a Plan

Quadratic Functions and Transformations

Write a quadratic function to represent the areas of all rectangles with a perimeter of 36 ft. Graph the function and describe the rectangle that has the largest area.

1. Write an equation that represents the area of a rectangle with a perimeter of 36 ft. Let x = width and y = length.

2. Solve your equation for y.

3. Write a quadratic function for the area of the rectangle.

$A = \square \cdot \square$

$= \square \cdot (\square)$

$= \square$

4. Graph the quadratic function you wrote.

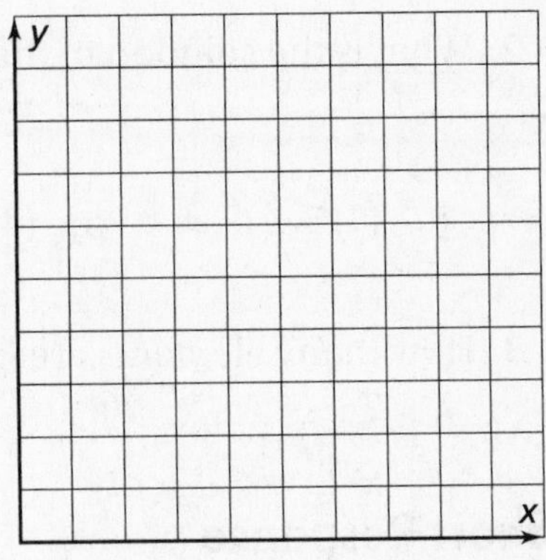

5. What point on the graph has a coordinate that represents the largest area?

6. How can you find the coordinates of this point? What are the coordinates?

____

____

7. Describe the rectangle that has the largest area. What is its area?

____

____

Name ______________________ Class ____________ Date ____________

4-1 Practice

Form G

Quadratic Functions and Transformations

Graph each function.

1. $y = 3x^2$
2. $f(x) = -5x^2$
3. $y = \frac{8}{3}x^2$
4. $f(x) = -\frac{5}{6}x^2$
5. $f(x) = \frac{87}{10}x^2$
6. $f(x) = \frac{4}{5}x^2$

Graph each function. Describe how it was translated from $f(x) = x^2$.

7. $f(x) = x^2 + 4$
8. $f(x) = (x - 3)^2$

Identify the vertex, axis of symmetry, the maximum or minimum value, and the domain and the range of each function.

9. $y = (x - 2)^2 + 3$
10. $f(x) = -0.2(x + 3)^2 + 2$

Graph each function. Identify the axis of symmetry.

11. $y = (x + 2)^2 - 1$
12. $y = -4(x - 3)^2 + 2$

Write a quadratic function to model each graph.

13.

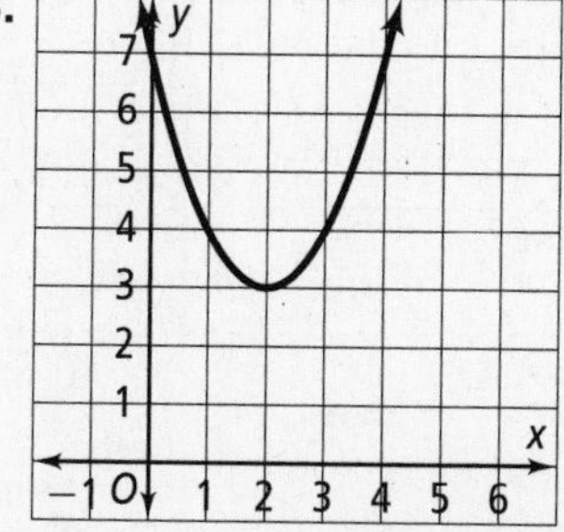

14.

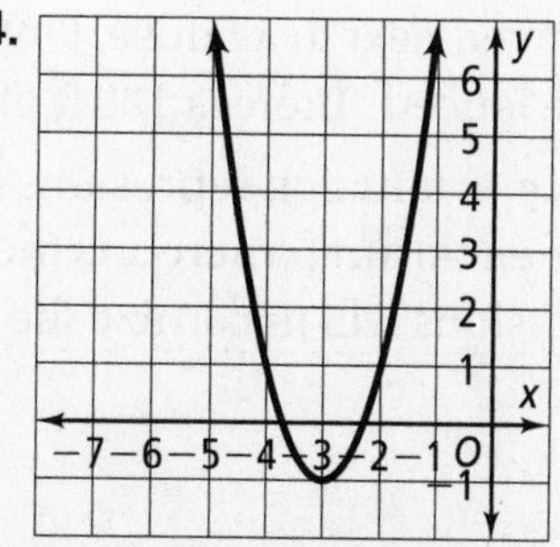

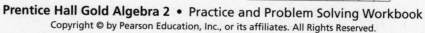

Name ______________________ Class ____________ Date ____________

4-1 Practice (continued) Form G

Quadratic Functions and Transformations

Describe how to transform the parent function $y = x^2$ to the graph of each function below. Graph both functions on the same axes.

15. $y = 3(x + 2)^2$

16. $y = -(x + 5)^2 + 1$

17. $y = \frac{1}{2}(x + 4)^2 - 2$

18. $y = -0.08(x - 0.04)^2 + 1.2$

Write the equation of each parabola in vertex form.

19. vertex $(3, -2)$, point $(2, 3)$

20. vertex $\left(\frac{1}{2}, 1\right)$, point $(2, -8)$

21. vertex $(-4, -24)$, point $(-5, -25)$

22. vertex $(-12.5, 35.5)$, point $(1, 400)$

23. The amount of cloth used to make four curtains is given by the function $A = -4x^2 + 40x$, where x is the width of one curtain in feet and A is the total area in square feet. Find the width that maximizes the area of the curtains. What is the maximum area?

24. The diagram shows the path of a model rocket launched from the ground. It reaches a maximum altitude of 384 ft when it is above a location 16 ft from the launch site. What quadratic function models the height of the rocket?

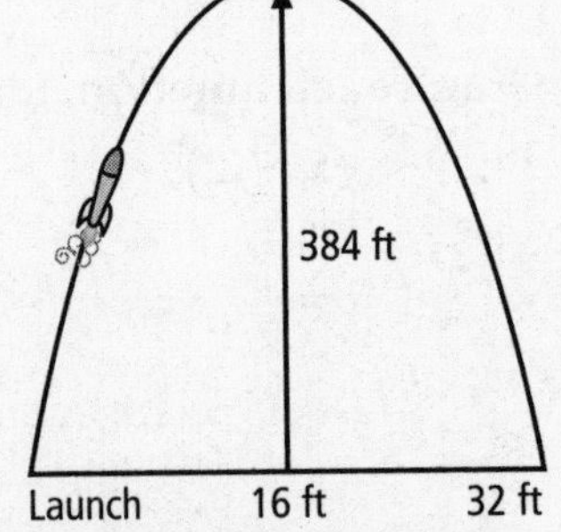

25. To make an enclosure for chickens, a rectangular area will be fenced next to a house. Only three sides will need to be fenced. There is 120 ft of fencing material.

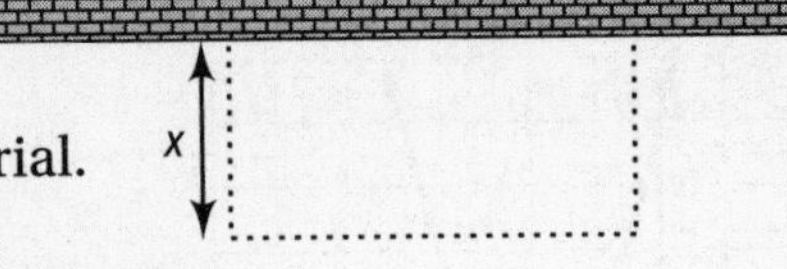

a. What quadratic function represents the area of the rectangular enclosure, where x is the distance from the house?

b. What dimensions will maximize the area of the enclosure?

Name ______________________ Class ____________ Date ____________

4-1 Standardized Test Prep

Quadratic Functions and Transformations

Multiple Choice

For Exercises 1–4, choose the correct letter.

1. What is the vertex of the function $y = 3(x - 7)^2 + 4$?

   (A) $(-7, -4)$ (B) $(-7, 4)$ (C) $(7, -4)$ (D) $(7, 4)$

2. Which is the graph of the function $f(x) = -2(x + 3)^2 + 5$?

   (F) 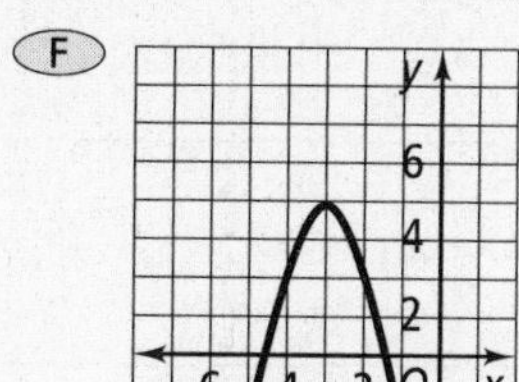

   (G) 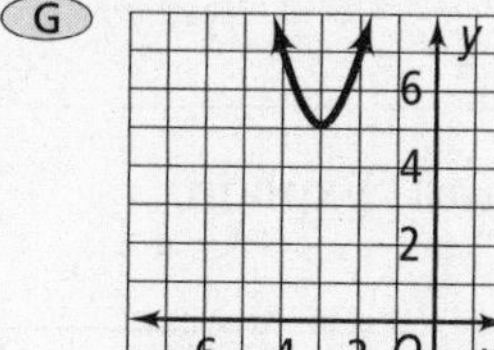

   (H) 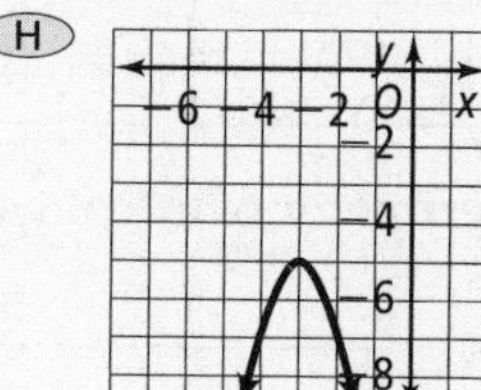

   (I) 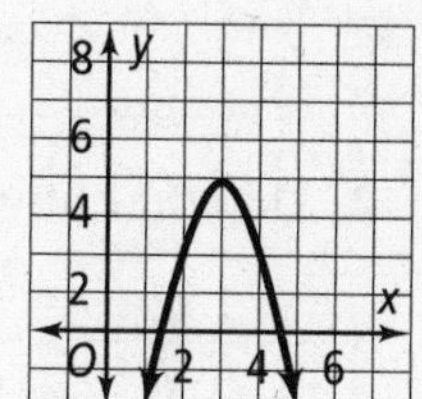

3. Which of the following best describes how to transform $y = x^2$ to the graph of $y = 4(x - 2.5)^2 - 3$?

   (A) Translate 2.5 units left, stretch by a factor of 4, translate 3 units down.

   (B) Translate 3 units right and 2.5 units down, stretch by a factor of 4.

   (C) Translate 2.5 units right, stretch by a factor of 4, translate 3 units down.

   (D) Stretch by a factor of 4, translate 2.5 units left and 3 units down.

4. What is the equation of the parabola with vertex $(-4, 6)$ passing through the point $(-2, -2)$?

   (F) $y = -2(x + 4)^2 - 6$ (H) $y = 2(x + 4)^2 + 6$

   (G) $y = 2(x - 4)^2 - 6$ (I) $y = -2(x + 4)^2 + 6$

Short Response

5. A baseball is hit so that its height above ground is given by the equation $h = -16t^2 + 96t + 4$, where h is the height in feet and t is the time in seconds after it is hit. Show your work.

   a. How long does it take the baseball to reach its highest point?

   b. How high will it go?

Name ______________________ Class ____________ Date ____________

4-2 Think About a Plan

Standard Form of a Quadratic Function

Landscaping A town is planning a playground. It wants to fence in a rectangular space using an existing wall. What is the greatest area it can fence in using 100 ft of donated fencing?

Understanding the Problem

1. Write an expression for the width of the playground. Let l be the length of the playground.

 ____

2. Do you know the perimeter of the playground? Explain.

 ____

3. What is the problem asking you to determine?

 ____

 ____

Planning the Solution

4. Write a quadratic equation to model the area of the playground.

 ____

5. What information can you get from the equation to find the maximum area? Explain.

 ____

 ____

Getting an Answer

6. What is the value of l that produces the maximum area?
7. What is the greatest area the town can fence in using 100 ft of fencing?

Name ______________________ Class ____________ Date ____________

4-2 Practice

Form G

Standard Form of a Quadratic Function

Identify the vertex, the axis of symmetry, the maximum or minimum value, and the range of each parabola.

1. $y = x^2 - 4x + 1$

2. $y = -x^2 + 2x + 3$

3. $y = -x^2 - 6x - 10$

4. $y = 3x^2 + 18x + 32$

5. $y = 2x^2 + 3x - 5$

6. $y = -3x^2 + 4x$

Graph each function.

7. $y = x^2 + 2x - 5$

8. $y = -x^2 + 3x + 1$

9. $y = 2x^2 + 4x - 4$

10. $y = -\frac{1}{2}x^2 - 3x + 3$

11. $y = 3x^2 - 8x$

12. $y = -3x^2 + 18x - 27$

Write each function in vertex form.

13. $y = x^2 - 8x + 19$

14. $y = x^2 - 2x - 6$

15. $y = x^2 + 3x$

16. $y = 2x^2 + x$

17. $y = 2x^2 - 12x + 11$

18. $y = -2x^2 - 4x + 6$

Name ______________________ Class ____________ Date ____________

4-2 Practice (continued)

Form G

Standard Form of a Quadratic Function

19. A small independent motion picture company determines the profit P for producing n DVD copies of a recent release is $P = -0.02n^2 + 3.40n - 16$. P is the profit in thousands of dollars and n is in thousands of units.

a. How many DVDs should the company produce to maximize the profit?

b. What will the maximize profit be?

Sketch each parabola using the given information.

20. vertex $(4, -2)$, y-intercept 6

21. vertex $(-3, 12)$, point $(-1, 0)$

For each function, the vertex of the function's graph is given. Find the unknown coefficients.

22. $y = x^2 + bx + c$; $(-4, -7)$

23. $y = ax^2 - 10x + c$; $(-5, 20)$

24. A local nursery sells a large number of ornamental trees every year. The owners have determined the cost per tree C for buying and caring for each tree before it is sold is $C = 0.001n^2 - 0.3n + 50$. In this function, C is the cost per tree in dollars and n is the number of trees in stock.

a. How many trees will minimize the cost per tree?

b. What will the minimum cost per tree be?

25. To line an irrigation ditch, a farmer will use rectangular metal sheets. Each side will be bent x feet from the edge at an angle of 90° to form the trough. If the sheets are 20 ft wide, how far from the edge (x) should the farmer bend them to maximize the area of a cross-section of the trough.

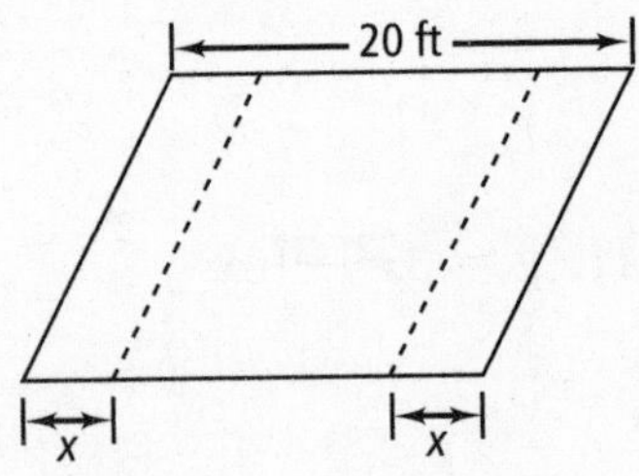

For each function, find the y-intercept.

26. $y = (x + 3)^2 - 5$

27. $y = -2(x - 2)^2 + 6$

28. $y = -(x + 1)^2 + 9$

29. $y = \frac{1}{2}(x + 4)^2 - 15$

Name ______________________ Class ____________ Date ____________

4-2 Standardized Test Prep

Standard Form of a Quadratic Function

Multiple Choice

For Exercises 1–6, choose the correct letter.

1. What is the vertex of the parabola $y = x^2 + 8x + 5$?

Ⓐ $(4, -11)$ Ⓑ $(-4, -11)$ Ⓒ $(-4, 5)$ Ⓓ $(4, 5)$

2. What is the maximum value of the function $y = -3x^2 + 12x - 8$?

Ⓕ 4 Ⓗ 8

Ⓖ -8 Ⓘ 2

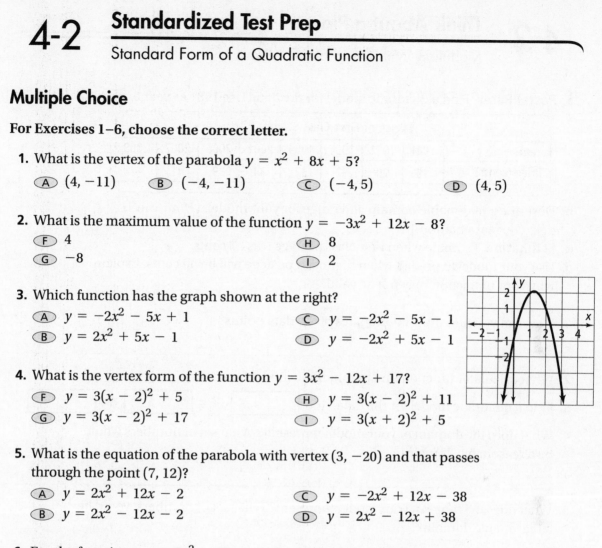

3. Which function has the graph shown at the right?

Ⓐ $y = -2x^2 - 5x + 1$ Ⓒ $y = -2x^2 - 5x - 1$

Ⓑ $y = 2x^2 + 5x - 1$ Ⓓ $y = -2x^2 + 5x - 1$

4. What is the vertex form of the function $y = 3x^2 - 12x + 17$?

Ⓕ $y = 3(x - 2)^2 + 5$ Ⓗ $y = 3(x - 2)^2 + 11$

Ⓖ $y = 3(x - 2)^2 + 17$ Ⓘ $y = 3(x + 2)^2 + 5$

5. What is the equation of the parabola with vertex $(3, -20)$ and that passes through the point $(7, 12)$?

Ⓐ $y = 2x^2 + 12x - 2$ Ⓒ $y = -2x^2 + 12x - 38$

Ⓑ $y = 2x^2 - 12x - 2$ Ⓓ $y = 2x^2 - 12x + 38$

6. For the function $y = -5x^2 - 10x + c$, the vertex is $(-1, 8)$. What is c?

Ⓕ -13 Ⓖ -3 Ⓗ 3 Ⓘ 13

Short Response

7. To increase revenue, a county wants to increase park fees. The overall income will go up, but there will be expenses involved in collecting the fees. For a $p\%$ increase in the fees, this cost C will be $C = 0.6p^2 - 7.2p + 48$, in thousands of dollars. What percent increase will minimize the cost to the county? Show your work.

Name ______________________ Class __________ Date __________

4-3 Think About a Plan

Modeling With Quadratic Functions

a. **Postal Rates** Find a quadratic model for the data. Use 1981 as year 0.

Price of First-Class Stamp

Year	1981	1991	1995	1999	2001	2006	2007	2008
Price (cents)	18	29	32	33	34	39	41	42

b. Describe a reasonable domain and range for your model. (*Hint*: This is a discrete, real situation.)

c. **Estimation** Estimate when first-class postage was 37 cents.

d. Use your model to predict when first-class postage will be 50 cents. Explain why your prediction may not be valid.

1. How can you find the x-coordinates of the data points?

____

2. What calculator function finds a quadratic model for data? __________

3. Find a quadratic model for the data. $y = \square x^2 + \square x + \square$

4. What does the domain of your model represent? What set of numbers would be a reasonable domain?

____

5. What does the range of your model represent? What set of numbers would be a reasonable domain?

____

6. How can you find the x-value that produces a given y-value?

____

____

7. Estimate the year when first-class postage was 37 cents. $\square$

8. Predict the year when first-class postage will be 50 cents. $\square$

9. Why might your prediction not be valid?

____

____

Name ______________________ Class ____________ Date ____________

4-3 Practice

Form G

Modeling With Quadratic Functions

Find an equation in standard form of the parabola passing through the points.

1. (1, −1), (2, −5), (3, −7)

2. (1, −4), (2, −3), (3, −4)

3. (2, −8), (3, −8), (6, 4)

4. (−1, −12), (2, −6), (4, −12)

5. (−1, −12), (0, −6), (3, 0)

6. (−2, −4), (1, −1), (3, 11)

7. (−1, −6), (0, 0), (2, 6)

8. (−3, 2), (1, −6), (4, 9)

9.

x	$f(x)$
−1	7
1	5
3	11

10.

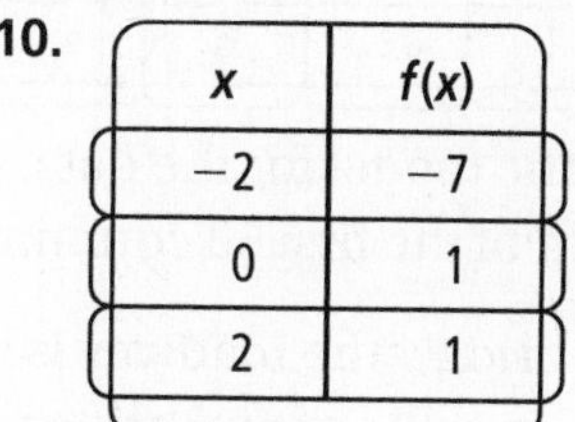

x	$f(x)$
−2	−7
0	1
2	1

11.

x	$f(x)$
−1	−6
1	4
2	12

12.

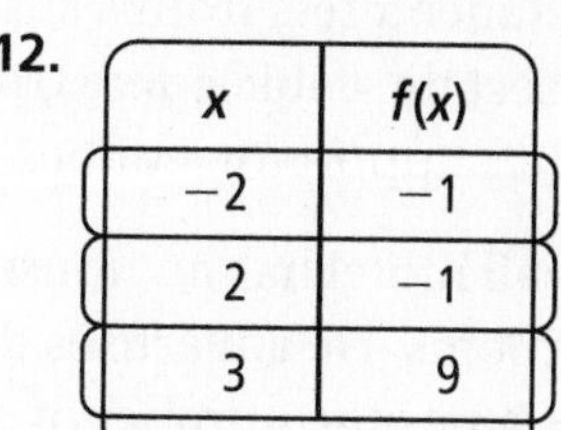

x	$f(x)$
−2	−1
2	−1
3	9

13. The table shows the number n of tickets to a school play sold t days after the tickets went on sale, for several days.

a. Find a quadratic model for the data.

b. Use the model to find the number of tickets sold on day 7.

c. When was the greatest number of tickets sold?

Day, t	Number of Tickets Sold, n
1	32
3	64
4	74

14. The table gives the number of pairs of skis sold in a sporting goods store for several months last year.

a. Find a quadratic model for the data, using January as month 1, February as month 2, and so on.

b. Use the model to predict the number of pairs of skis sold in November.

c. In what month were the fewest skis sold?

Month, t	Number of Pairs of Skis Sold, s
Jan	82
Mar	42
May	18

4-3 Practice (continued) Form G

Modeling With Quadratic Functions

Determine whether a quadratic model exists for each set of values. If so, write the model.

15. $f(-1) = -7, f(1) = 1, f(3) = 1$

16. $f(-1) = 13, f(0) = 6, f(2) = -8$

17. $f(2) = 2, f(-4) = -1, f(-2) = 0$

18. $f(2) = 6, f(0) = -4, f(-2) = -6$

19. a. Complete the table. It shows the sum of the counting numbers from 1 through n.

Number, n	1	2	3	4	5
Sum, s	1	3	6		

b. Write a quadratic model for the data.

c. Predict the sum of the first 50 counting numbers.

20. On a suspension bridge, the roadway is hung from cables hanging between support towers. The cable of one bridge is in the shape of the parabola $y = 0.1x^2 - 7x + 150$, where y is the height in feet of the cable above the roadway at the distance x feet from a support tower.

a. What is the closest the cable comes to the roadway?

b. How far from the support tower does this occur?

21. The owner of a small motel has an unusual idea to increase revenue. The motel has 20 rooms. He advertises that each night will cost a base rate of \$48 plus \$8 times the number of empty rooms that night. For example, if all rooms are occupied, he will have a total income of $20 \times \$48 = \$960$. But, if three rooms are empty, then his total income will be $(20 - 3) \times (\$48 + \$8 \cdot 3) = 17 \times \$72 = \$1224$.

a. Write a linear expression to show how many rooms are occupied if n rooms are empty.

b. Write a linear expression to show the price paid in dollars per room if n rooms are empty.

c. Multiply the expressions from parts (a) and (b) to obtain a quadratic model for the data. Write the result in standard form.

d. What will the owner's total income be if 10 rooms are empty?

e. What is the number of empty rooms that results in the maximum income for the owner?

Name ____________________ Class ____________ Date ____________

4-3 Standardized Test Prep

Modeling With Quadratic Functions

Multiple Choice

For Exercises 1–5, choose the correct letter.

1. Which parabola passes through the points (1, −2), (4, 1), and (5, −2)?

Ⓐ $y = -x^2 + x - 3$

Ⓑ $y = -x^2 + 6x - 7$

Ⓒ $y = x^2 - 4x + 1$

Ⓓ $y = x^2 - 4x - 1$

2. Which parabola passes through the points in the table at the right?

x	f(x)
−1	2
2	−4
4	2

Ⓕ $y = -x^2 - x + 2$

Ⓖ $y = \frac{1}{2}x^2 - \frac{5}{2}x - 1$

Ⓗ $y = 2x^2 - 4x - 4$

Ⓘ $y = x^2 - 3x - 2$

3. A baseball coach records the height at every second of a ball thrown in the air. Some of the data appears in the table below.

Time (s)	0	1	3
Height (ft)	0	64	96

Which equation is a quadratic model for the data?

Ⓐ $h = -16t^2 + 80t$

Ⓑ $h = -48t^2 + 112t$

Ⓒ $h = -32t^2 + 80t$

Ⓓ $h = -16t^2 + 64t$

4. Use the table in Exercise 3. What is the height of the ball at 2.5 s?

Ⓕ 80 ft

Ⓖ 88 ft

Ⓗ 100 ft

Ⓘ 112 ft

5. Which of the following sets of values cannot be modeled with a quadratic function?

Ⓐ (2, 3), (0, −1), (3, 2)

Ⓑ $f(2) = 7, f(-1) = -2, f(0) = 3$

Ⓒ (2, −7), (−1, 5), (3, −11)

Ⓓ $f(2) = -6, f(0) = -2, f(-1) = 3$

Short Response

6. The accountant for a small company studied the amount spent on advertising and the company's profit for several years. He made the table below. What is a quadratic model for the data? Show your work.

Advertising (Hundreds of Dollars)	1	2	3
Profit (Dollars)	269	386	501

Name ______________________ Class ____________ Date ____________

4-4 Think About a Plan

Factoring Quadratic Expressions

Agriculture The area in square feet of a rectangular field is $x^2 - 120x + 3500$. The width, in feet, is $x - 50$. What is the length, in feet?

Know

1. The area of the field equals the ☐ times the ☐.

2. The area of the field is ______________ ft^2.

3. The width of the field is ☐ ft.

Need

4. To solve the problem I need to:

____

____.

Plan

5. One factor is ☐.

6. What is the coefficient of the first term of the other factor?

How do you know?

____

7. What is the sign of the second term of the other factor? ☐

How do you know?

____

____

8. The product of 50 and ☐ is 3500.

9. The sum of 50 and ☐ is 120.

10. The other factor is ☐.

11. What is the length of the rectangular field, in feet?

Name ______________________ Class ____________ Date ____________

4-4 Practice

Form G

Factoring Quadratic Expressions

Factor each expression.

1. $x^2 + 11x + 28$

2. $x^2 + 11x + 24$

3. $s^2 + 13s + 42$

4. $x^2 - 10x + 21$

5. $y^2 - 8y + 15$

6. $x^2 - 12x + 32$

7. $-x^2 + 9x - 18$

8. $-w^2 + 12w - 35$

9. $-t^2 - 3t + 54$

10. $x^2 - 7x - 60$

Find the GCF of each expression. Then factor the expression.

11. $6x^2 - 9$

12. $16m^2 + 8m$

13. $2a^2 + 22a + 60$

14. $5x^2 + 25x - 70$

15. $\frac{1}{3}x^2 + \frac{1}{3}x - 4$

16. $-7x^2 + 7x + 14$

Factor each expression.

17. $5x^2 - 17x + 6$

18. $3x^2 + 10x + 8$

19. $2b^2 - 9b - 5$

20. $z^2 + 12z + 36$

21. $9x^2 - 6x + 1$

22. $4k^2 + 12k + 9$

23. $n^2 - 49$

24. $2x^2 - 50$

25. The area of a rectangular field is $x^2 - x - 72\ \text{m}^2$. The length of the field is $x + 8$ m. What is the width of the field in meters?

Name ______________________ Class ____________ Date ____________

4-4 Practice (continued)

Form G

Factoring Quadratic Expressions

26. The product of two integers is $w^2 - 3w - 40$, where w is a whole number. Write expressions for each of the two integers in terms of w.

27. John is j years old. The product of his younger brother's and older sister's ages is $j^2 - 2j - 15$. How old are John's brother and sister in terms of John's age?

Factor each expression completely.

28. $2x^2 + 9x + 10$

29. $6y^2 - 5y + 1$

30. $3x^2 + 8x - 3$

31. $4x^2 - 7x - 15$

32. $12t^2 + 10t - 12$

33. $-10x^2 + x + 21$

34. $-4k^2 + 2k + 30$

35. $\frac{1}{2}x^2 + \frac{1}{2}x - 10$

36. $x^2 - 16x + 64$

37. $m^2 + 22m + 121$

38. $16x^2 - 40x + 25$

39. $36x^2 + 12x + 1$

40. $-2x^2 - 32x - 128$

41. $-25p^2 + 30p - 9$

42. $r^2 - 144$

43. $\frac{1}{4}x^2 - \frac{1}{4}$

44. $-7s^2 + 175$

45. $-\frac{1}{25}z^2 + 1$

46. The radius of the outer circle in the illustration is R. The radius of the inner circle is r.

a. Write an expression for the area of the outer circle.

b. Write an expression for the area of the inner circle.

c. Write an expression representing the area of the ring, the shaded region in the illustration. Do not simplify.

d. Factor the expression in part (c).

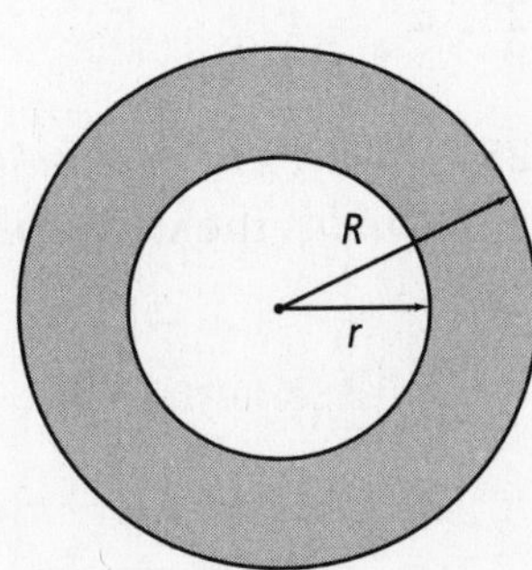

Name ______________________ Class ____________ Date ____________

4-4 Standardized Test Prep

Factoring Quadratic Expressions

Multiple Choice

For Exercises 1–6, choose the correct letter.

1. What is the complete factorization of $2x^2 + x - 15$?

(A) $(x - 5)(2x + 3)$
(B) $(x + 3)(2x - 5)$
(C) $(x - 3)(2x + 5)$
(D) $(x + 5)(2x - 3)$

2. What is the complete factorization of $-x^2 + 3x + 28$?

(F) $(x - 4)(x - 7)$
(G) $-(x - 4)(x + 7)$
(H) $-(x + 4)(x + 7)$
(I) $-(x - 7)(x + 4)$

3. What is the complete factorization of $6x^2 + 9x - 6$?

(A) $3(2x - 1)(x + 2)$
(B) $(3x + 2)(2x - 3)$
(C) $3(x - 2)(2x + 1)$
(D) $3(x - 2)(2x - 1)$

4. What is the complete factorization of $16x^2 - 56x + 49$?

(F) $(4x - 7)(4x + 7)$
(G) $(4x - 7)^2$
(H) $(4x + 7)^2$
(I) $16(x - 7)^2$

5. What is the complete factorization of $5x^2 - 20$?

(A) $(5x - 4)(x + 5)$
(B) $5(x + 4)(x - 4)$
(C) $5(x + 2)(x - 2)$
(D) $5(x - 2)^2$

6. What is the complete factorization of $x^2 - 14x + 24$?

(F) $(x - 8)(x - 3)$
(G) $(x - 4)(x - 6)$
(H) $(x + 2)(x - 12)$
(I) $(x - 12)(x - 2)$

Short Response

7. The area in square meters of a rectangular parking lot is $x^2 - 95x + 2100$. The width in meters is $x - 60$. What is the length of the parking lot in meters? Show your work.

Name ______________________ Class ____________ Date ____________

4-5 Think About a Plan

Quadratic Equations

Landscaping Suppose you have an outdoor pool measuring 25 ft by 10 ft. You want to add a cement walkway around the pool. If the walkway will be 1 ft thick and you have 304 ft^3 of cement, how wide should the walkway be?

Understanding the Problem

1. Draw a diagram of the pool and the walkway. Let $x =$ the width of the walkway in feet.
2. If you lay the pieces of walkway end to end, what is the total length of the walkway?
3. What is the thickness of the walkway?
4. What is the problem asking you to determine?

____

Planning the Solution

5. Write a quadratic equation to model the volume of the walkway.
6. What method can you use to find the solutions of your quadratic equation?

____

____

____

Getting an Answer

7. How many solutions of your quadratic equation do you need to find? Explain.

____

8. How wide should the walkway be?

Name ______________________ Class ____________ Date ____________

4-5 Practice

Form G

Quadratic Equations

Solve each equation by factoring. Check your answers.

1. $x^2 - 2x - 24 = 0$

2. $3x^2 = x + 4$

3. $x^2 - 6x + 9 = 0$

4. $3x^2 + 45 = 24x$

5. $4x^2 + 6x = 0$

6. $7x^2 = 21x$

7. $(x + 2)^2 = 49$

8. $x + 3 = 24x^2$

Solve each equation using tables. Give each answer to at most two decimal places.

9. $5x^2 + 7x - 6 = 0$

10. $x^2 - 2x = 1$

11. $2x^2 - x = 5$

12. $x^2 - 4x + 2 = 0$

13. $3x^2 + 7x = 1$

14. $2x^2 - 3x = 15$

Solve each equation by graphing. Give each answer to at most two decimal places.

15. $10x^2 = 4 - 3x$

16. $3x^2 + 2x = 2$

17. $4x^2 - x = 6$

18. $4x^2 + 3x = 6 - 2x$

19. $x^2 + 4 = 6x$

20. $5 - x = \frac{1}{2}x^2$

21. A woman drops a front door key to her husband from their apartment window several stories above the ground. The function $h = -16t^2 + 64$ gives the height h of the key in feet, t seconds after she releases it.

a. How long does it take the key to reach the ground?

b. What are the reasonable domain and range for the function h?

Name ______________________ Class __________ Date __________

4-5 Practice (continued)

Form G

Quadratic Equations

22. The function $C = 75x + 2600$ gives the cost, in dollars, for a small company to manufacture x items. The function $R = 225x - x^2$ gives the revenue, also in dollars, for selling x items. How many items should the company produce so that the cost and revenue are equal?

23. The function $a = 2.4t - 0.1t^2$ gives the amount a, in micromilligrams (mmg), of a drug in a patient's bloodstream t hours after being ingested in tablet form. When is the amount of the drug equal to 8 mmg? (*Hint:* Multiply the equation you write by 10 before solving.)

24. You use a rectangular piece of cardboard measuring 20 in. by 30 in. to construct a box. You cut squares with sides x in. from each corner of the piece of cardboard and then fold up the sides to form the bottom.

a. Write a function A representing the area of the base of the box in terms of x.

b. What is a reasonable domain for the function A?

c. Write an equation if the area of the base must be 416 in.^{2}.

d. Solve the equation in part (c) for values of x in the reasonable domain.

e. What are the dimensions of the base of the box?

Solve each equation by factoring, using tables, or by graphing. If necessary, round your answer to the nearest hundredth.

25. $9x^2 = 49$

26. $x^2 + 10x + 17 = 0$

27. $4x^2 + 1 = 8x$

28. $5x^2 - 2x - 7 = 0$

29. $4(x^2 - x) = 19$

30. $25x^2 + 20x + 4 = 0$

31. $3x^2 = 4x + 32$

32. $x^2 - 5x - 12 = 0$

Name ______________________ Class ______________ Date ______________

4-5 Standardized Test Prep

Quadratic Equations

Gridded Response

Solve each exercise and enter your answer in the grid provided.

1. What is the positive solution of the equation $x^2 = 2x + 35$? Solve by factoring.

2. What is the positive solution of the equation $5x^2 + 2x - 16 = 0$? Solve by factoring.

3. What is the positive solution of the equation $x^2 - 3x = 1$? Solve by using a table or by graphing. If necessary, round your answer to the nearest hundredth.

4. What is the positive solution of the equation $3x^2 - 5x - 7 = 0$? Solve by using a table or by graphing. If necessary, round your answer to the nearest hundredth.

5. What is the positive solution of the equation $\frac{1}{2}x^2 - 3x = 5$? Solve by using a table or by graphing. If necessary, round your answer to the nearest hundredth.

Answers

1.

2. 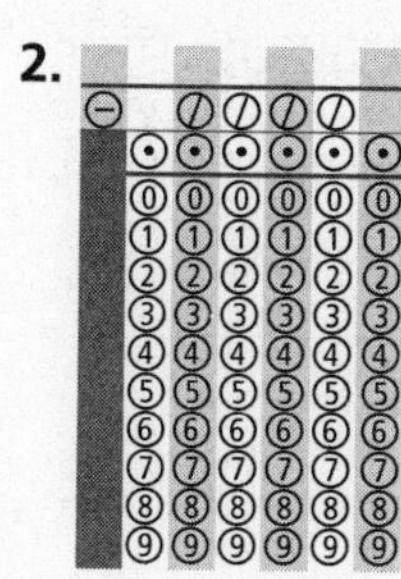

3. 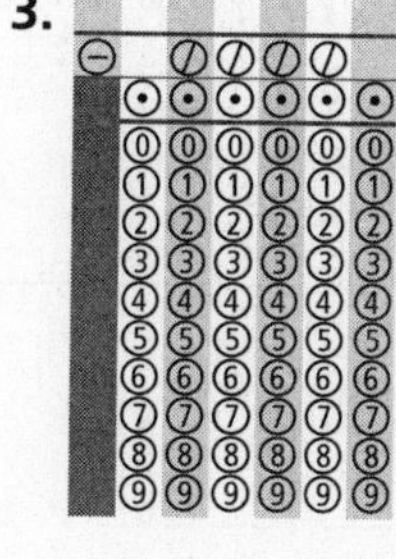

4. 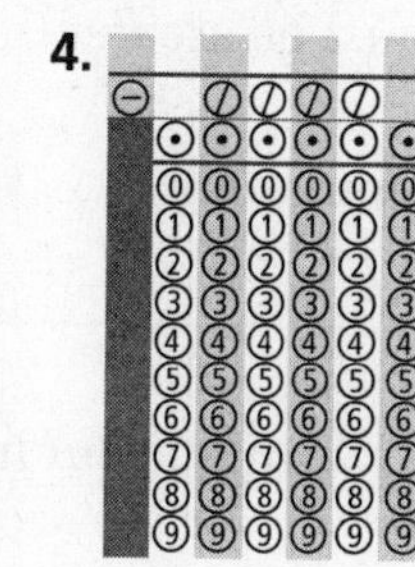

5. 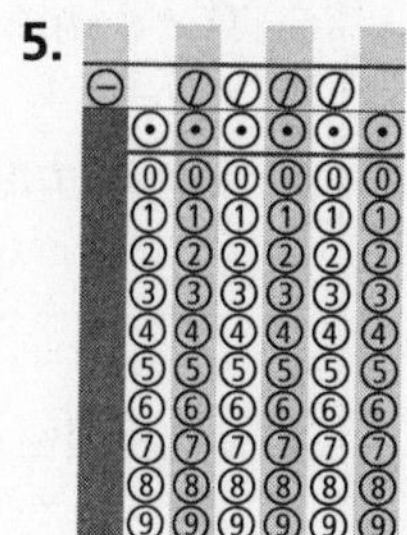

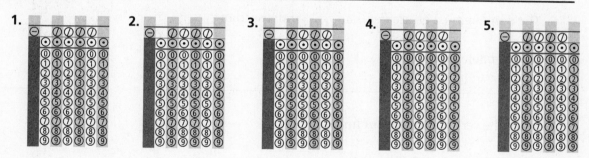

Name ______________________ Class __________ Date __________

4-6 Think About a Plan

Completing the Square

Geometry The table shows some possible dimensions of rectangles with a perimeter of 100 units. Copy and complete the table.

Width	Length	Area
1	49	49
2	48	
3		
4		
5		

a. Plot the points (width, area). Find a model for the data set.

b. What is another point in the data set? Use it to verify your model.

c. What is a reasonable domain for this function? Explain.

d. Find the maximum possible area. What are its dimensions?

e. Find an equation for area in terms of width without using the table. Do you get the same equation as in part (a)? Explain.

1. What points should you plot? Plot the points on the graph.

____

2. Use your graphing calculator to find a model for the data set. [ ]

3. What is another point in the data set? Use it to verify your model.

____

4. What does the domain of your function represent?

____

5. The domain must be greater than ____ and less than ____.

6. A reasonable domain is:

____

7. Write the vertex form of your function.

8. The maximum possible area is [ ].
The dimensions of this rectangle are [ ] by [ ].

9. If the width of the rectangle is x, then the length is [ ].

Area = [ ] times [ ] = [ ] · [ ] = [ ]

10. Is the equation in Exercise 9 the same as your model in Exercise 2? Explain.

____

Name ______________________ Class ____________ Date ____________

4-6 Practice

Form G

Completing the Square

Solve each equation by finding square roots.

1. $3x^2 = 75$

2. $5x^2 - 45 = 0$

3. $4x^2 - 49 = 0$

4. $6x^2 = 216$

5. $2x^2 = 14$

6. $3x^2 - 96 = 0$

7. A box is 4 in. high. Its length is 1.5 times its width. The volume of the box is 1350 in.^{2}. What are the width and length of the box?

Solve each equation.

8. $x^2 + 12x + 36 = 25$

9. $x^2 - 10x + 25 = 144$

10. $x^2 + 6x + 9 = \frac{49}{4}$

11. $x^2 - 22x + 121 = 225$

12. $16x^2 + 8x + 1 = 16$

13. $25x^2 - 30x + 9 = 81$

Complete the square.

14. $x^2 + 22x +$

15. $x^2 - 30x +$

16. $x^2 + 5x +$

17. $x^2 - \frac{1}{2}x +$

18. $25x^2 + 10x +$

19. $4x^2 - 12x +$

Solve each quadratic equation by completing the square.

20. $x^2 + 10x - 1 = 0$

21. $x^2 + 2x - 7 = 0$

22. $-x^2 + 6x + 10 = 0$

23. $x^2 + 5x = 3x + 11$

24. $3x^2 + 4x = 2x^2 + 3$

25. $x^2 - 2x - \frac{3}{4} = 0$

26. $-0.2x^2 + 0.4x + 0.8 = 0$

27. $4x^2 + 20x + 1 = 0$

Name ______________________ Class ____________ Date ____________

4-6 Practice (continued) Form G

Completing the Square

Rewrite each equation in vertex form.

28. $y = x^2 - 6x + 4$

29. $y = x^2 + 14x + 50$

30. $y = 3x^2 + 8x + 2$

31. $y = -2x^2 + 6x - 2$

Find the value of k that would make the left side of each equation a perfect square trinomial.

32. $x^2 + kx + 196 = 0$

33. $64x^2 - kx + 1 = 0$

34. $x^2 - kx + 16 = 0$

35. $4x^2 - kx + 9 = 0$

36. $16x^2 + kx + 9 = 0$

37. $\frac{1}{4}x^2 - kx + \frac{1}{25} = 0$

38. The quadratic function $d = -t^2 + 4t + 33$ models the depth of water in a flood channel after a rainstorm. The time in hours after it stops raining is t and d is the depth of the water in feet.
   a. Solve the equation $-t^2 + 4t + 33 = 0$.
   b. Approximate the positive solution found in part (a) to two decimal places.
   c. Interpret the answer to part (b) in terms of the problem.

39. While in orbit, a space scientist measures the pressure inside a container as it is being heated and then cooled. She records the information and discovers the pressure p, in pounds per square inch, is related to the time t in minutes after the experiment begins according to the equation $p = -0.2t^2 + 1.6t$.
   a. Complete the square in the expression $-0.2t^2 + 1.6t$.
   b. Rewrite the equation for p in vertex form.
   c. What is a reasonable domain for this function? Explain.
   d. When does the maximum pressure occur? What is the maximum pressure?

Name ______________________ Class ____________ Date ____________

4-6 Standardized Test Prep

Completing the Square

Multiple Choice

For Exercises 1–6, choose the correct letter.

1. What are the solutions of the equation $36x^2 - 12x + 1 = 4$?

(A) 4, 8 (B) $-\frac{1}{6}, \frac{1}{6}$ (C) $-\frac{1}{2}, \frac{1}{6}$ (D) $-\frac{1}{6}, \frac{1}{2}$

2. What are the solutions of the equation $2x^2 + 16x + 28 = 0$?

(F) $-4 \pm \sqrt{30}$ (G) $-4 \pm \sqrt{2}$ (H) $4 \pm \sqrt{2}$ (I) $4 \pm \sqrt{30}$

3. Which value completes the square for $x^2 - 3x$?

(A) $\frac{9}{4}$ (B) $\frac{3}{2}$ (C) 9 (D) $-\frac{9}{4}$

4. Which value for k would make the left side of $x^2 + kx + \frac{49}{64} = 0$ a perfect square trinomial?

(F) 7 (G) $\frac{7}{2}$ (H) $\frac{7}{4}$ (I) $\frac{7}{8}$

5. What are the solutions of the equation $x^2 = 8x - 1$?

(A) $-4 \pm \sqrt{17}$ (B) $-4 \pm \sqrt{15}$ (C) $4 \pm \sqrt{15}$ (D) $4 \pm \sqrt{17}$

6. Which equation is the vertex form of $y = -3x^2 + 12x - 7$?

(F) $y = -3(x - 2)^2 - 5$ (H) $y = -3(x + 2)^2 - 5$

(G) $y = -3(x - 2)^2 + 5$ (I) $y = -3(x + 2)^2 + 5$

Short Response

7. The equation $p = -x^2 + 8x + 5$ gives the price p, in dollars, for a product when x million units are produced.

a. What are the solutions of the equation $-x^2 + 8x + 5 = 0$?

b. What is the positive solution to part (a) rounded to two decimal places? What does this solution mean in terms of this problem?

Name ______________________ Class ____________ Date ____________

4-7 Think About a Plan

The Quadratic Formula

Sports A diver dives from a 10 m springboard. The equation $f(t) = -4.9t^2 + 4t + 10$ models her height above the pool at time t. At what time does she enter the water?

Understanding the Problem

1. What does the function represent?

____

2. What is the problem asking you to determine?

____

3. Do you need to use the height of the springboard to solve the problem? Explain.

____

____

Planning the Solution

4. What are three possible methods for solving this problem?

____

5. If a solution exists, which method will give an exact solution? Explain.

____

____

Getting an Answer

6. Is there more than one reasonable solution to the problem? Explain.

____

____

7. At what time does the diver enter the water?

____

Name ____________________ Class ____________ Date ____________

4-7 Practice

Form G

The Quadratic Formula

Solve each equation using the Quadratic Formula.

1. $x^2 - 8x + 15 = 0$

2. $x^2 + 12x + 35 = 0$

3. $3x^2 + 5x = 2$

4. $2x^2 + 3 = 7x$

5. $x^2 + 16 = 8x$

6. $x^2 = 4x - 1$

7. $x(2x - 5) = 12$

8. $-3x^2 - 8x + 16 = 0$

9. $x^2 + 4x = 3$

10. $x^2 + 10x + 22 = 0$

11. $4x(x + 1) = 7$

12. $x(2x - 3) = 9$

13. The principal at a high school is planning a concert to raise money for the music programs. He determines the profit p from ticket sales depends on the price t of a ticket according to the equation $p = -200t^2 + 3600t - 6400$. All amounts are in dollars. If the goal is to raise \$8500, what is the smallest amount the school should charge for a ticket to the concert?

14. The equation $y = x^2 - 12x + 45$ models the number of books y sold in a bookstore x days after an award-winning author appeared at an autograph-signing reception. What was the first day that at least 100 copies of the book were sold?

15. The height of the tide measured at a seaside community varies according to the number of hours t after midnight. If the height h, in feet, is currently given by the equation $h = -\frac{1}{2}t^2 + 6t - 9$, when will the tide first be at 6 ft?

16. The height h, in feet, of a model rocket t seconds after launch is given by $h = 256t - 16t^2$. As the rocket descends, it deploys a recovery parachute when it reaches 200 ft above the ground. At what time does the parachute deploy?

4-7 Practice (continued) — Form G

The Quadratic Formula

Evaluate the discriminant for each equation. Determine the number of real solutions.

17. $x^2 + 5x + 8 = 0$

18. $x^2 - 5x + 4 = 0$

19. $-9x^2 + 12x - 4 = 0$

20. $-3x^2 + 5x - 4 = 0$

21. $4x^2 + 4x = -1$

22. $6x^2 = x + 2$

23. $5x + 1 = 3x^2$

24. $4x^2 - x + 3 = 0$

25. $4x^2 + 36x + 81 = 0$

26. $5x^2 = 3x - 2$

27. $16x^2 - 56x + 49 = 0$

28. $4x^2 - 16x + 11 = 0$

29. In Exercise 16, the height of the rocket was given by $h = 256t - 16t^2$. Use the discriminant to answer the following questions.
   a. Will the rocket reach an altitude of 1000 ft?
   b. Will the rocket reach an altitude of 1024 ft?
   c. Will the rocket reach an altitude of 1048 ft?

30. The number n of people using the elevator in an office building every hour is given by $n = t^2 - 10t + 40$. In this equation, t is the number of hours after the building opens in the morning, $0 \leq t \leq 12$. Will the number of people using the elevator ever be less than 15 in any one hour? Use the discriminant to answer.

Solve each equation using any method. When necessary, round real solutions to the nearest hundredth.

31. $4x^2 + x - 3 = 0$

32. $5x^2 - 6x - 2 = 0$

33. $x^2 - 5x - 9 = 0$

34. $15x^2 - 2x - 1 = 0$

35. $2x^2 = 5x - 3$

36. $4x^2 + 3x = 5$

Name ______________________ Class __________ Date __________

4-7 Standardized Test Prep

The Quadratic Formula

Multiple Choice

For Exercises 1–6, choose the correct letter.

1. What is the solution of $3x^2 + 2x - 5 = 0$? Use the Quadratic Formula.

   (A) $-\frac{5}{3}, 1$ (B) $-1, \frac{5}{3}$ (C) $-\frac{1}{3}, 5$ (D) $-5, \frac{1}{3}$

2. What is the solution of $2x^2 - 8x + 3 = 0$? Use the Quadratic Formula.

   (F) $\frac{-4 \pm \sqrt{22}}{2}$ (G) $\frac{-4 \pm \sqrt{10}}{2}$ (H) $\frac{4 \pm \sqrt{10}}{2}$ (I) $\frac{4 \pm \sqrt{22}}{2}$

3. What is the solution of $x^2 - 5x = 5$? Use the Quadratic Formula.

   (A) $-5, 1$ (B) $-1, 5$ (C) $\frac{5 \pm \sqrt{5}}{2}$ (D) $\frac{5 \pm 3\sqrt{5}}{2}$

4. What is the solution of $x^2 = 6x - 3$? Use the Quadratic Formula.

   (F) $-3 \pm \sqrt{6}$ (G) -3 (H) 3 (I) $3 \pm \sqrt{6}$

5. What is the discriminant of the equation $3x^2 - 7x + 1 = 0$?

   (A) 61 (B) 37 (C) $\sqrt{37}$ (D) -19

6. What is the discriminant of the equation $4x^2 + 28x + 49 = 0$?

   (F) -5472 (G) -756 (H) 0 (I) 1568

Extended Response

7. The equation $d = n^2 - 12n + 43$ models the number of defective items d produced in a manufacturing process when there are n workers in a restricted area. Use the discriminant to answer the following questions. Show your work.
   a. Will the number of defective items ever be 10?
   b. Will the number of defective items ever be 7?
   c. Will the number of defective items ever be 5?

Name ______________________ Class ____________ Date ____________

4-8 Think About a Plan

Complex Numbers

A student wrote the numbers 1, 5, $1 + 3i$, and $4 + 3i$ to represent the vertices of a quadrilateral in the complex number plane. What type of quadrilateral has these vertices?

Know

1. The vertices of the quadrilateral are:

____.

2. You can write the vertices in the form $a + bi$ as:

____.

Need

3. To solve the problem I need to:

____.

Plan

4. How do you find the coordinates that represent each complex number?

____

____

5. What are the points you need to graph?

____

6. Graph your points in the complex plane. Connect the points with straight lines to form a quadrilateral.

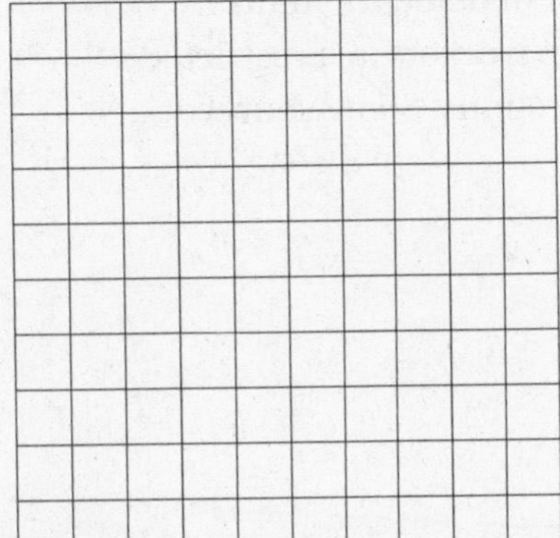

7. What type of quadrilateral did you draw? Explain how you know.

____

____

Name ______________________ Class ____________ Date ____________

4-8 Practice

Form G

Complex Numbers

Simplify each number by using the imaginary number *i*.

1. $\sqrt{-49}$

2. $\sqrt{-144}$

3. $\sqrt{-7}$

4. $\sqrt{-10}$

5. $\sqrt{-8}$

6. $\sqrt{-48}$

Plot each complex number and find its absolute value.

7. $-3i$

8. $6 - 4i$

9. $-4 + 8i$

Simplify each expression.

10. $(-2 + 3i) + (5 - 2i)$

11. $(-6 + 7i) + (6 - 7i)$

12. $(4 - 2i) - (-1 + 3i)$

13. $(-5 + 3i) - (-8 + 2i)$

14. $(4 - 3i)(-5 + 4i)$

15. $(2 - i)(-3 + 6i)$

16. $(5 - 3i)(5 + 3i)$

17. $(-1 + 3i)^2$

18. $(4 - i)^2$

19. $(-2i)(5i)(-i)$

20. $(6 - \sqrt{-16}) + (-4 + \sqrt{-25})$

21. $(-2 + \sqrt{-9}) + (-1 - \sqrt{-36})$

22. $(-5 + \sqrt{-4}) - (3 - \sqrt{-16})$

23. $(7 - \sqrt{-1}) - \sqrt{-81}$

24. $3i(2 + 2i)$

25. $2(3 - 7i) - i(-4 + 5i)$

26. $(2 + \sqrt{-4})(-1 + \sqrt{-9})$

27. $(5 + \sqrt{-1})(2 - \sqrt{-36})$

Name ______________________ Class ____________ Date ____________

4-8 Practice (continued) — Form G

Complex Numbers

Write each quotient as a complex number.

28. $\frac{5 + 2i}{4i}$

29. $\frac{3i}{-2 + i}$

30. $\frac{3 - 2i}{4 - 3i}$

31. $\frac{7}{5 - 2i}$

Find the factors of each expression. Check your answer.

32. $x^2 + 36$

33. $2x^2 + 8$

34. $5x^2 + 5$

35. $x^2 + \frac{1}{9}$

36. $16x^2 + 25$

37. $-4x^2 - 49$

Find all solutions to each quadratic equation.

38. $x^2 + 2x + 5 = 0$

39. $-x^2 + 2x - 10 = 0$

40. $2x^2 - 3x + 5 = 0$

41. $-4x^2 + 6x - 3 = 0$

42. $3x^2 + 2x + 5 = 0$

43. $2x^2 - 2x + 7 = 0$

44. a. Name the complex number represented by each point on the graph at the right.

b. Find the additive inverse of each number.

c. Find the complex conjugate of each number.

d. Find the absolute value of each number.

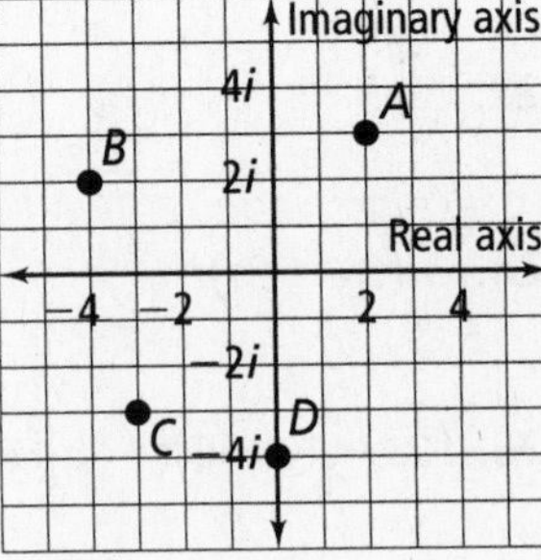

Name ______________________ Class ____________ Date ____________

4-8 Standardized Test Prep

Complex Numbers

Multiple Choice

For Exercises 1–8, choose the correct letter.

1. What is the simplified form of $(-8 + 5i) + (3 - 2i)$?

   (A) $-14 + 31i$ (B) $-5 + 3i$ (C) $-11 + 7i$ (D) $5 - 3i$

2. What is the simplified form of $(11 - 6i) - (-4 + 12i)$?

   (F) $7 + 6i$ (G) $7 - 18i$ (H) $15 + 6i$ (I) $15 - 18i$

3. What is the simplified form of $(5 + \sqrt{-36}) - (-4 - \sqrt{-49})$?

   (A) $9 - 13i$ (B) $9 + 85i$ (C) $1 - i$ (D) $9 + 13i$

4. What is the simplified form of $(-5i)(-3i)$?

   (F) $-15i$ (G) -15 (H) 15 (I) $15i$

5. What is the simplified form of $(-3 + 2i)(1 - 4i)$?

   (A) $-2 - 2i$ (B) $-11 - 10i$ (C) $5 + 14i$ (D) $-3 - 8i$

6. What is the simplified form of $(8 - 3i)^2$?

   (F) 73 (G) $16 - 6i$ (H) $55 - 48i$ (I) $55 + 48i$

7. What is $\frac{5 + 3i}{4 - 2i}$ written as a complex number?

   (A) $\frac{7}{10} + \frac{11}{10}i$ (B) $\frac{13}{10} + \frac{1}{10}i$ (C) $\frac{5}{4} - \frac{3}{2}i$ (D) $\frac{7}{10} - \frac{11}{10}i$

8. What is the factored form of the expression $4x^2 + 36$?

   (F) $4(x + 3i)^2$ (H) $4(x + 6i)^2$

   (G) $4(x + 3i)(x - 3i)$ (I) $4(x + 6i)(x - 6i)$

Short Response

9. What are the solutions of $2x^2 + 3x + 6 = 0$? Show your work.

Name ______________________ Class ____________ Date ____________

4-9 Think About a Plan

Quadratic Systems

Business A company's weekly revenue R is given by the formula $R = -p^2 + 30p$, where p is the price of the company's product. The company is considering hiring a distributor, which will cost the company $4p + 25$ per week.

a. Use a system of equations to find the values of the price p for which the company will still remain profitable if they hire this distributor.

b. Which value of p will maximize the profit after including the distributor cost?

1. What does it mean for the company to be profitable?

____

2. The weekly revenue is represented by the function [ ].

3. The distributor cost D is represented by the function [ ].

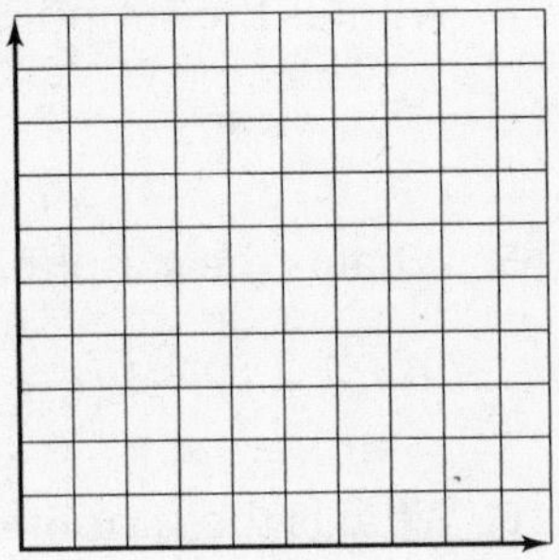

4. Solve this system of equations by graphing.

5. For what values of p will the company remain profitable?

6. How can you find the new weekly revenue of the company if they hire the distributor?

____

7. Write the new weekly revenue function and graph it.

[ ]

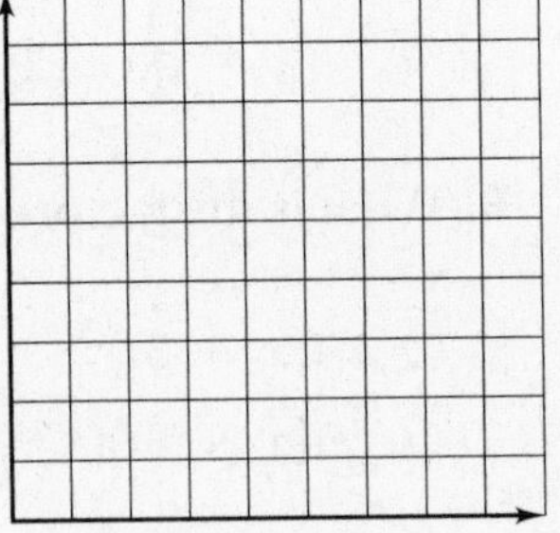

8. How can you find the value of p that will maximize the profit?

____

____

9. What value of p will maximize the profit?

10. What is the maximum profit?

Name ______________________ Class ____________ Date ____________

4-9 Practice

Form G

Quadratic Systems

Solve each system by graphing. Check your answers.

1. $\begin{cases} y = -x^2 + 3x + 2 \\ y = 3x + 2 \end{cases}$

2. $\begin{cases} y = x^2 + 2x - 3 \\ y = 2x + 1 \end{cases}$

3. $\begin{cases} y = -2x^2 + 4x + 3 \\ y = 2x - 1 \end{cases}$

4. $\begin{cases} y = 2x^2 - 5x \\ y = -3x + 4 \end{cases}$

Solve each system by substitution. Check your answers.

5. $\begin{cases} y = x^2 + 5x - 2 \\ y = 3x - 2 \end{cases}$

6. $\begin{cases} y = -x^2 + x + 12 \\ y = 2x - 8 \end{cases}$

7. $\begin{cases} y = x^2 - 2x - 3 \\ y = 2x - 3 \end{cases}$

8. $\begin{cases} y = 2x^2 - 5x + 6 \\ y = 3x - 2 \end{cases}$

9. $\begin{cases} y = -x^2 + 2x + 18 \\ y = 5x - 10 \end{cases}$

10. $\begin{cases} y = x^2 - 2x - 2 \\ y = -3x + 4 \end{cases}$

11. $\begin{cases} x + y = 5 \\ y + 1 = 3x^2 + 2x \end{cases}$

12. $\begin{cases} x + y = x^2 - 6 \\ x + y + 2 = 0 \end{cases}$

13. $\begin{cases} x = y - 5 \\ x^2 + 2x = y - 3 \end{cases}$

14. $\begin{cases} y + 4 = x^2 - 3x \\ y + 9 = 3x \end{cases}$

15. $\begin{cases} x^2 + y - 10 = 0 \\ x + y + 2 = 0 \end{cases}$

16. $\begin{cases} x + y = 7 \\ x^2 - y = -5x \end{cases}$

17. $\begin{cases} y + 5x = x^2 - 3 \\ y - 3x = -15 \end{cases}$

18. $\begin{cases} y - 2x = -x^2 - 4 \\ y + 2x = -1 \end{cases}$

Name ______________________ Class ____________ Date ____________

4-9 Practice (continued) *Form G*

Quadratic Systems

Solve each system.

19. $\begin{cases} y = -x^2 + 2x - 3 \\ y = x^2 + 4x - 3 \end{cases}$

20. $\begin{cases} y = x^2 + 2x - 3 \\ y = -x^2 - 2x + 3 \end{cases}$

21. $\begin{cases} y = 2x^2 + x - 5 \\ y = -x^2 - 2x - 5 \end{cases}$

22. $\begin{cases} y = -x^2 + x + 2 \\ y = x^2 - 3x - 4 \end{cases}$

23. $\begin{cases} y = x^2 + 1 \\ y = 2x^2 - 3 \end{cases}$

24. $\begin{cases} y = 2x^2 - 4 \\ y = x^2 - 4x + 1 \end{cases}$

Solve each system by graphing.

25. $\begin{cases} y < x^2 + 5 \\ y > 2x^2 - 4 \end{cases}$

26. $\begin{cases} y > x^2 - 4x \\ y < -x^2 + 6 \end{cases}$

27. $\begin{cases} y > x^2 - x \\ y < x^2 + 3 \end{cases}$

28. $\begin{cases} y \leq 4x^2 + 4x \\ y \geq x^2 + 4x \end{cases}$

29. In business, a break-even point is the point (x, y) at which the graphs of the revenue and cost functions intersect. For one manufacturing company, the revenue from producing x items is given by the function $y = 2x + 12$ and the cost of producing x items is given by $y = -x^2 + 10x + 5$. Find all break-even points.

30. Two skaters are practicing at the same time on the same rink. One skater follows the path $y = -2x + 32$, while the other skater follows the curve $y = -2x^2 + 18x$. Find all points where they might collide if they are not careful.

Name ______________________ Class ____________ Date ____________

4-9 Standardized Test Prep

Quadratic Systems

Multiple Choice

For Exercises 1–4, choose the correct letter.

1. What is the solution of the system? $\begin{cases} y = x^2 - 4x + 5 \\ y = -2x + 8 \end{cases}$

A. (0, 5), (2, 1)

B. (−1, 10), (4, 5)

C. (−2, 17), (1, 6)

D. (−1, 10), (3, 2)

2. What is the solution of the system? $\begin{cases} y = -x^2 - 2x + 4 \\ y = -x + 2 \end{cases}$

F. (−2, 4), (2, 0)

G. (−2, 4), (1, 1)

H. (−3, 5), (1, 1)

I. (−3, 1), (2, 0)

3. What is the solution of the system? $\begin{cases} y = x^2 - 4x + 3 \\ y = -2x + 6 \end{cases}$

A. (−1, 8), (3, 0)

B. (−2, 10), (3, 0)

C. (−1, 8), (4, 3)

D. (0, 3), (4, −2)

4. What is the solution of the system? $\begin{cases} y = -x^2 + 4x + 5 \\ y = x^2 - 2x - 3 \end{cases}$

F. (−2, −7), (2, 9)

G. (−1, 0), (4, 5)

H. (−1, 0), (3, 8)

I. (1, −4), (4, 5)

Short Response

5. What is the solution of the system? Solve by graphing. $\begin{cases} y < -x^2 + 3x \\ y > x^2 - x - 6 \end{cases}$

Name ______________________ Class ____________ Date ____________

5-1 Think About a Plan

Polynomial Functions

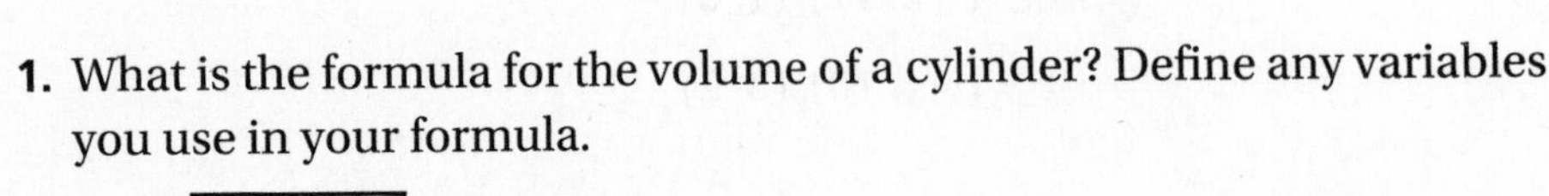

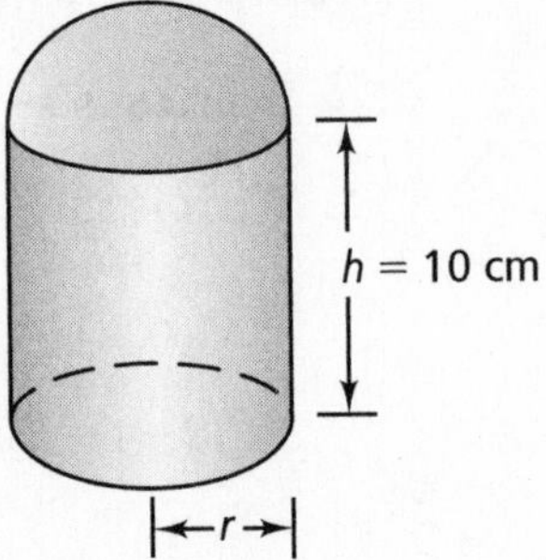

Packaging Design The diagram at the right shows a cologne bottle that consists of a cylindrical base and a hemispherical top.

a. Write an expression for the cylinder's volume.

b. Write an expression for the volume of the hemispherical top.

c. Write a polynomial to represent the total volume.

1. What is the formula for the volume of a cylinder? Define any variables you use in your formula.

   $V_c =$ ☐, where r is ____________ and h is ____________.

2. Write an expression for the volume of the cylinder using the information in the diagram.

   $V_c =$ ☐

3. What is the formula for the volume of a sphere? Define any variables you use in your formula.

   $V_s =$ ☐, where r is ____________.

4. Write an expression for the volume of the hemisphere.

   $V_h =$ ☐

5. How can you find the total volume of the bottle?

   ____.

6. Write a polynomial expression to represent the total volume of the bottle.

   $V =$ ☐ $+$ ☐

7. Is the polynomial expression you wrote in simplest form? Explain.

   ____

   ____.

Name ______________________ Class ____________ Date ____________

5-1 Practice

Form G

Polynomial Functions

Write each polynomial in standard form. Then classify it by degree and by number of terms.

1. $4x + x + 2$

2. $-3 + 3x - 3x$

3. $6x^4 - 1$

4. $1 - 2s + 5s^4$

5. $5m^2 - 3m^2$

6. $x^2 + 3x - 4x^3$

7. $-1 + 2x^2$

8. $5m^2 - 3m^3$

9. $5x - 7x^2$

10. $2 + 3x^3 - 2$

11. $6 - 2x^3 - 4 + x^3$

12. $6x - 7x$

13. $a^3(a^2 + a + 1)$

14. $x(x + 5) - 5(x + 5)$

15. $p(p - 5) + 6$

16. $(3c^2)^2$

17. $-(3 - b)$

18. $6(2x - 1)$

19. $\frac{2}{3} + s^2$

20. $\frac{2x^4 + 4x - 5}{4}$

21. $\frac{3 - z^5}{3}$

Determine the end behavior of the graph of each polynomial function.

22. $y = 3x^4 + 6x^3 - x^2 + 12$

23. $y = 50 - 3x^3 + 5x^2$

24. $y = -x + x^2 + 2$

25. $y = 4x^2 + 9 - 5x^4 - x^3$

26. $y = 12x^4 - x + 3x^7 - 1$

27. $y = 2x^5 + x^2 - 4$

28. $y = 5 + 2x + 7x^2 - 5x^3$

29. $y = 20 - 5x^6 + 3x - 11x^3$

30. $y = 6x + 25 + 4x^4 - x^2$

Describe the shape of the graph of each cubic function by determining the end behavior and number of turning points.

31. $y = x^3 + 4x$

32. $y = -2x^3 + 3x - 1$

33. $y = 5x^3 + 6x^2$

Determine the degree of the polynomial function with the given data.

34.

x	y
−2	−16
−1	1
0	4
1	5
2	16

35.

x	y
−2	52
−1	6
0	2
1	4
2	48

Name ______________________ Class ____________ Date ____________

5-1 Practice (continued) Form G

Polynomial Functions

Determine the sign of the leading coefficient and the degree of the polynomial function for each graph.

36. 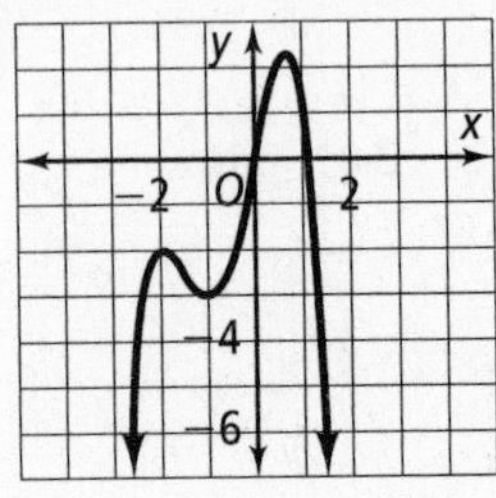

37. 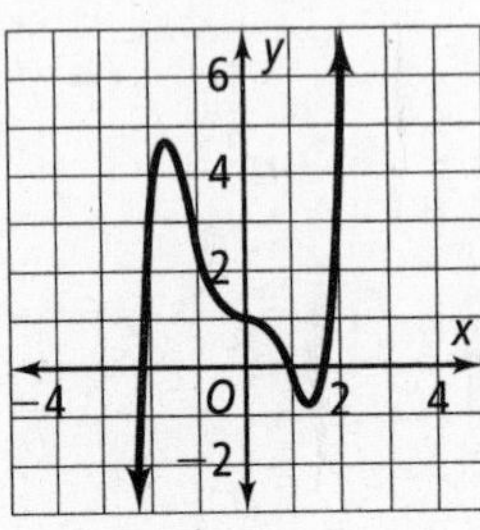

38. 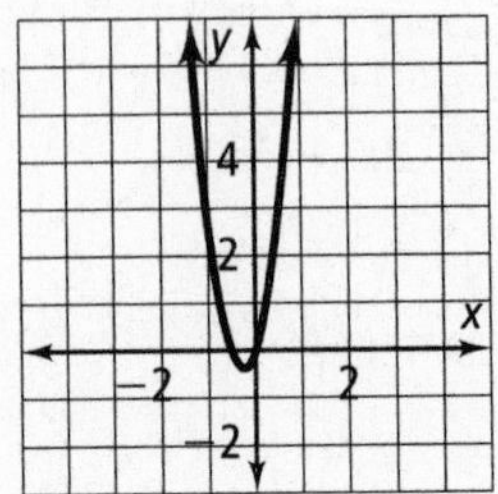

39. **Error Analysis** A student claims the function $y = 3x^4 - x^3 + 7$ is a fourth-degree polynomial with end behavior of down and down. Describe the error the student made. What is wrong with this statement?

40. The table at the right shows data representing a polynomial function.
   a. What is the degree of the polynomial function?
   b. What are the second differences of the y-values?
   c. What are the differences when they are constant?

x	y
−3	−999
−2	−140
−1	−7
0	0
1	1
2	116
3	945

Classify each polynomial by degree and by number of terms. Simplify first if necessary.

41. $4x^5 - 5x^2 + 3 - 2x^2$

42. $b(b - 3)^2$

43. $(7x^2 + 9x - 5) + (9x^2 - 9x)$

44. $(x + 2)^3$

45. $(4s^4 - s^2 - 3) - (3s - s^2 - 5)$

46. 13

47. **Open-Ended** Write a third-degree polynomial function. Make a table of values and a graph.

48. **Writing** Explain why finding the degree of a polynomial is easier when the polynomial is written in standard form.

Name ______________________ Class ____________ Date ____________

5-1 Standardized Test Prep

Polynomial Functions

Multiple Choice

For Exercises 1–7, choose the correct letter.

1. Which expression is a binomial?

Ⓐ $2x$ Ⓑ $\frac{x}{2}$ Ⓒ $3x^2 + 2x + 4$ Ⓓ $x - 9$

2. Which polynomial function has an end behavior of up and down?

Ⓕ $-6x^7 + 4x^2 - 3$ Ⓗ $6x^7 - 4x^2 + 3$

Ⓖ $-7x^6 + 3x - 2$ Ⓘ $7x^6 - 3x + 2$

3. What is the degree of the polynomial $5x + 4x^2 + 3x^3 - 5x$?

Ⓐ 1 Ⓑ 2 Ⓒ 3 Ⓓ 4

4. What is the degree of the polynomial represented by the data in the table at the right?

Ⓕ 2 Ⓖ 3 Ⓗ 4 Ⓘ 5

x	y
−3	77
−2	24
−1	1
0	−4
1	−3
2	−8
3	−31

5. For the table of values at the right, if the *n*th differences are constant, what is the constant value?

Ⓐ −12 Ⓑ 12 Ⓒ 1 Ⓓ 6

6. What is the standard form of the polynomial $9x^2 + 5x + 27 + 2x^3$?

Ⓕ $27 + 5x + 9x^2 + 2x^3$ Ⓗ $9x^2 + 5x + 27 + 2x^3$

Ⓖ $9x^2 + 5x + 2x^3 + 27$ Ⓘ $2x^3 + 9x^2 + 5x + 27$

7. What is the number of terms in the polynomial $(2a - 5)(a^2 - 1)$?

Ⓐ 2 Ⓑ 3 Ⓒ 4 Ⓓ 5

Short Response

8. Simplify $(9x^3 - 4x + 2) - (x^3 + 3x^2 + 1)$. Then name the polynomial by degree and the number of terms.

Name ______________________ Class __________ Date __________

5-2 Think About a Plan

Polynomials, Linear Factors, and Zeros

Measurement The volume in cubic feet of a CD holder can be expressed as $V(x) = -x^3 - x^2 + 6x$, or, when factored, as the product of its three dimensions. The depth is expressed as $2 - x$. Assume that the height is greater than the width.

a. Factor the polynomial to find linear expressions for the height and the width.

b. Graph the function. Find the x-intercepts. What do they represent?

c. What is a realistic domain for the function?

d. What is the maximum volume of the CD holder?

1. What do you know about the factors of the polynomial?

____.

2. Factor the polynomial.

$V(x) = -x^3 - x^2 + 6x = (\square)(\square)(\square)$

3. What are the height and width of the CD holder? How do you know which factor is the height and which factor is the width?

____

____.

4. Graph the function on a graphing calculator. How can you find the x-intercepts?

____.

5. What are the x-intercepts? What do they represent?

____.

6. What are the limits of each of the factors? What is a realistic domain for the function? Explain.

____

____

____.

7. How can you find the maximum volume of the CD holder?

____

____.

8. What is the maximum volume of the CD holder?

Name ______________________ Class ____________ Date ____________

5-2 Practice

Form G

Polynomials, Linear Factors, and Zeros

Write each polynomial in factored form. Check by multiplication.

1. $2x^3 + 10x^2 + 12x$

2. $x^4 - x^3 - 6x^2$

3. $-3x^3 + 18x^2 - 27x$

4. $x^3 - 2x^2 + x$

5. $x^3 + 7x^2 + 15x + 9$

6. $2x^4 + 23x^3 + 60x^2 - 125x - 500$

Find the zeros of each function. Then graph the function.

7. $y = (x + 1)(x - 1)(x - 3)$

8. $y = (x + 2)(x - 3)$

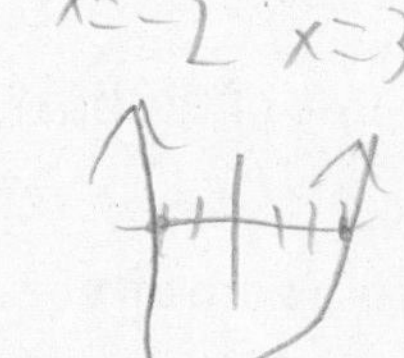

9. $y = x(x - 2)(x + 5)$

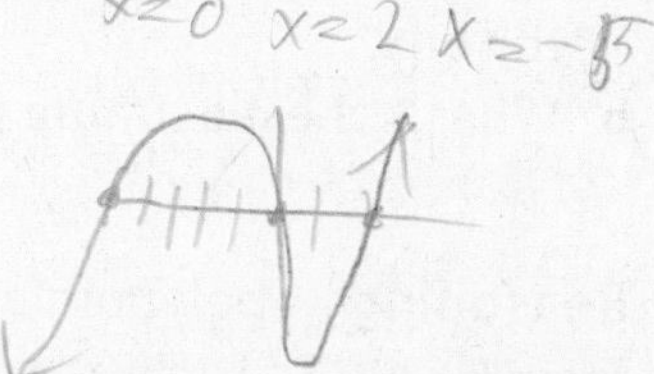

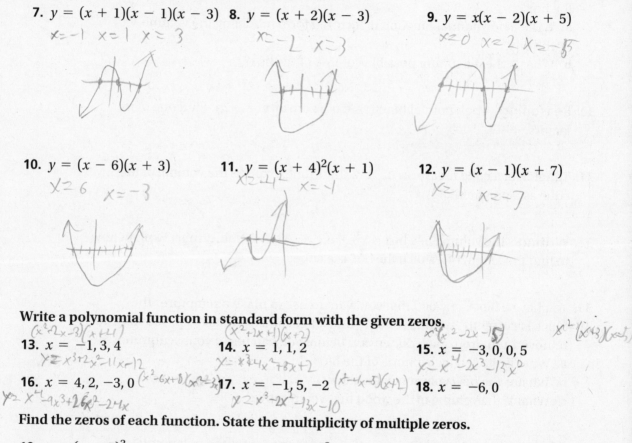

10. $y = (x - 6)(x + 3)$

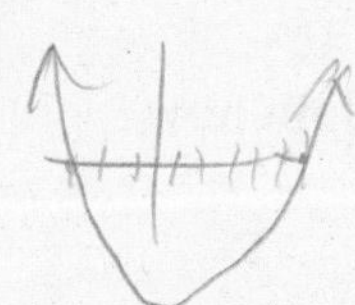

11. $y = (x + 4)^2(x + 1)$

12. $y = (x - 1)(x + 7)$

Write a polynomial function in standard form with the given zeros.

13. $x = -1, 3, 4$

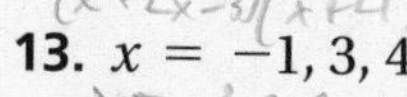

14. $x = 1, 1, 2$

15. $x = -3, 0, 0, 5$

16. $x = 4, 2, -3, 0$

17. $x = -1, 5, -2$

18. $x = -6, 0$

Find the zeros of each function. State the multiplicity of multiple zeros.

19. $y = (x - 5)^3$

20. $y = x(x - 8)^2$

21. $y = (x - 2)(x + 7)^3$

22. $y = x^4 - 8x^3 + 16x^2$

23. $y = 9x^3 - 81x$

24. $y = (2x + 5)(x - 3)^2$

Name ______________________________ Class ____________ Date ____________

5-2 Practice (continued)

Form G

Polynomials, Linear Factors, and Zeros

Find the relative maximum and relative minimum of the graph of each function.

25. $f(x) = x^3 - 7x^2 + 10x$

26. $f(x) = x^3 - x^2 - 9x + 9$

27. $f(x) = x^4 + x^3 - 3x^2 - 5x - 2$

28. $f(x) = x^2 - 6x + 9$

29. A rectangular box has a square base. The combined length of a side of the square base, and the height is 20 in. Let x be the length of a side of the base of the box.

a. Write a polynomial function in factored form modeling the volume V of the box.

b. What is the maximum possible volume of the box?

30. Reasoning A polynomial function has a zero at $x = -2a$. Find one of its factors.

31. The side of a cube measures $3x + 2$ units long. Express the volume of the cube as a polynomial.

32. Writing The volume of a box is $x^3 - 3x^2 + 3x - 1$ cubic units. Explain how to find the length of a side if the box is a cube.

33. You have a block of wood that you want to use to make a sculpture. The block is currently $3x$ units wide, $4x$ units high, and $5x$ units deep. You need to remove 1 unit from each dimension before you can begin your sculpture.

a. What is the original volume of the block?

b. What is the new volume of the block?

c. What is the volume of the wood that you remove?

34. What are the zeros and the multiplicity of each zero for the polynomial function $x^4 - 2x^2 + 1$?

35. Error Analysis On your homework, you wrote that the polynomial function from the given zeros $x = 3, 0, -9, 1$ is $y = x^4 + 5x^3 - 33x^2 + 27x$. Your friend wrote that the polynomial function is $y = x^3 + 5x^2 - 33x + 27$. Who is correct? What mistake was made?

Name ____________________ Class __________ Date __________

5-2 Standardized Test Prep

Polynomials, Linear Factors, and Zeros

Multiple Choice

For Exercises 1–6, choose the correct letter.

1. What are the zeros of the polynomial function $y = (x - 3)(2x + 1)(x - 1)$?

Ⓐ $\frac{1}{2}, 1, 3$ Ⓑ $-1, 1, 3$ Ⓒ $-\frac{1}{2}, 1, 3$ Ⓓ $-3, \frac{1}{2}, -1$

2. What is the factored form of $2x^3 + 5x^2 - 12x$?

Ⓕ $(x + 4)(2x - 3)$ Ⓗ $x(x + 4)(2x - 3)$

Ⓖ $(x - 4)(2x + 3)$ Ⓘ $x(x - 4)(2x + 3)$

3. Which is the cubic polynomial in standard form with roots 3, −6, and 0?

Ⓐ $x^2 - 3x - 18$ Ⓒ $x^3 - 3x^2 - 18x$

Ⓑ $x^2 + 3x - 18$ Ⓓ $x^3 + 3x^2 - 18x$

4. What is the relative minimum and relative maximum of $f(x) = 6x^3 - 5x + 12$?

Ⓕ min = 0, max = 0 Ⓗ min = −1.5, max = 12

Ⓖ min = −5, max = 6 Ⓘ min = 10.2, max = 13.8

5. What is the multiplicity of the zero of the polynomial function $f(x) = (x + 5)^4$?

Ⓐ 4 Ⓑ 5 Ⓒ 20 Ⓓ 625

6. For the polynomial function $y = (x - 2)^3$, how does the graph behave at the x-intercept?

Ⓕ linear Ⓖ quadratic Ⓗ cubic Ⓘ quartic

Short Response

7. A rectangular box is 24 in. long, 12 in. wide, and 18 in. high. If each dimension is increased by x in., what is the polynomial function in standard form that models the volume V of the box? Show your work.

Name ____________________ Class __________ Date __________

5-3 Think About a Plan

Solving Polynomial Equations

Geometry The width of a box is 2 m less than the length. The height is 1 m less than the length. The volume is 60 m^3. What is the length of the box?

Know

1. The volume of the box is [ ].

2. The formula for the volume of a rectangular prism is [ ].

3. The width of the box is equal to [ ] − 2 m.

4. The height of the box is equal to [ ] − 1 m.

Need

5. To solve the problem I need to:

____

____.

Plan

6. Define a variable. Let $x =$ [ ].

7. What variable expressions represent the width and height of the box?

[ ] and [ ]

8. What equation expresses the volume of the box in two ways?

9. How can you use a graphing calculator to help you solve the equation?

____

____.

10. What is the solution of the equation?

11. What are the dimensions of the box? Are the solutions reasonable?

____

____.

Name ______________________ Class ____________ Date ____________

5-3 Practice

Form G

Solving Polynomial Equations

Find the real or imaginary solutions of each equation by factoring.

1. $8x^3 - 27 = 0$

2. $x^3 + 64 = 0$

3. $2x^3 + 54 = 0$

4. $2x^3 - 250 = 0$

5. $4x^3 - 32 = 0$

6. $27x^3 + 1 = 0$

7. $64x^3 - 1 = 0$

8. $x^3 - 27 = 0$

9. $x^4 - 5x^2 + 4 = 0$

10. $x^4 - 12x^2 + 11 = 0$

11. $x^4 - 10x^2 + 16 = 0$

12. $x^4 - 8x^2 + 16 = 0$

13. $x^4 - 9x^2 + 14 = 0$

14. $x^4 + 13x^2 + 36 = 0$

15. $x^4 - 10x^2 + 9 = 0$

16. $x^4 + 3x^2 - 4 = 0$

Find the real solutions of each equation by graphing.

17. $2x^4 = 9x^2 - 4$

18. $x^2 - 16x = -1$

19. $6x^3 + 10x^2 + 5x = 0$

20. $36x^3 + 6x^2 = 9x$

21. $15x^4 = 11x^3 + 14x^2$

22. $x^4 = 81x^2$

For Exercises 23 and 24, write an equation to model each situation. Then solve each equation by graphing.

23. The volume V of a container is 84 ft^3. The width, the length, and the height are x, $x + 1$, and $x - 4$ respectively. What are the container's dimensions?

24. The product of three consecutives integers $n - 1$, n, and $n + 1$ is -336. What are the integers?

5-3 Practice (continued) — Form G

Solving Polynomial Equations

Solve each equation.

25. $x^4 - x = 0$

26. $3x^4 + 18 = 21x^2$

27. $2x^4 - 26x^2 - 28 = 0$

28. $5x^4 + 50x^2 + 80 = 0$

29. $x^4 - 81 = 0$

30. $x^4 = 25$

31. $x^5 = x^3 + 12x$

32. $x^4 + 12x^2 = 8x^3$

33. Over 3 years, you save your earnings from a summer job. The polynomial $1600x^3 + 1200x^2 + 800x$ represents your savings, with interest, at the end of the 3 years. The annual interest rate equals $x - 1$. Find the interest rate needed so that you will have \$4000 at the end of 3 years.

34. Error Analysis Your friend claims that the zeros of $3x^3 + 7x^2 - 22x - 8 = 0$ are -4, 2, and -1. What did your friend do wrong? What are the correct factors?

35. The container at the right consists of a cylinder on top of a hemisphere. The container holds 500 cm^3. What is the radius of the container, to the nearest hundredth of a centimeter?

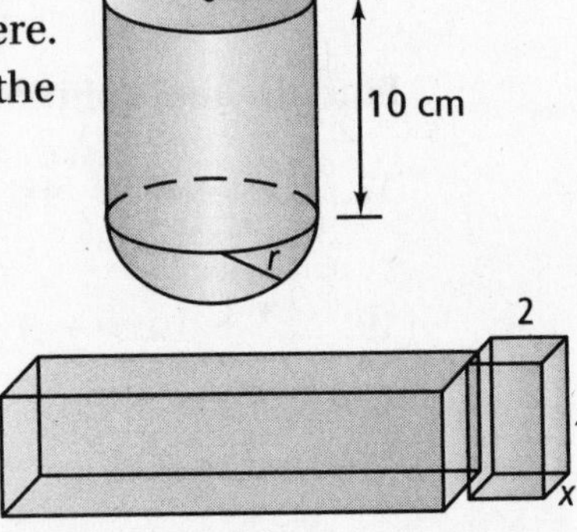

36. Suppose a 2-in. slice is cut from one face of the cheese block as shown. The remaining block has a volume of 224 in.^3.

a. What are the dimensions of the new block?

b. What are the dimensions of the old block?

c. What is the original volume?

d. What is the volume of the cut slice?

37. Reasoning A test question asks you to find three integers whose product is 412. Do you have enough information to solve this problem? Explain.

38. Your mother is 25 years older than you. Your father is 3 years older than your mother. The product of all three ages is 32,130. How old is your father?

Name ______________________ Class ____________ Date ____________

5-3 Standardized Test Prep

Solving Polynomial Equations

Multiple Choice

For Exercises 1–6, choose the correct letter.

1. If you factor $x^3 - 8$ in the form $(x - a)(x^2 + bx + c)$, what is the value of a?

(A) 2 (B) -2 (C) 4 (D) -4

2. The product of three integers x, $x + 2$, and $x - 5$ is 240. What are the integers?

(F) 5.9, 7.9, 0.9 (G) 7.5, 9.5, 2.5 (H) 5, 6, 8 (I) 8, 10, 3

3. Over 3 years, you save \$550, \$600, and \$650 from babysitting jobs. The polynomial $550x^3 + 600x^2 + 650x$ represents your total bank account balance after 3 years. The annual interest rate is $x - 1$. What is the interest rate needed so that you will have \$2000 after 3 years?

(A) 0.06% (B) 1.06% (C) 5.52% (D) 24%

4. Which polynomial equation has the zeros 5, -3, and $\frac{1}{2}$?

(F) $x^3 + 4x^2 + 4x - 45$ (H) $2x^3 - 5x^2 - 28x + 15$

(G) $x^3 - 4x^2 + 4x + 15$ (I) $2x^3 + 5x^2 - 28x - 45$

5. Your brother is 3 years older than you. Your sister is 4 years younger than you. The product of your ages is 1872. How old is your sister?

(A) 9 years (B) 13 years (C) 16 years (D) 17 years

6. What are the real roots of $x^3 + 8 = 0$?

(F) 2 (G) -2 (H) $-2 \pm \sqrt{3}$ (I) $-2 \pm \sqrt{5}$

Short Response

7. You have a block of wood with a depth of x units, a length of $5x$ units, and a height of $2x$ units. You need to cut a slice off the top of the block to decrease the height by 2 units. The new block will have a volume of 480 cubic units.

a. What are the dimensions of the new block?

b. What is the volume of the slice?

Name ______________________ Class ____________ Date ____________

5-4 Think About a Plan

Dividing Polynomials

Geometry The expression $\frac{1}{3}(x^3 + 5x^2 + 8x + 4)$ represents the volume of a square pyramid. The expression $x + 1$ represents the height of the pyramid. What expression represents the side length of the base? (*Hint:* The formula for the volume of a pyramid is $V = \frac{1}{3}Bh$.)

Understanding the Problem

1. What expression represents the height of the pyramid?

2. What does B represent in the formula for the volume of a pyramid?

____

3. What is the problem asking you to determine?

____

Planning the Solution

4. How can you find an expression that represents B?

____

____.

5. How can polynomial division help you solve this problem?

____

____.

6. How can you find the side length of the base once you find an expression for B?

____.

Getting an Answer

7. What expression represents B, the area of the base?

8. What expression represents the side length of the base?

Name ____________________ Class __________ Date __________

5-4 Practice

Form G

Dividing Polynomials

Divide using long division. Check your answers.

1. $(x^2 - 13x - 48) \div (x + 3)$
2. $(2x^2 + x - 7) \div (x - 5)$
3. $(x^3 + 5x^2 - 3x - 1) \div (x - 1)$
4. $(3x^3 - x^2 - 7x + 6) \div (x + 2)$
5. $(x^2 - 3x + 1) \div (x - 4)$
6. $(x^3 - 4x^2 + 3x + 2) \div (x + 2)$

Determine whether each binomial is a factor of $x^3 + 3x^2 - 10x - 24$.

7. $x + 4$
8. $x - 3$
9. $x + 6$
10. $x + 2$

Divide using synthetic division.

11. $(x^3 - 8x^2 + 17x - 10) \div (x - 5)$
12. $(x^3 + 5x^2 - x - 9) \div (x + 2)$
13. $(-2x^3 + 15x^2 - 22x - 15) \div (x - 3)$
14. $(x^3 + 7x^2 + 15x + 9) \div (x + 1)$
15. $(x^3 + 2x^2 + 5x + 12) \div (x + 3)$
16. $(x^3 - 5x^2 - 7x + 25) \div (x - 5)$
17. $(x^4 - x^3 + x^2 - x + 1) \div (x - 1)$
18. $(2x^4 + 7x^3 - 11x^2 + 21x + 5) \div (x + 5)$
19. $(x^4 - 5x^3 + 5x^2 + 7x - 12) \div (x - 4)$
20. $(2x^4 + 23x^3 + 60x^2 - 125x - 500) \div (x + 4)$

Use synthetic division and the given factor to completely factor each polynomial function.

21. $y = x^3 + 3x^2 - 13x - 15; (x + 5)$
22. $y = x^3 - 3x^2 - 10x + 24; (x - 2)$
23. $y = x^3 + x^2 - 10x + 8; (x - 1)$
24. $y = x^3 + 4x^2 - 9x - 36; (x + 3)$
25. The expression $V(x) = x^3 - 13x + 12$ represents the volume of a rectangular safe in cubic feet. The length of the safe is $x + 4$. What linear expressions with integer coefficients could represent the other dimensions of the safe? Assume that the height is greater than the width.

Use synthetic division and the Remainder Theorem to find $P(a)$.

26. $P(x) = 3x^3 - 4x^2 - 5x + 1; a = 2$
27. $P(x) = x^3 + 7x^2 + 12x - 3; a = -5$
28. $P(x) = x^3 + 6x^2 + 10x + 3; a = -3$
29. $P(x) = 2x^4 - 9x^3 + 7x^2 - 5x + 11; a = 4$

Name ______________________ Class ______________ Date ______________

5-4 Practice (continued) — Form G

Dividing Polynomials

Divide.

30. $(6x^3 + 2x^2 - 11x + 12) \div (3x + 4)$

31. $(x^4 + 2x^3 + x - 3) \div (x - 1)$

32. $(2x^4 + 3x^3 - 4x^2 + x + 1) \div (2x - 1)$

33. $(x^5 - 1) \div (x - 1)$

34. $(x^4 - 3x^2 - 10) \div (x - 2)$

35. $(3x^3 - 2x^2 + 2x + 1) \div \left(x + \frac{1}{3}\right)$

36. The volume in cubic inches of a box can be expressed as the product of its three dimensions: $V(x) = x^3 - 16x^2 + 79x - 120$. The length is $x - 8$. Find linear expressions with integer coefficients for the other dimensions. Assume that the width is greater than the height.

37. **Writing** What are the divisor, quotient, and remainder represented by the synthetic division below?

-5	1	0	-19	30
		-5	25	-30
	1	-5	6	0

38. **Reasoning** What does it mean if $P(-4)$ for the polynomial function $P(x) = x^3 + 11x^2 + 34x + 24$ equals zero?

39. **Error Analysis** Using synthetic division, you say that the quotient of $4x^3 - 3x^2 + 15$ divided by $x - 1$ is $4x^2 - 7x + 7$ R 8. Your friend says that the quotient is $4x^2 + x + 1$ R 16. Who is correct? What mistake was made?

40. What is $P(-2)$ for $P(x) = 3x^3 - 6x^2 + 2x - 12$?

41. The expression $x^3 + 16x^2 + 68x + 80$ represents the volume of a flower box in cubic inches. The expression $x + 4$ represents the depth of the box. Assume that the length is greater than the height and that linear expressions with integer coefficients represent both.
   a. What are the other dimensions of the flower box?
   b. If $x = 3$, what are the dimensions of the flower box?

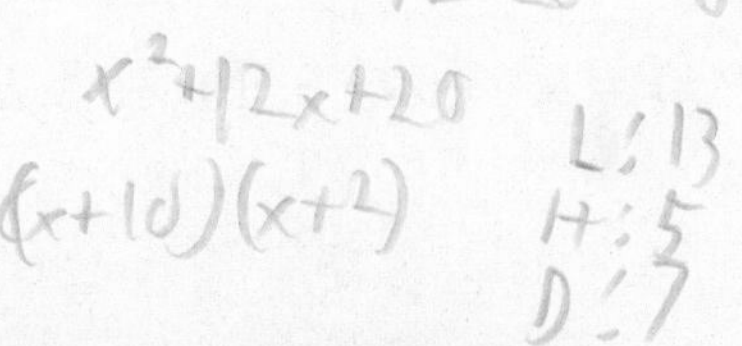

Name ______________________ Class ____________ Date ____________

5-4 Standardized Test Prep

Dividing Polynomials

Gridded Response

Solve each exercise and enter your answer in the grid provided.

1. What is $P(-2)$ given that $P(x) = x^4 - 3x^2 + 5x + 10$?

2. What is the missing value in the following synthetic division?

−4	1	0	−5	4	12
		−4	☐	−44	160
	1	−4	11	−40	172

3. What is the remainder when $x^6 - 4x^4 + 4x^2 - 10$ is divided by $x + 3$?

4. How many unique factors does $x^4 + 4x^3 - 3x^2 - 14x - 8$ have, including $(x + 4)$?

5. How many terms are there in the simplified form of $\dfrac{x^4 - 2x^3 - 23x^2 - 12x + 36}{x - 6}$?

Answers

1. 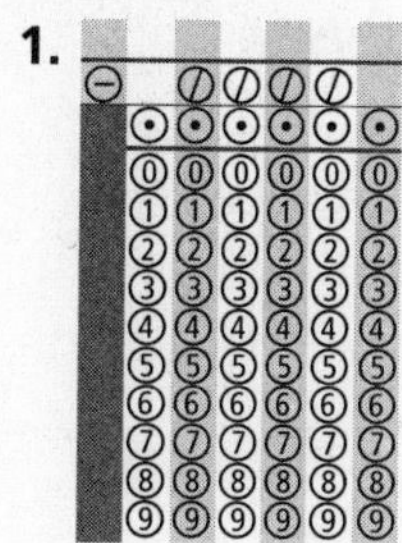

2.

3. 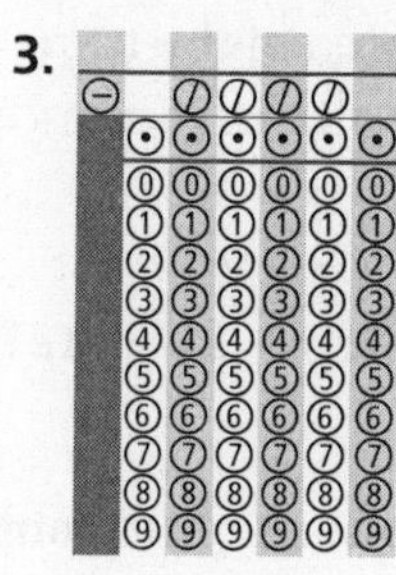

4. 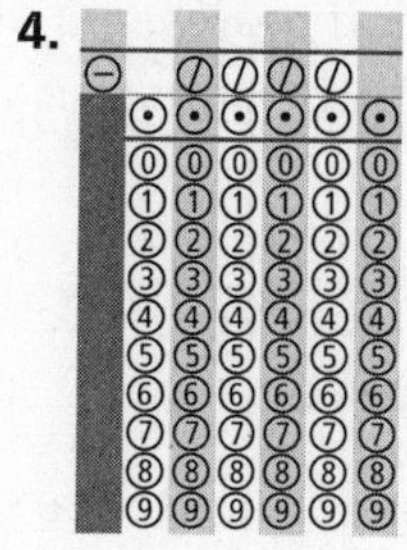

5. 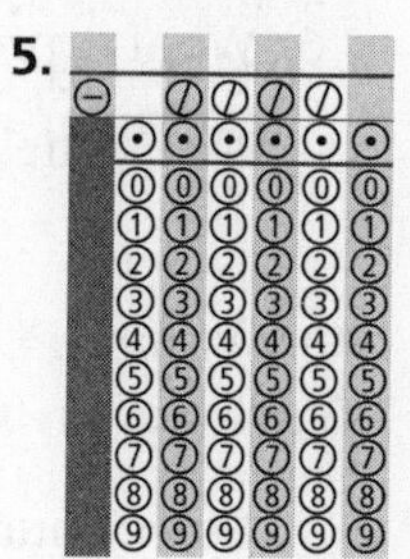

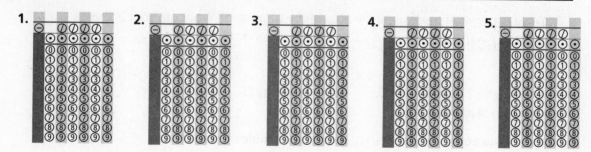

Name ______________________ Class ____________ Date ____________

5-5 Think About a Plan

Theorems About Roots of Polynomial Equations

Gardening A gardener is designing a new garden in the shape of a trapezoid. She wants the shorter base to be twice the height and the longer base to be 4 feet longer than the shorter base. If she has enough topsoil to create a 60 ft^2 garden, what dimensions should she use for the garden?

Understanding the Problem

1. What is the formula for the area of a trapezoid?

2. How can drawing a diagram help you solve the problem?

____

____.

3. What is the problem asking you to determine?

____

Planning the Solution

4. Define a variable. Let x = [   ].

5. What variable expression represents the shorter base? The longer base?

[   ] [   ]

6. What expression represents the area of the trapezoid? What number is this equal to? Write the equation you obtain in standard form.

Getting an Answer

7. Solve your equation. Are the solutions reasonable?

____.

8. What are the dimensions of the garden?

____

Name ______________________ Class ____________ Date ____________

5-5 Practice

Form G

Theorems About Roots of Polynomial Equations

Use the Rational Root Theorem to list all possible rational roots for each equation. Then find any actual rational roots.

1. $x^3 + 5x^2 - 2x - 15 = 0$

2. $36x^3 + 144x^2 - x - 4 = 0$

3. $2x^3 + 5x^2 + 4x + 1 = 0$

4. $12x^4 + 14x^3 - 5x^2 - 14x - 4 = 0$

5. $5x^3 - 11x^2 + 7x - 1 = 0$

6. $x^3 + 81x^2 - 49x - 49 = 0$

A polynomial function $P(x)$ with rational coefficients has the given roots. Find two additional roots of $P(x) = 0$.

7. $2 + 3i$ and $\sqrt{7}$

8. $3 - \sqrt{2}$ and $1 + \sqrt{3}$

9. $-4i$ and $6 - i$

10. $5 - \sqrt{6}$ and $-2 + \sqrt{10}$

11. $\sqrt{5}$ and $-\sqrt{13}$

12. $1 - \sqrt{10}$ and $2 + \sqrt{2}$

Write a polynomial function with rational coefficients so that $P(x) = 0$ has the given roots.

13. 4 and 6

14. -5 and -1

15. $3i$ and $\sqrt{6}$

16. $2 + i$ and $1 - \sqrt{5}$

17. -5 and $3i$

18. i and $5i$

What does Descartes' Rule of Signs say about the number of positive real roots and negative real roots for each polynomial function?

19. $P(x) = 3x^3 + x^2 - 8x - 12$

20. $P(x) = 2x^4 - x^3 - 3x + 7$

21. $P(x) = 4x^5 - x^4 - x^3 + 6x^2 - 5$

22. $P(x) = x^3 + 4x^2 + x - 6$

Name ______________________ Class ____________ Date ____________

5-5 Practice (continued)

Form G

Theorems About Roots of Polynomial Equations

Find all rational roots for $P(x) = 0$.

23. $P(x) = x^3 - 5x^2 + 2x + 8$

24. $P(x) = x^3 + x^2 - 17x + 15$

25. $P(x) = 2x^3 + 13x^2 + 17x - 12$

26. $P(x) = x^3 - x^2 - 34x - 56$

27. $P(x) = x^3 - 18x + 27$

28. $P(x) = x^4 - 5x^2 + 4$

29. $P(x) = x^3 - 6x^2 + 13x - 10$

30. $P(x) = x^3 - 5x^2 + 4x + 10$

31. $P(x) = x^3 - 5x^2 + 17x - 13$

32. $P(x) = x^3 + x + 10$

33. $P(x) = x^3 - 5x^2 - x + 5$

34. $P(x) = x^3 - 12x + 16$

35. $P(x) = x^3 - 2x^2 - 5x + 6$

36. $P(x) = x^3 - 8x^2 - 200$

37. $P(x) = x^3 + x^2 - 5x + 3$

38. $P(x) = 4x^3 - 12x^2 - x + 3$

39. $P(x) = x^3 + x^2 - 7x + 2$

40. $P(x) = 12x^3 + 31x^2 - 17x - 6$

Write a polynomial function $P(x)$ with rational coefficients so that $P(x) = 0$ has the given roots.

41. $\sqrt{3}, 2, -i$

42. $5, 2i$

43. $-1, 3 + i$

44. $-\sqrt{7}, i$

45. $-4, 4i$

46. $6, 3 - 2i$

47. Error Analysis A student claims that $2i$ is the only imaginary root of a polynomial equation that has real coefficients. Explain the student's mistake.

48. You are building a rectangular sandbox for a children's playground. The width of the sandbox is 4 times its height. The length of the sandbox is 8 ft more than 2 times its height. You have 40 ft^3 of sand available to fill this sandbox. What are the dimensions of the sandbox?

49. Writing According to the Rational Root Theorem, what is the relationship between the polynomial equation $2x^4 - x^3 - 7x^2 + 5x + 3 = 0$ and rational roots of the form $\frac{p}{q}$, where $\frac{p}{q}$ is in simplest form?

Name ______________________ Class __________ Date __________

5-5 Standardized Test Prep

Theorems About Roots of Polynomial Equations

Multiple Choice

For Exercises 1–5, choose the correct letter.

1. A fourth-degree polynomial with integer coefficients has roots at 1 and $3 + \sqrt{5}$. Which number *cannot* also be a root of this polynomial?

(A) -1 (B) -3 (C) $3 - \sqrt{5}$ (D) $3 + \sqrt{2}$

2. A quartic polynomial $P(x)$ has rational coefficients. If $\sqrt{7}$ and $6 + i$ are roots of $P(x) = 0$, what is one additional root?

(F) 7 (G) $-\sqrt{7}$ (H) $i - 6$ (I) $6i$

3. What is a quartic polynomial function with rational coefficients that has roots i and $2i$?

(A) $x^4 - 5x^2 - 4$ (B) $x^4 - 5x^2 + 4$ (C) $x^4 + 5x^2 + 4$ (D) $x^4 + 5x^2 - 4$

4. What does Descartes' Rule of Signs tell you about the real roots of $6x^4 + 29x^3 + 40x^2 + 7x - 12$?

(F) 1 positive real root and 1 or 3 negative real roots

(G) 0 positive real roots and 1 negative real root

(H) 1 or 3 positive real roots and 1 negative real root

(I) 0 or 1 positive real roots and 3 negative real roots

5. What is a rational root of $x^3 + 3x^2 - 6x - 8 = 0$?

(A) 1 (B) -1 (C) 8 (D) -8

Extended Response

6. A third-degree polynomial with rational coefficients has roots -4 and $-4i$. If the leading coefficient of the polynomial is $\frac{3}{2}$, what is the polynomial? Show your work.

Name ______________________ Class ____________ Date ____________

5-6 Think About a Plan

The Fundamental Theorem of Algebra

Bridges A twist in a river can be modeled by the function $f(x) = \frac{1}{3}x^3 + \frac{1}{2}x^2 - x$, $-3 \leq x \leq 2$. A city wants to build a road that goes directly along the x-axis. How many bridges would it have to build?

Know

1. The function has exactly ☐ complex roots.

2. ____

____

3. ____

____

Need

4. To solve the problem I need to:

____

____.

Plan

5. Graph the function on a graphing calculator. What viewing window should you use?

____

6. What does the graph tell you?

____.

7. How many bridges would the city have to build? ☐
Explain.

____

____.

Name ______________________ Class ____________ Date ____________

5-6 Practice

Form G

The Fundamental Theorem of Algebra

Without using a calculator, find all the complex roots of each equation.

1. $x^5 - 3x^4 - 8x^3 - 8x^2 - 9x - 5 = 0$
2. $x^3 - 2x^2 + 4x - 8 = 0$
3. $x^3 + x^2 - x + 2 = 0$
4. $x^4 - 2x^3 - x^2 - 4x - 6 = 0$
5. $x^4 + 3x^3 - 21x^2 - 48x + 80 = 0$
6. $x^5 - 3x^4 + x^3 + x^2 + 4 = 0$

Find all the zeros of each function.

7. $y = 5x^3 - 5x$
8. $f(x) = x^3 - 16x$
9. $g(x) = 12x^3 - 2x^2 - 2x$
10. $y = 6x^3 + x^2 - x$
11. $f(x) = 5x^3 + 6x^2 + x$
12. $y = -4x^3 + 100x$

For each equation, state the number of complex roots, the possible number of real roots, and the possible rational roots.

13. $2x^2 + 5x + 3 = 0$
14. $3x^2 + 11x - 10 = 0$
15. $2x^4 - 18x^2 + 5 = 0$
16. $4x^3 - 12x + 9 = 0$
17. $6x^5 - 28x + 15 = 0$
18. $x^3 - x^2 - 2x + 7 = 0$
19. $x^3 - 6x^2 - 7x - 12 = 0$
20. $2x^4 + x^2 - x + 6 = 0$
21. $4x^5 - 5x^4 + x^3 - 2x^2 + 2x - 6 = 0$
22. $7x^6 + 3x^4 - 9x^2 + 18 = 0$
23. $5 + x + x^2 + x^3 + x^4 + x^5 = 0$
24. $6 - x + 2x^3 - x^3 + x^4 - 8x^5 = 0$

Find the number of complex roots for each equation.

25. $x^8 - 5x^6 + x^4 + 2x - 16 = 0$
26. $x^{10} - 100 = 0$
27. $2x^4 + x^3 - 3x^2 + 4x - 2 = 0$
28. $-4x^3 + x^2 - 3x + 10 = 0$
29. $x^6 + 2x^5 + 3x^4 + 4x^3 + 5x^2 + 6x + 10 = 0$
30. $-3x^5 + 4x^4 + 5x^2 - 15 = 0$

Name ______________________ Class ____________ Date ____________

5-6 Practice (continued) — Form G

The Fundamental Theorem of Algebra

Find all the zeros of each function.

31. $f(x) = x^3 - 9x^2 + 27x - 27$

32. $y = 2x^3 - 8x^2 + 18x - 72$

33. $y = x^3 - 10x - 12$

34. $y = x^3 - 4x^2 + 8$

35. $f(x) = 2x^3 + x - 3$

36. $y = x^3 - 2x^2 - 11x + 12$

37. $g(x) = x^3 + 4x^2 + 7x + 28$

38. $f(x) = x^3 + 3x^2 + 6x + 4$

39. $g(x) = x^4 - 5x^2 - 36$

40. $y = x^4 - 7x^2 + 12$

41. $y = 9x^4 + 5x^2 - 4$

42. $y = 4x^4 - 11x^2 - 3$

43. Error Analysis Your friend says that the equation $4x^7 - 3x^3 + 4x^2 - x + 2 = 0$ has 5 complex roots. You say that the equation has 7 complex roots. Who is correct? What mistake was made?

44. A section of roller coaster can be modeled by the function $f(x) = x^5 - 5x^4 - 31x^3 + 113x^2 + 282x - 360$. A walkway bridge will be placed at one of the zeros. What are the possible locations for the walkway bridge?

45. Writing Using the Fundamental Theorem of Algebra, explain how $x^3 = 0$ has 3 roots and 3 linear factors.

46. How many complex roots does the equation $x^4 = 256$ have? What are they?

47. Reasoning Can a fifth-degree polynomial with rational coefficients have 4 real roots and 1 irrational root? Explain why or why not.

Name ______________________ Class ______________ Date ______________

5-6 Standardized Test Prep

The Fundamental Theorem of Algebra

Multiple Choice

For Exercises 1–6, choose the correct letter.

1. Which number is a zero of $f(x) = x^3 + 6x^2 + 9x$ with multiplicity 1?

   A) -3 B) 0 C) 1 D) 3

2. One root of the equation $x^3 + x^2 - 2 = 0$ is 1. What are the other two roots?

   F) $-1 \pm i$ G) $1 \pm 2i$ H) $\pm 1 + 2i$ I) $\pm 1 - i$

3. A polynomial with real coefficients has 3, $2i$, and $-i$ as three of its zeros. What is the least possible degree of the polynomial?

   A) 3 B) 4 C) 5 D) 6

4. How many times does the graph of $x^3 + 27$ cross the x-axis?

   F) 0 G) 1 H) 2 I) 4

5. Which of the following is the polynomial with zeros at 1, $-\frac{3}{2}$, $2i$, and $-2i$?

   A) $2x^4 + x^3 + 5x^2 + 4x - 12$ C) $2x^4 + x^3 - 11x^2 - 4x + 12$

   B) $2x^4 - x^3 + 5x^2 - 4x - 12$ D) $2x^4 - x^3 - 11x^2 + 4x + 12$

6. A polynomial with real coefficients has roots of 6, -2, $-4i$, and $\sqrt{5}$. Which of the following *must* be another root of this polynomial?

   F) -6 G) $-\sqrt{5}$ H) 2 I) $4i$

Short Response

7. One root of the equation $x^4 - 4x^3 - 6x^2 + 4x + 5 = 0$ is -1. How many complex roots does this equation have? What are all the roots? Show your work.

Name ____________________ Class __________ Date __________

5-7 Think About a Plan

The Binomial Theorem

Geometry The side length of a cube is given by the expression $(2x + 8)$. Write a binomial expression for the area of a face of the cube and the volume of the cube. Then use the Binomial Theorem to expand and rewrite the expressions in standard form.

Understanding the Problem

1. What is the formula for the area of a face of a cube?

2. What is the formula for the volume of a cube?

3. What is the problem asking you to determine?

____

____

Planning the Solution

4. What is a binomial expression for the area of a face of this cube?

5. What is a binomial expression for the volume of this cube?

6. How can you use the Binomial Theorem to expand these expressions?

____

____

____.

Getting an Answer

7. What is an expression for the area of a face of the cube written in standard form?

8. What is an expression for the volume of the cube written in standard form?

Name ______________________ Class ____________ Date ____________

5-7 Practice

Form G

The Binomial Theorem

Expand each binomial.

1. $(x + 2)^4$
2. $(a + 2)^7$
3. $(x + y)^7$
4. $(d - 2)^9$
5. $(2x - 3)^8$
6. $(x - 1)^9$
7. $(2x^2 - 2y^2)^6$
8. $(x^5 + 2y)^7$
9. $(n - 3)^3$
10. $(2n + 2)^4$
11. $(n - 6)^5$
12. $(n - 1)^6$
13. $(2a + 2)^3$
14. $(x^2 - y^2)^4$
15. $(2x + 3y)^5$
16. $(2x^2 + y^2)^6$
17. $(x^2 - y^2)^3$
18. $(2b + c)^4$
19. $(3m - 2n)^5$
20. $(x^3 - y^4)^6$

Find the specified term of each binomial expansion.

21. third term of $(x + 3)^{12}$
22. second term of $(x + 3)^9$
23. twelfth term of $(2 + x)^{11}$
24. third term of $(x - 2)^{12}$
25. eighth term of $(x - 2y)^{15}$
26. seventh term of $(x - 2y)^6$
27. fifth term of $(x^2 + y^2)^{13}$
28. fourth term of $(x^2 - 2y)^{11}$
29. The term $126c^4d^5$ appears in the expansion of $(c + d)^n$. What is n?
30. The coefficient of the second term in the expansion of $(r + s)^n$ is 7. Find the value of n, and write the complete term.

State the number of terms in each expansion and give the first two terms.

31. $(d + e)^{12}$
32. $(x - y)^{15}$
33. $(2a + b)^5$
34. $(x - 3y)^7$
35. $(4 - 2x)^8$
36. $(x^2 + y)^6$
37. The side of a number cube is $x + 4$ units long. Write a binomial for the volume of the number cube. Use the Binomial Theorem to expand and rewrite the expression in standard form.

Name ______________________ Class ____________ Date ____________

5-7 Practice (continued) — Form G

The Binomial Theorem

Expand each binomial.

38. $(x + 1)^7$

39. $(x + 4)^8$

40. $(x - 3y)^6$

41. $(x + 2)^5$

42. $(x^2 - y^2)^5$

43. $(3 + y)^5$

44. $(x^2 + 3)^6$

45. $(x - 5)^7$

46. $(x - 4y)^4$

47. **Open-Ended** Write a binomial in the form $(a + b)^n$ that has 3 as the coefficient of the first term.

48. Use Pascal's Triangle to determine the binomial of the expanded expression $x^6 + 6x^5 + 15x^4 + 20x^3 + 15x^2 + 6x + 1$.

49. **Error Analysis** Your friend expands the binomial $(x - 2)^6$ as $x^6 + 12x^5 + 30x^4 + 160x^3 + 240x^2 + 192x + 64$. What mistake did your friend make? What is the correct expansion?

50. **Reasoning** Without writing any of the previous terms, how do you know that 2187 is the eighth term of the expansion of the binomial $(x + 3)^7$?

51. In the expansion of $(3x - y)^6$, one of the terms contains the factor y^4.

a. What is the exponent of $3x$ in this term?

b. What is the coefficient of this term?

52. You are shipping a cubic glass sculpture. Each side of the sculpture is x in. long. To adequately protect the sculpture, the shipping box must leave room for 5 in. of padding on either side in every dimension. Write and expand a binomial for the volume of the shipping box.

Name ______________________ Class ____________ Date ____________

5-7 Standardized Test Prep

The Binomial Theorem

Multiple Choice

For Exercises 1–7, choose the correct letter.

1. What is the expanded form of $(a - b)^3$?

(A) $a^3 + a^2b + ab^2 + b^3$

(B) $a^3 - a^2b + ab^2 - b^3$

(C) $a^3 + 3a^2b + 3ab^2 + b^3$

(D) $a^3 - 3a^2b + 3ab^2 - b^3$

2. What is the third term in the expansion of $(x - y)^7$?

(F) $21x^5y^2$ (G) $-7x^6y$ (H) $7x^6y$ (I) $-21x^5y^2$

3. What is the coefficient of the third term in the expansion of $(2x - y)^5$?

(A) -80 (B) 32 (C) 40 (D) 80

4. Which term in the expansion of $(2a - 3b)^6$ has coefficient 2160?

(F) second term (G) third term (H) fourth term (I) fifth term

5. What is n if $-448x^5y^3$ appears in the expansion of $(x - 2y)^n$?

(A) 6 (B) 7 (C) 8 (D) 9

6. What is the 6th term in the 12th line of Pascal's Triangle?

(F) 252 (G) 462 (H) 792 (I) 1287

7. What is the expanded form of $(2x - y)^5$?

(A) $32x^5 + 80x^4y + 80x^3y^2 + 40x^2y^3 + 10xy^4 + y^5$

(B) $32x^5 - 80x^4y + 80x^3y^2 - 40x^2y^3 + 10xy^4 - y^5$

(C) $2x^5 + 5x^4y + 20x^3y^2 + 20x^2y^3 + 10xy^4 + y^5$

(D) $2x^5 - 5x^4y + 20x^3y^2 - 20x^2y^3 + 10xy^4 - y^5$

Short Response

8. The coefficient of the fourth term in the expansion of $(x + y)^n$ is 84.

a. What is the value of n?

b. What is the complete term?

Name ______________________ Class ____________ Date ____________

5-8 Think About a Plan

Polynomial Models in the Real World

Air Travel The table shows the percent of on-time flights for selected years. Find a polynomial function to model the data.

Year	1998	2000	2002	2004	2006
On-time Flights (%)	76.04	73.1	81.07	77.6	76.19

1. How can you plot the data? (*Hint*: Let x equal the number of years after 1990.)

____

2. What types of models can you find for the data? ______________________

3. Which model will fit the data points exactly? ______________________

4. Find r^2 or R^2 for the models you listed in Exercise 2.

____

5. What does the value of r^2 or R^2 tell you about each model?

____

____.

6. Graph each model on your graphing calculator. Sketch and label each model.

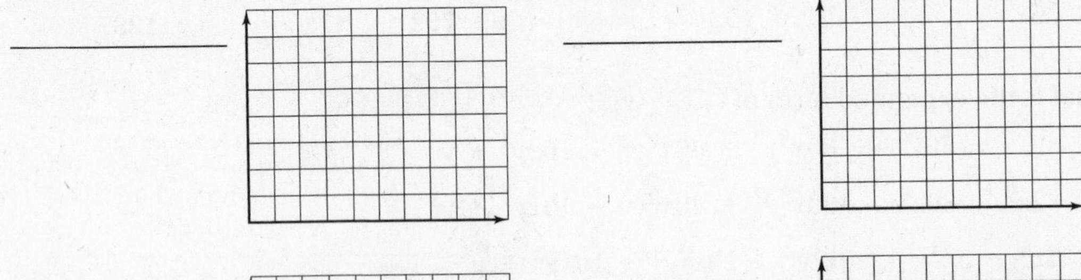

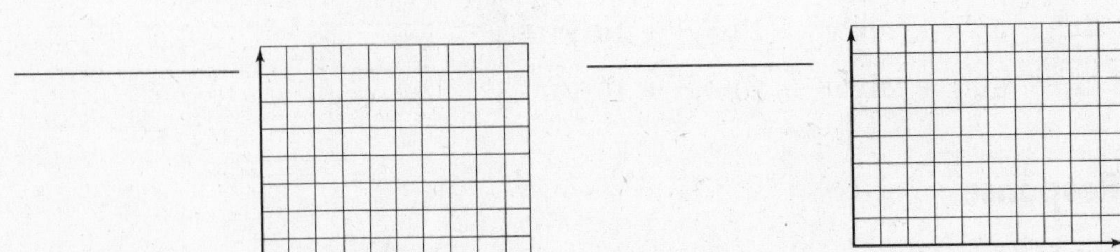

7. Which model seems more likely to represent the percent of on-time flights over time?

____

____

____.

Name ______________________ Class ____________ Date ____________

5-8 Practice

Form G

Polynomial Models in the Real World

Find a polynomial function whose graph passes through each set of points.

1. $(4, -1)$ and $(-3, 13)$
2. $\left(1, -\frac{9}{2}\right)$ and $(6, -2)$
3. $(7, -5)$ and $(-1, 3)$
4. $(0, -3)$, $(-2, -7)$, and $(2, 9)$
5. $(-3, 15)$, $(1, 11)$, and $(0, 6)$
6. $(-2, -12)$, $(1, -6)$, and $(2, -24)$
7. $(4, -1)$, $(-2, -13)$, and $(1, 2)$
8. $(0, 9)$, $(2, 21)$ $(-1, 0)$, and $(3, 36)$

Find a polynomial function that best models each set of values.

9. Let $x =$ the number of years after 1985.

World Gold

Year	Production (millions of troy ounces)
1985	49.3
1990	70.2
1995	71.8
2000	82.6

SOURCES: *The World Almanac* and *World Gold*

10. Let $x =$ the number of years after 1970.

Life Expectancy

Year of Birth	Female (years)
1970	74.7
1980	77.4
1990	78.8
2000	79.7

SOURCE: U.S. Bureau of the Census

11. Let $x =$ the number of years after 1985.

U.S. Energy

Year	Total Production ($\times 10^{15}$ Btu)
1985	64.9
1990	70.8
1995	71.0

SOURCE: Energy Information Administration

12. Let $x =$ the number of years after 1980.

Social Security Benefits

Year	Monthly Average (dollars)
1980	321.10
1990	550.50
2000	844.60

SOURCE: *www.infoplease.com*

Find a cubic and a quartic model for each set of values. Then determine which model best represents the values.

13.

x	−2	−1	0	1	2
y	−7	−3	3	5	−3

14.

x	−2	−1	0	1	2
y	2	−6	2	8	42

Name ______________________ Class ____________ Date ____________

5-8 Practice (continued) *Form G*

Polynomial Models in the Real World

Use your models from Exercises 9–12 to make predictions.

15. Estimate world gold production for 2010, 2020, and 2025.

16. Estimate the life expectancy for women born in 1986, 1992, and 2005.

17. Estimate the U.S. energy production for 2002, 2005, and 2010.

18. Estimate the average monthly Social Security benefits for 1970, 1996, and 1999.

19. Find a cubic function to model the data below. (*Hint*: Use x to represent the gestation period.) Then use the function to estimate the longevity of an animal with a gestation period of 151 days.

Gestation and Longevity of Certain Animals

Animal	Rat	Squirrel	Pig	Cow	Elephant
Gestation (in days)	21	44	115	280	624
Longevity (in years)	3	9	10	12	40

Source: *www.infoplease.com*

20. Error Analysis Your teacher gives the class the table at the right and asks you to find a polynomial model for the data set. Then he asks the class to estimate the percent of U.S. foreign-born population in 1920. Your friend uses $x = -10$ and estimates the percent as 16.1. What did your friend do wrong? What is the correct estimate?

U.S. Population

Year	Foreign-Born (percent)
1910	14.7
1930	11.6
1950	6.9
1970	4.7
1990	8.0
2000	10.4
2004	11.7

Source: Bureau of the Census

21. Reasoning Using the data set from Exercise 12 and the model you determined, find the average monthly Social Security benefits for the year 2050. Do you have much confidence in this prediction? Explain.

22. Find a cubic model for the following set of values: $(0, -4)$, $(-1, -6)$, $(5, -264)$, and $(2, -18)$. Using the regression coefficient, determine whether the model is a good fit.

Name ______________________ Class ____________ Date ____________

5-8 Standardized Test Prep

Polynomial Models in the Real World

Multiple Choice

For Exercises 1–4, choose the correct letter.

1. Which of the following is the polynomial function whose graph passes through (0, 4), (−2, 30), and (1, 6)?

   (A) $y = -9x + 10$
   (B) $y = 5x^2 - 3x + 4$
   (C) $y = 9x - 10$
   (D) $y = -5x^2 + 3x - 4$

2. Which model type best represents the set of values at the right?

x	−2	−1	0	1	2
y	−17	4	1	−2	−5

   (F) linear
   (G) cubic
   (H) quadratic
   (I) quartic

3. Which polynomial function best models the data set at the right?

   (A) $y = 0.00006006x^4 + 0.000119x^3 - 0.025x^2 + 2.13x + 71.6$
   (B) $y = 0.00002163x^4 + 0.001267x^3 - 0.155x^2 + 8.24x + 81.2$
   (C) $y = 0.00000312x^4 + 0.000197x^3 - 0.219x^2 + 5.22x + 86.3$
   (D) $y = 0.00000606x^4 + 0.000217x^3 - 0.079x^2 + 3.90x + 83.5$

Paying Taxes for 1 Day

Year	Time Spent (minute
1940	83
1950	117
1960	130
1970	141
1980	145
1990	145
2000	160

SOURCE: Tax Foundation

4. Using a cubic model for the data set at the right, what is the estimated Consumer Price Index for 1965?

   (F) 102.5
   (G) 130.034
   (H) 116.564
   (I) 147.384

Consumer Prices

Year	Index
1920	60.0
1930	50.0
1940	42.0
1950	72.1
1960	88.7
1970	116.3
1980	248.8
1990	391.4
2000	515.8

SOURCE: Bureau of Labor Statistics

Short Response

5. Find both a cubic and quartic model for the set of values at the right. Which model is a better fit? How do you know?

x	1.2	1.4	1.6	1.8	2.0	2.2
y	3.1	−4.2	4.1	7.5	−8.9	10

Name ______________________ Class ____________ Date ____________

5-9 Think About a Plan

Transforming Polynomial Functions

Physics The formula $K = \frac{1}{2}mv^2$ represents the kinetic energy of an object. If the kinetic energy of a ball is 10 lb-ft^2/s^2 when it is thrown with a velocity of 4 ft/s, how much kinetic energy is generated if the ball is thrown with a velocity of 8 ft/s?

Know

1. The kinetic energy of a ball is [ ] when the velocity of the ball is [ ].

2. ____

____

Need

3. To solve the problem I need to:

____.

Plan

4. What equation can you use to find the value of m for the ball?

5. Solve the equation.

6. What equation can you use to find the kinetic energy generated if the ball is thrown with a velocity of 8 ft/s?

7. Simplify.

8. Is the solution reasonable? Explain.

____

____

____.

Name ______________________ Class ____________ Date ____________

5-9 Practice

Form G

Transforming Polynomial Functions

Determine the cubic function that is obtained from the parent function $y = x^3$ after each sequence of transformations.

1. a reflection in the x-axis; a vertical translation 3 units down; and a horizontal translation 2 units right

2. a vertical stretch by a factor of 4; a reflection in the x-axis; and a horizontal translation $\frac{1}{2}$ unit left

3. a vertical stretch by a factor of $\frac{1}{3}$; a reflection in the y-axis; and a vertical translation 6 units up

4. a vertical stretch by a factor of 3; a reflection in the x-axis; a vertical translation 2 units down; and a horizontal translation 2 units left

Find all the real zeros of each function.

5. $y = 2(x + 1)^3 - 3$

6. $y = -3(x - 2)^3 + 24$

7. $y = -\frac{1}{2}(x + 4)^3 - 1$

8. $y = 8(-x - 2)^3 + 5$

9. $y = -(x + 5)^3 + 1$

10. $y = 4(x - 6)^3 - 2$

Find a quartic function with the given x-values as its only real zeros.

11. $x = 2$ and $x = 8$

12. $x = 3$ and $x = -1$

13. $x = 1$ and $x = 3$

14. $x = -2$ and $x = 6$

15. $x = 5$ and $x = -2$

16. $x = -1$ and $x = 2$

17. $x = -3$ and $x = -5$

18. $x = -4$ and $x = 4$

19. **Physics** If you stretch a spring to 5 ft, it has 310 ft-lb of potential energy (PE). Potential energy varies directly as the square of the stretched length (l). The potential energy can be represented by the formula $PE = \frac{1}{2}kl^2$, where k is the spring constant.
    a. What is the value of the spring constant for this spring?
    b. How many ft-lbs of PE would an 8 ft length of spring have?

Name ________________________ Class ____________ Date ____________

5-9 Practice (continued) — Form G

Transforming Polynomial Functions

Determine whether each function can be obtained from the parent function $y = x^n$, using basic transformations. If so, describe the sequence of transformations.

20. $y = 2(x - 3)^3 + 4$

21. $y = x^4 + x - 3$

22. $y = -\frac{1}{3}x^2$

23. $y = (-x + 5)^3$

24. $y = \frac{2}{x^3}$

25. $y = 4(x)^4 - 12$

26. Graph the parent function $y = x^3$ after it has been transformed by the following changes.

- vertical stretch by a factor of $2\frac{1}{4}$
- reflection across the x-axis
- vertical translation 4 units up

27. Error Analysis Your friend set up a problem to find a quartic function with the only real zeros of $x = -4$ and $x = 1$. She wrote down $y = (x + 4)(x - 1)(x^2 - 1)$. Will she get a correct quartic function? Why or why not?

28. Open-Ended Transform the parent function $y = x^3$ by vertical stretch, reflection across the x-axis, horizontal translation, and vertical translation.

29. You are swinging a bucket in a circle at a velocity of 7.8 ft/s. The radius of the circle you are making is 1.25 ft. The acceleration is equal to one over the radius multiplied by the velocity squared.

a. What is the acceleration of the bucket?

b. What is the velocity if the acceleration is 25 ft/sec^2?

Name ______________________ Class __________ Date __________

5-9 Standardized Test Prep

Transforming Polynomial Functions

Multiple Choice

For Exercises 1–5, choose the correct letter.

1. Which of the following describes the transformation of the parent function $y = x^3$ shown in the graph at the right?

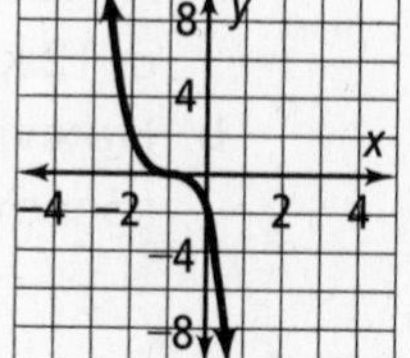

Ⓐ reflection across x-axis, vertical stretch by a factor of 2, and horizontal translation 1 unit left

Ⓑ reflection across y-axis, vertical translation 1 unit up

Ⓒ horizontal translation 2 units left, vertical translation 1 unit down

Ⓓ vertical stretch by a factor of $\frac{1}{2}$, horizontal translation 1 unit right, and vertical translation 2 units down

2. What are all the real zeros for $y = 5(x - 4)^3 + 6$?

Ⓕ $\sqrt[3]{\frac{-6}{5}} - 4$ Ⓖ $\sqrt[3]{\frac{6}{5}} - 4$ Ⓗ $\sqrt[3]{\frac{-6}{5}} + 4$ Ⓘ $\sqrt[3]{\frac{6}{5}} + 4$

3. Which of the following polynomial functions *cannot* be obtained from the parent function $y = x^n$ using basic transformations?

Ⓐ $y = 6(x + 2)^3 - 3$ Ⓑ $y = (-x - 1)^4$ Ⓒ $y = \frac{x^2}{5}$ Ⓓ $y = x^2 + x$

4. Which quartic function has $x = 3$ and $x = 9$ as its only real zeros?

Ⓕ $y = (x + 6)^4 - 81$ Ⓗ $y = (x + 3)^4 - 81$

Ⓖ $y = (x - 6)^4 - 81$ Ⓘ $y = (x - 3)^4 - 81$

5. Which graph represents the polynomial $y = 2(-x + 6)^3 - 1$?

Ⓐ 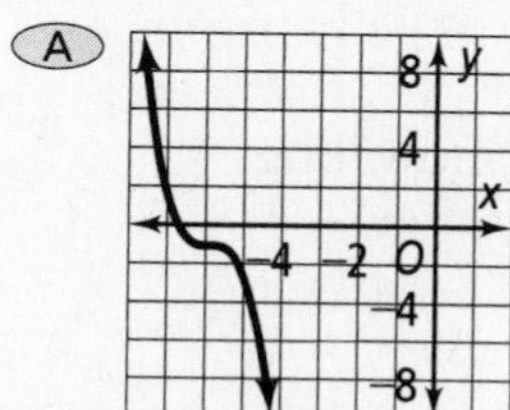

Ⓑ 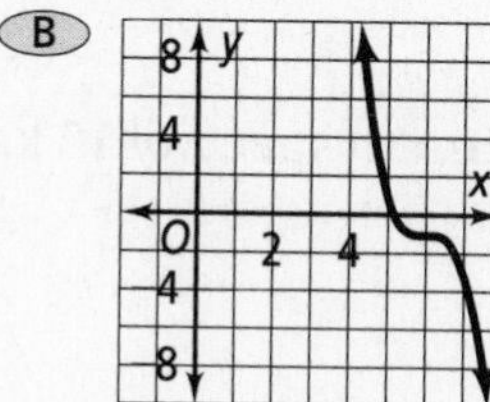

Ⓒ 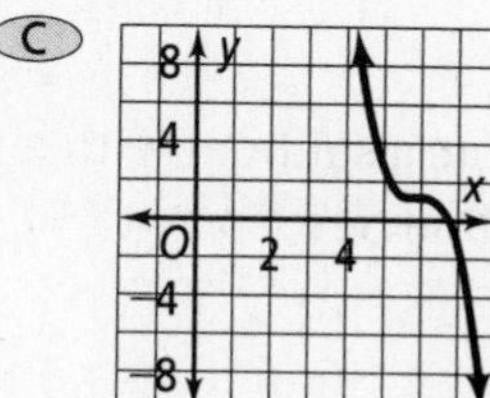

Ⓓ 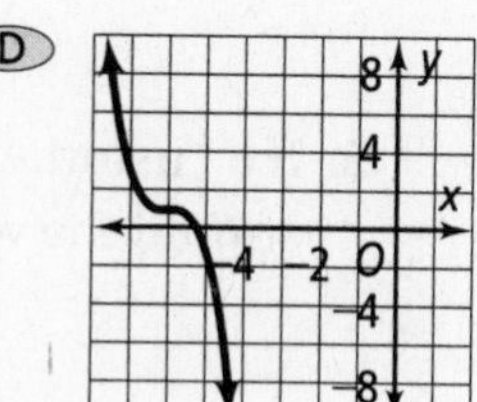

Short Response

6. The formula $s = \frac{1}{2}at^2$ represents the distance an object will travel in a specific amount of time if it travels at a constant acceleration. You roll a ball 20 ft in 6 s. How long will it take to roll the ball 45 ft? Show your work.

Name ______________________ Class ____________ Date ____________

6-1 Think About a Plan

Roots and Radical Expressions

Boat Building Boat builders share an old rule of thumb for sailboats. The maximum speed K in knots is 1.35 times the square root of the length L in feet of the boat's waterline.

a. A customer is planning to order a sailboat with a maximum speed of 12 knots. How long should the waterline be?

b. How much longer would the waterline have to be to achieve a maximum speed of 15 knots?

1. Write an equation to relate the maximum speed K in knots to the length L in feet of a boat's waterline.

2. How can you find the length of a sailboat's waterline if you know its maximum speed?

____.

3. A customer is planning to order a sailboat with a maximum speed of 12 knots. How long should the waterline be?

4. How can you find how much longer the waterline would have to be to achieve a maximum speed of 15 knots, compared to a maximum speed of 12 knots?

____

____.

5. If a customer wants a sailboat with a maximum speed of 15 knots, how long should the waterline be?

6. How much longer would the waterline have to be to achieve a maximum speed of 15 knots?

Name ______________________ Class ____________ Date ____________

6-1 Practice

Form G

Roots and Radical Expressions

Find all the real square roots of each number.

1. 400 **2.** −196 **3.** 10,000 **4.** 0.0625

Find all the real cube roots of each number.

5. 216 **6.** −343 **7.** −0.064 **8.** $\frac{1000}{27}$

Find all the real fourth roots of each number.

9. −81 **10.** 256 **11.** 0.0001 **12.** 625

Find each real root.

13. $\sqrt{144}$ **14.** $-\sqrt{25}$ **15.** $\sqrt{-0.01}$ **16.** $\sqrt[3]{0.001}$

17. $\sqrt[4]{0.0081}$ **18.** $\sqrt[3]{27}$ **19.** $\sqrt[3]{-27}$ **20.** $\sqrt{0.09}$

Simplify each radical expression. Use absolute value symbols when needed.

21. $\sqrt{81x^4}$ **22.** $\sqrt{121y^{10}}$ **23.** $\sqrt[3]{8g^6}$

24. $\sqrt[3]{125x^9}$ **25.** $\sqrt[5]{243x^5y^{15}}$ **26.** $\sqrt[3]{(x-9)^3}$

27. $\sqrt{25(x+2)^4}$ **28.** $\sqrt[3]{\frac{64x^9}{343}}$ **29.** $\sqrt[3]{-0.008}$

30. $\sqrt[4]{\frac{x^4}{81}}$ **31.** $\sqrt{36x^2y^6}$ **32.** $\sqrt[4]{(m-n)^4}$

33. A cube has volume $V = s^3$, where s is the length of a side. Find the side length for a cube with volume 8000 cm^3.

34. The temperature T in degrees Celsius (°C) of a liquid t minutes after heating is given by the formula $T = 8\sqrt{t}$. When is the temperature 48°C?

Name ______________________ Class ____________ Date ____________

6-1 Practice (continued)

Form G

Roots and Radical Expressions

Find the two real solutions of each equation.

35. $x^2 = 4$

36. $x^4 = 81$

37. $x^2 = 0.16$

38. $x^2 = \frac{16}{49}$

39. $x^4 = \frac{16}{625}$

40. $x^2 = \frac{121}{625}$

41. $x^2 = 0.000009$

42. $x^4 = 0.0001$

43. The number of new customers n that visit a dry cleaning shop in one year is directly related to the amount a (in dollars) spent on advertising. This relationship is represented by $n^3 = 13{,}824a$. To attract 480 new customers, how much should the owners spend on advertising during the year?

44. Geometry The volume V of a sphere with radius r is given by the formula $V = \frac{4}{3}\pi r^3$.

a. What is the radius of a sphere with volume 36π cubic inches?

b. If the volume increases by a factor of 8, what is the new radius?

45. A clothing manufacturer finds the number of defective blouses d is a function of the total number of blouses n produced at her factory. This function is $d = 0.000005n^2$.

a. What is the total number of blouses produced if 45 are defective?

b. If the number of defective blouses increases by a factor of 9, how does the total number of blouses change?

46. The velocity of a falling object can be found using the formula $v^2 = 64h$, where v is the velocity (in feet per second) and h is the distance the object has already fallen.

a. What is the velocity of the object after a 10-foot fall?

b. How much does the velocity increase if the object falls 20 feet rather than 10 feet?

Name ______________________ Class ____________ Date ____________

6-1 Standardized Test Prep

Roots and Radical Expressions

Multiple Choice

For Exercises 1–6, choose the correct letter.

1. What is the real square root of 0.0064?

Ⓐ 0.4
Ⓑ 0.08
Ⓒ 0.04
Ⓓ no real square root

2. What is the real cube root of −64?

Ⓕ 4
Ⓖ −4
Ⓗ −8
Ⓘ no real cube root

3. What is the real fourth root of $-\frac{16}{81}$?

Ⓐ $\frac{2}{3}$
Ⓑ $-\frac{2}{3}$
Ⓒ $-\frac{4}{9}$
Ⓓ no real fourth root

4. What is the value of $\sqrt[3]{-0.027}$?

Ⓕ −0.3 Ⓖ 0.3 Ⓗ −0.03 Ⓘ 0.03

5. What is the simplified form of the expression $\sqrt{4x^2y^4}$?

Ⓐ $2xy^2$ Ⓑ $2|x|y^2$ Ⓒ $4xy^2$ Ⓓ $2|xy|$

6. What are the real solutions of the equation $x^4 = 81$?

Ⓕ −9, 9 Ⓖ 3 Ⓗ −3, 3 Ⓘ −3

Short Response

7. The volume V of a cube with side length s is $V = s^3$. A cubical storage bin has volume 5832 cubic inches. What is the length of the side of the cube? Show your work.

Name ______________________ Class ______________ Date ______________

6-2 Think About a Plan

Multiplying and Dividing Radical Expressions

Satellites The circular velocity v, in miles per hour of a satellite orbiting Earth is given by the formula $v = \sqrt{\frac{1.24 \times 10^{12}}{r}}$, where r is the distance in miles from the satellite to the center of the Earth. How much greater is the velocity of a satellite orbiting at an altitude of 100 mi than the velocity of a satellite orbiting at an altitude of 200 mi? (The radius of the Earth is 3950 mi.)

Know

1. The first satellite orbits at an altitude of ☐.

2. The second satellite orbits at an altitude of ☐.

3. The distance from the surface of the Earth to its center is ☐.

Need

4. To solve the problem I need to find:

____

____.

Plan

5. Rewrite the formula for the circular velocity of a satellite using a for the altitude of the satellite.

6. Use your formula to find the velocity of a satellite orbiting at an altitude of 100 mi.

7. Use your formula to find the velocity of a satellite orbiting at an altitude of 200 mi.

8. How much greater is the velocity of a satellite orbiting at an altitude of 100 mi than one orbiting at an altitude of 200 mi?

Name ______________________ Class ____________ Date ____________

6-2 Practice

Form G

Multiplying and Dividing Radical Expressions

Multiply, if possible. Then simplify.

1. $\sqrt{4} \cdot \sqrt{25}$
2. $\sqrt{81} \cdot \sqrt{36}$
3. $\sqrt{3} \cdot \sqrt[3]{27}$
4. $\sqrt[3]{45} \cdot \sqrt[3]{75}$
5. $\sqrt{18} \cdot \sqrt{50}$
6. $\sqrt[3]{-16} \cdot \sqrt[3]{4}$

Simplify. Assume that all variables are positive.

7. $\sqrt{36x^3}$
8. $\sqrt[3]{125y^2z^4}$
9. $\sqrt{18k^6}$
10. $\sqrt[3]{-16a^{12}}$
11. $\sqrt{x^2y^{10}z}$
12. $\sqrt[4]{256s^7t^{12}}$
13. $\sqrt[3]{216x^4y^3}$
14. $\sqrt{75r^3}$
15. $\sqrt[4]{625u^5v^8}$

Multiply and simplify. Assume that all variables are positive.

16. $\sqrt{4} \cdot \sqrt{6}$
17. $\sqrt{9x^2} \cdot \sqrt{9y^5}$
18. $\sqrt[3]{50x^2z^5} \cdot \sqrt[3]{15y^3z}$
19. $4\sqrt{2x} \cdot 3\sqrt{8x}$
20. $\sqrt{xy} \cdot \sqrt{4xy}$
21. $9\sqrt{2} \cdot 3\sqrt{y}$
22. $\sqrt{12x^2y} \cdot \sqrt{3xy^4}$
23. $\sqrt[3]{-9x^2y^4} \cdot \sqrt[3]{12xy}$
24. $7\sqrt{3y^2} \cdot 2\sqrt{6x^3y}$

Divide and simplify. Assume that all variables are positive.

25. $\dfrac{\sqrt{75}}{\sqrt{3}}$
26. $\dfrac{\sqrt{63xy^3}}{\sqrt{7y}}$
27. $\dfrac{\sqrt{54x^5y^3}}{\sqrt{2x^2y}}$
28. $\dfrac{\sqrt{6x}}{\sqrt{3x}}$
29. $\dfrac{\sqrt[3]{4x^2}}{\sqrt[3]{x}}$
30. $\sqrt[4]{\dfrac{243k^3}{3k^7}}$
31. $\dfrac{\sqrt{(2x)^2}}{\sqrt{(5y)^4}}$
32. $\dfrac{\sqrt[3]{18y^2}}{\sqrt[3]{12y}}$
33. $\sqrt{\dfrac{162a}{6a^3}}$

Name ______________________ Class ____________ Date ____________

6-2 Practice (continued)

Form G

Multiplying and Dividing Radical Expressions

Rationalize the denominator of each expression. Assume that all variables are positive.

34. $\frac{\sqrt{y}}{\sqrt{5}}$

35. $\frac{\sqrt{18x^2y}}{\sqrt{2y^3}}$

36. $\frac{\sqrt[3]{7xy^2}}{\sqrt[3]{4x^2}}$

37. $\sqrt{\frac{9x}{2}}$

38. $\frac{\sqrt{xy}}{\sqrt{3x}}$

39. $\sqrt[3]{\frac{x^2}{3y}}$

40. $\frac{\sqrt[4]{2x}}{\sqrt[4]{3x^2}}$

41. $\sqrt{\frac{x}{8y}}$

42. $\sqrt[3]{\frac{3a}{4b^2c}}$

43. What is the area of a rectangle with length $\sqrt{175}$ in. and width $\sqrt{63}$ in.?

44. The area of a rectangle is 30 m^2. If the length is $\sqrt{75}$ m, what is the width?

45. The volume of a right circular cone is $V = \frac{1}{3}\pi r^2 h$, where r is the radius of the base and h is the height of the cone. Solve the formula for r. Rationalize the denominator.

46. The volume of a sphere of radius r is $V = \frac{4}{3}\pi r^3$.
   a. Use the formula to find r in terms of V. Rationalize the denominator.
   b. Use your answer to part (a) to find the radius of a sphere with volume 100 cubic inches. Round to the nearest hundredth.

Simplify each expression. Rationalize all denominators. Assume that all variables are positive.

47. $\sqrt{14} \cdot \sqrt{21}$

48. $\sqrt[3]{150} \cdot \sqrt[3]{20}$

49. $\sqrt{3}\left(\sqrt{12} - \sqrt{6}\right)$

50. $\frac{6\sqrt{2x}}{5\sqrt{3}}$

51. $\frac{8}{\sqrt[3]{2x^2}}$

52. $\frac{5\sqrt[3]{xy^4}}{\sqrt[3]{25xy^2}}$

Name ______________________ Class ____________ Date ____________

6-2 Standardized Test Prep

Multiplying and Dividing Radical Expressions

Multiple Choice

For Exercises 1–5, choose the correct letter. Assume that all variables are positive.

1. What is the simplest form of $\sqrt[3]{-49x} \cdot \sqrt[3]{7x^2}$?

   (A) $7x\sqrt{7x}$ (B) $-7x$ (C) $7x$ (D) $-7\sqrt[3]{x^2}$

2. What is the simplest form of $\sqrt{80x^7y^6}$?

   (F) $2x^3y^3\sqrt{20x}$ (G) $4x^6y^6\sqrt{5x^3}$ (H) $4\sqrt{5x^7y^6}$ (I) $4x^3y^3\sqrt{5x}$

3. What is the simplest form of $\sqrt[3]{25xy^2} \cdot \sqrt[3]{15x^2}$?

   (A) $5x\sqrt[3]{3y^2}$ (B) $5x\sqrt[3]{3y}$ (C) $15xy\sqrt[3]{y}$ (D) $5xy\sqrt{15x}$

4. What is the simplest form of $\dfrac{\sqrt{75x^5}}{\sqrt{12xy^2}}$?

   (F) $\dfrac{5\sqrt{3x^4}}{2\sqrt{3y^2}}$ (G) $\dfrac{5x^2}{2y}$ (H) $\dfrac{5x\sqrt{x}}{2y}$ (I) $\dfrac{5x^2y}{2}$

5. What is the simplest form of $\dfrac{2\sqrt[3]{x^2y}}{\sqrt[3]{4xy^2}}$?

   (A) $\dfrac{\sqrt[3]{x^2y}}{2y}$ (B) $\dfrac{x\sqrt[3]{2y}}{y}$ (C) $\dfrac{\sqrt[3]{2xy^2}}{y}$ (D) $\dfrac{\sqrt[3]{2y}}{xy}$

Short Response

6. The volume V of a wooden beam is $V = ls^2$, where l is the length of the beam and s is the length of one side of its square cross section. If the volume of the beam is 1200 in.^{3} and its length is 96 in., what is the side length? Show your work.

Name ______________________ Class __________ Date __________

6-3 Think About a Plan

Binomial Radical Expressions

Geometry Show that the right triangle with legs of length $\sqrt{2} - 1$ and $\sqrt{2} + 1$ is similar to the right triangle with legs of length $6 - \sqrt{32}$ and 2.

Understanding the Problem

1. What is the length of the shortest leg of the first triangle? Explain.

____

2. What is the length of the shortest leg of the second triangle? Explain.

____

____

3. Which legs in the two triangles are corresponding legs?

____

____

____

Planning the Solution

4. Write a proportion that can be used to show that the two triangles are similar.

Getting an Answer

5. Simplify your proportion to show that the two triangles are similar.

Name ____________________ Class ____________ Date ____________

6-3 Practice

Form G

Binomial Radical Expressions

Add or subtract if possible.

1. $9\sqrt{3} + 2\sqrt{3}$
2. $5\sqrt{2} + 2\sqrt{3}$
3. $3\sqrt{7} - 7\sqrt[3]{x}$
4. $14\sqrt[3]{xy} - 3\sqrt[3]{xy}$
5. $8\sqrt[3]{x} + 2\sqrt[3]{y}$
6. $5\sqrt[3]{xy} + \sqrt[3]{xy}$
7. $\sqrt{3x} - 2\sqrt{3x}$
8. $6\sqrt{2} - 5\sqrt[3]{2}$
9. $7\sqrt{x} + x\sqrt{7}$

Simplify.

10. $3\sqrt{32} + 2\sqrt{50}$
11. $\sqrt{200} - \sqrt{72}$
12. $\sqrt[3]{81} - 3\sqrt[3]{3}$
13. $2\sqrt[4]{48} + 3\sqrt[4]{243}$
14. $3\sqrt{75} + 2\sqrt{12}$
15. $\sqrt[3]{250} - \sqrt[3]{54}$
16. $\sqrt{28} - \sqrt{63}$
17. $3\sqrt[4]{32} - 2\sqrt[4]{162}$
18. $\sqrt{125} - 2\sqrt{20}$

Multiply.

19. $(1 - \sqrt{5})(2 - \sqrt{5})$
20. $(1 + 4\sqrt{10})(2 - \sqrt{10})$
21. $(1 - 3\sqrt{7})(4 - 3\sqrt{7})$
22. $(4 - 2\sqrt{3})^2$
23. $(\sqrt{2} + \sqrt{7})^2$
24. $(2\sqrt{3} - 3\sqrt{2})^2$
25. $(4 - \sqrt{3})(2 + \sqrt{3})$
26. $(3 + \sqrt{11})(4 - \sqrt{11})$
27. $(3\sqrt{2} - 2\sqrt{3})^2$

Multiply each pair of conjugates.

28. $(3\sqrt{2} - 9)(3\sqrt{2} + 9)$
29. $(1 - \sqrt{7})(1 + \sqrt{7})$
30. $(5\sqrt{3} + \sqrt{2})(5\sqrt{3} - \sqrt{2})$
31. $(3\sqrt{2} - 2\sqrt{3})(3\sqrt{2} + 2\sqrt{3})$
32. $(\sqrt{11} + 5)(\sqrt{11} - 5)$
33. $(2\sqrt{7} + 3\sqrt{3})(2\sqrt{7} - 3\sqrt{3})$

Name ______________________ Class ____________ Date ____________

6-3 Practice (continued) Form G

Binomial Radical Expressions

Rationalize each denominator. Simplify the answer.

34. $\frac{3 - \sqrt{10}}{\sqrt{5} - \sqrt{2}}$

35. $\frac{2 + \sqrt{14}}{\sqrt{7} + \sqrt{2}}$

36. $\frac{2 + \sqrt[3]{x}}{\sqrt[3]{x}}$

Simplify. Assume that all the variables are positive.

37. $\sqrt{28} + 4\sqrt{63} - 2\sqrt{7}$

38. $6\sqrt{40} - 2\sqrt{90} - 3\sqrt{160}$

39. $3\sqrt{12} + 7\sqrt{75} - \sqrt{54}$

40. $4\sqrt[3]{81} + 2\sqrt[3]{72} - 3\sqrt[3]{24}$

41. $3\sqrt{225x} + 5\sqrt{144x}$

42. $6\sqrt{45y^2} + 4\sqrt{20y^2}$

43. $(3\sqrt{y} - \sqrt{5})(2\sqrt{y} + 5\sqrt{5})$

44. $(\sqrt{x} - \sqrt{3})(\sqrt{x} + \sqrt{3})$

45. A park in the shape of a triangle has a sidewalk dividing it into two parts.

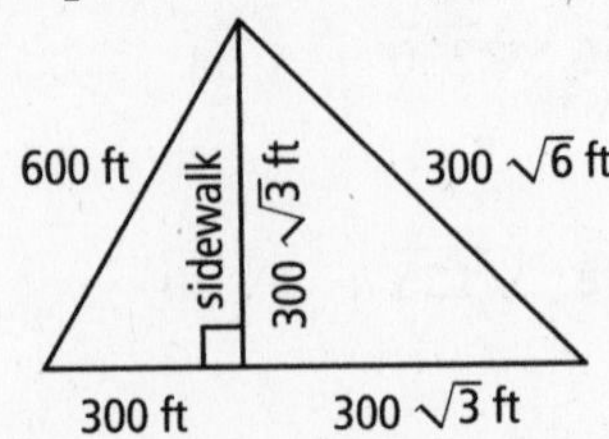

a. If a man walks around the perimeter of the park, how far will he walk?

b. What is the area of the park?

46. The area of a rectangle is 10 in.². The length is $(2 + \sqrt{2})$ in. What is the width?

47. One solution to the equation $x^2 + 2x - 2 = 0$ is $-1 + \sqrt{3}$. To show this, let $x = -1 + \sqrt{3}$ and answer each of the following questions.

a. What is x^2?

b. What is $2x$?

c. Using your answers to parts (a) and (b), what is the sum $x^2 + 2x - 2$?

Name ______________________ Class ____________ Date ____________

6-3 Standardized Test Prep

Binomial Radical Expressions

Multiple Choice

For Exercises 1–5, choose the correct letter.

1. What is the simplest form of $2\sqrt{72} - 3\sqrt{32}$?

   (A) $2\sqrt{72} - 3\sqrt{32}$ (B) $24\sqrt{2}$ (C) $-2\sqrt{2}$ (D) 0

2. What is the simplest form of $(2 - \sqrt{7})(1 + 2\sqrt{7})$?

   (F) $-12 + 3\sqrt{7}$ (H) $16 + 5\sqrt{7}$

   (G) $-12 - 3\sqrt{7}$ (I) $3 + \sqrt{7}$

3. What is the simplest form of $(\sqrt{2} + \sqrt{7})(\sqrt{2} - \sqrt{7})$?

   (A) $9 + 2\sqrt{14}$ (B) $9 - 2\sqrt{14}$ (C) -5 (D) 9

4. What is the simplest form of $\frac{7}{2 + \sqrt{5}}$?

   (F) $-14 + 7\sqrt{5}$ (H) $-14 - 7\sqrt{5}$

   (G) $14 + 7\sqrt{5}$ (I) $14 - 7\sqrt{5}$

5. What is the simplest form of $8\sqrt[3]{5} - \sqrt[3]{40} - 2\sqrt[3]{135}$?

   (A) $16\sqrt[3]{5}$ (B) $12\sqrt[3]{5}$ (C) $4\sqrt[3]{5}$ (D) 0

Short Response

6. A hiker drops a rock from the rim of the Grand Canyon. The distance it falls d in feet after t seconds is given by the function $d = 16t^2$. How far has the rock fallen after $(3 + \sqrt{2})$ seconds? Show your work.

Name ______________________ Class ____________ Date ____________

6-4 Think About a Plan

Rational Exponents

Science A desktop world globe has a volume of about 1386 cubic inches. The radius of the Earth is approximately equal to the radius of the globe raised to the 10th power. Find the radius of the Earth. (*Hint:* Use the formula $V = \frac{4}{3}\pi r^3$ for the volume of a sphere.)

Know

1. The volume of the globe is ☐.

2. The radius of the Earth is equal to ______________________.

Need

3. To solve the problem I need to find ______________________.

Plan

4. Write an equation relating the radius of the globe r_G to the radius of the Earth r_E.

5. How can you represent the radius of the globe in terms of the radius of the Earth?

6. Write an equation to represent the volume of the globe.

7. Use your previous equation and your equation from Exercise 5 to write an equation to find the radius of the Earth.

8. Solve your equation to find the radius of the Earth.

Name ______________________ Class ____________ Date ____________

6-4 Practice

Form G

Rational Exponents

Simplify each expression.

1. $125^{\frac{1}{3}}$
2. $64^{\frac{1}{2}}$
3. $32^{\frac{1}{5}}$
4. $7^{\frac{1}{2}} \cdot 7^{\frac{1}{2}}$
5. $(-5)^{\frac{1}{3}} \cdot (-5)^{\frac{1}{3}} \cdot (-5)^{\frac{1}{3}}$
6. $3^{\frac{1}{2}} \cdot 75^{\frac{1}{2}}$
7. $11^{\frac{1}{3}} \cdot 11^{\frac{1}{3}} \cdot 11^{\frac{1}{3}}$
8. $7^{\frac{1}{2}} \cdot 28^{\frac{1}{2}}$
9. $8^{\frac{1}{4}} \cdot 32^{\frac{1}{4}}$
10. $12^{\frac{1}{2}} \cdot 27^{\frac{1}{2}}$
11. $12^{\frac{1}{3}} \cdot 45^{\frac{1}{3}} \cdot 50^{\frac{1}{3}}$
12. $18^{\frac{1}{2}} \cdot 98^{\frac{1}{2}}$

Write each expression in radical form.

13. $x^{\frac{4}{3}}$
14. $(2y)^{\frac{1}{3}}$
15. $a^{1.5}$
16. $b^{\frac{1}{5}}$
17. $z^{\frac{2}{3}}$
18. $(ab)^{\frac{1}{4}}$
19. $m^{2.4}$
20. $t^{-\frac{2}{7}}$
21. $a^{-1.6}$

Write each expression in exponential form.

22. $\sqrt{x^3}$
23. $\sqrt[3]{m}$
24. $\sqrt{5y}$
25. $\sqrt[3]{2y^2}$
26. $\left(\sqrt[4]{b}\right)^3$
27. $\sqrt{-6}$
28. $\sqrt{(6a)^4}$
29. $\sqrt[5]{n^4}$
30. $\sqrt[4]{(5ab)^3}$

31. The rate of inflation i that raises the cost of an item from the present value P to the future value F over t years is found using the formula $i = \left(\frac{F}{P}\right)^{\frac{1}{t}} - 1$. Round your answers to the nearest tenth of a percent.
   a. What is the rate of inflation for which a television set costing \$1000 today will become one costing \$1500 in 3 years?
   b. What is the rate of inflation that will result in the price P doubling (that is, $F = 2P$) in 10 years?

Name ______________________ Class __________ Date __________

6-4 Practice (continued)

Form G

Rational Exponents

Write each expression in simplest form. Assume that all variables are positive.

32. $\left(81^{\frac{1}{4}}\right)^4$

33. $\left(32^{\frac{1}{5}}\right)^5$

34. $(256^4)^{\frac{1}{4}}$

35. 7^0

36. $8^{\frac{2}{3}}$

37. $(-27)^{\frac{2}{3}}$

38. $x^{\frac{1}{2}} \cdot x^{\frac{1}{3}}$

39. $2y^{\frac{1}{2}} \cdot y$

40. $(8^2)^{\frac{1}{3}}$

41. 3.6^0

42. $\left(\frac{1}{16}\right)^{\frac{1}{4}}$

43. $\left(\frac{27}{8}\right)^{\frac{2}{3}}$

44. $\sqrt[8]{0}$

45. $\left(3x^{\frac{1}{2}}\right)\left(4x^{\frac{2}{3}}\right)$

46. $\dfrac{12y^{\frac{1}{3}}}{4y^{\frac{1}{2}}}$

47. $\left(3a^{\frac{1}{2}}b^{\frac{1}{3}}\right)^2$

48. $\left(y^{\frac{2}{3}}\right)^{-9}$

49. $\left(a^{\frac{2}{3}}b^{-\frac{1}{2}}\right)^{-6}$

50. $y^{\frac{2}{5}} \cdot y^{\frac{3}{8}}$

51. $\left(\dfrac{x^{\frac{4}{7}}}{x^{\frac{2}{3}}}\right)$

52. $\left(2a^{\frac{1}{4}}\right)^3$

53. $81^{-\frac{1}{2}}$

54. $\left(2x^{\frac{2}{5}}\right)\left(6x^{\frac{1}{4}}\right)$

55. $\left(9x^4y^{-2}\right)^{\frac{1}{2}}$

56. $\left(\dfrac{27x^6}{64y^4}\right)^{\frac{1}{3}}$

57. $\dfrac{x^{\frac{1}{2}}y^{\frac{2}{3}}}{x^{\frac{1}{3}}y^{\frac{1}{2}}}$

58. $y^{\frac{5}{8}} \div y^{\frac{1}{2}}$

59. $x^{\frac{1}{4}} \cdot x^{\frac{1}{6}} \cdot x^{\frac{1}{3}}$

60. $\left(\dfrac{x^{-\frac{1}{3}}y}{x^{\frac{2}{3}}y^{-\frac{1}{2}}}\right)^2$

61. $\left(\dfrac{12x^8}{75y^{10}}\right)^{\frac{1}{2}}$

62. In a test kitchen, researchers have measured the radius of a ball of dough made with a new quick-acting yeast. Based on their data, the radius r of the dough ball, in centimeters, is given by $r = 5(1.05)^{\frac{t}{3}}$ after t minutes. Round the answers to the following questions to the nearest tenth of a cm.
   a. What is the radius after 5 minutes?
   b. What is the radius after 20 minutes?
   c. What is the radius after 43 minutes?

Name ______________________ Class ______________ Date ______________

6-4 Standardized Test Prep

Rational Exponents

Multiple Choice

For Exercises 1–5, choose the correct letter.

1. What is $12^{\frac{1}{3}} \cdot 45^{\frac{1}{3}} \cdot 50^{\frac{1}{3}}$ in simplest form?

Ⓐ $\sqrt{27{,}000}$ Ⓑ 30 Ⓒ $107^{\frac{1}{3}}$ Ⓓ 27,000

2. What is $x^{\frac{1}{3}} \cdot y^{\frac{2}{3}}$ in simplest form?

Ⓕ $x^3\sqrt{y^3}$ Ⓖ $\sqrt{xy^3}$ Ⓗ $\sqrt[3]{(xy)^2}$ Ⓘ $\sqrt[3]{xy^2}$

3. What is $x^{\frac{1}{3}} \cdot x^{\frac{1}{2}} \cdot x^{\frac{1}{4}}$ in simplest form?

Ⓐ $x^{\frac{13}{12}}$ Ⓑ $x^{\frac{1}{24}}$ Ⓒ $x^{\frac{1}{9}}$ Ⓓ $x^{\frac{5}{24}}$

4. What is $\left(\dfrac{x^{\frac{2}{3}}y^{\frac{1}{3}}}{x^{\frac{1}{2}}y^{\frac{3}{4}}}\right)^6$ in simplest form?

Ⓕ $xy^{\frac{5}{2}}$ Ⓖ $x^7y^{\frac{5}{2}}$ Ⓗ $\dfrac{1}{xy^{\frac{5}{2}}}$ Ⓘ $\dfrac{x}{y^{\frac{5}{2}}}$

5. What is $(-32x^{10}y^{35})^{-\frac{1}{5}}$ in simplest form?

Ⓐ $2x^2y^7$ Ⓑ $-\dfrac{2}{x^2y^7}$ Ⓒ $-\dfrac{1}{2x^2y^7}$ Ⓓ $\dfrac{2}{x^2y^7}$

Short Response

6. The surface area S, in square units, of a sphere with volume V, in cubic units, is given by the formula $S = \pi^{\frac{1}{3}}(6V)^{\frac{2}{3}}$. What is the surface area of a sphere with volume $\frac{4}{3}$ mi^3? Show your work.

Name ______________________ Class ____________ Date ____________

6-5 Think About a Plan

Solving Square Root and Other Radical Equations

Traffic Signs A stop sign is a regular octagon, formed by cutting triangles off the corners of a square. If a stop sign measures 36 in. from top to bottom, what is the length of each side?

Understanding the Problem

1. How can you use the diagram at the right to find a relationship between s and x?

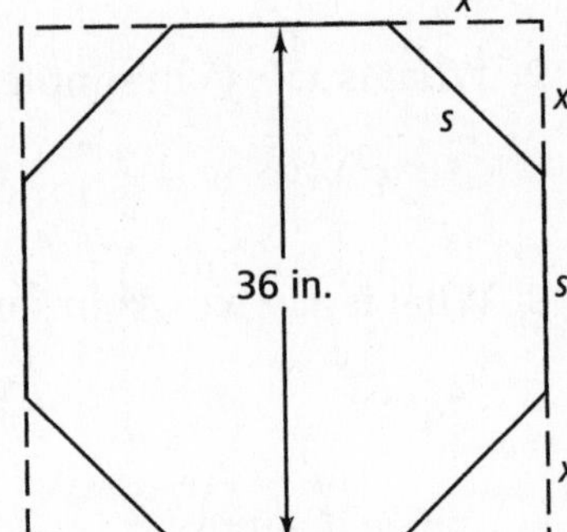

____

____.

2. How can you use the diagram at the right to find another relationship between s and x?

____

____.

3. What is the problem asking you to determine?

____

Planning the Solution

4. What are two equations that relate s and x?

5. How can you use your equations to find s?

____.

Getting an Answer

6. Solve your equations for s.

7. Is your answer reasonable? Explain.

____

____.

Name ______________________ Class ____________ Date ____________

6-5 Practice

Form G

Solving Square Root and Other Radical Equations

Solve.

1. $5\sqrt{x} + 2 = 12$
2. $3\sqrt{x} - 8 = 7$
3. $\sqrt{4x} + 2 = 8$
4. $\sqrt{2x - 5} = 7$
5. $\sqrt{3x - 3} - 6 = 0$
6. $\sqrt{5 - 2x} + 5 = 12$
7. $\sqrt{3x - 2} - 7 = 0$
8. $\sqrt{4x + 3} + 2 = 5$
9. $\sqrt{33 - 3x} = 3$
10. $\sqrt[3]{2x + 1} = 3$
11. $\sqrt[3]{13x - 1} - 4 = 0$
12. $\sqrt[3]{2x - 4} = -2$

Solve.

13. $(x - 2)^{\frac{1}{3}} = 5$
14. $(2x + 1)^{\frac{1}{3}} = -3$
15. $2x^{\frac{3}{4}} = 16$
16. $2x^{\frac{1}{3}} - 2 = 0$
17. $x^{\frac{1}{2}} - 5 = 0$
18. $4x^{\frac{3}{2}} - 5 = 103$
19. $(7x - 3)^{\frac{1}{2}} = 5$
20. $4x^{\frac{1}{2}} - 5 = 27$
21. $x^{\frac{1}{6}} - 2 = 0$
22. $(2x + 1)^{\frac{1}{3}} = 1$
23. $(x - 2)^{\frac{2}{3}} - 4 = 5$
24. $3x^{\frac{4}{3}} + 5 = 53$

25. The formula $P = 4\sqrt{A}$ relates the perimeter P, in units, of a square to its area A, in square units. What is the area of the square window shown below?

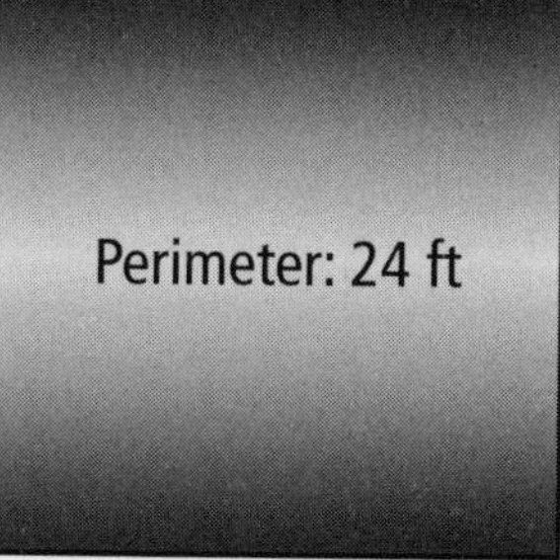

26. The formula $A = 6V^{\frac{2}{3}}$ relates the surface area A, in square units, of a cube to the volume V, in cubic units. What is the volume of a cube with surface area 486 in.^{2}?

27. A mound of sand at a rock-crushing plant is growing over time. The equation $t = \sqrt[3]{5V - 1}$ gives the time t, in hours, at which the mound has volume V, in cubic meters. When is the volume equal to 549 m^3?

Name ______________________ Class ____________ Date ____________

6-5 Practice (continued)

Form G

Solving Square Root and Other Radical Equations

28. City officials conclude they should budget s million dollars for a new library building if the population increases by p thousand people in a ten-year census. The formula $s = 2 + \frac{1}{3}(p + 1)^{\frac{2}{5}}$ expresses the relationship between population and library budget for the city. How much can the population increase without the city going over budget if they have \$5 million for a new library building?

Solve. Check for extraneous solutions.

29. $\sqrt{x + 1} = x - 1$

30. $\sqrt{2x + 1} = -3$

31. $(x + 7)^{\frac{1}{2}} = x - 5$

32. $(2x - 4)^{\frac{1}{2}} = x - 2$

33. $\sqrt{x + 2} = x - 18$

34. $\sqrt{x} + 6 = x$

35. $(2x + 1)^{\frac{1}{2}} = -5$

36. $(x + 2)^{\frac{1}{2}} = 10 - x$

37. $\sqrt{x + 1} = x + 1$

38. $\sqrt{9 - 3x} = 3 - x$

39. $\sqrt[3]{2x - 4} = -2$

40. $2\sqrt[5]{5x + 2} - 1 = 3$

41. $\sqrt{4x + 2} = \sqrt{3x + 4}$

42. $\sqrt{7x - 6} - \sqrt{5x + 2} = 0$

43. $2(x - 1)^{\frac{1}{2}} = (26 + x)^{\frac{1}{2}}$

44. $(x - 1)^{\frac{1}{2}} - (2x + 1)^{\frac{1}{4}} = 0$

45. $\sqrt{2x} - \sqrt{x + 1} = 1$

46. $\sqrt{7x - 1} = \sqrt{5x + 5}$

47. $(7 - x)^{\frac{1}{2}} = (2x + 13)^{\frac{1}{2}}$

48. $(x - 7)^{\frac{1}{2}} = (x + 5)^{\frac{1}{4}}$

49. $\sqrt{x + 9} - \sqrt{x} = 1$

50. $\sqrt[3]{8x} - \sqrt[3]{6x - 2} = 0$

51. A clothing manufacturer uses the model $a = \sqrt{f + 4} - \sqrt{36 - f}$ to estimate the amount of fabric to order from a mill. In the formula, a is the number of apparel items (in hundreds) and f is the number of units of fabric needed. If 400 apparel items will be manufactured, how many units of fabric should be ordered?

52. What are the lengths of the sides of the trapezoid shown at the right if the perimeter of the trapezoid is 17 cm?

Name ____________________ Class __________ Date __________

6-5 Standardized Test Prep

Solving Square Root and Other Radical Equations

Gridded Response

Solve each exercise and enter your answer in the grid provided.

1. What is the solution? $\sqrt{2x - 4} - 3 = 1$

2. What is the solution? $5x^{\frac{1}{2}} - 8 = 7$

3. What is the solution? $\sqrt{2x - 6} = 3 - x$

4. What is the solution? $\sqrt{5x - 3} = \sqrt{2x + 3}$

5. Kepler's Third Law of Orbital Motion states that the period P (in Earth years) it takes a planet to complete one orbit of the sun is a function of the distance d (in astronomical units, AU) from the planet to the sun. This relationship is $P = d^{\frac{3}{2}}$. If it takes Neptune 165 years to orbit the sun, what is the distance (in AU) of Neptune from the sun? Round your answer to two decimal places.

Answers

1. 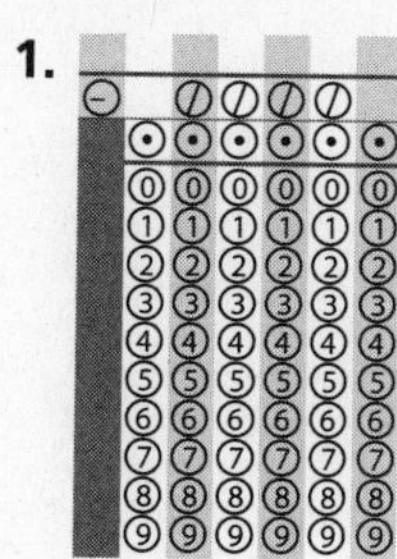

2. 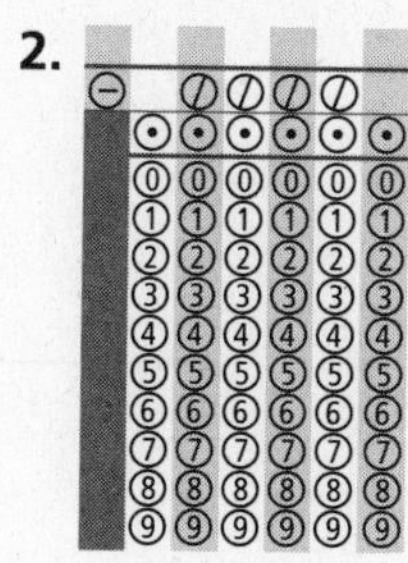

3. 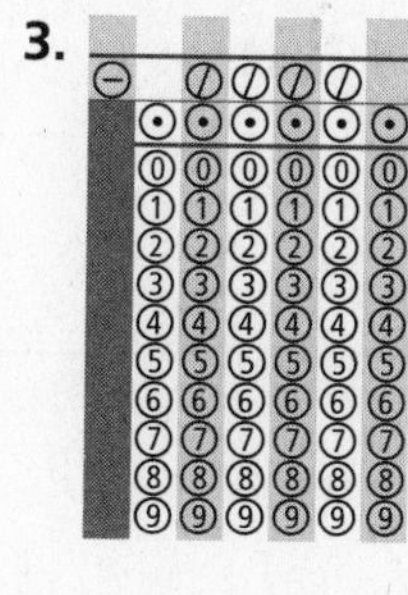

4. 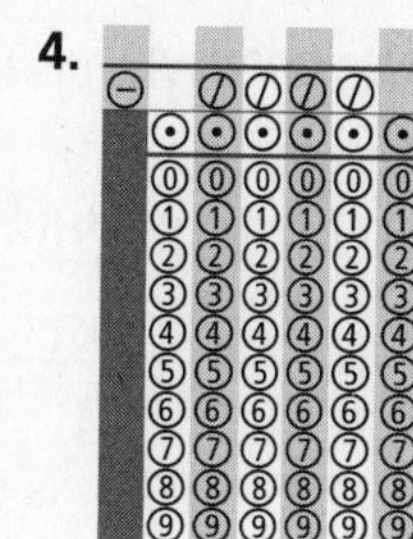

5. 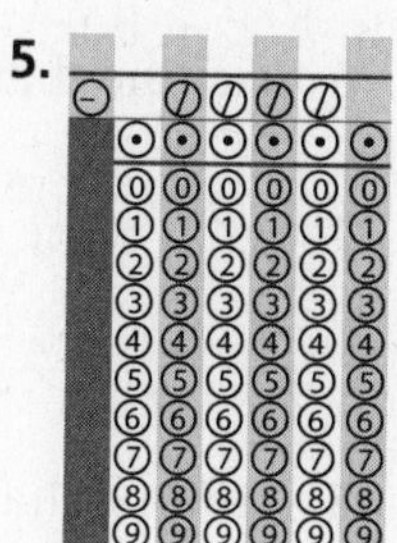

Name ____________________ Class __________ Date __________

6-6 Think About a Plan

Function Operations

Sales A salesperson earns a 3% bonus on weekly sales over $5000. Consider the following functions.

$$g(x) = 0.03x \qquad h(x) = x - 5000$$

a. Explain what each function above represents.

b. Which composition, $(h \circ g)(x)$ or $(g \circ h)(x)$, represents the weekly bonus? Explain.

1. What does x represent in the function $g(x)$?

____

2. What does the function $g(x)$ represent?

____

3. What does x represent in the function $h(x)$?

____

4. What does the function $h(x)$ represent?

____

5. What is the meaning of $(h \circ g)(x)$?

______________________________.

6. Assume that x is $7000. What is $(h \circ g)(x)$?

7. What is the meaning of $(g \circ h)(x)$?

______________________________.

8. Assume that x is $7000. What is $(g \circ h)(x)$?

9. Which composition represents the weekly bonus? Explain

____

____

______________________________.

Name ______________________ Class ____________ Date ____________

6-6 Practice

Form G

Function Operations

Let $f(x) = 4x - 1$ and $g(x) = 2x^2 + 3$. Perform each function operation and then find the domain.

1. $(f + g)(x)$
2. $(f - g)(x)$
3. $(g - f)(x)$
4. $(f \cdot g)(x)$
5. $\frac{f}{g}(x)$
6. $\frac{g}{f}(x)$

Let $f(x) = 2x$ and $g(x) = \sqrt{x} - 1$. Perform each function operation and then find the domain of the result.

7. $(f + g)(x)$
8. $(f - g)(x)$
9. $(g - f)(x)$
10. $(f \cdot g)(x)$
11. $\frac{f}{g}(x)$
12. $\frac{g}{f}(x)$

Let $f(x) = -3x + 2$, $g(x) = \frac{x}{5}$, $h(x) = -2x^2 + 9$, and $j(x) = 5 - x$. Find each value or expression.

13. $(f \circ j)(3)$
14. $(j \circ h)(-1)$
15. $(h \circ g)(-5)$
16. $(g \circ f)(a)$
17. $f(x) + j(x)$
18. $f(x) - h(x)$
19. $(g \circ f)(-5)$
20. $(f \circ g)(-2)$
21. $3f(x) + 5g(x)$
22. $g(f(2))$
23. $g(f(x))$
24. $f(g(1))$

25. **A video game store adds a 25% markup on each of the games that it sells. In addition to the manufacturer's cost, the store also pays a $1.50 shipping charge on each game.**
    a. **Write a function to represent the price $f(x)$ per video game after the store's markup.**
    b. **Write a function $g(x)$ to represent the manufacturer's cost plus the shipping charge.**
    c. **Suppose the manufacturer's cost for a video game is $13. Use a composite function to find the cost at the store if the markup is applied after the shipping charge is added.**
    d. **Suppose the manufacturer's cost for a video game is $13. Use a composite function to find the cost at the store if the markup is applied before the shipping charge is added.**

6-6 Practice (continued)

Form G

Function Operations

26. The formula $V = \frac{4}{3}\pi r^3$ expresses the relationship between the volume V and radius r of a sphere. A weather balloon is being inflated so that the radius is changing with respect to time according to the equation $r = t + 1$, where t is the time, in minutes, and r is the radius, in feet.
   a. Write a composite function $f(t)$ to represent the volume of the weather balloon after t minutes. Do not expand the expression.
   b. Find the volume of the balloon after 5 minutes. Round the answer to two decimal places. Use 3.14 for π.

27. A boutique prices merchandise by adding 80% to its cost. It later decreases by 25% the price of items that do not sell quickly.
   a. Write a function $f(x)$ to represent the price after the 80% markup.
   b. Write a function $g(x)$ to represent the price after the 25% markdown.
   c. Use a composition function to find the price of an item, after both price adjustments, that originally costs the boutique $150.
   d. Does the order in which the adjustments are applied make a difference? Explain.

28. A department store has marked down its merchandise by 25%. It later decreases by $5 the price of items that have not sold.
   a. Write a function $f(x)$ to represent the price after the 25% markdown.
   b. Write a function $g(x)$ to represent the price after the $5 markdown.
   c. Use a composition function to find the price of a $50 item after both price adjustments.
   d. Does the order in which the adjustments are applied make a difference? Explain.

Let $g(x) = x^2 - 5$ and $h(x) = 3x + 2$. Perform each function operation.

29. $(h \circ g)(x)$

30. $g(x) \cdot h(x)$

31. $-2g(x) + h(x)$

Name ______________________ Class ____________ Date ____________

6-6 Standardized Test Prep

Function Operations

Multiple Choice

For Exercises 1–5, choose the correct letter.

1. Let $f(x) = -2x + 5$ and $g(x) = x^3$. What is $(g - f)(x)$?

(A) $x^3 - 2x + 5$
(B) $x^3 + 2x - 5$
(C) $-x^3 - 2x + 5$
(D) $-x^3 + 2x - 5$

2. Let $f(x) = 3x$ and $g(x) = x^2 + 1$. What is $(f \cdot g)(x)$?

(F) $9x^2 + 3x$
(G) $9x^2 + 1$
(H) $3x^3 + 3x$
(I) $3x^3 + 1$

3. Let $f(x) = x^2 - 2x - 15$ and $g(x) = x + 3$. What is the domain of $\frac{f}{g}(x)$?

(A) all real numbers
(B) $x \neq 5, -3$
(C) $x \neq -3$
(D) $x > 0$

4. Let $f(x) = \sqrt{x} + 1$ and $g(x) = 2x + 1$. What is $(g \circ f)(x)$?

(F) $2\sqrt{x} + 3$
(G) $2x\sqrt{x} + 2x + \sqrt{x} + 1$
(H) $\sqrt{2x + 1} + 1$
(I) $2x + \sqrt{x} + 2$

5. Let $f(x) = \frac{1}{x}$ and $g(x) = x^2 - 2$. What is $(f \circ g)(-3)$?

(A) $\frac{17}{9}$
(B) $\frac{1}{7}$
(C) $-\frac{17}{9}$
(D) $-\frac{7}{3}$

Short Response

6. Suppose the function $f(x) = 0.035x$ represents the number of U.S. dollars equivalent to x Russian rubles and the function $g(x) = 90x$ represents the number of Japanese yen equivalent to x U.S. dollars. Write a composite function that represents the number of Japanese yen equivalent to x Russian rubles. Show your work.

Name ______________________ Class ____________ Date ____________

6-7 Think About a Plan

Inverse Relations and Functions

Geometry Write a function that gives the length of the hypotenuse of an isosceles right triangle with side length *s*. Evaluate the inverse of the function to find the side length of an isosceles right triangle with a hypotenuse of 6 in.

Know

1. An equation that relates the length of each side *s* and the length of the hypotenuse *h* of an isosceles right triangle is [ ].

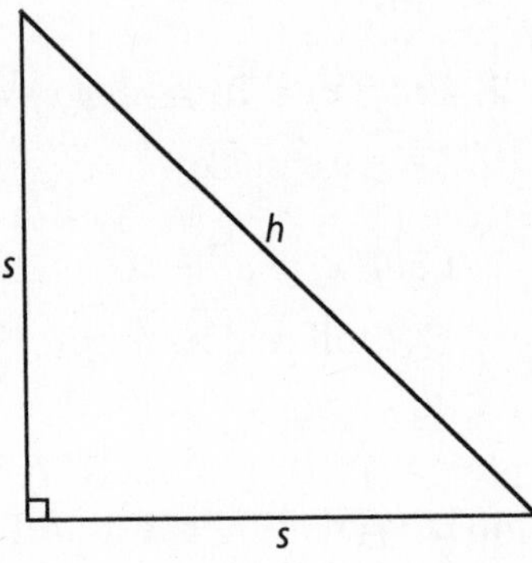

Need

2. To solve the problem I need to:

____

____

____.

Plan

3. A function that gives the length of the hypotenuse *h* in terms of the side length *s* is [ ].

4. An inverse function that gives the side length *s* in terms of the length of the hypotenuse *h* is [ ].

5. What is the value of the inverse function for $h = 6$ in.?

6. Is the side length reasonable? Explain.

____.

Name _______________ Class _______________ Date _______________

6-7 Practice

Form G

Inverse Relations and Functions

Find the inverse of each relation. Graph the given relation and its inverse.

1.

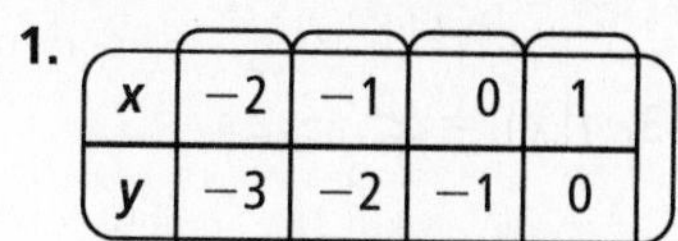

x	−2	−1	0	1
y	−3	−2	−1	0

2.

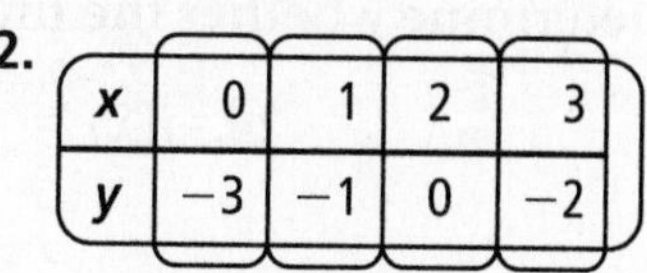

x	0	1	2	3
y	−3	−1	0	−2

3.

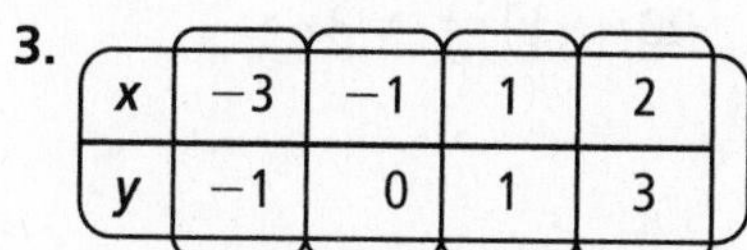

x	−3	−1	1	2
y	−1	0	1	3

4.

x	−3	−2	−1	0
y	3	2	1	0

Find the inverse of each function. Is the inverse a function?

5. $y = x^2 + 2$

6. $y = x + 2$

7. $y = 3(x + 1)$

8. $y = -x^2 - 3$

9. $y = 2x - 1$

10. $y = 1 - 3x^2$

11. $y = 5x^2$

12. $y = (x + 3)^2$

13. $y = 6x^2 - 4$

14. $y = 3x^2 - 2$

15. $y = (x + 4)^2 - 4$

16. $y = -x^2 + 4$

Graph each relation and its inverse.

17. $y = \frac{x + 3}{3}$

18. $y = \frac{1}{2}x + 5$

19. $y = 2x + 5$

20. $y = \frac{1}{2}x^2$

21. $y = (x + 2)^2$

22. $y = (2x - 1)^2 - 2$

Name ______________________ Class ____________ Date ____________

6-7 Practice (continued)

Form G

Inverse Relations and Functions

For each function, find the inverse and the domain and range of the function and its inverse. Determine whether the inverse is a function.

23. $f(x) = \frac{1}{6}x$

24. $f(x) = -\frac{1}{5}x + 2$

25. $f(x) = x^2 - 2$

26. $f(x) = x^2 + 4$

27. $f(x) = \sqrt{x - 1}$

28. $f(x) = \sqrt{3x}$

29. $f(x) = 3 - x$

30. $f(x) = (x + 1)^2$

31. $f(x) = \frac{1}{\sqrt{x}}$

32. The equation $f(x) = 198{,}900x + 635{,}600$ can be used to model the number of utility trucks under 6000 pounds that are sold each year in the U.S. with $x = 0$ representing the year 1992. Find the inverse of the function. Use the inverse to estimate in which year the number of utility trucks under 6000 pounds sold in the U.S. will be 6,000,000. Source: *www.infoplease.com*

33. The formula $s = 0.04n + 2500$ gives an employee's monthly salary s, in dollars, after selling n dollars in merchandise at an appliance store.

a. Find the inverse of the function. Is the inverse a function?

b. Use the inverse to find the amount of merchandise sold if the employee's salary was \$2820 last month.

34. The formula for the surface area A of a sphere of radius r is $A = 4\pi r^2$ for $r \geq 0$.

a. Find the inverse of the formula. Is the inverse a function?

b. Use the inverse to find the radius of a sphere with surface area 10,000 m^3.

Let $f(x) = 2x + 5$. Find each value.

35. $(f^{-1} \circ f)(-1)$

36. $(f \circ f^{-1})(3)$

37. $(f \circ f^{-1})\left(-\frac{1}{2}\right)$

Name ______________________ Class ____________ Date ____________

6-7 Standardized Test Prep

Inverse Relations and Functions

Multiple Choice

For Exercises 1–4, choose the correct letter.

1. What is the inverse of the relation?

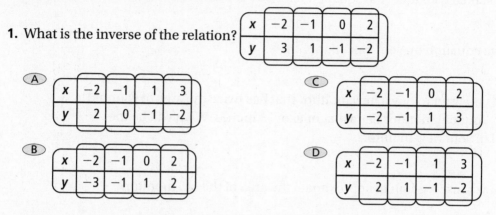

x	−2	−1	0	2
y	3	1	−1	−2

A 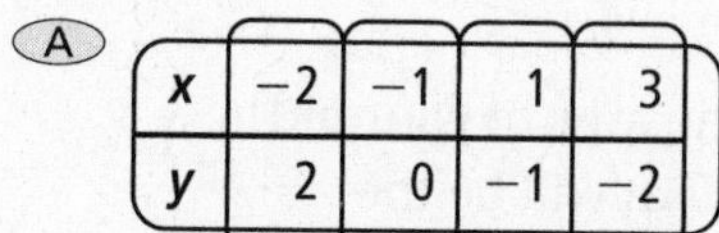

x	−2	−1	1	3
y	2	0	−1	−2

C 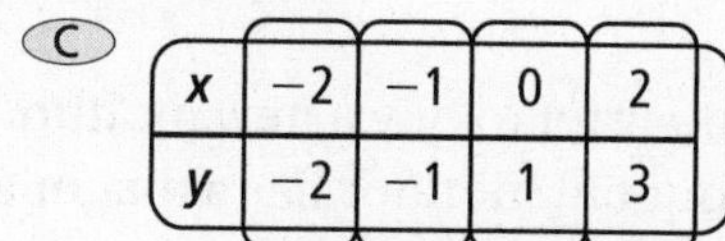

x	−2	−1	0	2
y	−2	−1	1	3

B 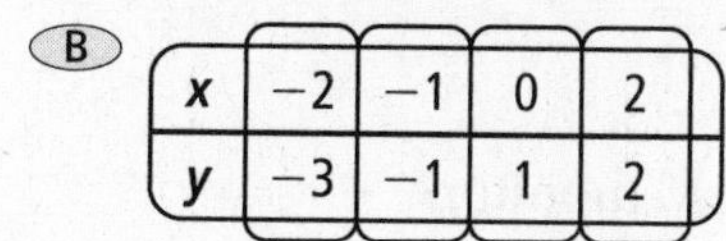

x	−2	−1	0	2
y	−3	−1	1	2

D 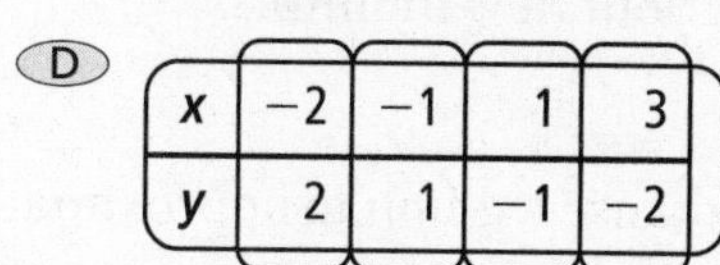

x	−2	−1	1	3
y	2	1	−1	−2

2. What is the inverse of the function? $y = 5(x - 3)$

F $y = \frac{x + 3}{5}$ G $y = \frac{1}{5}x + 3$ H $y = 5(x + 3)$ I $y = \frac{1}{5}x - 3$

3. What function with domain $x \geq 5$ is the inverse of $y = \sqrt{x} + 5$?

A $y = x^2 + 5$ B $y = x^2 - 5$ C $y = (x - 5)^2$ D $y = (x + 5)^2$

4. What is the domain and range of the inverse of the function? $y = \sqrt{x - 5}$

F domain is the set of all real numbers ≥ 0; range is the set of all real numbers ≥ 5

G domain is the set of all real numbers ≥ 5; range is the set of all real numbers ≥ 0

H domain and range is the set of all real numbers ≥ 5

I domain and range is the set of all real numbers

Extended Response

5. A high school principal uses the formula $y = 150x + 180$ to predict a student's score on a state achievement test using the student's 11th-grade GPA number x.

a. What is the inverse of the formula?

b. Is the inverse a function?

c. Using the inverse, what GPA does a student need to get a passing score of 510 on the state exam?

Name ______________________ Class ______________ Date ______________

6-8 Think About a Plan

Graphing Radical Functions

Electronics The size of a computer monitor is given as the length of the screen's diagonal d in inches. The equation $d = \frac{5}{6}\sqrt{3A}$ models the length of a diagonal of a monitor screen with area A in square inches.

a. Graph the equation on your calculator.

b. Suppose you want to buy a new monitor that has twice the area of your old monitor. Your old monitor has a diagonal of 15 inches. What will be the diagonal of your new monitor?

1. How can you use a graph to approximate the area of the old monitor?

____

____.

2. Graph the equation on your calculator. Make a sketch of the graph.

d / A

3. What is the area of the old monitor?

4. How can you check your answer algebraically?

____.

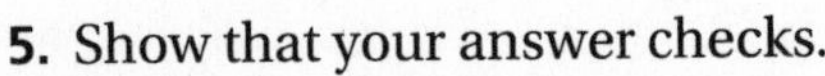

5. Show that your answer checks.

6. How can you find the diagonal of a new monitor with twice the area of the old monitor?

____.

7. Use your method to find the diagonal of your new monitor.

8. What will be the diagonal of your new monitor?

Name ______________________ Class ____________ Date ____________

6-8 Practice

Form G

Graphing Radical Functions

Graph each function.

1. $y = \sqrt{x} + 3$

2. $y = \sqrt{x} - 1$

3. $y = \sqrt{x + 5}$

4. $y = \sqrt{x - 3}$

5. $y = -2\sqrt{x} - 2$

6. $y = \frac{1}{4}\sqrt{x - 1} + 5$

Solve each square root equation by graphing. Round the answer to the nearest hundredth, if necessary. If there is no solution, explain why.

7. $\sqrt{x + 6} = 9$

8. $\sqrt{4x - 3} = 5$

9. $\sqrt{3x - 5} = \sqrt{1 - x}$

10. If you know the area A of a circle, you can use the equation $r = \sqrt{\frac{A}{\pi}}$ to find the radius r.

a. Graph the equation.

b. What is the radius of a circle with an area of 350 ft^2?

Graph each function.

11. $y = -\sqrt[3]{x} + 2$

12. $y = 2\sqrt[3]{x - 3}$

13. $y = \sqrt[3]{x + 3} - 1$

Name ______________________ Class ____________ Date ____________

6-8 Practice (continued) — Form G

Graphing Radical Functions

Rewrite each function to make it easy to graph using transformations of its parent function. Describe the graph.

14. $y = \sqrt{81x + 162}$

15. $y = -\sqrt{4x + 20}$

16. $y = \sqrt[3]{125x - 250}$

17. $y = -\sqrt{64x + 192}$

18. $y = -\sqrt[3]{8x - 56} + 4$

19. $y = \sqrt{25x + 75} - 1$

20. $y = \sqrt{0.25x + 1}$

21. $y = 5 - \sqrt{4x + 2}$

22. $y = \sqrt[3]{27x - 54}$

23. To find the radius r of a sphere of volume V, use the equation $r = \sqrt[3]{\frac{3V}{4\pi}}$.

a. Graph the equation.

b. A balloon used for advertising special events has a volume of 225 ft^3. What is the radius of the balloon?

24. An exercise specialist has studied your exercise routine and says the formula $t = 1.85\sqrt{c + 10}$ expresses the amount of time t, in minutes, it takes you to burn c calories (cal) while exercising.

a. Graph the equation.

b. According to this formula, how long should it take you to burn 100 cal? 200 cal? 300 cal?

25. You can use the equation $t = \frac{1}{4}\sqrt{d}$ to find the time t, in seconds, it takes an object to fall d feet after being dropped.

a. Graph the equation.

b. How long does it take the object to fall 400 feet?

Name ______________________ Class __________ Date __________

6-8 Standardized Test Prep

Graphing Radical Functions

Multiple Choice

For Exercises 1–4, choose the correct letter.

1. What is the graph of $y = \sqrt{x} + 4$?

A 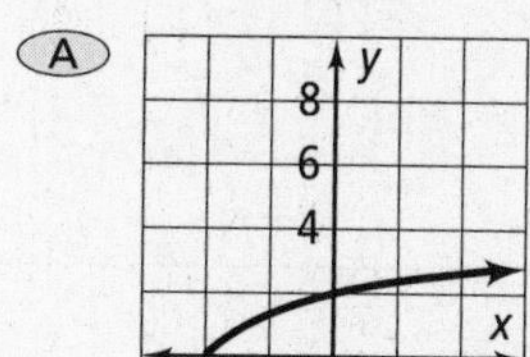

B 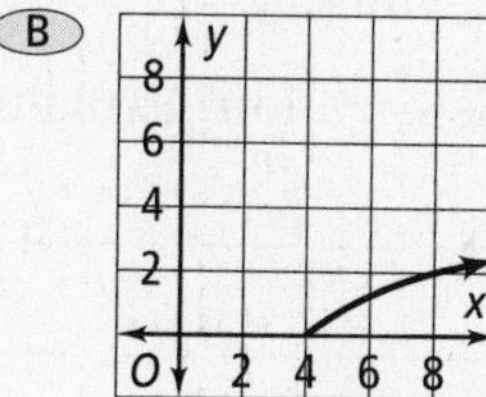

C 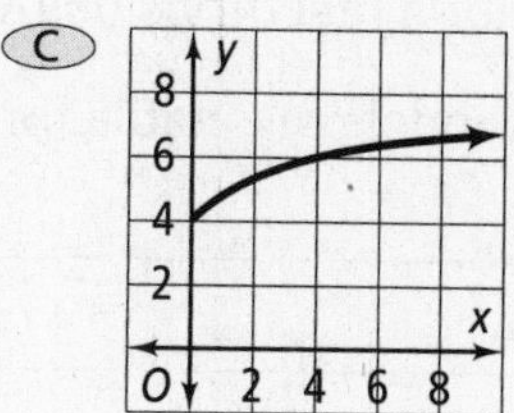

D 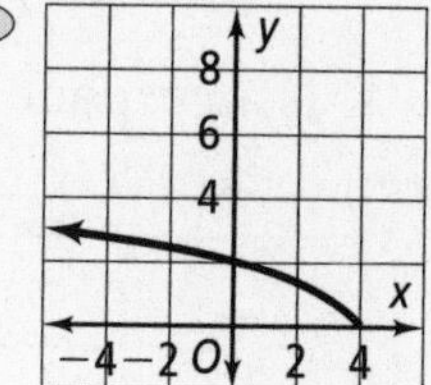

2. What is the graph of $y = \sqrt{x - 3} - 2$?

F 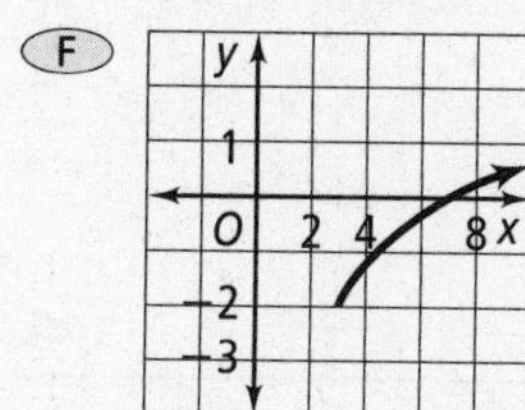

G 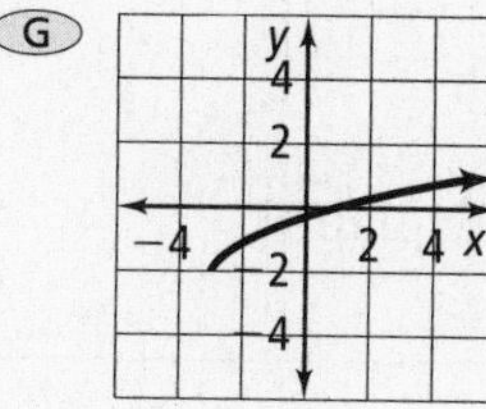

H 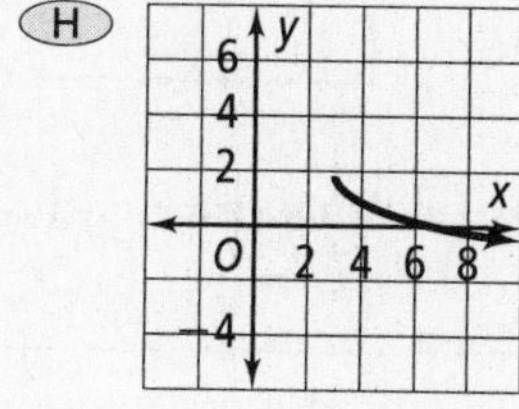

I 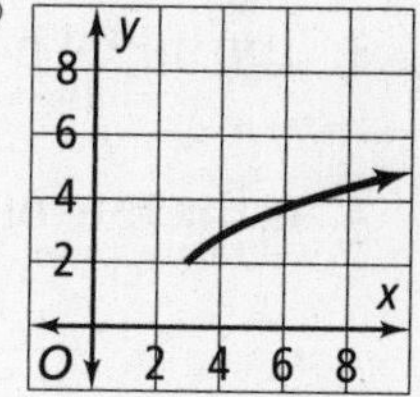

3. What is the graph of $y = 1 - \sqrt[3]{x + 3}$?

A 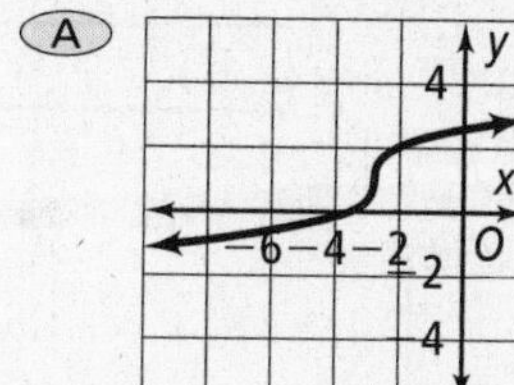

B 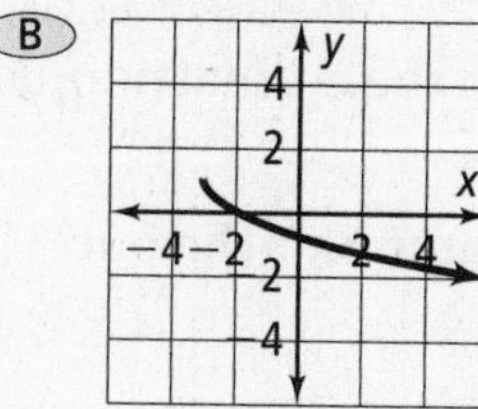

C 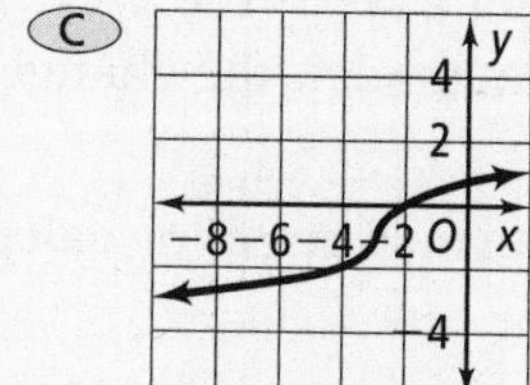

D 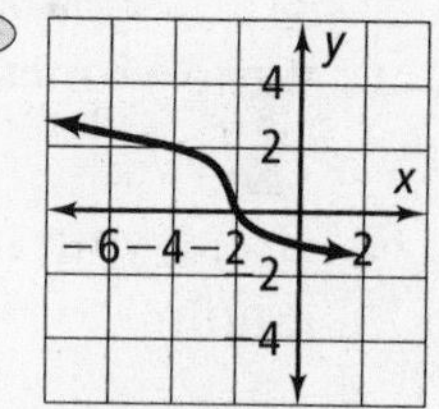

4. What is the description of $y = \sqrt{9x - 3}$ to make it easy to graph using transformations of its parent function?

F the graph of $y = 3\sqrt{x}$, shifted right 3 units

G the graph of $y = 3\sqrt{x}$, shifted right $\frac{1}{3}$ unit

H the graph of $y = \sqrt{x}$, shifted right 3 units and up 9 units

I the graph of $y = \sqrt{x}$, shifted right $\frac{1}{3}$ unit and up 9 units

Short Response

5. What is the graph of $y = 2\sqrt{x - 1} + 3$?

Name ______________________ Class ______________ Date ______________

7-1 Think About a Plan

Exploring Exponential Models

Population The population of a certain animal species decreases at a rate of 3.5% per year. You have counted 80 of the animals in the habitat you are studying.

a. Write a function that models the change in the animal population.

b. Graphing Calculator Graph the function. Estimate the number of years until the population first drops below 15 animals.

1. Is an exponential model reasonable for this situation? Explain.

____

____.

2. Write the function that models exponential growth or decay. $A(t) =$ [ ]

3. The initial population is [ ].

4. Is the rate of change positive or negative? Explain.

____.

5. The rate of change is [ ].

6. Write a function that models the change in the animal population. $P(t) =$ [ ]

7. Graph your function on a graphing calculator. Sketch your graph.

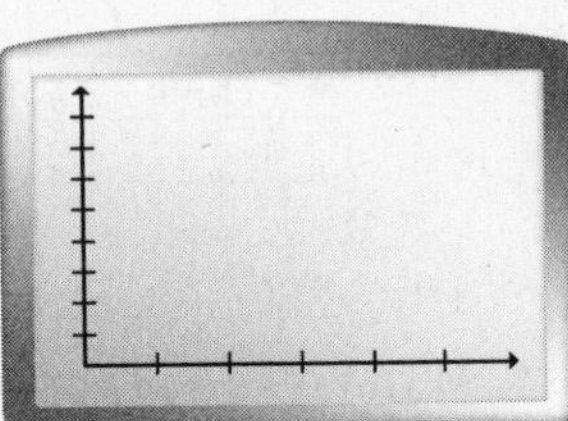

8. How can you find the *x*-value that produces a given *y*-value?

____.

9. Use your graph to estimate the number of years until the population first drops below 15 animals.

Name ______________________ Class ____________ Date ____________

7-1 Practice

Exploring Exponential Models

Form G

Graph each function.

1. $y = (0.3)^x$

2. $y = 3^x$

3. $y = 2\left(\frac{1}{5}\right)^x$

4. $y = \frac{1}{2}(3)^x$

5. $s(t) = 2.5^t$

6. $f(x) = \frac{1}{2}(5)^x$

Without graphing, determine whether the function represents exponential growth or exponential decay. Then find the *y*-intercept.

7. $y = 0.99\left(\frac{1}{3}\right)^x$

8. $y = 20(1.75)^x$

9. $y = 185\left(\frac{5}{4}\right)^x$

10. $f(x) = \frac{2}{3}\left(\frac{1}{2}\right)^x$

11. $f(x) = 0.25(1.05)^x$

12. $y = \frac{1}{5}\left(\frac{6}{5}\right)^x$

13. Suppose you deposit $1500 in a savings account that pays interest at an annual rate of 6%. No money is added or withdrawn from the account.

a. How much will be in the account after 5 years?

b. How much will be in the account after 20 years?

c. How many years will it take for the account to contain $2500?

d. How many years will it take for the account to contain $4000?

Write an exponential function to model each situation. Find each amount after the specified time.

14. A population of 1,236,000 grows 1.3% per year for 10 years.

15. A population of 752,000 decreases 1.4% per year for 18 years.

16. A new car that sells for $18,000 depreciates 25% each year for 4 years.

Name ____________________ Class ____________ Date ____________

7-1 Practice (continued)

Form G

Exploring Exponential Models

For each annual rate of change, find the corresponding growth or decay factor.

17. +45%

18. −10%

19. −40%

20. +200%

21. +28%

22. +100%

23. −5%

24. +3%

25. In 2009, there were 1570 bears in a wildlife refuge. In 2010, the population had increased to approximately 1884 bears. If this trend continues and the bear population is increasing exponentially, how many bears will there be in 2018?

26. The value of a piece of equipment has a decay factor of 0.80 per year. After 5 years, the equipment is worth $98,304. What was the original value of the equipment?

27. Your friend drops a rubber ball from 4 ft. You notice that its rebound is 32.5 in. on the first bounce and 22 in. on the second bounce.

a. What exponential function would be a good model for the height of the ball?

b. How high will the ball bounce on the fourth bounce?

28. An investment of $75,000 increases at a rate of 12.5% per year. What is the value of the investment after 30 years?

29. A new truck that sells for $29,000 depreciates 12% each year. What is the value of the truck after 7 years?

30. The price of a new home is $350,000. The value of the home appreciates 2% each year. How much will the home be worth in 10 years?

31. The population of an endangered bird is decreasing at a rate of 0.75% per year. There are currently about 200,000 of these birds.

a. What exponential function would be a good model for the population of these endangered birds?

b. How many birds will there be in 100 years?

Name ______________________ Class ____________ Date ____________

7-1 Standardized Test Prep

Exploring Exponential Models

Multiple Choice

For Exercises 1 and 2, choose the correct letter.

1. Which of the following functions represents exponential decay and has a y-intercept of 2?

Ⓐ $y = 2\left(\frac{4}{3}\right)^x$

Ⓑ $y = \frac{1}{2}(0.95)^x$

Ⓒ $y = \frac{1}{4}(2)^x$

Ⓓ $y = 2\left(\frac{2}{5}\right)^x$

2. Suppose you deposit \$3000 in a savings account that pays interest at an annual rate of 4%. If no other money is added or withdrawn from the account, how much will be in the account after 10 years?

Ⓕ \$3122.18

Ⓖ \$4994.50

Ⓗ \$4440.73

Ⓘ \$86,776.40

Extended Response

3. In 2009 there was an endangered population of 270 cranes in a western state. Due to wildlife efforts, the population is increasing at a rate of 5% per year.

a. What exponential function would be a good model for this population of cranes? Explain in words or show work for how you determined the exponential function.

b. If this trend continues, how many cranes will there be in this population in 2020? Show your work.

Name ______________________ Class ______________ Date ____________

7-2 Think About a Plan

Properties of Exponential Functions

Investment How long would it take to double your principal in an account that pays 6.5% annual interest compounded continuously?

Know

1. The equation for continuously compounded interest is ☐.

2. The principal is ☐.

3. The interest rate is ☐.

Need

4. To solve the problem I need to:

____.

Plan

5. If the principal is P, then twice the principal is ☐.

6. What equation can you use to find the time it takes to double your principal?

7. Solve your equation for t.

8. Is your solution reasonable? Explain.

____

____.

Name ______________________ Class ____________ Date ____________

7-2 Practice

Form G

Properties of Exponential Functions

Graph each function.

1. $y = 2^x$

2. $y = 5(0.12)^x$

3. $y = 5^x$

4. $y = -0.1(5)^x$

5. $y = \left(\frac{1}{5}\right)^x$

6. $y = -5\left(\frac{1}{3}\right)^x$

Graph each function as a transformation of its parent function.

7. $y = 2^{x+1}$

8. $y = -(2)^{x+1}$

9. $y = 5^{-x}$

10. $y = -0.1(5)^{-x}$

11. $y = 2(2)^{x+2}$

12. $y = 2^x + 1$

13. A cake is 190°F when you remove it from the oven. You must let it cool to 75°F before you can frost it. The table at the right shows the temperature readings for the cake.

a. Given a room temperature of 68°F, what is an exponential model for this data set?

b. How long must the cake cool before you can frost it?

Time (min)	Temp (°F)
0	190
5	149
10	122
15	104
20	92

Use the graph of $y = e^x$ to evaluate each expression to four decimal places.

14. e^2

15. $e^{-2.5}$

16. $e^{\frac{1}{3}}$

Name ______________________ Class ____________ Date ____________

7-2 Practice (continued) Form G

Properties of Exponential Functions

Find the amount in a continuously compounded account for the given conditions.

17. principal: \$5000
annual interest rate: 6.9%
time: 30 yr

18. principal: \$20,000
annual interest rate: 3.75%
time: 2 yr

19. How long would it take to double your principal at an annual interest rate of 7% compounded continuously?

20. Error Analysis A student says that the graph of $f(x) = 2^{x+3} + 4$ is a shift of 3 units up and 4 units to the right of the parent function. Describe and correct the student's error.

21. The isotope Hg-197 is used in kidney scans. It has a half-life of 64.128 h. After that time, half the isotope will have decayed. Write the exponential decay function for a 12-mg sample. Find the amount remaining after 72 h.

22. The isotope Sr-85 is used in bone scans. It has a half-life of 64.9 days. Write the exponential decay function for an 8-mg sample. Find the amount remaining after 100 days.

23. Suppose you invest \$2000 at an annual interest of 5.5% compounded continuously.

a. How much will you have in the account in 10 years?

b. How long will it take for the account to reach \$5000?

The parent function for each graph below is of the form $y = ab^x$. Write the parent function. Then write a function for the translation indicated.

24.

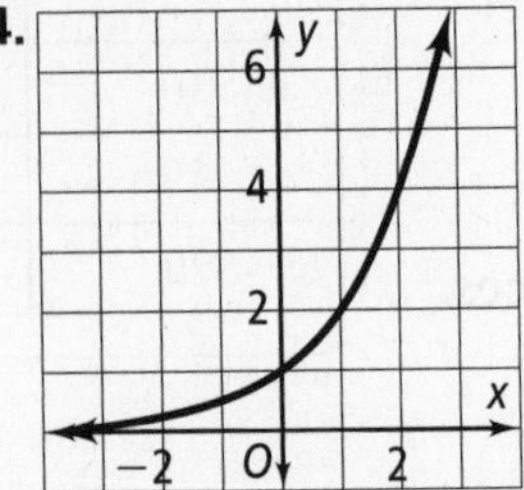

translation: left 3 units, up 1 unit

25.

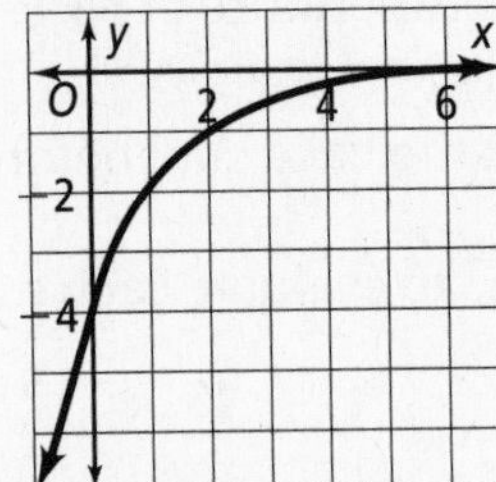

translation: right 2 units, up 3 units

Name ______________________ Class ____________ Date ____________

7-2 Standardized Test Prep

Properties of Exponential Functions

Gridded Response

Solve each exercise and enter your answer in the grid provided.

1. Suppose you deposit $6000 in a savings account that pays interest at an annual rate of 4% compounded continuously. How many years will it take for the balance in your savings account to reach $8000? Round your answer up to the nearest number of years.

2. Suppose you make $1500 at your summer job and you decide to invest this money in a savings account that pays interest at an annual rate of 5.5% compounded continuously. How many dollars will be in the account after 5 years? Express the answer to the nearest whole dollar.

3. The half-life of a radioactive substance is the time it takes for half of the material to decay. Phosphorus-32 is used to study a plant's use of fertilizer. It has a half-life of 14.3 days. How many milligrams of phosphorus-32 remain after 92 days from a 100-mg sample? Express the answer to the nearest whole milligram.

4. A scientist notes the bacteria count in a petrie dish is 40. Three hours later, she notes the count has increased to 75. Using an exponential model, how many hours will it take for the bacteria count to grow from 75 to 120? Express the answer to the nearest tenth of an hour.

Answers

1. 

2. 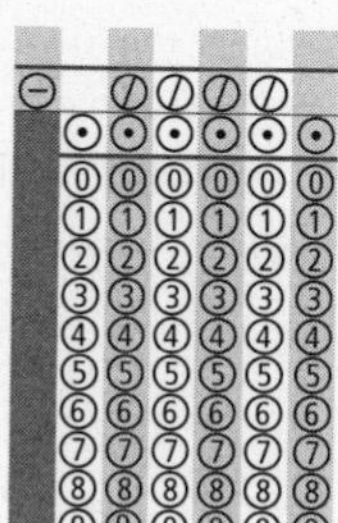

3. 

4. 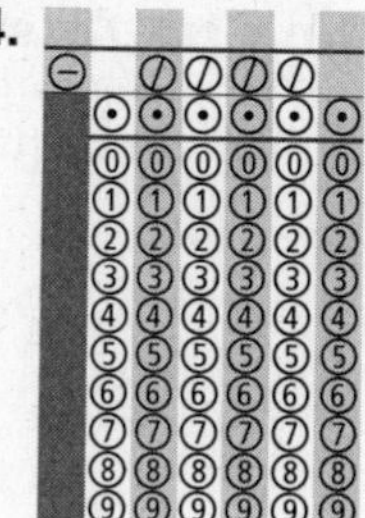

Name ______________________ Class ____________ Date ____________

7-3 Think About a Plan

Logarithmic Functions as Inverses

Chemistry Find the concentration of hydrogen ions in seawater, if the pH level of seawater is 8.5.

Understanding the Problem

1. What is the pH of seawater?

2. How do you represent the concentration of hydrogen ions?

3. What is the problem asking you to determine?

____

Planning the Solution

4. Write the formula for the pH of a substance.

5. Write an equation relating the pH of seawater to the concentration of hydrogen ions in seawater.

Getting an Answer

6. Solve your equation to find the concentration of hydrogen ions in seawater.

Name ______________________ Class ____________ Date ____________

7-3 Practice

Form G

Logarithmic Functions as Inverses

Write each equation in logarithmic form.

1. $9^2 = 81$
2. $\frac{1}{64} = \left(\frac{1}{4}\right)^3$
3. $8^3 = 512$
4. $\left(\frac{1}{3}\right)^{-2} = 9$
5. $2^9 = 512$
6. $4^5 = 1024$
7. $5^4 = 625$
8. $10^{-3} = 0.001$

Evaluate each logarithm.

9. $\log_2 128$
10. $\log_4 32$
11. $\log_9 (27)$
12. $\log_2 (-32)$
13. $\log_{\frac{1}{3}} \frac{1}{9}$
14. $\log 100{,}000$
15. $\log_7 7^6$
16. $\log_3 \frac{1}{81}$

In 2004, an earthquake of magnitude 7.0 shook Papua, Indonesia. Compare the intensity level of that earthquake to the intensity level of each earthquake below.

17. magnitude 6.1 in Costa Rica, in 2009

18. magnitude 5.1 in Greece, in 2008

19. magnitude 7.8 in the Fiji Islands, in 2007

20. magnitude 8.3 in the Kuril Islands, in 2006

Graph each logarithmic function.

21. $y = \log x$
22. $y = \log_3 x$
23. $y = \log_6 x$

Name ______________________ Class ____________ Date ____________

7-3 Practice (continued) *Form G*

Logarithmic Functions as Inverses

Describe how the graph of each function compares with the graph of the parent function, $y = \log_b x$.

24. $y = \log_3 x - 2$

25. $y = \log_8 (x - 2)$

26. $y = \log_6 (x + 1) - 5$

27. $y = \log_2 (x - 4) + 1$

Write each equation in exponential form.

28. $\log_4 256 = 4$

29. $\log_7 1 = 0$

30. $\log_2 32 = 5$

31. $\log 10 = 1$

32. $\log_5 5 = 1$

33. $\log_8 \frac{1}{64} = -2$

34. $\log_9 59{,}049 = 5$

35. $\log_{17} 289 = 2$

36. $\log_{56} 1 = 0$

37. $\log_{12} \frac{1}{144} = -2$

38. $\log_2 \frac{1}{1024} = -10$

39. $\log_3 6561 = 8$

40. A single-celled bacterium divides every hour. The number N of bacteria after t hours is given by the formula $\log_2 N = t$. After how many hours will there be 32 bacteria?

For each pH given, find the concentration of hydrogen ions $[H^+]$. Use the formula $pH = -\log[H^+]$.

41. 7.2

42. 7.3

43. 8.2

44. 6.2

45. 5.6

46. 4.6

47. 7.0

48. 2.9

Find the inverse of each function.

49. $y = \log_2 x$

50. $y = \log_{0.7} x$

51. $y = \log_{100} x$

52. $y = \log_8 x$

53. $y = \log_2 (4x)$

54. $y = \log (x + 4)$

Find the domain and range of each function.

55. $y = \log_3 x - 2$

56. $y = 2 \log_5 x$

57. $y = \log (x + 1)$

Name ______________________ Class ____________ Date ____________

7-3 Standardized Test Prep

Logarithmic Functions as Inverses

Multiple Choice

For Exercises 1–4, choose the correct letter.

1. Which of the following is the logarithmic form of the equation $4^{-3} = \frac{1}{64}$?

(A) $\log_{-3}\left(\frac{1}{64}\right) = 4$

(B) $\log_{-3} 4 = \frac{1}{64}$

(C) $\log_4\left(\frac{1}{64}\right) = -3$

(D) $\log_{\frac{1}{64}} 4 = -3$

2. What is the value of $\log_2 8$?

(F) 64

(G) 8

(H) 16

(I) 3

3. How does the graph of $y = \log_5(x - 3)$ compare with the graph of the parent function, $y = \log_5 x$?

(A) translated 3 units to the left

(B) translated 3 units down

(C) translated 3 units to the right

(D) translated 3 units up

4. In 2009, an earthquake of magnitude 6.7 shook the Kermadec Islands off the coast of New Zealand. Also in 2009, an earthquake of magnitude 5.1 occurred in the Alaska Peninsula. How many times stronger was the Kermadec earthquake than the Alaska earthquake?

(F) 39.811

(G) 20.593

(H) 5.77

(I) 0.025

Short Response

5. A single-celled bacterium divides every hour. The number N of bacteria after t hours is given by the formula $\log_2 N = t$.

a. After how many hours will there be 64 bacteria?

b. Explain in words or show work for how you determined the number of hours.

Name ____________________ Class ____________ Date ____________

7-4 Think About a Plan

Properties of Logarithms

Construction The foreman of a construction team puts up a sound barrier that reduces the intensity of the noise by 50%. By how many decibels is the noise reduced? Use the formula $L = 10 \log \frac{I}{I_0}$ to measure loudness. (*Hint*: Find the difference between the expression for loudness for intensity *I* and the expression for loudness for intensity 0.5*I*.)

Know

1. You can represent the intensity of the original noise by [ ].

2. You can represent the intensity of the reduced noise by [ ].

3. The formula for loudness is [ ].

Need

4. To solve the problem I need to find:

____

____.

Plan

5. What is an expression for the loudness of the original construction noise?

6. What is an expression for the loudness of the reduced construction noise?

7. Use your expressions to find the difference between the loudness of the original construction noise and the loudness of the reduced construction noise.

8. The sound barrier reduced the loudness by [ ].

Name ______________________ Class ____________ Date ____________

7-4 Practice

Form G

Properties of Logarithms

Write each expression as a single logarithm.

1. $\log_5 4 + \log_5 3$
2. $\log_6 25 - \log_6 5$
3. $\log_2 4 + \log_2 2 - \log_2 8$
4. $5\log_7 x - 2\log_7 x$
5. $\log_4 60 - \log_4 4 + \log_4 x$
6. $\log 7 - \log 3 + \log 6$
7. $2\log x - 3\log y$
8. $\frac{1}{2}\log r + \frac{1}{3}\log s - \frac{1}{4}\log t$
9. $\log_3 4x + 2\log_3 5y$
10. $5\log 2 - 2\log 2$
11. $\frac{1}{3}\log 3x + \frac{2}{3}\log 3x$
12. $2\log 4 + \log 2 + \log 2$
13. $(\log 3 - \log 4) - \log 2$
14. $5\log x + 3\log x^2$
15. $\log_6 3 - \log_6 6$
16. $\log 2 + \log 4 - \log 7$
17. $\log_3 2x - 5\log_3 y$
18. $\frac{1}{3}(\log_2 x - \log_2 y)$
19. $\frac{1}{2}\log x + \frac{1}{3}\log y - 2\log z$
20. $3(4\log t^2)$
21. $\log_5 y - 4(\log_5 r + 2\log_5 t)$

Expand each logarithm. Simplify if possible.

22. $\log xyz$
23. $\log_2 \frac{x}{yz}$
24. $\log 6x^3y$
25. $\log 7(3x - 2)^2$
26. $\log \sqrt{\frac{2rst}{5w}}$
27. $\log \frac{5x}{4y}$
28. $\log_5 5x^{-5}$
29. $\log \frac{2x^2y}{3k^3}$
30. $\log_4 (3xyz)^2$

Use the Change of Base Formula to evaluate each expression. Round your answer to the nearest thousandth.

31. $\log_4 32$
32. $\log_3 5$
33. $\log_2 15$
34. $\log_6 17$
35. $\log_6 10$
36. $\log_5 6$
37. $\log_8 1$
38. $\log_9 11$

39. The concentration of hydrogen ions in a batch of homemade ketchup is 10^{-4}. What is the pH level of the ketchup?

Name ______________________ Class ____________ Date ____________

7-4 Practice (continued)

Form G

Properties of Logarithms

Determine if each statement is *true* or *false*. Justify your answer.

40. $\log 12 = \log 4 + \log 3$

41. $\log \frac{3}{5} = \frac{\log 3}{\log 5}$

42. $\log_6 12 + \log_6 3 = 2$

43. $\frac{1}{2}\log_4 4x = \log_4 2x$

Use the properties of logarithms to evaluate each expression.

44. $\log_2 8 - \log_2 4$

45. $\log_2 160 - \log_2 5$

46. $\log_6 27 + \log_6 8$

47. $\log_7 14 - \log_7 2$

48. $\log_4 64 + 2\log_4 2$

49. $\frac{1}{4}\log_3 162 - \log_3 \sqrt[4]{2}$

State the property or properties used to rewrite each expression.

50. $\log 6 - \log 3 = \log 2$

51. $6 \log 2 = \log 64$

52. $\log 3x = \log 3 + \log x$

53. $\frac{1}{3}\log_2 x = \log_2 \sqrt[3]{x}$

54. $\frac{2}{3}\log 7 = \log \sqrt[3]{49}$

55. $\log_4 20 - 3\log_4 x = \log_4 \frac{20}{x^3}$

The formula for loudness in decibels (dB) is $L = 10 \log \frac{I}{I_0}$, where I is the intensity of a sound in watts per square meter (W/m^2) and I_0 is 10^{-12} W/m^2, the intensity of a barely audible sound.

56. A sound has an intensity of 5.92×10^{25} W/m^2. What is the loudness of the sound in decibels? Use $I_0 = 10^{-12}$ W/m^2.

57. Suppose you decrease the intensity of a sound by 45%. By how many decibels would the loudness be decreased?

58. Writing Explain why $\log\left(\frac{9}{4}\right) \neq \frac{\log 9}{\log 4}$.

Name ______________________ Class ____________ Date ____________

7-4 Standardized Test Prep

Properties of Logarithms

Multiple Choice

For Exercises 1–4, choose the correct letter.

1. Which statement correctly demonstrates the Power Property of Logarithms?

(A) $\frac{1}{2}\log_5 9 = \log_5 81$

(B) $\frac{1}{2}\log_5 9 = \log_5 \frac{9}{2}$

(C) $\frac{1}{2}\log_5 9 = \log_5 18$

(D) $\frac{1}{2}\log_5 9 = \log_5 3$

2. Which expression is the correct expansion of $\log_4 (3x)^2$?

(F) $\frac{1}{2}(\log_4 3 - \log_4 x)$

(G) $2(\log_4 3 + \log_4 x)$

(H) $2(\log_4 3 - \log_4 x)$

(I) $2\log_4 3 + \log_4 x$

3. Which expression is equivalent to $\log_7 16$?

(A) $\frac{\log_7 16}{\log 10}$

(B) $\frac{\log_{16} 10}{\log_7 10}$

(C) $\frac{\log 16}{\log 7}$

(D) $\frac{\log 7}{\log 16}$

4. Which statement correctly expresses $4\log_3 x + 7\log_3 y$ as a single logarithm?

(F) $\log_3 x^4y^7$

(G) $\log_3 (4x + 7y)$

(H) $\log_3 (x^4 + y^7)$

(I) $\log_3 (4x - 7y)$

Short Response

5. The pH of a substance equals $-\log[H^+]$, where $[H^+]$ is the concentration of hydrogen ions. The concentration of hydrogen ions in pure water is 10^{-7} and the concentration of hydrogen ions in a sodium hydroxide solution is 10^{-14}.

a. Without using a calculator, what is the difference of the pH levels of pure water and the sodium hydroxide solution?

b. Explain in words or show work for how you determined the difference of the pH levels.

Name ______________________ Class ____________ Date ____________

7-5 Think About a Plan

Exponential and Logarithmic Equations

Seismology An earthquake of magnitude 7.6 occurred in 2001 in Gujarat, India. It was 251 times as strong as the greatest earthquake ever to hit Pennsylvania. What is the magnitude of the Pennsylvania earthquake? (*Hint*: Refer to the Richter scale on page 453.)

Know

1. The magnitude of the Gujarat earthquake is [ ].

2. The ratio of the intensity of the Gujarat earthquake to the intensity of Pennsylvania's greatest earthquake is [ ].

Need

3. To solve the problem I need to find:

____.

Plan

4. Let I_1 and M_1 be the intensity and magnitude of the Gujarat earthquake. Let I_2 and M_2 be the intensity and magnitude of Pennsylvania's greatest earthquake. What equation should you use to model this situation?

5. What does $\frac{I_1}{I_2}$ represent? ____

____

6. What can you substitute for $\frac{I_1}{I_2}$ in your equation?

7. Solve your equation for the magnitude of Pennsylvania's greatest earthquake.

8. The magnitude of Pennsylvania's greatest earthquake was [ ].

Name ______________________ Class ____________ Date ____________

7-5 Practice

Form G

Exponential and Logarithmic Equations

Solve each equation.

1. $8^{2x} = 32$
2. $7^{n} = 343$
3. $9^{2x} = 27$
4. $25^{2n+1} = 625$
5. $36^{-2x+1} = 216$
6. $64^{x} = 4096$

Solve each equation. Round answers to the nearest hundredth.

7. $5^{2x} = 20$
8. $8^{n+1} = 3$
9. $4^{n-2} = 3$
10. $4^{3n} = 5$
11. $15^{2n-3} = 245$
12. $4^{x} - 5 = 12$

Solve by graphing. Round to the nearest hundredth.

13. $2^{n+5} = 120$
14. $5^{n+1} = 175$
15. $8^{x} = 58$
16. $10^{n} = 3$
17. $10^{3y} = 5$
18. $10^{k-2} = 20$
19. $5^{x} = 4$
20. $2^{4x} = 8$
21. $3^{x+5} = 15$

Use a table to solve each equation. Round to the nearest hundredth.

22. $8^{2n} = 3$
23. $12^{2n-1} = 64$
24. $12^{n-2} = 8$
25. $10^{x} = 182$
26. $8^{n} = 12$
27. $10^{2x} = 9$
28. $5^{n+1} = 3$
29. $10^{n-2} = 0.3$
30. $3^{3n} = 50$
31. The equation $y = 281(1.01)^{x}$ is a model for the population of the United States y, in millions of people, x years after the year 2000. Estimate when the United States population will reach 400 million people.

Solve each equation. Check your answers.

32. $\log x = 2$
33. $\log 4x = -1$
34. $\log 3x = 2$
35. $\log 4x = 2$
36. $4 \log x = 4$
37. $8 \log x = 16$
38. $2 \log x = 2$
39. $\log (2x + 5) = 3$
40. $\log (3x - 2) = 3$
41. $\log (x - 25) = 2$
42. $2 \log (2x + 5) = 4$
43. $3 \log (1 - 2x) = 6$

Name ______________________ Class ____________ Date ____________

7-5 Practice (continued) — Form G

Exponential and Logarithmic Equations

Solve each equation.

44. $\log x - \log 4 = 3$

45. $\log x - \log 4 = -2$

46. $2\log x - \log 4 = 2$

47. $\log 3x - \log 5 = 1$

48. $2\log x - \log 3 = 1$

49. $\log 8 - \log 2x = -1$

50. $2\log 3x - \log 9 = 1$

51. $2\log x - \log 5 = -2$

52. $\log(x + 21) + \log x = 2$

53. The function $y = 1000(1.005)^x$ models the value of $1000 deposited at an interest rate of 6% per year (0.005 per month) x months after the money is deposited.

a. Use a graph (on your graphing calculator) to predict how many months it will be until the account is worth $1100.

b. Predict how many years it will be until the account is worth $5000.

54. Suppose the population of a country is currently 8,100,000. Studies show this country's population is increasing 2% each year.

a. What exponential function would be a good model for this country's population?

b. Using the equation you found in part (a), how many years will it take for the country's population to reach 9 million? Round your answer to the nearest hundredth.

55. Suppose you deposit $2500 in a savings account that pays you 5% interest per year.

a. How many years will it take for you to double your money?

b. How many years will it take for your account to reach $8,000?

Mental Math **Solve each equation.**

56. $5^x = \frac{1}{25}$

57. $4^x = 64$

58. $10^x = 0.0001$

59. $\log_3 81 = x$

60. $\log_2 \frac{1}{32} = x$

61. $\log 1{,}000{,}000 = x$

Use the properties of exponential and logarithmic functions to solve each system. Check your answers.

62. $\begin{cases} -2^{10-x} + y = 0 \\ y = 8^{x+2} \end{cases}$

63. $\begin{cases} 3^{2x-y} = 1 \\ 4^{x+y} - 8 = 0 \end{cases}$

64. $\begin{cases} \log_2(x - 2y) = 3 \\ \log_2(x + y) = \log_2 8 \end{cases}$

Name ______________________ Class ____________ Date ____________

7-5 Standardized Test Prep

Exponential and Logarithmic Equations

Multiple Choice

For Exercises 1–5, choose the correct letter.

1. If $9^x = 243$, what is the value of x?

Ⓐ 2　　Ⓑ 5　　Ⓒ 2.5　　Ⓓ 10

2. If $2^{3x+2} = 64$, what is the value of x?

Ⓕ $\frac{8}{3}$　　Ⓖ $\frac{4}{3}$　　Ⓗ 2　　Ⓘ $\frac{3}{4}$

3. If $\log(3x + 25) = 2$, what is the value of x?

Ⓐ 25　　Ⓑ 75　　Ⓒ $41\frac{2}{3}$　　Ⓓ 100

4. Which best approximates the solution of $16^{2x} = 124$?

Ⓕ 0.869　　Ⓖ 1.150　　Ⓗ 1.739　　Ⓘ 3.477

5. Which equation represents the solution of $2^{3x+1} = 7$?

Ⓐ $x = 3\left(\frac{\log 7}{\log 2} - 1\right)$　　Ⓒ $x = \frac{1}{3}\left(\frac{\log 2}{\log 7} - 1\right)$

Ⓑ $x = \frac{\log 7}{3\log 2} - 1$　　Ⓓ $x = \frac{1}{3}\left(\frac{\log 7}{\log 2} - 1\right)$

Short Response

6. In 2007, the population of Tallahassee, Florida was 168,979. Some researchers believe that the population of Tallahassee will increase at a rate of 1% each year for the 10 years following this.

a. If the researchers are correct, how many years will it take for the population of Tallahassee to reach 180,000?

b. Explain in words or show your work for how you determined the number of years found in part (a).

Name ____________________ Class __________ Date __________

7-6 Think About a Plan

Natural Logarithms

Archaeology A fossil bone contains 25% of its original carbon-14. What is the approximate age of the bone?

Understanding the Problem

1. What is the amount of carbon-14 remaining in the fossil bone?

____

2. If a is the amount of carbon-14 originally in an object and t is the object's age in years, what equation gives the amount of carbon-14 in the object?

3. What is the problem asking you to determine?

____

Planning the Solution

4. What number should you substitute for y in the equation above?

5. Write an equation you can use to determine the approximate age of the bone.

Getting an Answer

6. How can logarithms help you solve your equation?

____

____.

7. Solve your equation to find the approximate age of the bone.

Name ______________________ Class ____________ Date ____________

7-6 Practice

Form G

Natural Logarithms

Write each expression as a single natural logarithm.

1. $\ln 16 - \ln 8$

2. $3 \ln 3 + \ln 9$

3. $a \ln 4 - \ln b$

4. $\ln z - 3 \ln x$

5. $\frac{1}{2} \ln 9 + \ln 3x$

6. $4 \ln x + 3 \ln y$

7. $\frac{1}{3} \ln 8 + \ln x$

8. $3 \ln a - b \ln 2$

9. $2 \ln 4 - \ln 8$

Solve each equation. Check your answers. Round your answer to the nearest hundredth.

10. $4 \ln x = -2$

11. $2 \ln (3x - 4) = 7$

12. $5 \ln (4x - 6) = -6$

13. $-7 + \ln 2x = 4$

14. $3 - 4 \ln (8x + 1) = 12$

15. $\ln x + \ln 3x = 14$

16. $2 \ln x + \ln x^2 = 3$

17. $\ln x + \ln 4 = 2$

18. $\ln x - \ln 5 = -1$

19. $\ln e^x = 3$

20. $3 \ln e^{2x} = 12$

21. $\ln e^{x+5} = 17$

22. $\ln 3x + \ln 2x = 3$

23. $5 \ln (3x - 2) = 15$

24. $7 \ln (2x + 5) = 8$

25. $\ln (3x + 4) = 5$

26. $\ln \frac{2x}{41} = 2$

27. $\ln (2x - 1)^2 = 4$

Use natural logarithms to solve each equation. Round your answer to the nearest hundredth.

28. $e^x = 15$

29. $4e^x = 10$

30. $e^{x+2} = 50$

31. $4e^{3x-1} = 5$

32. $e^{x-4} = 2$

33. $5e^{6x+3} = 0.1$

34. $e^x = 1$

35. $e^{\frac{x}{5}} = 32$

36. $3e^{3x-5} = 49$

37. $7e^{5x+8} = 0.23$

38. $6 - e^{12x} = 5.2$

39. $e^{\frac{x}{2}} = 25$

40. $e^{2x} = 25$

41. $e^{\ln 5x} = 20$

42. $e^{\ln x} = 21$

43. $e^{x+6} + 5 = 1$

7-6 Practice (continued) Form G

Natural Logarithms

The formula $P = 50e^{-\frac{t}{25}}$ gives the power output P, in watts, needed to run a certain satellite for t days. Find how long a satellite with the given power output will operate.

44. 10 W

45. 12 W

46. 14 W

The formula for the maximum velocity v of a rocket is $v = -0.0098t + c \ln R$, where c is the exhaust velocity in km/s, t is the firing time, and R is the mass ratio of the rocket. A rocket must reach 7.7 km/s to attain a stable orbit 300 km above Earth.

47. What is the maximum velocity of a rocket with a mass ratio of 18, an exhaust velocity of 2.2 km/s, and a firing time of 25 s?

48. Can the rocket in Exercise 47 achieve a stable orbit? Explain your answer.

49. What mass ratio would be needed to achieve a stable orbit for a rocket with an exhaust velocity of 2.5 km/s and a firing time of 29 s?

50. A rocket with an exhaust velocity of 2.4 km/s and a 28 second firing time can reach a maximum velocity of 7.8 km/s. What is the mass ratio of the rocket?

By measuring the amount of carbon-14 in an object, a paleontologist can determine its approximate age. The amount of carbon-14 in an object is given by $y = ae^{-0.00012t}$, where a is the amount of carbon-14 originally in the object, and t is the age of the object in years.

51. A fossil of a bone contains 32% of its original carbon-14. What is the approximate age of the bone?

52. A fossil of a bone contains 83% of its original carbon-14. What is the approximate age of the bone?

Simplify each expression.

53. $\ln e^4$

54. $5 \ln e^5$

55. $\frac{\ln e^2}{2}$

56. $\ln e^{100}$

Name ______________________ Class ____________ Date ____________

7-6 Standardized Test Prep

Natural Logarithms

Multiple Choice

For Exercises 1–4, choose the correct letter. Do not use a calculator.

1. What is $3 \ln 5 - \ln 2$ written as a single natural logarithm?

   (A) $\ln 7.5$ (B) $\ln 27$ (C) $\ln\left(\frac{5}{2}\right)^3$ (D) $\ln 62.5$

2. What is the solution of $e^{x+1} = 13$?

   (F) $x = \ln 13 + 1$ (G) $x = \ln 13 - 1$ (H) $x = \ln 13$ (I) $x = \ln 12$

3. What is the solution of $\ln(x - 2)^2 = 6$?

   (A) $2 + e^3$ (B) $2 - e^3$ (C) $2 \pm e^3$ (D) $2 \pm e^6$

4. What is the solution of $e^{\frac{x}{2}+1} + 3 = 8$?

   (F) $x = 2\ln 5 - 1$ (G) $x = 2\ln 5 - 2$ (H) $x = 2\ln 4$ (I) $x = \frac{1}{2}(\ln 5 - 1)$

Short Response

5. The maximum velocity v of a rocket is $v = -0.0098t + c\ln R$. The rocket fires for t seconds and the velocity of the exhaust is c km/s. The ratio of the mass of the rocket filled with fuel to the mass of the rocket without fuel is R. A spacecraft can attain a stable orbit 300 km above Earth if it reaches a velocity of 7.7 km/s.

   a. What is the velocity of a spacecraft whose booster rocket has a mass ratio of 16, an exhaust velocity of 3.2 km/s, and a firing time of 40 s?

   b. Can this rocket attain a stable orbit 300 km above Earth? Explain in words or show work for how you determined your answer.

Name ______________________ Class ____________ Date ____________

8-1 Think About a Plan

Inverse Variation

The spreadsheet shows data that could be modeled by an equation of the form $PV = k$. Estimate P when $V = 62$.

	A	B
1	P	V
2	140.00	100
3	147.30	95
4	155.60	90
5	164.70	85
6	175.00	80
7	186.70	75

Understanding the Problem

1. The data can be modeled by [ ].

2. What is the problem asking you to determine?

____

____

Planning the Solution

3. What does it mean that the data can be modeled by an inverse variation?

______________________________.

4. How can you estimate the constant of the inverse variation?

____

______________________________.

5. What is the constant of the inverse variation?

6. Write an equation that you can use to find P when $V = 62$.

Getting an Answer

7. Solve your equation.

8. What is an estimate for P when $V = 62$?

Name ______________________ Class ____________ Date ____________

8-1 Practice

Form G

Inverse Variation

Is the relationship between the values in each table a *direct variation*, an *inverse variation*, or *neither*? Write equations to model the direct and inverse variations.

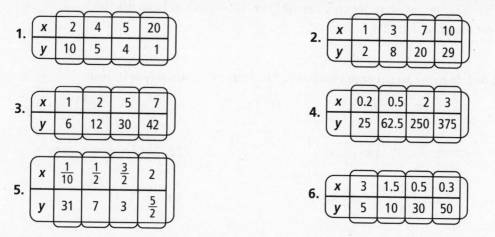

1.
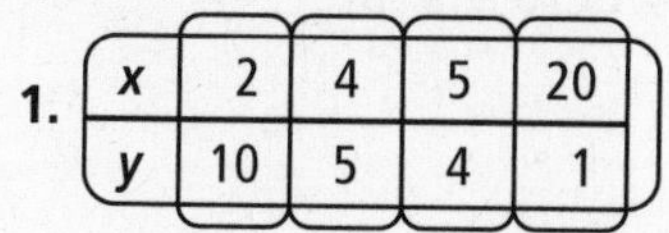

x	2	4	5	20
y	10	5	4	1

2.
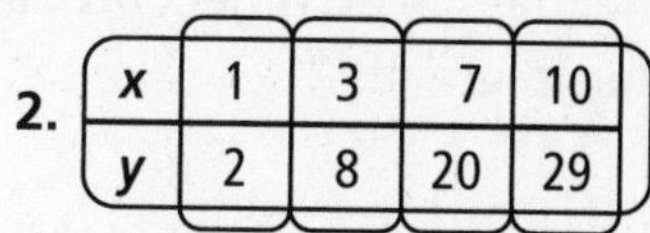

x	1	3	7	10
y	2	8	20	29

3.
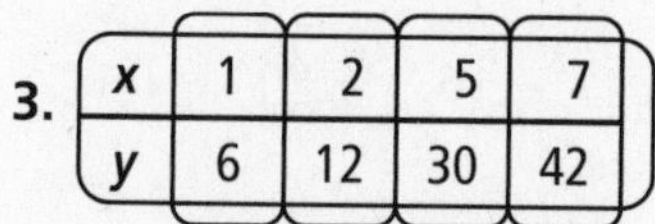

x	1	2	5	7
y	6	12	30	42

4.

x	0.2	0.5	2	3
y	25	62.5	250	375

5.

x	$\frac{1}{10}$	$\frac{1}{2}$	$\frac{3}{2}$	2
y	31	7	3	$\frac{5}{2}$

6.

x	3	1.5	0.5	0.3
y	5	10	30	50

Suppose that x and y vary inversely. Write a function that models each inverse variation. Graph the function and find y when $x = 10$.

7. $x = 7$ when $y = 2$

8. $x = 4$ when $y = 0.2$

9. $x = \frac{1}{3}$ when $y = \frac{9}{10}$

10. The students in a school club decide to raise money by selling hats with the school mascot on them. The table below shows how many hats they can expect to sell based on how much they charge per hat in dollars.

Price per Hat (p)	5	6	8	9
Hats Sold (h)	72	60	45	40

a. What is a function that models the data?

b. How many hats can the students expect to sell if they charge \$7.50 per hat?

11. The minimum number of carpet rolls n needed to carpet a house varies directly as the house's square footage h and inversely with the square footage r in one roll. It takes a minimum of two 1200-ft^2 carpet rolls to cover 2300 ft^2 of floor. What is the minimum number of 1200-ft^2 carpet rolls you would need to cover 2500 ft^2 of floor? Round your answer up to the nearest half roll.

8-1 Practice (continued)

Form G

Inverse Variation

12. On Earth, the mass m of an object varies directly with the object's potential energy E and inversely with its height above the Earth's surface h. What is an equation for the mass of an object on Earth? (*Hint:* $E = gmh$, where g is the acceleration due to gravity.)

Each ordered pair is from an inverse variation. Find the constant of variation.

13. $\left(3, \frac{1}{3}\right)$ **14.** $(0.2, 6)$ **15.** $(10, 5)$ **16.** $\left(\frac{5}{7}, \frac{2}{5}\right)$

17. $(-13, 22)$ **18.** $\left(\frac{1}{2}, 10\right)$ **19.** $\left(\frac{1}{3}, \frac{6}{7}\right)$

20. $(4.8, 2.9)$ **21.** $\left(\frac{5}{8}, -\frac{2}{5}\right)$ **22.** $(4.75, 4)$

Write the function that models each variation. Find z when $x = 6$ and $y = 4$.

23. z varies jointly with x and y. When $x = 7$ and $y = 2$, $z = 28$.

24. z varies directly with x and inversely with the cube of y. When $x = 8$ and $y = 2$, $z = 3$.

Each pair of values is from an inverse variation. Find the missing value.

25. $(2, 4), (6, y)$ **26.** $\left(\frac{1}{3}, 6\right), \left(x, -\frac{1}{2}\right)$ **27.** $(1.2, 4.5), (2.7, y)$

28. One load of gravel contains 240 ft^3 of gravel. The area A that the gravel will cover is inversely proportional to the depth d to which the gravel is spread.

a. Write a model for the relationship between the area and depth for one load of gravel.

b. A designer plans a playground with gravel 6 in. deep over the entire play area. If the play area is a rectangle 40 ft wide and 24 ft long, how many loads of gravel will be needed?

Name ______________________ Class ____________ Date ____________

8-1 Standardized Test Prep

Inverse Variation

Multiple Choice

For Exercises 1–5, choose the correct letter.

1. Which equation represents inverse variation between x and y?

   (A) $4y = kx$ (B) $xy = 4k$ (C) $y = 4kx$ (D) $4k = \frac{x}{y}$

2. The ordered pair (3.5, 1.2) is from an inverse variation. What is the constant of variation?

   (F) 2.3 (G) 2.9 (H) 4.2 (I) 4.7

3. Suppose x and y vary inversely, and $x = 4$ when $y = 9$. Which function models the inverse variation?

   (A) $y = \frac{36}{x}$ (B) $x = \frac{y}{36}$ (C) $y = \frac{x}{36}$ (D) $\frac{x}{y} = 36$

4. Suppose x and y vary inversely, and $x = -3$ when $y = \frac{1}{3}$. What is the value of y when $x = 9$?

   (F) -9 (G) -1 (H) $-\frac{1}{9}$ (I) $\frac{1}{9}$

5. In which function does t vary jointly with q and r and inversely with s?

   (A) $t = \frac{kq}{rs}$ (B) $t = \frac{ks}{qr}$ (C) $t = \frac{s}{kqr}$ (D) $t = \frac{kqr}{s}$

Short Response

6. A student suggests that the graph at the right represents the inverse variation $y = \frac{3}{x}$. Is the student correct? Explain.

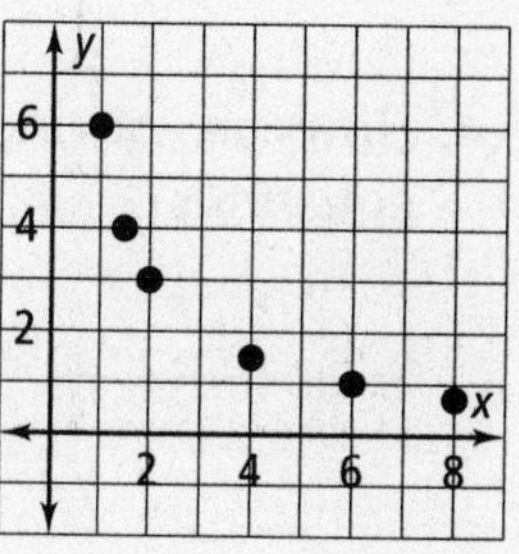

Name ______________________________ Class ______________ Date ______________

8-2 Think About a Plan

The Reciprocal Function Family

a. Gasoline Mileage Suppose you drive an average of 10,000 miles each year. Your gasoline mileage (mi/gal) varies inversely with the number of gallons of gasoline you use each year. Write and graph a model for your average mileage m in terms of the gallons g of gasoline used.

b. After you begin driving on the highway more often, you use 50 gal less per year. Write and graph a new model to include this information.

c. Calculate your old and new mileage assuming that you originally used 400 gal of gasoline per year.

1. Write a formula for gasoline mileage in words.

____.

2. Write and graph an equation to model your average mileage m in terms of the gallons g of gasoline used.

3. Write and graph an equation to model your average mileage m in terms of the gallons g of gasoline used if you use 50 gal less per year.

4. How can you find your old and your new mileage from your equations?

____.

5. What is your old mileage?

6. What is your new mileage?

Name ____________________ Class ____________ Date ____________

8-2 Practice

Form G

The Reciprocal Function Family

Graph each function. Identify the *x*- and *y*-intercepts and the asymptotes of the graph. Also, state the domain and the range of the function.

1. $y = \frac{12}{x}$

2. $y = \frac{5}{x}$

3. $y = -\frac{4}{x}$

Use a graphing calculator to graph the equations $y = \frac{1}{x}$ and $y = \frac{a}{x}$ using the given value of *a*. Then identify the effect of *a* on the graph.

4. $a = 3$

5. $a = -5$

6. $a = 0.4$

Sketch the asymptotes and the graph of each function. Identify the domain and range.

7. $y = \frac{1}{x} + 3$

8. $y = \frac{3}{4x} + \frac{1}{2}$

9. $y = \frac{3}{x - 1} + 2$

Write an equation for the translation of $y = -\frac{3}{x}$ that has the given asymptotes.

10. $x = -1$; $y = 3$

11. $x = 4$; $y = -2$

12. $x = 0$; $y = 6$

Name ______________________ Class ____________ Date ____________

8-2 Practice (continued)

Form G

The Reciprocal Function Family

13. The length of a pipe in a panpipe ℓ (in feet) is inversely proportional to its pitch p (in hertz). The inverse variation is modeled by the equation $p = \frac{495}{\ell}$. Find the length required to produce a pitch of 220 Hz.

Write each equation in the form $y = \frac{k}{x}$.

14. $y = \frac{4}{5x}$

15. $y = -\frac{7}{2x}$

16. $xy = -0.03$

Sketch the graph of each function.

17. $xy = 6$

18. $xy + 10 = 0$

19. $4xy = -1$

20. The junior class is buying keepsakes for Class Night. The price of each keepsake p is inversely proportional to the number of keepsakes s bought. The keepsake company also offers 10 free keepsakes in addition to the class's order. The equation $p = \frac{1800}{s + 10}$ models this inverse variation.
    a. If the class buys 240 keepsakes, what is the price for each one?
    b. If the class pays $5.55 for each keepsake, how many can they get, including the free keepsakes?
    c. If the class buys 400 keepsakes, what is the price for each one?
    d. If the class buys 50 keepsakes, what is the price for each one?

Graph each pair of functions. Find the approximate point(s) of intersection.

21. $y = \frac{3}{x - 4}$; $y = 2$

22. $y = \frac{2}{x + 5}$; $y = -1.5$

Name ______________________ Class ____________ Date ____________

8-2 Standardized Test Prep

The Reciprocal Function Family

Multiple Choice

For Exercises 1–3, choose the correct letter.

1. What is an equation for the translation of $y = -\frac{4.5}{x}$ that has asymptotes at $x = 3$ and $y = -5$?

(A) $y = -\frac{4.5}{x - 3} - 5$ (C) $y = -\frac{4.5}{x - 5} + 3$

(B) $y = -\frac{4.5}{x + 3} - 5$ (D) $y = -\frac{4.5}{x + 5} + 3$

2. What is the equation of the vertical asymptote of $y = \frac{2}{x - 5}$?

(F) $x = -5$ (G) $x = 0$ (H) $x = 2$ (I) $x = 5$

3. Which is the graph of $y = \frac{1}{x + 1} - 2$?

(A)
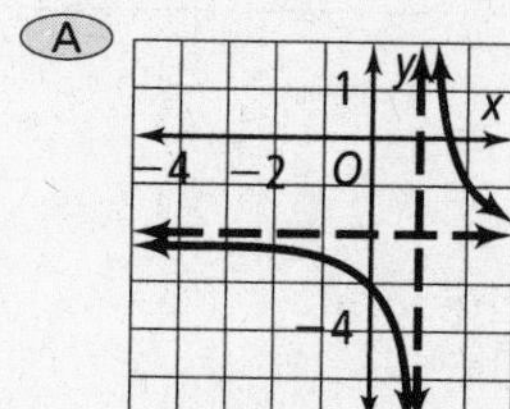

(B)
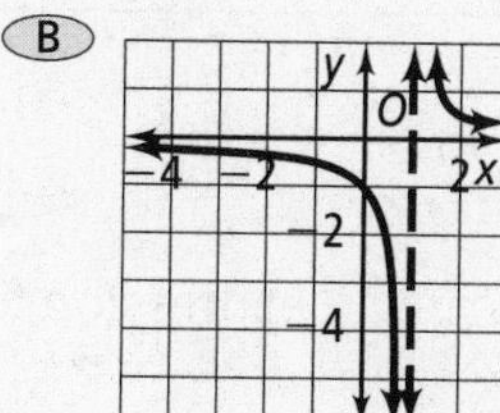

(C)
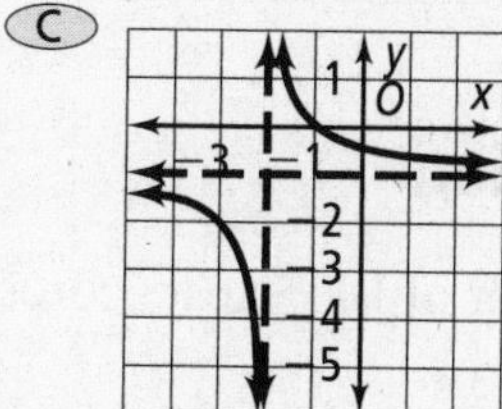

(D)
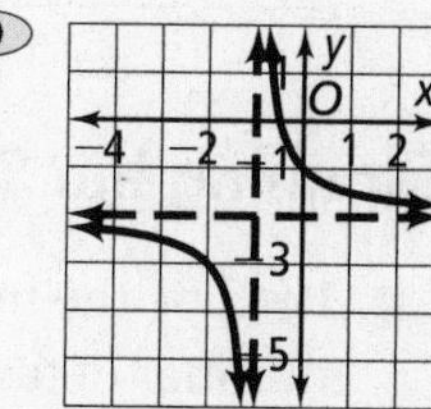

Extended Response

4. A race pilot's average rate of speed over a 720-mi course is inversely proportional to the time in minutes t the pilot takes to fly a complete race course. The pilot's final score s is the average speed minus any penalty points p earned.

a. Write a function to model the pilot's score for a given t and p. (*Hint:* $d = rt$)

b. Graph the function for a pilot who has 2 penalty points.

c. What is the maximum time a pilot with 2 penalty points can take to finish the course and still earn a score of at least 3?

Name ______________________ Class ____________ Date ____________

8-3 Think About a Plan

Rational Functions and Their Graphs

Grades A student earns an 82% on her first test. How many consecutive 100% test scores does she need to bring her average up to 95%? Assume that each test has equal impact on the average grade.

Understanding the Problem

1. One test score is [ ].

2. The average of all the test scores is [ ].

3. What is the problem asking you to determine?

____

____.

Planning the Solution

4. Let x be the number of 100% test scores. Write an expression for the total number of test scores.

5. Write an expression for the sum of the test scores.

6. How can you model the student's average as a rational function?

Getting an Answer

7. How can a graph help you answer this question?

____

____.

8. What does a fractional answer tell you? Explain.

____

____.

9. How many consecutive 100% test scores does the student need to bring her average up to 95%?

Name ______________________ Class ____________ Date ____________

8-3 Practice

Form G

Rational Functions and Their Graphs

Find the domain, points of discontinuity, and *x*- and *y*-intercepts of each rational function. Determine whether the discontinuities are removable or nonremovable.

1. $y = \frac{(x-4)(x+3)}{x+3}$

2. $y = \frac{(x-3)(x+1)}{x-2}$

3. $y = \frac{2}{x+1}$

4. $y = \frac{4x}{x^4+16}$

Find the vertical asymptotes and holes for the graph of each rational function.

5. $y = \frac{5-x}{x^2-1}$

6. $y = \frac{x^2-2}{x+2}$

7. $y = \frac{x}{x(x-1)}$

8. $y = \frac{x+3}{x^2-9}$

9. $y = \frac{x-2}{(x+2)(x-2)}$

10. $y = \frac{x^2-4}{x^2+4}$

11. $y = \frac{x^2-25}{x-4}$

12. $y = \frac{(x-2)(2x+3)}{(5x+4)(x-3)}$

Find the horizontal asymptote of the graph of each rational function.

13. $y = \frac{2}{x-6}$

14. $y = \frac{x+2}{x-4}$

15. $y = \frac{2x^2+3}{x^2-6}$

16. $y = \frac{3x-12}{x^2-2}$

Sketch the graph of each rational function.

17. $y = \frac{3}{x-2}$

18. $y = \frac{3}{(x-2)(x+2)}$

19. $y = \frac{x}{x^2+4}$

20. $y = \frac{x+2}{x-1}$

8-3 Practice (continued) Form G

Rational Functions and Their Graphs

21. How many milliliters of 0.75% sugar solution must be added to 100 mL of 1.5% sugar solution to form a 1.25% sugar solution?

22. A soccer player has made 3 of his last 24 shots on goal, or 12.5%. How many more consecutive goals does he need to raise his shots-on-goal average to at least 20%?

23. Error Analysis A student listed the asymptotes of the function $y = \frac{x^2 + 5x + 6}{x(x^2 + 4x + 4)}$ as shown at the right. Explain the student's error(s). What are the correct asymptotes?

> horizontal asymptote
> none
>
> vertical asymptote
> x = 0

Sketch the graph of each rational function.

24. $y = \frac{x}{x(x - 6)}$

25. $y = \frac{2x}{x - 6}$

26. $y = \frac{x^2 - 1}{x^2 - 4}$

27. $y = \frac{2x^2 + 10x + 12}{x^2 - 9}$

28. You start a business word-processing papers for other students. You spend $3500 on a computer system and office furniture. You figure additional costs at $.02 per page.

a. Write a rational function modeling the total average cost per page. Graph the function.

b. What is the total average cost per page if you type 1000 pages? If you type 2000?

c. How many pages must you type to bring your total average cost to less than $1.50 per page?

d. What are the vertical and horizontal asymptotes of the graph of the function?

Name ______________________ Class ____________ Date ____________

8-3 Standardized Test Prep

Rational Functions and Their Graphs

Multiple Choice

For Exercises 1–4, choose the correct letter.

1. What function has a graph with a removable discontinuity at $\left(5, \frac{1}{9}\right)$?

Ⓐ $y = \frac{(x - 5)}{(x + 4)(x - 5)}$

Ⓑ $y = \frac{4}{x - 5}$

Ⓒ $y = \frac{4x - 1}{5x + 1}$

Ⓓ $y = \frac{x + 1}{5x - 4}$

2. What is the vertical asymptote of the graph of $y = \frac{(x + 2)(x - 3)}{x(x - 3)}$?

Ⓕ $x = -3$ Ⓖ $x = -2$ Ⓗ $x = 0$ Ⓘ $x = 3$

3. What best describes the horizontal asymptote(s), if any, of the graph of $y = \frac{x^2 + 2x - 8}{(x + 6)^2}$?

Ⓐ $y = -6$

Ⓑ $y = 0$

Ⓒ $y = 1$

Ⓓ The graph has no horizontal asymptote.

4. Which rational function has a graph that has vertical asymptotes at $x = a$ and $x = -a$, and a horizontal asymptote at $y = 0$?

Ⓕ $y = \frac{(x - a)(x + a)}{x}$

Ⓖ $y = \frac{1}{x^2 - a^2}$

Ⓗ $y = \frac{x^2}{x^2 - a^2}$

Ⓘ $y = \frac{x - a}{x + a}$

Short Response

5. How many milliliters of 0.30% sugar solution must you add to 75 mL of 4% sugar solution to get a 0.50% sugar solution? Show your work.

Name ______________________ Class ____________ Date ____________

8-4 Think About a Plan

Rational Expressions

Manufacturing A toy company is considering a cube or sphere-shaped container for packaging a new product. The height of the cube would equal the diameter of the sphere. Compare the ratios of the volumes to the surface areas of the containers. Which packaging will be more efficient? For a sphere, $SA = 4\pi r^2$.

Understanding the Problem

1. Let x be the height of the cube. What are expressions for the cube's volume and surface area?

   Volume: ☐ Surface area: ☐

2. Let x be the diameter of the sphere. What are expressions for the sphere's volume and surface area?

   Volume: ☐ Surface area: ☐

3. What is the problem asking you to do?

   ____

   ____.

Planning the Solution

4. Write an expression for the ratio of the cube's volume to its surface area. Simplify your expression.

5. Write an expression for the ratio of the sphere's volume to its surface area. Simplify your expression.

Getting an Answer

6. Compare the ratios of the volumes to the surface areas of the containers. Which packaging will be more efficient?

   ____.

Name ______________________ Class ____________ Date ____________

8-4 Practice

Form G

Rational Expressions

Simplify each rational expression. State any restrictions on the variables.

1. $\frac{4x + 6}{2x + 3}$

2. $\frac{2y}{y^2 + 6y}$

3. $\frac{20 + 40x}{20x}$

4. $\frac{7x - 28}{x^2 - 16}$

5. $\frac{3y^2 - 3}{y^2 - 1}$

6. $\frac{3x^2 - 12}{x^2 - x - 6}$

7. $\frac{x^2 + 3x - 18}{x^2 - 36}$

8. $\frac{x^2 + 13x + 40}{x^2 - 2x - 35}$

Multiply. State any restrictions on the variables.

9. $\frac{5a}{5a + 5} \cdot \frac{10a + 10}{a}$

10. $\frac{2x + 4}{10x} \cdot \frac{15x^2}{x + 2}$

11. $\frac{x^2 - 5x}{x^2 + 3x} \cdot \frac{x + 3}{x - 5}$

12. $\frac{x^2 - 6x}{x^2 - 36} \cdot \frac{x + 6}{x^2}$

13. $\frac{5y - 20}{3y + 15} \cdot \frac{7y + 35}{10y + 40}$

14. $\frac{x - 2}{(x + 2)^2} \cdot \frac{x + 2}{2x - 4}$

15. $\frac{3x^3}{x^2 - 25} \cdot \frac{x^2 + 6x + 5}{x^2}$

16. $\frac{y^2 - 2y}{y^2 + 7y - 18} \cdot \frac{y^2 - 81}{y^2 - 11y + 18}$

Divide. State any restrictions on the variables.

17. $\frac{7x^4}{24y^5} \div \frac{21x}{12y^4}$

18. $\frac{6x + 6}{7} \div \frac{4x + 4}{x - 2}$

19. $\frac{5y}{2x^2} \div \frac{5y^2}{8x^2}$

20. $\frac{3y + 3}{6y + 12} \div \frac{18}{5y + 5}$

21. $\frac{y^2 - 49}{(y - 7)^2} \div \frac{5y + 35}{y^2 - 7y}$

22. $\frac{x^2 + 10x + 16}{x^2 - 6x - 16} \div \frac{x + 8}{x^2 - 64}$

23. $\frac{y^2 - 5y + 4}{y^2 - 1} \div \frac{y^2 - 9}{y^2 + 5y + 4}$

24. $\frac{x^2 - 4}{x^2 + 6x + 9} \div \frac{x^2 + 4x + 4}{x^2 - 9}$

8-4 Practice (continued) Form G

Rational Expressions

25. A farmer must decide whether to build a cylindrical grain silo or a rectangular grain silo. The cylindrical silo has radius r. The rectangular silo has width r and length $2r$. Both silos have the same height h.

a. Write and simplify an expression for the ratio of the volume of the cylindrical silo to its surface area, including the circular floor and ceiling.

b. Write and simplify an expression for the ratio of the volume of the rectangular silo to its surface area, including the rectangular floor and ceiling.

c. Compare the ratios of volume to surface area for the two silos.

d. Compare the volumes of the two silos.

e. Reasoning Assume the average cost of construction materials per square foot of surface area is the same for either silo. How can you measure the cost-effectiveness of each silo?

Simplify each rational expression. State any restrictions on the variables.

26. $\dfrac{2x^2 + 11x + 5}{3x^2 + 17x + 10}$

27. $\dfrac{6x^2 + 5xy - 6y^2}{3x^2 - 5xy + 2y^2}$

Multiply or divide. State any restrictions on the variables.

28. $\dfrac{x^2 + 2x + 1}{x^2 - 1} \cdot \dfrac{x^2 + 3x + 2}{x^2 + 4x + 4}$

29. $\dfrac{x^2 - 3x - 10}{2x^2 - 11x + 5} \div \dfrac{x^2 - 5x + 6}{2x^2 - 7x + 3}$

30. Reasoning A rectangle has area $\dfrac{10b}{6b - 6}$ and length $\dfrac{b + 2}{2b - 2}$. Write an expression for the width of the rectangle.

31. Open-Ended Write three rational expressions that simplify to $\dfrac{x + 1}{x - 1}$.

Name ______________________ Class ____________ Date ____________

8-4 Standardized Test Prep

Rational Expressions

Multiple Choice

For Exercises 1–4, choose the correct letter.

1. Which expression equals $\frac{x^2 - 4x - 5}{x^2 + 6x + 5}$?

(A) $x + 1$ (B) $-10x - 10$ (C) $\frac{x - 5}{x + 5}$ (D) $\frac{4x - 5}{6x + 5}$

2. Which expression equals $\frac{42a^2b^4}{12a^5b^{-2}}$?

(F) $\frac{7b^6}{2a^3}$ (G) $\frac{30a^7}{b^2}$ (H) $\frac{7ab^3}{2}$ (I) $\frac{30b^2}{a^3}$

3. Which expression equals $\frac{t^2 - 1}{t - 2} \cdot \frac{t^2 - 3t + 2}{t^2 + 4t + 3}$?

(A) $\frac{t^2 - 2t + 1}{t + 3}$ (B) $\frac{t^2 - 1}{t + 3}$ (C) $\frac{(t + 1)^2(t + 3)}{(t - 2)^2}$ (D) $\frac{2t^2 - 3t + 1}{t^2 + 5t + 1}$

4. What is the area of the triangle shown at the right?

(F) $\frac{2x + 8}{x^2 - 6x + 9}$ (H) $\frac{x + 4}{x^2 - 6x + 9}$

(G) $\frac{x^2 + 6x + 9}{x + 4}$ (I) $\frac{2x^2 + 12x + 18}{x + 4}$

$\frac{x + 3}{x - 3}$

c

$\frac{2x + 8}{x^2 - 9}$

Short Response

5. What is the quotient $\frac{y + 2}{2y^2 - 3y - 2} \div \frac{y^2 - 4}{y^2 + y - 6}$ expressed in simplest form? State any restrictions on the variable. Show your work.

Name ______________________ Class ______________ Date ______________

8-5 Think About a Plan

Adding and Subtracting Rational Expressions

Optics To read small font, you use the magnifying lens with the focal length 3 in. How far from the magnifying lens should you place the page if you want to hold the lens at 1 foot from your eyes? Use the thin-lens equation.

Know

1. The focal length of the magnifying lens is [ ].

2. The distance from the lens to your eyes is [ ].

3. The thin-lens equation is [ ].

Need

4. To solve the problem I need to find:

____.

Plan

5. What variables in the thin-lens equation have values that are known?

____

____

6. Solve the thin-lens equation for the variable whose value is unknown.

7. Substitute the known values into your equation and simplify.

8. How far from the page should you hold the magnifying lens?

Name ______________________ Class ____________ Date ____________

8-5 Practice

Form G

Adding and Subtracting Rational Expressions

Find the least common multiple of each pair of polynomials.

1. $3x(x + 2)$ and $6x(2x - 3)$

2. $2x^2 - 8x + 8$ and $3x^2 + 27x - 30$

3. $4x^2 + 12x + 9$ and $4x^2 - 9$

4. $2x^2 - 18$ and $5x^3 + 30x^2 + 45x$

Simplify each sum or difference. State any restrictions on the variables.

5. $\frac{x^2}{5} + \frac{x^2}{5}$

6. $\frac{6y - 4}{y^2 - 5} + \frac{3y + 1}{y^2 - 5}$

7. $\frac{2y + 1}{3y} + \frac{5y + 4}{3y}$

8. $\frac{12}{xy^3} - \frac{9}{xy^3}$

9. $-\frac{2}{n + 4} - \frac{n^2}{n^2 - 16}$

10. $\frac{3}{8x^3y^3} - \frac{1}{4xy}$

11. $\frac{6}{5x^2y} + \frac{5}{10xy^2}$

12. $\frac{x + 2}{x^2 + 4x + 4} + \frac{2}{x + 2}$

13. $\frac{4}{x^2 - 25} + \frac{6}{x^2 + 6x + 5}$

14. $\frac{y}{4y + 8} - \frac{1}{y^2 + 2y}$

Simplify each complex fraction.

15. $\dfrac{\frac{2}{x}}{\frac{3}{y}}$

16. $\dfrac{1 + \frac{2}{x}}{4 - \frac{6}{x}}$

17. $\dfrac{\frac{1}{x - 2}}{2 + \frac{1}{x}}$

18. $\dfrac{\frac{3}{x + 1}}{\frac{5}{x - 1}}$

19. $\dfrac{\frac{4}{x^2 - 1}}{\frac{3}{x + 1}}$

20. $\dfrac{1 + \frac{2}{3}}{\frac{4}{9}}$

21. $\dfrac{\frac{2}{x} + 6}{\frac{1}{y}}$

22. $\dfrac{\frac{x + 3}{x - 3}}{\frac{x^2 - 9}{3x - 9}}$

23. $\dfrac{\frac{5}{x + 3}}{2 + \frac{1}{x + 3}}$

Name ____________________ Class __________ Date __________

8-5 Practice (continued) — Form G

Adding and Subtracting Rational Expressions

24. The total resistance for a parallel circuit is given by $\frac{1}{R} = \frac{1}{R_1} + \frac{1}{R_2} + \frac{1}{R_3}$.

a. If $R = 1$ ohm, $R_2 = 6$ ohms, and $R_3 = 8$ ohms, find R_1.
b. If $R_1 = 3$ ohms, $R_2 = 4$ ohms, and $R_3 = 6$ ohms, find R.

Add or subtract. Simplify where possible. State any restrictions on the variables.

25. $\frac{3}{7x^2y} + \frac{4}{21xy^2}$

26. $\frac{xy - y}{x - 2} - \frac{y}{x + 2}$

27. $\frac{3}{x^2 - x - 6} + \frac{2}{x^2 + 6x + 5}$

28. $\frac{6}{y^2 + 5y} + \frac{3y}{4y + 20} - \frac{1}{4}$

29. A teacher uses an overhead projector with a focal length of x cm. She sets a transparency $x + 20$ cm below the projector's lens. Write an expression in simplest form to represent how far from the lens she should place the screen to place the image in focus. Use the thin-lens equation $\frac{1}{f} = \frac{1}{d_i} + \frac{1}{d_o}$.

30. Open-Ended Write two complex fractions that simplify to $\frac{x + 5}{x^2}$.

31. Writing Explain the differences in the process of adding two rational expressions using the lowest common denominator (LCD) and adding them using a common denominator that is not the LCD. Include an example in your explanation.

Name ______________________ Class ____________ Date ____________

8-5 Standardized Test Prep

Adding and Subtracting Rational Expressions

Multiple Choice

For Exercises 1–4, choose the correct letter.

1. Which is the least common denominator of fractions that have denominators $5x + 10$ and $25x^2 - 100$?

   Ⓐ $5(x - 2)$
   Ⓑ $5(x^2 - 20)$
   Ⓒ $25(x^2 - 4)$
   Ⓓ $75(x + 2)(x^2 - 4)$

2. Which expression equals $\dfrac{\frac{2}{m} + 6}{\frac{1}{n}}$?

   Ⓕ $\dfrac{12n}{m}$
   Ⓖ $\dfrac{2n + 6mn}{m}$
   Ⓗ $\dfrac{6m + 2}{mn}$
   Ⓘ $\dfrac{m}{2n + 6mn}$

3. Which expression equals $\dfrac{4}{x^2 - 3x} + \dfrac{6}{3x - 9}$?

   Ⓐ $\dfrac{2(x + 2)}{x(x - 3)}$
   Ⓑ $\dfrac{10}{x^2 - 9}$
   Ⓒ $\dfrac{4x + 18}{3x(x - 3)}$
   Ⓓ $\dfrac{2}{x}$

4. The harmonic mean of two numbers a and b equals $\dfrac{2}{\frac{1}{a} + \frac{1}{b}}$. Which expression equals the harmonic mean of x and $x + 1$?

   Ⓕ $\dfrac{2}{x^2 + x}$
   Ⓖ $\dfrac{4x + 2}{x^2 + x}$
   Ⓗ $2x + 1$
   Ⓘ $\dfrac{2x^2 + 2x}{2x + 1}$

Short Response

5. Subtract $3 - \dfrac{1}{x^2 + 5}$. Write your answer in simplest form. State any restrictions on the variable. Show your work.

Name ______________________ Class ____________ Date ____________

8-6 Think About a Plan

Solving Rational Equations

Storage One pump can fill a tank with oil in 4 hours. A second pump can fill the same tank in 3 hours. If both pumps are used at the same time, how long will they take to fill the tank?

Understanding the Problem

1. How long does it take the first pump to fill the tank?

2. How long does it take the second pump to fill the tank?

3. What is the problem asking you to determine?

____

____

Planning the Solution

4. If V is the volume of the tank, what expressions represent the portion of the tank that each pump can fill in one hour?

First pump: [ ] Second pump: [ ]

5. What expression represents the part of the tank the two pumps can fill in one hour if they are used at the same time?

6. Let t be the number of hours. Write an equation to find the time it takes for the two pumps to fill one tank.

Getting an Answer

7. Solve your equation to find how long the pumps will take to fill the tank if both pumps are used at the same time.

Name ______________________ Class ____________ Date ____________

8-6 Practice

Solving Rational Equations

Form G

Solve each equation. Check each solution.

1. $\frac{x}{3} + \frac{x}{2} = 10$

2. $\frac{1}{x} - \frac{x}{9} = 0$

3. $-\frac{4}{x+1} = \frac{5}{3x+1}$

4. $\frac{4}{x} = \frac{x}{4}$

5. $\frac{3x}{4} = \frac{5x+1}{3}$

6. $\frac{3}{2x-3} = \frac{1}{5-2x}$

7. $\frac{x-4}{3} = \frac{x-2}{2}$

8. $\frac{2x-1}{x+3} = \frac{5}{3}$

9. $\frac{2y}{5} + \frac{2}{6} = \frac{y}{2} - \frac{1}{6}$

10. $\frac{1}{2x+2} + \frac{5}{x^2-1} = \frac{1}{x-1}$

11. $\frac{2}{x+3} + \frac{5}{3-x} = \frac{6}{x^2-9}$

12. An airplane flies from its home airport to a city 510 mi away and back. The total flying time for the round-trip flight is 3.9 h. The plane travels the first half of the trip at 255 mi/h with no wind.
    a. How strong is the wind on the return flight? Round your answer to the nearest tenth.
    b. Is the wind on the return flight a headwind or a tailwind?

Use a graphing calculator to solve each equation. Check each solution.

13. $\frac{x-1}{6} = \frac{x}{4}$

14. $\frac{x-2}{10} = \frac{x-7}{5}$

15. $\frac{4}{x+3} = \frac{10}{2x-1}$

16. $\frac{3}{3-x} = \frac{4}{2-x}$

17. $\frac{3y}{5} + \frac{1}{2} = \frac{y}{10}$

18. $5 - \frac{4}{x+1} = 6$

19. $\frac{2}{3} + \frac{3x-1}{6} = \frac{5}{2}$

20. $\frac{4}{x-1} = \frac{5}{x-2}$

21. $\frac{1}{x} - \frac{2}{x+3} = 0$

Solve each equation for the given variable.

22. $h = \frac{2A}{b}; b$

23. $\frac{1}{f} = \frac{1}{d_i} + \frac{1}{d_o}; d_o$

24. $\frac{h}{t} + 16t = v_o; h$

25. $m = \frac{y_2 - y_1}{x_2 - x_1}; x_1$

26. $\frac{xy}{z} + 2x = \frac{z}{y}; x$

27. $\frac{S - 2wh}{2w + 2h} = \ell; S$

8-6 Practice (continued)

Form G

Solving Rational Equations

28. One delivery driver can complete a route in 6 h. Another driver can complete the same route in 5 h.

a. Let *N* be the total number of deliveries on the route. Write expressions to represent the number of deliveries each driver can make in 1 hour.

b. Write an expression to represent the number of hours needed to make *N* deliveries if the drivers work together.

c. If the drivers work together, about how many hours will they take to complete the route? Round your answer to the nearest tenth.

29. A fountain has two drainage valves. With the first valve open, the fountain drains completely in 4 h. With only the second valve open, the fountain drains completely in 5.25 h. About how many hours will the fountain take to drain with both valves open? Round your answer to the nearest tenth.

30. A pen factory has two machines making pens. Together, the machines make 1500 pens during an 8-h shift. Machine A makes pens at 2.5 times the rate of Machine B. About how many hours would Machine A need to make 1500 pens by itself? Round your answer to the nearest tenth.

31. Error Analysis Describe and correct the error made in solving the equation.

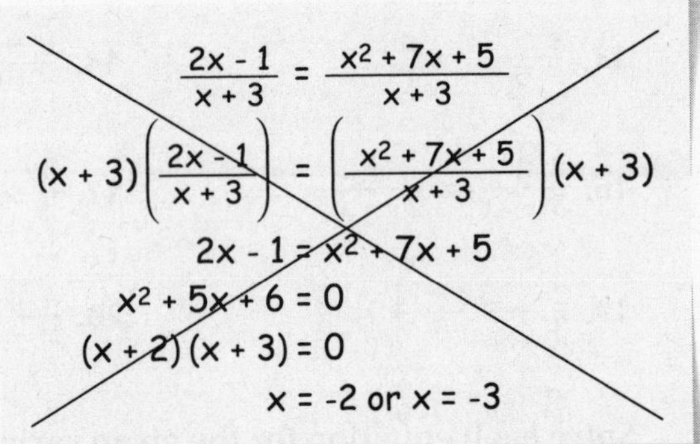

$\frac{2x - 1}{x + 3} = \frac{x^2 + 7x + 5}{x + 3}$
$(x + 3)\left(\frac{2x - 1}{x + 3}\right) = \left(\frac{x^2 + 7x + 5}{x + 3}\right)(x + 3)$
$2x - 1 = x^2 + 7x + 5$
$x^2 + 5x + 6 = 0$
$(x + 2)(x + 3) = 0$
$x = -2$ or $x = -3$

32. The formula $V = hH\left(\frac{b_1 + b_2}{6}\right)$ gives the volume of a pyramid with a trapezoidal base.

a. Solve this equation for b_2.

b. Find b_2 if $b_1 = 5$ cm, $h = 8$ cm, $H = 9$ cm, and $V = 216$ cm^3.

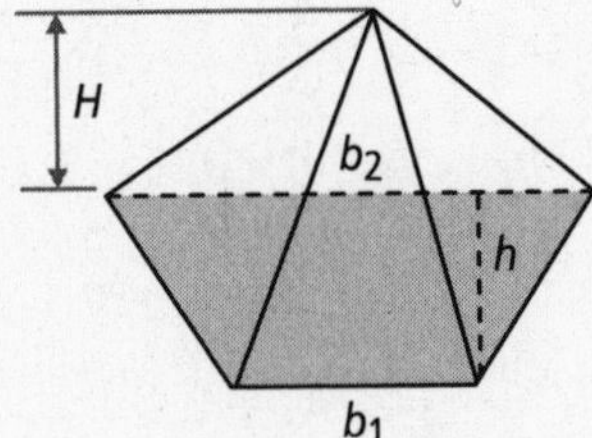

Name ______________________ Class ____________ Date ____________

8-6 Standardized Test Prep

Solving Rational Equations

Gridded Response

For Exercises 1–8, what are the solutions of each rational equation? Enter your answer in the grid provided. If necessary, enter your answer as a fraction.

1. $\frac{3-x}{6} = \frac{6-x}{12}$

2. $\frac{2}{6x+2} = \frac{x}{3x^2+11}$

3. $\frac{3}{2x-4} = \frac{5}{3x+7}$

4. $\frac{2}{x+2} + \frac{5}{x-2} = \frac{6}{x^2-4}$

5. $\frac{7}{x^2-5x} + \frac{2}{x} = \frac{3}{2x-10}$

6. $\frac{1}{4-5x} = \frac{3}{x+9}$

7. $\frac{7}{2} = \frac{7x}{8} - 4$

8. $4 + \frac{2y}{y-5} = \frac{8}{y-5}$

Answers

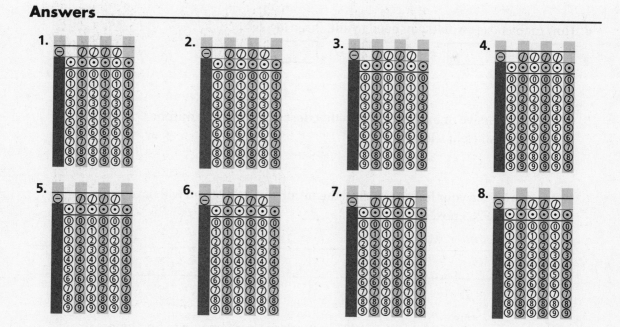

1. 

2. 

3. 

4. 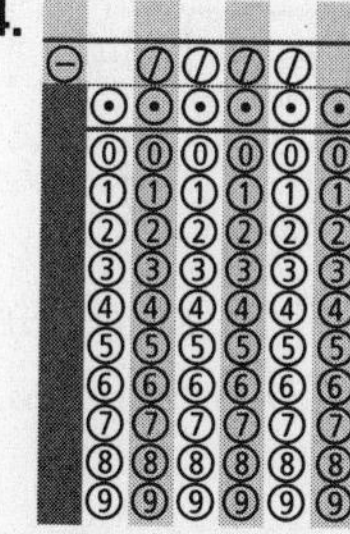

5. 

6. 

7. 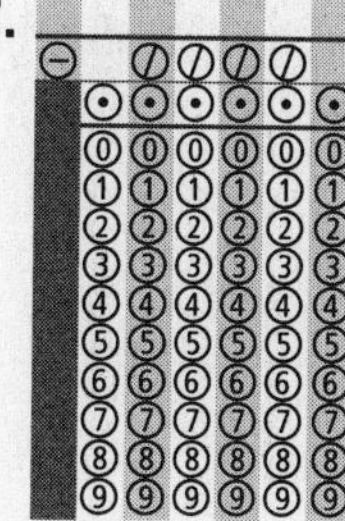

8.

Name ______________________ Class ____________ Date ____________

9-1 Think About a Plan

Mathematical Patterns

Geometry Suppose you are stacking boxes in levels that form squares. The numbers of boxes in successive levels form a sequence. The figure at the right shows the top four levels as viewed from above.

a. How many boxes of equal size would you need for the next lower level?

b. How many boxes of equal size would you need to add three levels?

c. Suppose you are stacking a total of 285 boxes. How many levels will you have?

1. How many boxes are in each of the first four levels?

Level 1: ☐ Level 2: ☐ Level 3: ☐ Level 4: ☐

2. How many boxes of equal size would you need for the next lower level?

3. What is a recursive or explicit formula that describes the number of boxes in the *n*th level?

4. How many boxes would you need to add three levels?

☐ + ☐ + ☐ = ☐

5. What is a recursive or explicit formula that describes the total number of boxes in a stack of *n* levels?

6. How can you use your formula to find the number of levels you will have with a stack of 285 boxes?

____

____.

7. Suppose you are stacking a total of 285 boxes. Use your formula to find how many levels you will have. Show your work.

8. You need ☐ levels to make a stack of 285 boxes.

Name ______________________ Class ____________ Date ____________

9-1 Practice

Form G

Mathematical Patterns

Find the first six terms of each sequence.

1. $a_n = -2n + 1$

2. $a_n = n^2 - 1$

3. $a_n = 2n^2 + 1$

4. $a_n = 1^n + 1$

5. $a_n = 2^n + 2$

6. $a_n = 2n^2 - n$

7. $a_n = 4n + n^2$

8. $a_n = \frac{1}{3}n^3$

9. $a_n = (-2)^n$

Write a recursive definition for each sequence.

10. $-14, -8, -2, 4, 10, \ldots$

11. $6, 5.7, 5.4, 5.1, 4.8, \ldots$

12. $1, -2, 4, -8, 16, \ldots$

13. $1, 3, 9, 27, \ldots$

14. $1, \frac{1}{2}, \frac{1}{4}, \frac{1}{8}, \frac{1}{16}, \ldots$

15. $\frac{2}{3}, 1, 1\frac{1}{3}, 1\frac{2}{3}, 2, \ldots$

16. $36, 39, 42, 45, 48, \ldots$

17. $36, 30, 24, 18, 12, \ldots$

18. $9.6, 4.8, 2.4, 1.2, 0.6, \ldots$

Write an explicit formula for each sequence. Find the twentieth term.

19. $7, 14, 21, 28, 35, \ldots$

20. $2, 8, 14, 20, 26, \ldots$

21. $5, 6, 7, 8, 9, \ldots$

22. $-1, 0, 1, 2, 3, \ldots$

23. $3, 5, 7, 9, 11, \ldots$

24. $0.8, 1.6, 2.4, 3.2, 4, \ldots$

25. $\frac{1}{4}, \frac{1}{2}, \frac{3}{4}, 1, \frac{5}{4}, \ldots$

26. $\frac{1}{2}, \frac{1}{4}, \frac{1}{6}, \frac{1}{8}, \frac{1}{10}, \ldots$

27. $\frac{2}{3}, 1\frac{2}{3}, 2\frac{2}{3}, 3\frac{2}{3}, 4\frac{2}{3}, \ldots$

Find the eighth term of each sequence.

28. $1, 3, 5, 7, 9, \ldots$

29. $400, 200, 100, 50, 25, \ldots$

30. $0, -2, -4, -6, -8, \ldots$

31. $1, 2, 4, 8, 16, \ldots$

32. $44, 39, 34, 29, 24, \ldots$

33. $0.7, 0.8, 0.9, 1.0, 1.1, \ldots$

34. $4, 11, 18, 25, 32, \ldots$

35. $1\frac{1}{4}, 2\frac{1}{2}, 5, 10, 20, \ldots$

36. $-6, -9, -12, -15, -18, \ldots$

37. A man swims 1.5 mi on Monday, 1.6 mi on Tuesday, 1.8 mi on Wednesday, 2.1 mi on Thursday, and 2.5 mi on Friday. If the pattern continues, how many miles will he swim on Saturday?

Name ______________________ Class ____________ Date ____________

9-1 Practice (continued)

Form G

Mathematical Patterns

Determine whether each formula is *explicit* or *recursive*. Then find the first five terms of each sequence.

38. $a_n = \frac{1}{3}n$

39. $a_n = n^2 - 6$

40. $a_1 = 5, a_n = 3a_{n-1} - 7$

41. $a_n = \frac{1}{2}(n - 1)$

42. $a_1 = 5, a_n = 3 - a_{n-1}$

43. $a_1 = -4, a_n = 2a_{n-1}$

44. Error Analysis Your friend says the explicit formula for the sequence 1, 8, 27, 64 is $a_n = n^2$. Is she correct? Explain.

45. Writing Explain how to find an explicit formula for a sequence.

46. The first figure of a fractal contains one segment. For each successive figure, six segments replace each segment.

a. How many segments are in each of the first four figures of the sequence?

b. Write a recursive definition for the sequence.

47. The sum of the measures of the exterior angles of any polygon is 360°. All the angles have the same measure in a regular polygon.

a. Find the measure of one exterior angle in a regular hexagon (six angles).

b. Write an explicit formula for the measure of one exterior angle in a regular polygon with n angles.

c. Why would this formula not be meaningful for $n = 1$ or $n = 2$?

48. Reasoning In order to find a term in a sequence, its position in the sequence is doubled and then two is added. What are the first ten terms in the sequence?

49. Writing Explain the difference between a recursive and an explicit formula.

50. Open-Ended Write five terms in a sequence. Describe the sequence using a recursive or explicit formula.

Name ______________________ Class ____________ Date ____________

9-1 Standardized Test Prep

Mathematical Patterns

Multiple Choice

For Exercises 1–6, choose the correct letter.

1. What are the first five terms of the sequence?

$$a_n = 3^n - 1$$

(A) 2, 5, 8, 11, 14
(B) 3, 9, 27, 81, 243
(C) 2, 8, 26, 80, 242
(D) 2, 4, 8, 16, 32

2. The formula $a_n = 3n + 2$ best represents which sequence?

(F) 3, 6, 9, 12, 15
(G) 5, 8, 11, 14, 17
(H) 4, 7, 10, 13, 16
(I) 5, 9, 29, 83, 245

3. Which pattern can be represented by $a_n = n^2 - 3$?

(A) −1, 0, 5, 12, 21 (B) 4, 7, 12, 19, 28 (C) 1, 4, 9, 16, 25 (D) −2, 1, 6, 13, 22

4. The sequence 4, 16, 36, 64, 100, . . . can best be represented by which formula?

(F) $a_n = 4n$ (G) $a_n = 4n^2$ (H) $a_n = 4n^3$ (I) $a_n = 2n^4$

5. For the sequence 0, 6, 16, 30, 48, . . . , what is the 40th term?

(A) 3198 (B) 3200 (C) 4000 (D) 16,000

6. A student sets up a savings plan to transfer money from his checking account to his savings account. The first week \$10 is transferred, the second week \$12 is transferred, the third week \$16 is transferred, and the fourth week \$24 is transferred. If this pattern continues and he starts with \$100 in his checking account, how many weeks will pass before his balance is zero?

(F) 4 (G) 5 (H) 6 (I) 7

Short Response

7. After training for and running a marathon, an athlete wants to reduce her daily run by half each day. The marathon is about 26 mi. How many days will it take after the marathon before she runs less than a mile a day? Show your work.

Name ______________________ Class ____________ Date ____________

9-2 Think About a Plan

Arithmetic Sequences

Transportation Suppose a trolley stops at a certain intersection every 14 min. The first trolley of the day gets to the stop at 6:43 A.M. How long do you have to wait for a trolley if you get to the stop at 8:15 A.M.? At 3:20 P.M.?

Know

1. If you define 12:00 A.M. as minute 0, then 6:43 A.M. is [ ] from 0.

2. 8:15 A.M. is [ ] from 0 and 3:20 P.M. is [ ] from 0.

3. The trolley stops every [ ].

Need

4. To solve the problem I need to find:

____

____.

Plan

5. What is an explicit formula for the number of minutes after 12:00 A.M. that the trolley gets to the stop?

6. Use your formula to find the smallest n that gives the minutes just after 8:15 A.M. that the trolley arrives at the stop.

7. Using this n in your formula, when does the trolley stop? How long do you have to wait for this trolley?

8. Use your formula to find the smallest n that gives the minutes just after 3:20 P.M. that the trolley arrives at the stop.

9. Using this n in your formula, when does the trolley stop? How long do you have to wait for this trolley?

Name ______________________ Class ____________ Date ____________

9-2 Practice

Form G

Arithmetic Sequences

Determine whether each sequence is arithmetic. If so, identify the common difference.

1. 2, 3, 5, 8, . . .

2. 0, −3, −6, −9, . . .

3. 0.9, 0.5, 0.1, −0.3, . . .

4. 3, 8, 13, 18, . . .

5. 14, −15, −44, −73, . . .

6. 3.2, 3.5, 3.8, 4.1, . . .

7. −34, −28, −22, −16, . . .

8. 2.3, 2.5, 2.7, 2.9, . . .

9. 127, 140, 153, 166, . . .

10. 11, 13, 17, 25, . . .

Find the 43rd term of each sequence.

11. 12, 14, 16, 18, . . .

12. 13.1, 3.1, −6.9, −16.9, . . .

13. 19.5, 19.9, 20.3, 20.7, . . .

14. 27, 24, 21, 18, . . .

15. 2, 13, 24, 35, . . .

16. 21, 15, 9, 3, . . .

17. 1.3, 1.4, 1.5, 1.6, . . .

18. −2.1, −2.3, −2.5, −2.7, . . .

19. 45, 48, 51, 54, . . .

20. −0.073, −0.081, −0.089, . . .

Find the missing term of each arithmetic sequence.

21. . . . 23, ■, 49, . . .

22. 14, ■, 28, . . .

23. . . . 29, ■, 33, . . .

24. . . . 14, ■, 15, . . .

25. . . . −45, ■, −39, . . .

26. . . . −5, ■, −2, . . .

27. −2, ■, 2, . . .

28. . . . −6, ■, 2, . . .

29. −34, ■, 77, . . .

30. . . . −45, ■, −12, . . .

31. −2, ■, 456, . . .

32. . . . 34, ■, 345, . . .

33. A teacher donates the same amount of money each year to help protect the rainforest. At the end of the second year, she has donated enough money to protect 8 acres. At the end of the third year, she has donated enough money to protect 12 acres. How many acres will the teacher's donations protect at the end of the tenth year?

34. Writing Explain how you know that the sequence 109, 105, 101, 97, 93, . . . is arithmetic.

Name ______________________ Class ____________ Date ____________

9-2 Practice (continued)

Form G

Arithmetic Sequences

Find the arithmetic mean a_n of the given terms.

35. $a_{n-1} = 5, a_{n+1} = 11$

36. $a_{n-1} = 17, a_{n+1} = 3$

37. $a_{n-1} = -8, a_{n+1} = -9$

38. $a_{n-1} = -0.6, a_{n+1} = 3.8$

39. $a_{n-1} = y - z, a_{n+1} = y$

40. $a_{n-1} = 2t + 3, a_{n+1} = 4t - 1$

41. Open-Ended Write an arithmetic sequence of at least five terms with a positive common difference.

42. Error Analysis On your homework, you write that the missing term in the arithmetic sequence 31, ___, 41, . . . is $35\frac{1}{2}$. Your friend says the missing term is 36. Who is correct? What mistake was made?

43. Reasoning Explain why 84 is the missing term in the sequence 89, 86.5, ___, 81.5, ...

44. Writing Describe the general process of finding a missing term in an arithmetic sequence.

45. You are making an arrangement of cubes in concentric rings for a sculpture. The number of cubes in each ring follows the pattern below.

1, 9, 17, 25, 33, . . .

a. Is this an arithmetic sequence? Explain.
b. What are the next three terms?
c. If the sequence continues to the 100th term in this pattern, what will that term be?

46. Each year, a volunteer organization expects to add 5 more people to the number of shut-ins for whom the group provides home maintenance services. This year, the organization provides the service for 32 people.

a. Write a recursive formula for the number of people the organization expects to serve each year.
b. Write the first five terms of the sequence.
c. Write an explicit formula for the number of people the organization expects to serve each year.
d. How many people would the organization expect to serve in the 20th year?

Name ______________________ Class ____________ Date ____________

9-2 Standardized Test Prep

Arithmetic Sequences

Multiple Choice

For Exercises 1–6, choose the correct letter.

1. Which sequence is an arithmetic sequence?

(A) 7, 10, 13, 16, 19, . . .

(B) 7, 8, 10, 13, 17, . . .

(C) 7, 14, 28, 56, 112, . . .

(D) 1, 7, 14, 22, 31, 41, . . .

2. An arithmetic sequence begins 4, 9, ... What is the 20th term?

(F) 76 (G) 80 (H) 84 (I) 99

3. What are the missing terms of the arithmetic sequence 5, __, __, 62, . . . ?

(A) 19, 24 (B) 19, 34 (C) 24, 43 (D) 43, 62

4. What is the missing term of the arithmetic sequence 25, __, 45, . . . ?

(F) 30 (G) 35 (H) 37 (I) 40

5. The seventh and ninth terms of an arithmetic sequence are 197 and 173. What is the eighth term?

(A) 161 (B) 180 (C) 185 (D) 221

6. An artist is creating a tile mosaic. She uses 4 green tiles in the first row, 11 green tiles in the second row, 18 green tiles in the third row, and 25 green tiles in the fourth row. If she continues the pattern, how many green tiles will she use in the 20th row?

(F) 32 (G) 58 (H) 134 (I) 137

Extended Response

7. What is the 100th term in the arithmetic sequence beginning with 3, 19, . . . ? Show your work.

Name ______________________ Class ____________ Date ____________

9-3 Think About a Plan

Geometric Sequences

Athletics During your first week of training for a marathon, you run a total of 10 miles. You increase the distance you run each week by twenty percent. How many miles do you run during your twelfth week of training?

Understanding the Problem

1. How can you write a sequence of numbers to represent this situation?

____

____.

2. Is the sequence arithmetic, geometric, or neither? ____________________

3. What is the first term of the sequence?

4. What is the common ratio of the sequence?

5. What is the problem asking you to determine?

____

____

Planning the Solution

6. Write a formula for the sequence.

Getting an Answer

7. Evaluate your formula to find the number of miles you run during your twelfth week of training.

Name ______________________ Class ____________ Date ____________

9-3 Practice

Form G

Geometric Sequences

Determine whether each sequence is geometric. If so, find the common ratio.

1. 3, 9, 27, 81, . . .

2. 4, 8, 16, 32, . . .

3. 4, 8, 12, 16, . . .

4. 4, −8, 16, −32, . . .

5. 1, 0.5, 0.25, 0.125, . . .

6. 100, 30, 9, 2.7, . . .

7. −5, 0, 5, 10, . . .

8. 64, −32, 16, −8, . . .

9. 1, 4, 9, 16, . . .

Find the tenth term of each geometric sequence.

10. 2, 4, 8, . . .

11. 1, 3, 9, . . .

12. −2, 6, −18, . . .

13. −3, 9, −27, . . .

14. −3, −12, −48, . . .

15. −5, 25, −125, . . .

16. $\frac{1}{3}, \frac{1}{9}, \frac{1}{27}, \ldots$

17. 0.3, 0.6, 1.2, . . .

18. $\frac{1}{4}, \frac{1}{2}, 1, \ldots$

19. When a pendulum swings freely, the length of its arc decreases geometrically. Find each missing arc length.

a. 20th arc is 20 in.; 22nd arc is 18.5 in.

b. 8th arc is 27 mm; 10th arc is 3 mm

c. 5th arc is 25 cm; 7th arc is 1 cm

d. 100th arc is 18 ft; 98th arc is 2 ft

Find the missing term of each geometric sequence. It could be the geometric mean or its opposite.

20. 4, ■, 16, . . .

21. 9, ■, 16, . . .

22. 2, ■, 8, . . .

23. 3, ■, 12, . . .

24. 2, ■, 50, . . .

25. 4, ■, 5.76, . . .

26. 625, ■, 25, . . .

27. $\frac{1}{3}$, ■, 3, . . .

28. 0.5, ■, 0.125, . . .

29. Writing Explain how you know that the sequence 400, 200, 100, 50 is geometric.

30. Open-Ended Write a geometric sequence of at least seven terms.

31. Error Analysis A student says that the geometric sequence 30, __, 120 can be completed with 90. Is she correct? Explain.

Name ______________________ Class ____________ Date ____________

9-3 Practice (continued) — Form G

Geometric Sequences

Identify each sequence as *arithmetic, geometric,* or *neither*. Then find the next two terms.

32. $9, 3, 1, \frac{1}{3}, \ldots$

33. $1, 0, -2, -5, \ldots$

34. $2, -2, 2, -2, \ldots$

35. $-3, 2, 7, 12, \ldots$

36. $1, -2, -5, -8, \ldots$

37. $1, -2, 3, -4, \ldots$

Write an explicit formula for each sequence. Then generate the first five terms.

38. $a_1 = 3, r = -2$

39. $a_1 = 5, r = 3$

40. $a_1 = -1, r = 4$

41. $a_1 = -2, r = -3$

42. $a_1 = 32, r = -0.5$

43. $a_1 = 2187, r = \frac{1}{3}$

44. $a_1 = 9, r = 2$

45. $a_1 = -4, r = 4$

46. $a_1 = 0.1, r = -2$

47. The deer population in an area is increasing. This year, the population was 1.025 times last year's population of 2537.

a. Assuming that the population increases at the same rate for the next few years, write an explicit formula for the sequence.

b. Find the expected deer population for the fourth year of the sequence.

48. You enlarge the dimensions of a picture to 150% several times. After the first increase, the picture is 1 in. wide.

a. Write an explicit formula to model the width after each increase.

b. How wide is the photo after the 2nd increase?

c. How wide is the photo after the 3rd increase?

d. How wide is the photo after the 12th increase?

Find the missing terms of each geometric sequence. (*Hint:* The geometric mean of positive first and fifth terms is the third term. Some terms might be negative.)

49. 12, ■, ■, ■, 0.75

50. −9, ■, ■, ■, −2304

For the geometric sequence 6, 18, 54, 162, . . . , find the indicated term.

51. 6th term

52. 19th term

53. *n*th term

Name ______________________ Class ____________ Date ____________

9-3 Standardized Test Prep

Geometric Sequences

Multiple Choice

For Exercises 1–6, choose the correct letter.

1. What is the 10th term of the geometric sequence 1, 4, 16, . . .?

Ⓐ 40 Ⓑ 180,224 Ⓒ 262,144 Ⓓ 2,883,584

2. Which sequence is a geometric sequence?

Ⓕ 1, 3, 5, 7, 9, . . .

Ⓗ 2, 4, 8, 16, 32, . . .

Ⓖ 12, 9, 6, 3, 0, . . .

Ⓘ −2, −6, −10, −14, −18, . . .

3. Which could be the missing term of the geometric sequence 5, __, 125, . . .?

Ⓐ 25 Ⓑ 50 Ⓒ 75 Ⓓ 100

4. What could be the missing term of the geometric sequence −12, __, $-\frac{3}{4}$, . . .?

Ⓕ −4 Ⓖ −6.375 Ⓗ 3 Ⓘ 4

5. In the explicit formula for the 9th term of the geometric sequence 1, 6, 36, . . . what number is *a*?

Ⓐ 1 Ⓑ 6 Ⓒ 36 Ⓓ 1,679,616

6. In each successive round of a backgammon tournament, the number of players decreases by half. If the tournament starts with 32 players, which rule could predict the number of players in the *n*th round?

Ⓕ $32 = (0.5)^n$ Ⓖ $32 = 0.5r^{n-1}$ Ⓗ $a_n = 15^{n-1}$ Ⓘ $a_n = (32)(0.5)^{n-1}$

Short Response

7. What is the 6th term of the geometric sequence 100, 50, . . .? Show your work using the explicit formula.

Name ______________________ Class ____________ Date ____________

9-4 Think About a Plan

Arithmetic Series

Architecture In a 20-row theater, the number of seats in a row increases by three with each successive row. The first row has 18 seats.

a. Write an arithmetic series to represent the number of seats in the theater.

b. Find the total seating capacity of the theater.

c. Front-row tickets for a concert cost \$60. After every 5 rows, the ticket price goes down by \$5. What is the total amount of money generated by a full house?

1. Write the explicit formula for an arithmetic sequence.

2. What are a_1 and d for the sequence that represents the number of seats in each row?

$a_1 =$ ☐ $d =$ ☐

3. Write an explicit formula for the arithmetic sequence that represents the number of seats in each row.

4. Write an arithmetic series to represent the number of seats in the theater.

5. How can you use a graphing calculator to evaluate the series?

____

____.

6. Find the total seating capacity of the theater.

7. Write a series for the number of seats in each set of 5 rows.

8. Use your graphing calculator to evaluate each series. ____________________

9. What are the ticket prices for each set of 5 rows? ____________________

10. What is the total amount of money generated by a full house?

Name ______________________ Class ____________ Date ____________

9-4 Practice

Form G

Arithmetic Series

Find the sum of each finite arithmetic series.

1. $1 + 3 + 5 + 7 + 9$

2. $5 + 8 + 11 + \cdots + 26$

3. $4 + 9 + 14 + \cdots + 44$

4. $(-10) + (-25) + (-40) + \cdots + (-85)$

5. $17 + 25 + 33 + \cdots + 65$

6. $125 + 126 + 127 + \cdots + 131$

7. A bookshelf has 7 shelves of different widths. Each shelf is narrower than the shelf below it. The bottom three shelves are 36 in., 31 in., and 26 in. wide.

a. The shelf widths decrease by the same amount from bottom to top. What is the width of the top shelf?

b. What is the total shelf space of all seven shelves?

Write each arithmetic series in summation notation.

8. $4 + 8 + 12 + 16$

9. $10 + 7 + 4 + \cdots + (-5)$

10. $1 + 3 + 5 + \cdots + 13$

11. $3 + 7 + 11 + \cdots + 31$

12. $(-20) + (-25) + (-30) + \cdots + (-65)$

13. $15 + 25 + 35 + \cdots + 75$

Find the sum of each finite series.

14. $\sum_{n=1}^{4} (n - 1)$

15. $\sum_{n=2}^{6} (2n - 1)$

16. $\sum_{n=3}^{8} (n + 25)$

17. $\sum_{n=2}^{5} (5n + 3)$

18. $\sum_{n=1}^{4} (2n + 0.5)$

19. $\sum_{n=1}^{6} (3 - n)$

20. $\sum_{n=5}^{10} n$

21. $\sum_{n=1}^{4} (-n - 3)$

22. $\sum_{n=3}^{6} (3n + 2)$

Use a graphing calculator to find the sum of each series.

23. $\sum_{n=1}^{15} (n + 3)$

24. $\sum_{n=1}^{12} (2n - 1)$

25. $\sum_{n=1}^{20} 2n^2$

26. $\sum_{n=1}^{25} (n^3 + 2n)$

27. $\sum_{n=1}^{50} (n^2 - 4n)$

28. $\sum_{n=5}^{25} (5n^3 + 3n)$

Name ______________________ Class ____________ Date ____________

9-4 Practice (continued) — Form G

Arithmetic Series

Determine whether each list is a *sequence* or a *series* and *finite* or *infinite*.

29. 7, 12, 17, 22, 27

30. $3 + 5 + 7 + 9 + \ldots$

31. 8, 8.2, 8.4, 8.6, 8.8, 9.0, . . .

32. $1 + 5 + 9 + \cdots + 21$

33. 40, 20, 10, 5, 2.5, 1.25, . . .

34. $10 + 20 + 30 + 40 + 50$

35. An embroidery pattern calls for five stitches in the first row and for three more stitches in each successive row. The 25th row, which is the last row, has 77 stitches. Find the total number of stitches in the pattern.

36. A marching band formation consists of 6 rows. The first row has 9 musicians, the second has 11, the third has 13 and so on. How many musicians are in the last row and how many musicians are there in all?

37. Writing Explain how you can identify the difference between a series and a sequence.

38. a. Open-Ended Write three explicit formulas for arithmetic sequences.

b. Write the first seven terms of each related series.

c. Use summation notation to rewrite the series.

d. Evaluate each series.

39. Error Analysis A student identifies the series $10 + 15 + 20 + 25 + 30$ as an infinite arithmetic series. Is he correct? Explain.

40. Mental Math Use mental math to evaluate $\sum_{1}^{3}(2n + 1)$.

41. To train new employees, an employer offers a bonus after 30 work days as follows. An employee must turn in one report on the first day; the number of reports for each subsequent day must increase by two. What is the minimum number of reports an employee will have to turn in over the 30 days to earn the bonus?

Name ______________________ Class ____________ Date ____________

9-4 Standardized Test Prep

Arithmetic Series

Multiple Choice

For Exercises 1–6, choose the correct letter.

1. What is the sum of the odd integers 1 to 99?

Ⓐ 2450 Ⓑ 2500 Ⓒ 2550 Ⓓ 4950

2. Which of the following is an infinite series?

Ⓕ 3, 8, 13, 18, 23

Ⓖ $3 + 8 + 13 + 18 + 23$

Ⓗ $3 + 8 + 13 + 18 + 23 + \dots$

Ⓘ 3, 8, 13, 18, 23, . . .

3. The high school choir is participating in a fundraising sales contest. The choir will receive a bonus if they make 20 sales in their first week and improve their sales by 3 in every subsequent week. What is the minimum number of sales the choir could make in the first 12 weeks to qualify for the bonus?

Ⓐ 13 Ⓑ 53 Ⓒ 438 Ⓓ 5015

4. What is summation notation for the series $5 + 7 + 9 + \cdots + 105$?

Ⓕ $\sum_{n=1}^{51}(2n + 3)$ Ⓖ $\sum_{n=1}^{51}(n + 3)$ Ⓗ $\sum_{n=1}^{50}(2n + 3)$ Ⓘ $\sum_{n=7}^{51}(n + 3)$

5. What is the upper limit of the summation $\sum_{n=1}^{100}(n - 2)$?

Ⓐ 1 Ⓑ 2 Ⓒ 98 Ⓓ 100

6. What is the sum of the series $\sum_{n=1}^{30}(2n + 2)$?

Ⓕ 62 Ⓖ 66 Ⓗ 990 Ⓘ 1980

Short Response

7. What is the sum of the finite arithmetic series $2 + 4 + 6 + \cdots + 50$? Show your work.

Name ______________________ Class ____________ Date ____________

9-5 Think About a Plan

Geometric Series

Communications Many companies use a telephone chain to notify employees of a closing due to bad weather. Suppose a company's CEO calls three people. Then each of these people calls three others, and so on.

a. Make a diagram to show the first three stages in the telephone chain. How many calls are made at each stage?

b. Write the series that represents the total number of calls made through the first six stages.

c. How many employees have been notified after stage six?

1. What type of diagram can you make to represent the telephone chain? ____________

2. Make a diagram to show the first three stages in the telephone chain.

3. What expression represents the number of calls made at stage n?

4. Write the series that represents the total number of calls made through the first six stages. ______________________

5. What is the sum of this series?

6. Write the sum formula.

7. Use the sum formula to find how many employees have been notified after stage six.

8. Does your answer agree with your sum from Exercise 5?

Name ______________________ Class ____________ Date ____________

9-5 Practice

Form G

Geometric Series

Evaluate each finite series for the specified number of terms.

1. $40 + 20 + 10 + \ldots; n = 10$

2. $4 + 12 + 36 + \ldots; n = 15$

3. $15 + 12 + 9.6 + \ldots; n = 40$

4. $27 + 9 + 3 + \ldots; n = 100$

5. $0.2 + 0.02 + 0.002 + \ldots; n = 8$

6. $100 + 200 + 400 + \ldots; n = 6$

7. This month, your friend deposits $400 to save for a vacation. She plans to deposit 10% more each successive month for the next 11 months. How much will she have saved after the 12 deposits?

Determine whether each infinite geometric series *diverges* or *converges.* State whether each series has a sum.

8. $3 + \frac{3}{2} + \frac{3}{4} + \ldots$

9. $4 + 2 + 1 + \ldots$

10. $17 + 15.3 + 13.77 + \ldots$

11. $6 + 11.4 + 21.66 + \ldots$

12. $-20 - 8 - 3.2 - \ldots$

13. $50 + 70 + 98 + \ldots$

Evaluate each infinite geometric series.

14. $8 + 4 + 2 + 1 + \ldots$

15. $1 + \frac{1}{3} + \frac{1}{9} + \frac{1}{27} + \ldots$

16. $120 + 96 + 76.8 + 61.44 + \ldots$

17. $1000 + 750 + 562.5 + 421.875 + \ldots$

18. Suppose your business made a profit of $5500 the first year. If the profit increased 20% per year, find the total profit over the first 5 yr.

19. The end of a pendulum travels 50 cm on its first swing. Each swing after the first, it travels 99% as far as the preceding swing. How far will the pendulum travel before it stops?

20. A seashell has chambers that are each 0.82 times the length of the enclosing chamber. The outer chamber is 32 mm around. Find the total length of the shell's spiraled chambers.

21. The first year a toy manufacturer introduces a new toy, its sales total $495,000. The company expects its sales to drop 10% each succeeding year. Find the total expected sales in the first 6 years. Find the total expected sales if the company offers the toy for sale for as long as anyone buys it.

Name ______________________ Class ____________ Date ____________

9-5 Practice (continued)

Form G

Geometric Series

Determine whether each series is *arithmetic* or *geometric*. Then evaluate the series for the specified number of terms.

22. $2 + 5 + 8 + 11 + \ldots; n = 9$

23. $\frac{1}{8} + \frac{1}{16} + \frac{1}{32} + \frac{1}{64} + \ldots; n = 8$

24. $-3 + 6 - 12 + 24 - \ldots; n = 10$

25. $-2 + 2 + 6 + 10 + \ldots; n = 12$

26. $4 + 8 + 16 + 32 + \ldots; n = 15$

27. $5 + 10 + 15 + 20 + \ldots; n = 20$

Evaluate each infinite series that has a sum.

28. $\sum_{n=1}^{\infty} 5\left(\frac{2}{3}\right)^{n-1}$

29. $\sum_{n=1}^{\infty} (-2.1)^{n-1}$

30. $\sum_{n=1}^{\infty} \left(-\frac{1}{2}\right)^{n-1}$

31. $\sum_{n=1}^{\infty} 2\left(\frac{5}{3}\right)^{n-1}$

32. Open Ended Write an infinite geometric series that converges to 2. Show your work.

Find the specified value for each infinite geometric series.

33. $a_1 = 5$, $S = \frac{25}{3}$, find r

34. $S = 108$, $r = \frac{1}{3}$, find a_1

35. $a_1 = 3$, $S = 12$, find r

36. $S = 840$, $r = 0.5$, find a_1

37. Error Analysis Your friend says that an infinite geometric series cannot have a sum because it's infinite. You say that it is possible for an infinite geometric series to have a sum. Who is correct? Explain.

38. Writing Describe in general terms how you would find the sum of a finite geometric series.

Name ______________________ Class ____________ Date ____________

9-5 Standardized Test Prep

Geometric Series

Gridded Response

Solve each exercise and enter your answer in the grid provided.

1. What is the value of a_1 in the series $\sum_{n=0}^{20} 3\left(\frac{1}{2}\right)^n$?

2. What is the sum of the geometric series $2 + 6 + 18 + \cdots + 486$?

3. A community organizes a phone tree in order to alert each family of emergencies. In the first stage, one person calls five families. In the second stage, each of the five families calls another five families, and so on. How many stages need to be reached before 600 families or more are called?

4. What is the approximate whole number sum for the finite geometric series $\sum_{n=0}^{5} 8\left(\frac{1}{4}\right)^n$?

5. What is the sum of the geometric series $1 + \frac{1}{3} + \frac{1}{9} + \ldots$? Enter your answer as a fraction.

Answers

1.

2.

3.

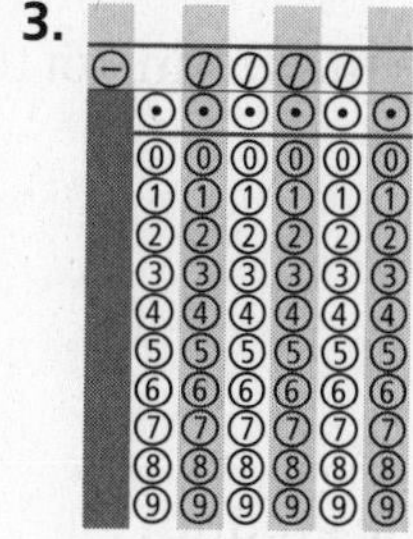

4.

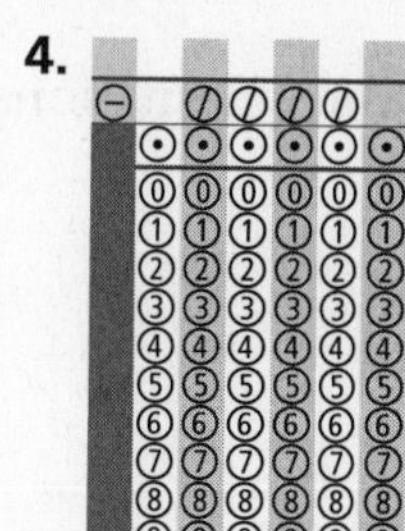

5.

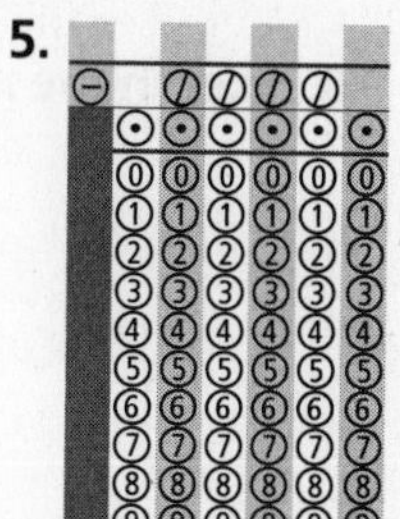

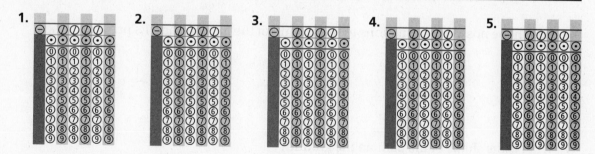

Name ______________________ Class ____________ Date ____________

10-1 Think About a Plan

Exploring Conic Sections

Sound An airplane flying faster than the speed of sound creates a cone-shaped pressure disturbance in the air. This is heard by people on the ground as a sonic boom. What is the shape of the path on the ground?

Know

1. The pressure disturbance is shaped like a ______.

2. The ground near the airplane is shaped like a ______.

Need

3. To solve the problem I need to find:

____

____.

Plan

4. How can a drawing or model help you solve this problem?

____

____.

5. Is there only one possible path on the ground? Explain.

____

____.

6. Sketch the possible orientations to the ground of the airplane and its pressure cone.

7. What is the shape of the path on the ground?

____

____.

Name ______________________ Class ____________ Date ____________

10-1 Practice

Form G

Exploring Conic Sections

Graph each equation. Identify the conic section and describe the graph and its lines of symmetry. Then find the domain and range.

1. $9x^2 + 4y^2 = 36$

2. $x^2 - y^2 = 4$

3. $8x^2 + 8y^2 = 40$

Identify the center and intercepts of each conic section. Give the domain and range of each graph. (On graphing calculator screens, each interval represents two units.)

4.

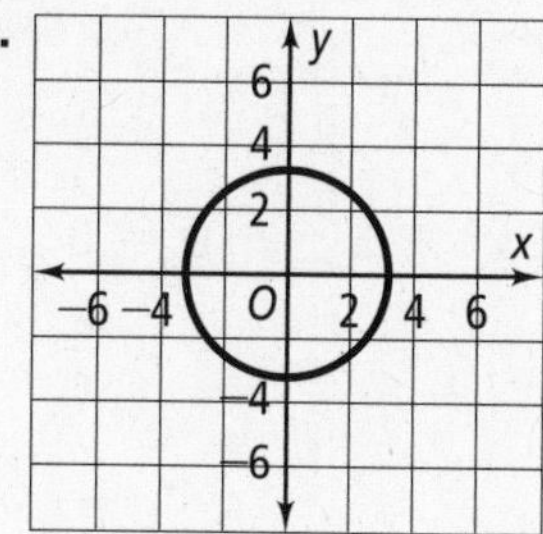

5.

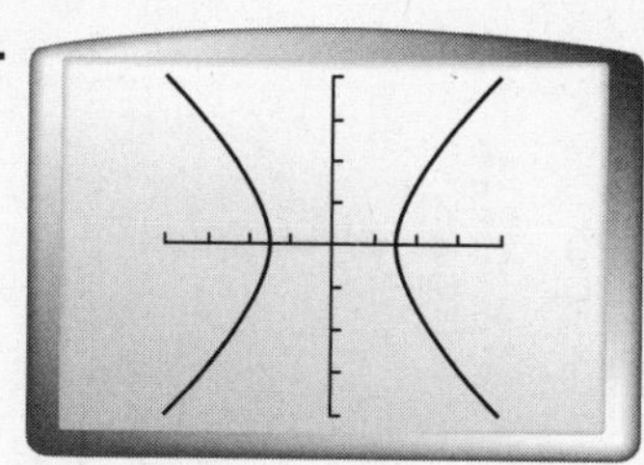

6.

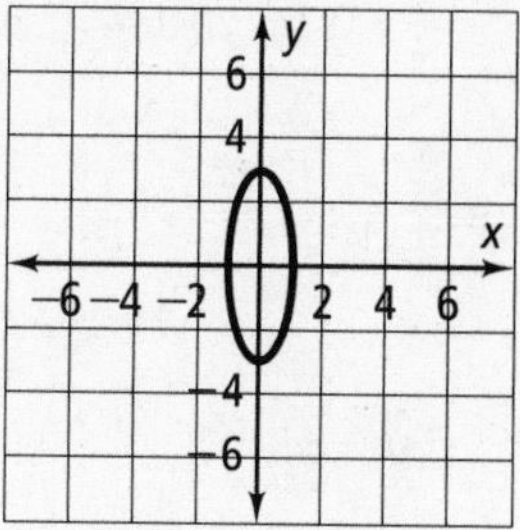

7.

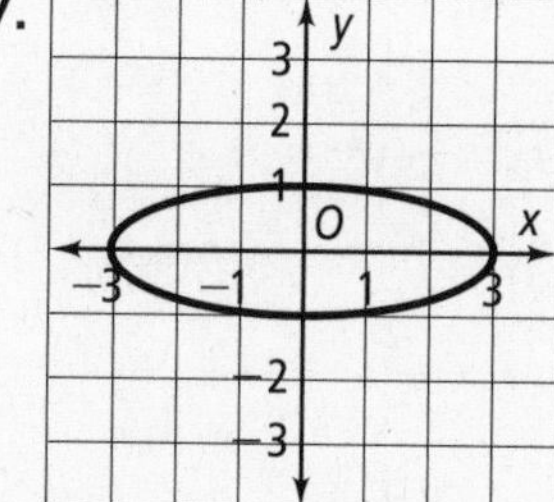

8.

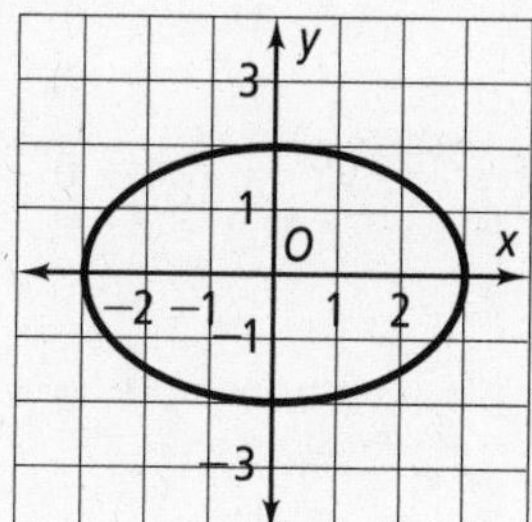

9.

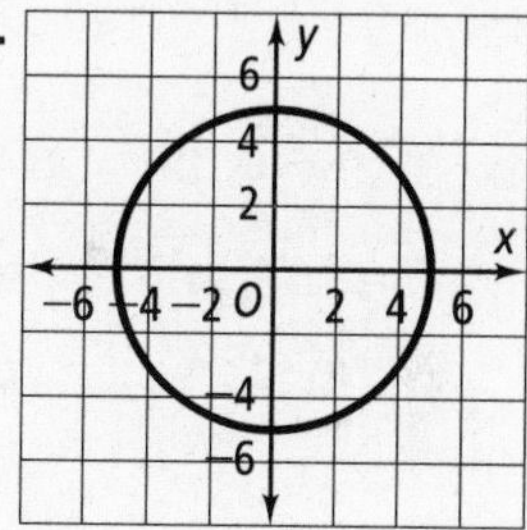

Match each equation with a graph in Exercises 4–9.

10. $x^2 + 9y^2 = 9$

11. $x^2 + y^2 = 25$

12. $9x^2 + y^2 = 9$

13. $x^2 + y^2 = 9$

14. $4x^2 + 9y^2 = 36$

15. $x^2 - y^2 = 9$

Name ______________________ Class ____________ Date ____________

10-1 Practice (continued) Form G

Exploring Conic Sections

Graph each equation. Describe the graph and its lines of symmetry. Then find the domain and range.

16. $25x^2 - y^2 - 25 = 0$

17. $y^2 - x^2 = 9$

18. $4y^2 - 9x^2 = 36$

19. $x^2 + y^2 = 4$

20. $x^2 + y^2 = 36$

21. $3x^2 + 3y^2 - 9 = 0$

22. $4x^2 + 9y^2 - 36 = 0$

23. $6x^2 + y^2 - 12 = 0$

24. $9x^2 + y^2 = 9$

25. Error Analysis One student identifies four types of conic sections. Another says there are only three types (hyperbola, circle, and ellipse). Who is correct? Explain how conic sections are found.

Mental Math Each given point is on the graph of the given equation. Use symmetry to find at least one more point on the graph.

26. $(1, 2)$; $y^2 = 4x$

27. $(2, 0)$; $x^2 + y^2 - 4 = 0$

28. $(0, -3)$; $x^2 + 2y^2 = 18$

29. $(-1, 0)$; $4x^2 + 4y^2 = 4$

30. Reasoning A student wants to graph a circle with the equation $x^2 + y^2 = 25$. What points could he use to determine a sketch of the graph?

Name ______________________ Class ____________ Date ____________

10-1 Standardized Test Prep

Exploring Conic Sections

Multiple Choice

For Exercises 1–6, choose the correct letter.

1. What shape is the conic section $x^2 + y^2 = 16$?

(A) circle (B) ellipse (C) parabola (D) hyperbola

2. Which line is not a line of symmetry for $x^2 + y^2 = 25$?

(F) $y = x$ (H) $y = x + 2$

(G) $2y = 3x$ (I) $3y = 3x$

3. Which equation represents the graph at the right?

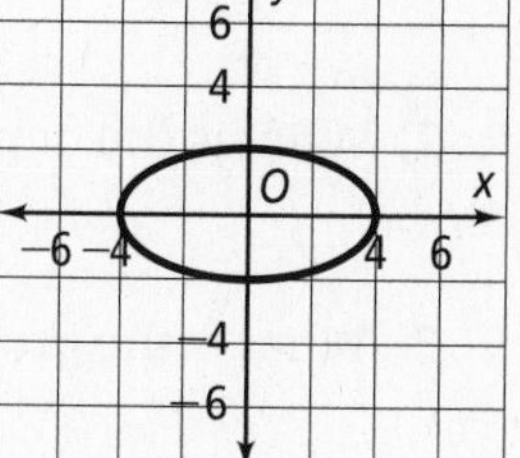

(A) $4y^2 + 4x^2 = 4$ (C) $x^2 + 4y^2 = 16$

(B) $4x^2 + y^2 = 16$ (D) $y^2 + x^2 = 16$

4. What are the lines of symmetry of a circle with the center at the origin?

(F) the x-axis (H) the y-axis

(G) the x- and y-axis (I) all lines that pass through the center

5. What is the range of $16x^2 + 9y^2 = 144$?

(A) $-3 \leq y \leq 3$ (B) $-4 \leq y \leq 4$ (C) $-16 \leq y \leq 16$ (D) $-144 \leq y \leq 144$

6. What is the domain of $x^2 + y^2 = 64$?

(F) $-8 \leq x \leq 8$ (G) $0 \leq x \leq 8$ (H) $-8 \leq y \leq 8$ (I) $-64 \leq x \leq 64$

Short Response

7. Describe the graph of $x^2 - y^2 = 16$. What is the center? What are the lines of symmetry? What are the domain and range?

Name ______________________________ Class ______________ Date ______________

10-2 Think About a Plan

Parabolas

Sound Broadcasters use a parabolic microphone on football sidelines to pick up field audio for broadcasting purposes. A certain parabolic microphone has a reflector dish with a diameter of 28 inches and a depth of 14 inches. If the receiver of the microphone is located at the focus of the reflector dish, how far from the vertex should the receiver be positioned?

Understanding the Problem

1. What is the diameter of the reflector dish?

2. What is the depth of the reflector dish?

3. What is the problem asking you to determine?

____

Planning the Solution

4. Sketch a graph of a vertical parabola to represent the reflector dish. Place the vertex at the origin.

5. You know the coordinates of two other points on the parabola. Plot and label them on your graph.

6. What is the equation for a vertical parabola with vertex at the origin?

7. How can you find the location of the focus from the equation for the parabola?

____

____.

Getting an Answer

8. What is the location of the focus?

9. If the receiver of the microphone is located at the focus of the reflector dish, how far from the vertex should the receiver be positioned?

Name ______________________ Class ____________ Date ____________

10-2 Practice

Form G

Parabolas

Write an equation of a parabola with vertex at the origin and the given focus.

1. focus at $(-2, 0)$

2. focus at $(0, 4)$

3. focus at $(0, -3)$

4. focus at $(3, 0)$

5. focus at $(-5, 0)$

6. focus at $(0, 5)$

Identify the vertex, the focus, and the directrix of the parabola with the given equation. Then sketch the graph of the parabola.

7. $y = \frac{1}{12}x^2$

8. $x = -\frac{1}{4}y^2$

9. $y = \frac{1}{2}(x - 1)^2$

10. $x = -\frac{1}{4}(y + 1)^2 + 2$

Write an equation of a parabola with vertex at the origin and the given directrix.

11. directrix $x = 3$

12. directrix $y = 4$

13. directrix $x = -2$

14. directrix $y = -3$

15. directrix $x = 6$

16. directrix $y = -7$

17. The center of a pipe with a diameter of 0.5 in. is located 10 in. from a mirror with a parabolic cross section used as a solar collector. The center of the pipe is at the focus of the parabola.

a. Write an equation to model the cross section of the mirror.

b. The pipe receives 25 times more sunlight than it would without the mirror. The amount of light collected by the mirror is directly proportional to its diameter. Find the width of the mirror.

Name ______________________ Class ____________ Date ____________

10-2 Practice (continued) Form G

Parabolas

Identify the vertex, the focus, and the directrix of the parabola with the given equation. Then sketch the graph of the parabola.

18. $y + 1 = -\frac{1}{4}(x - 3)^2$

19. $x = 2y^2$

20. $y^2 - 4x - 2y = 3$

Write an equation of a parabola with the given vertex and focus.

21. vertex (0, 0); focus (−2, 0)

22. vertex (0, 0); focus (0, 4)

23. vertex (2, 3); focus (6, 3)

24. vertex (4, 7); focus (4, 4)

25. vertex (5, 2); focus (5, 9)

26. vertex (2, 9); focus (3, 9)

27. Writing What is the relationship between the focus of a parabola and the directrix of a parabola?

28. Open-Ended Write an equation for a horizontal parabola and an equation for a vertical parabola.

29. Error Analysis A student writes the equation of a parabola with vertex (5, −7) and focus (5, 3) as $x = \frac{1}{40}(x - 5)^2 + 7$. Is this correct? Why or why not?

30. Reasoning How can you find the value for c for the parabola $x = \frac{1}{10}(y + 6)^2 + 2$?

Name ______________________ Class ____________ Date ____________

10-2 Standardized Test Prep

Parabolas

Multiple Choice

For Exercises 1–5, choose the correct letter.

1. Which is an equation of the parabola with the vertex at the origin and focus (0, 3)?

(A) $y = \frac{1}{4}x^2$ (B) $y = \frac{1}{12}x^2$ (C) $x = \frac{1}{12}y^2$ (D) $x = \frac{1}{3}y^2$

2. What is the focus of the parabola with the equation $y = -\frac{1}{16}x^2$?

(F) $(0, -4)$ (G) $(-4, 0)$ (H) $\left(0, -\frac{1}{16}\right)$ (I) $\left(-\frac{1}{4}, 0\right)$

3. Which is the equation of a parabola with vertex at the origin and directrix $x = 2.5$?

(A) $x = -\frac{1}{10}y^2$ (B) $x = \frac{1}{10}y^2$ (C) $x = \frac{1}{2.5}y^2$ (D) $x = -\frac{5}{2}y^2$

4. What is the directrix of $x = 2.25y^2$?

(F) $x = \frac{1}{4}$ (G) $x = -\frac{1}{4}$ (H) $x = \frac{1}{9}$ (I) $x = -\frac{1}{9}$

5. What is the vertex of $y = x^2 - 8x + 10$?

(A) $(-4, 8)$ (B) $(8, 10)$ (C) $(10, 16)$ (D) $(4, -6)$

Short Response

6. What are the vertex, focus, and directrix of the parabola with equation $y = x^2 - 14x + 5$? Show your work.

Name ______________________ Class ______________ Date ______________

10-3 Think About a Plan

Circles

Machinery Three gears, *A*, *B*, and *C*, mesh with each other in a motor assembly. Gear *A* has a radius of 4 in., *B* has a radius of 3 in., and *C* has a radius of 1 in. If the largest gear is centered at $(-4, 0)$, the smallest gear is centered at $(4, 0)$, and Gear *B* is centered at the origin, what is the equation of each circle in standard form?

Understanding the Problem

1. The radius of gear $A = \square$ in.

2. The radius of gear $B = \square$ in.

3. The radius of gear $C = \square$ in.

4. The centers of the gears are at what points?

5. What is the problem asking you to determine?

____

Planning the Solution

6. What do you need to find an equation for each gear?

____

Getting an Answer

7. Fill in the table below to find the equation of the circle that represents each gear.

Gear	(h, k)	r	Equation
A			
B			
C			

Name _______________ Class _______________ Date _______________

10-3 Practice

Circles

Form G

Write an equation of a circle with the given center and radius. Check your answers.

1. center (0, 0), radius 3
2. center (0, 1), radius 2
3. center (−1, 0), radius 6
4. center (2, 0), radius 1
5. center (1, −5), radius 2.5
6. center (2, 3), diameter 1

Write an equation for each translation.

7. $x^2 + y^2 = 9$; right 4 and down 2
8. $x^2 + y^2 = 12$; left 2 and up 5
9. $x^2 + y^2 = 49$; right 1 and up 7
10. $x^2 + y^2 = 1$; right 5 and up 5
11. $x^2 + y^2 = 25$; up 10
12. $x^2 + y^2 = 36$; left 8 and down 6

Write an equation for each circle. Each interval represents one unit.

13. 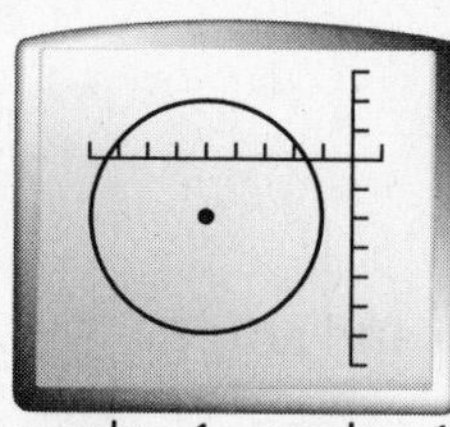

x scale = 1 y scale = 1

14. 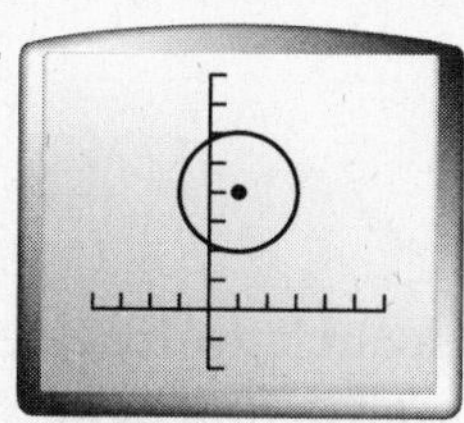

x scale = 1 y scale = 1

15. 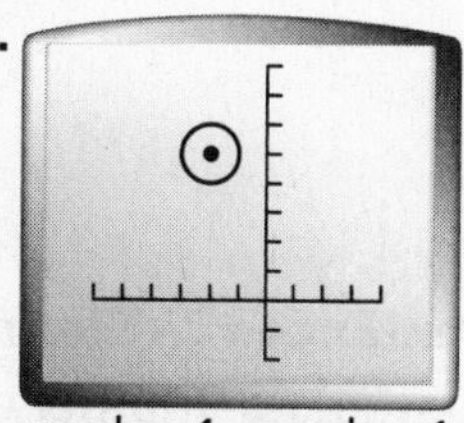

x scale = 1 y scale = 1

16. 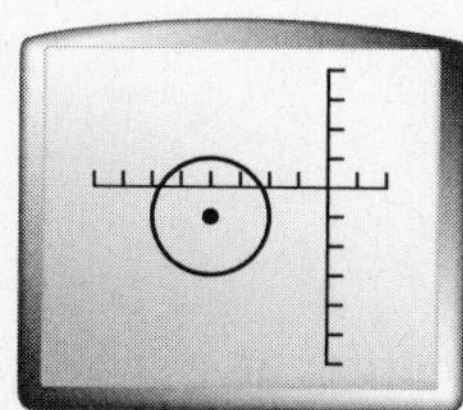

x scale = 1 y scale = 1

17. 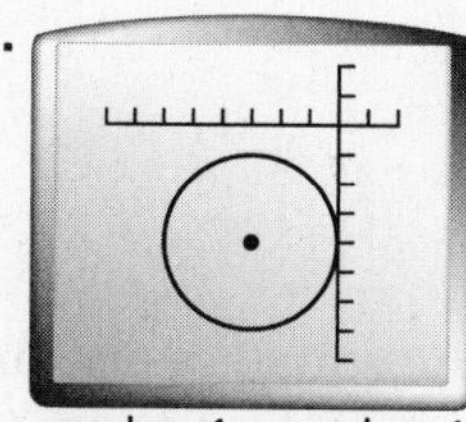

x scale = 1 y scale = 1

18. 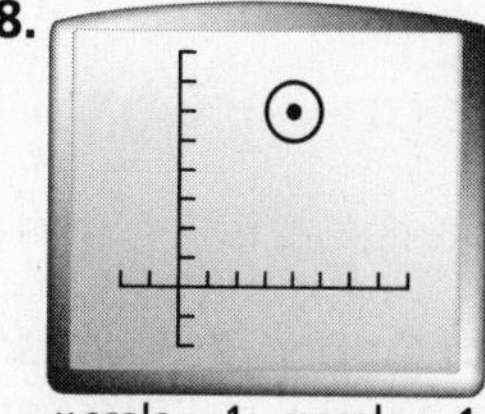

x scale = 1 y scale = 1

For each equation, find the center and radius of the circle.

19. $(x + 1)^2 + (y - 8)^2 = 1$
20. $x^2 + (y + 3)^2 = 9$
21. $(x + 3)^2 + (y + 1)^2 = 2$
22. $(x - 6)^2 + y^2 = 5$
23. $(x - 6)^2 + (y - 9)^2 = 4$
24. $x^2 + y^2 = 144$

10-3 Practice (continued)

Form G

Circles

Use the center and the radius to graph each circle.

25. $(x + 9)^2 + (y - 2)^2 = 81$

26. $x^2 + (y + 3)^2 = 121$

27. $(x - 8)^2 + (y + 9)^2 = 64$

28. $(x + 8)^2 + y^2 = 49$

29. Writing Describe in words how to change the equation of a circle with the center at the origin and radius 5 to a circle with the center 3 units right and 2 units up.

30. Open-Ended Write an equation for a circle with center at the origin and an equation for another circle that is a translation of the first.

31. Error Analysis A classmate writes the equation of a circle with the center at (8.5, 0) and diameter 25 as $x + (y - 8.5)^2 = 156.25$. Is she correct? Why or why not?

32. Reasoning How can you determine if the graph of the circle $(x + 8)^2 + (y + 9)^2 = 49$ is correctly drawn?

Name ______________________ Class ____________ Date ____________

10-3 Standardized Test Prep

Circles

Multiple Choice

For Exercises 1–5, choose the correct letter.

1. Which is an equation of the circle with center at the origin and radius 3?

(A) $x^2 + y^2 = 3$
(B) $x^2 + y^2 = 81$
(C) $x^2 + y^2 = 9$
(D) $(x - 3)^2 + (y - 3)^2 = 9$

2. What is the equation for the translation of $x^2 + y^2 = 16$ two units left and one unit down?

(F) $x^2 + y^2 = 16$
(G) $(x - 2)^2 + (y - 1)^2 = 16$
(H) $2x^2 + y^2 = 16$
(I) $(x + 2)^2 + (y + 1)^2 = 16$

3. Which equation represents a circle with a center at (7, −9) and a diameter of 8?

(A) $(x - 7)^2 + (y - 9)^2 = 64$
(B) $(x - 7)^2 + (y + 9)^2 = 64$
(C) $(x - 7)^2 + (y + 9)^2 = 16$
(D) $(x + 7)^2 + (y - 9)^2 = 16$

4. What is the center of the circle $(x - 3)^2 + (y + 2)^2 = 81$?

(F) (−3, 2)
(G) (3, −2)
(H) (3, 2)
(I) (9, 9)

5. What is the radius of the circle $(x + 8)^2 + (y - 3)^2 = 100$?

(A) 10
(B) 20
(C) 50
(D) 100

Short Response

6. What are the radius and center of a circle with the equation $(x + 7)^2 + (y - 8)^2 = 144$?

Name ______________________ Class ____________ Date ____________

10-4 Think About a Plan

Ellipses

Aerodynamics Scientists used the Transonic Tunnel at NASA Langley Research Center, Virginia, to study the dynamics of air flow. The elliptical opening of the Transonic Tunnel is 82 ft wide and 58 ft high. What is an equation of the ellipse?

Know

1. The width of the tunnel opening is ______.

2. The height of the tunnel opening is ______.

Need

3. To solve the problem I need to find:

____.

Plan

4. How can a drawing help you solve this problem?

____

____.

5. Make a sketch of an ellipse that represents the tunnel opening. Where should you put the origin? ______________________

6. How do the width and height of the tunnel opening relate to the equation of the ellipse?

____

____.

7. How can you write the equation of the ellipse in standard form?

____

____.

8. Write the equation of the ellipse in standard form.

Name ______________________ Class ____________ Date ____________

10-4 Practice

Form G

Ellipses

Write an equation of an ellipse in standard form with center at the origin and with the given vertex and co-vertex listed respectively.

1. (6, 0), (0, −5)

2. (0, 10), (−7, 0)

3. (0, 2), (−1, 0)

4. (4, 0), (0, 2)

5. (9, 0), (0, −6)

6. (11, 0), (0, −10)

7. (−7, 0), (0, −5)

8. (−2, 0), (0, −1)

Find the foci for each equation of an ellipse. Then graph the ellipse.

9. $\frac{x^2}{36} + \frac{y^2}{81} = 1$

10. $x^2 + \frac{y^2}{36} = 1$

11. $\frac{x^2}{9} + \frac{y^2}{100} = 1$

12. $16x^2 + 25y^2 = 1600$

13. $4x^2 + y^2 = 49$

14. $\frac{x^2}{64} + \frac{y^2}{144} = 1$

Find the distance between the foci of an ellipse. The lengths of the major and minor axes are listed.

15. 10 and 8

16. 20 and 16

17. 30 and 16

18. 40 and 20

19. 25 and 15

20. 50 and 26

Write an equation of an ellipse for the given foci and co-vertices.

21. foci (±5, 0), co-vertices (0, ±2)

22. foci (0, ±2), co-vertices (±1, 0)

23. foci (±1, 0), co-vertices (0, ±2)

24. foci (0, ±3), co-vertices (±3, 0)

25. foci (0, ±4), co-vertices (±4, 0)

26. foci (±4, 0), co-vertices (0, ±2)

27. foci (±2, 0), co-vertices (0, ±4)

28. foci (±1, 0), co-vertices (0, ±5)

10-4 Practice (continued)

Form G

Ellipses

29. Blinn College is building a new track for cycling teams. The track is to be elliptical. The available land is 200 yd long and 100 yd wide. Find the equation of the largest ellipse possible.

Write an equation of an ellipse in standard form with center at the origin and with the given characteristics.

30. height 3, width 1

31. vertices $(\pm 2, 0)$, co-vertices $(0, \pm 1)$

32. height 28 ft, width 20 ft

33. height 20 ft, width 28 ft

34. height 50 ft, width 40 ft

35. height 9 cm, width 12 cm

36. foci $(\pm 3, 0)$, co-vertices $(0, \pm 3)$

37. foci $(0, \pm 2)$, co-vertices $(\pm 1, 0)$

38. vertex $(-7, 0)$, co-vertex $(0, -5)$

39. vertex $(-2, 0)$, co-vertex $(0, -1)$

40. Reasoning A student claims that an ellipse with the foci $(\pm 3, 0)$ and vertices $(\pm 5, 0)$ has co-vertices $(0, \pm 4)$. Is the student correct? Why or why not?

Write an equation for each ellipse.

41.

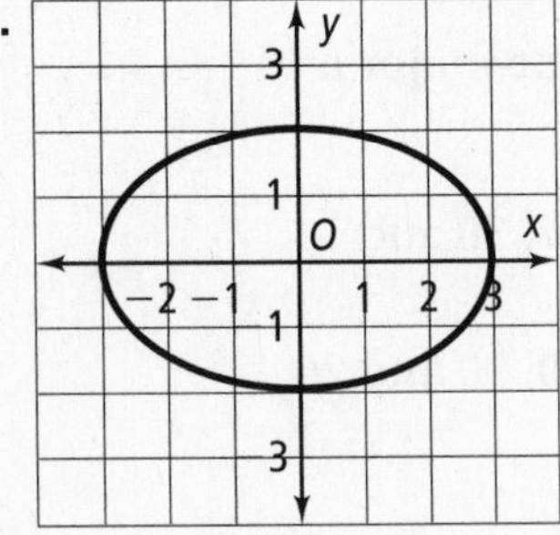

42.

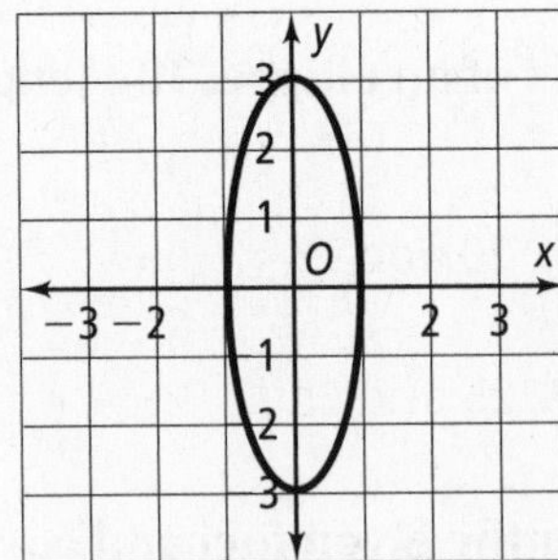

43.

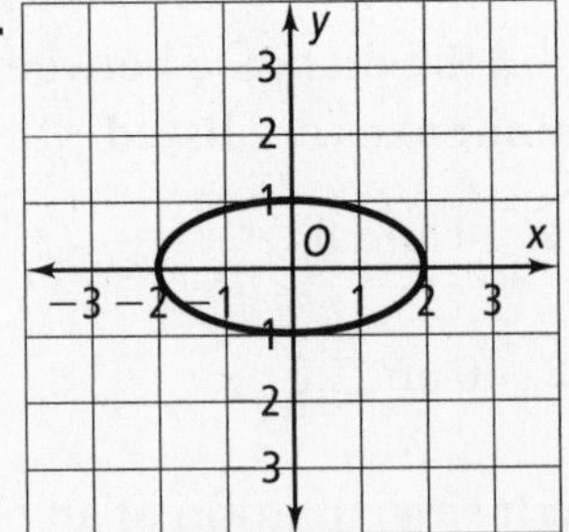

44. Writing What do the major and minor axes of an ellipse have in common?

Name ____________________ Class __________ Date __________

10-4 Standardized Test Prep

Ellipses

Gridded Response

Solve each exercise and enter your answer on the grid provided.

1. In the equation for a horizontal ellipse $\frac{x^2}{16} + \frac{y^2}{9} = 1$, what is the positive value of the x-coordinates of the vertices?

2. What is the positive y-coordinate of the foci of the ellipse with the equation $25x^2 + 16y^2 = 400$?

3. In the equation for a vertical ellipse $\frac{x^2}{49} + \frac{y^2}{100} = 1$, what is the positive value of the y-coordinates of the vertices?

4. An ellipse has foci at $(\pm 7, 0)$ and vertices at $(\pm 16, 0)$. What is the value of c?

5. Suppose you are planning a party at an elliptical park with one game at each foci. The major axis of the ellipse is 80 yd and the minor axis is 28 yd. How many yards will the games be from one another? Round to the nearest whole number.

Answers

1.

2. 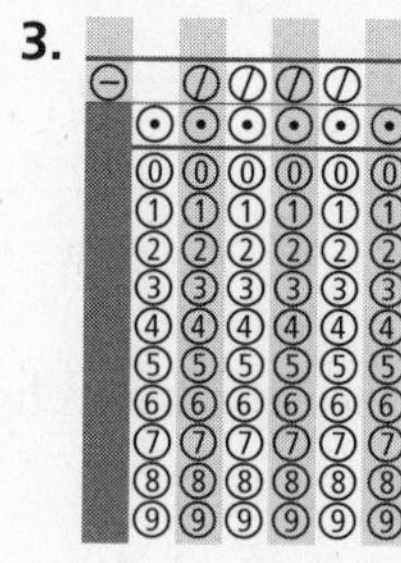

3. 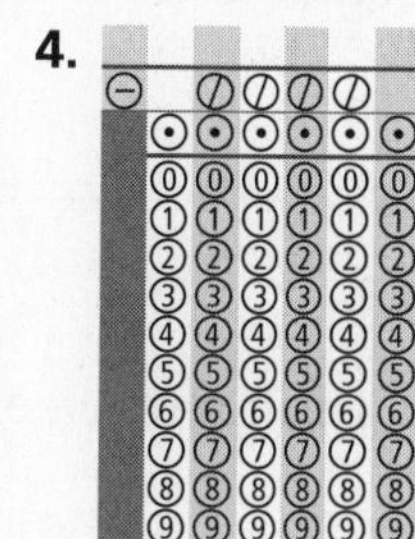

4.

5.

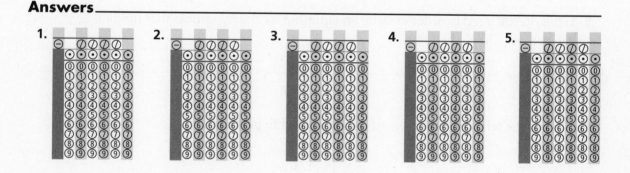

Name ____________________ Class __________ Date __________

10-5 Think About a Plan

Hyperbolas

Comets The path of a comet around the sun followed one branch of a hyperbola. Find an equation that models its path around the sun, given that $a = 40$ million miles and $c = 250$ million miles. Use the horizontal model.

Know

1. a is equal to ______.

2. c is equal to ______.

Need

3. To solve the problem I need to find:

____

______________________________.

Plan

4. What is the equation for a horizontal hyperbola?

5. What do you need in order to write an equation for the hyperbola that models the comet?

____

6. What is the relationship between a, b, and c in a hyperbola?

7. How can you use the relationship between a, b, and c to find an equation for the hyperbola?

______________________________.

8. Write an equation for a horizontal hyperbola that models the path of the comet.

Name ______________________ Class ____________ Date ____________

10-5 Practice

Form G

Hyperbolas

Find the equation of a hyperbola with the given values, foci, or vertices. Assume that the transverse axis is horizontal.

1. $a = 7, b = 2$

2. $a = 12, b = 11$

3. $b = 9, c = 12$

4. $a = 10, c = 13$

5. $a = 7, c = 9$

6. $a = 15, b = 22$

7. $b = 14, c = 20$

8. $b = 30, c = 40$

9. foci $(\pm 9, 0)$, vertices $(\pm 4, 0)$

10. foci $(\pm 8, 0)$, vertices $(\pm 2, 0)$

11. foci $(\pm 13, 0)$, vertices $(\pm 12, 0)$

12. foci $(\pm 11, 0)$, vertices $(\pm 5, 0)$

Find the vertices, foci, and asymptotes of each hyperbola. Then sketch the graph.

13. $\frac{x^2}{4} - \frac{y^2}{4} = 1$

14. $\frac{y^2}{9} - \frac{x^2}{25} = 1$

15. $\frac{x^2}{25} - \frac{y^2}{4} = 1$

16. $y^2 - \frac{x^2}{9} = 1$

17. $4y^2 - 36x^2 = 144$

18. $x^2 - 9y^2 = 9$

Name ______________________ Class ____________ Date ____________

10-5 Practice (continued) — Form G

Hyperbolas

19. The graph at the right shows a 2-dimensional view of a satellite dish and the small reflector inside it. The vertex of the small reflector is 6 in. from focus F_1 and 20 in. from focus F_2. What equation best models the small reflector?

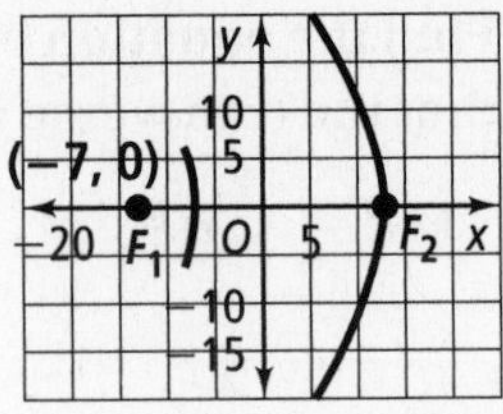

Write the equation of a hyperbola with the given foci and vertices.

20. foci $(\pm 7, 0)$, vertices $(\pm 3, 0)$

21. foci $(0, \pm 12)$, vertices $(0, \pm 10)$

22. foci $(0, \pm 3)$, vertices $(0, \pm 2)$

23. foci $(\pm 9, 0)$, vertices $(\pm 5, 0)$

Graph each equation.

24. $20x^2 - 8y^2 = 160$

25. $27y^2 - 9x^2 = 243$

26. $6x^2 - 28y^2 = 168$

27. Writing How can you tell from the standard form of the equation of a hyperbola whether the hyperbola is horizontal or vertical?

28. Error Analysis On a test, a student wrote (5, 0) for the foci of the hyperbola with the equation $\frac{y^2}{9} - \frac{x^2}{16} = 1$. The teacher gave the student partial credit. What did the student do right? What did the student do wrong?

29. Reasoning Describe how you can find the asymptotes when you have the a and c values for a vertical hyperbola.

Name ______________________ Class ____________ Date ____________

10-5 Standardized Test Prep

Hyperbolas

Multiple Choice

For Exercises 1–4, choose the correct letter.

1. A hyperbola has vertices $(\pm 5, 0)$ and one focus at $(6, 0)$. What is the equation of the hyperbola in standard form?

(A) $\frac{x^2}{25} + \frac{y^2}{11} = 1$

(B) $\frac{x^2}{5} - \frac{y^2}{11} = 1$

(C) $\frac{x^2}{11} - \frac{y^2}{25} = 1$

(D) $\frac{x^2}{25} - \frac{y^2}{11} = 1$

2. A hyperbola with a horizontal transverse axis has asymptotes $y = \pm\frac{3}{4}x$. Which of the following could be the equation of the hyperbola in standard form?

(F) $\frac{x^2}{3} + \frac{y^2}{4} = 1$

(G) $\frac{x^2}{16} - \frac{y^2}{9} = 1$

(H) $\frac{x^2}{4} - \frac{y^2}{3} = 1$

(I) $\frac{x^2}{25} - \frac{y^2}{16} = 1$

3. What are the vertices of the hyperbola with the equation $8x^2 - 9y^2 = 72$?

(A) $(\pm 3, 0)$ (B) $(\pm 2\sqrt{2}, 0)$ (C) $(\pm 8, 0)$ (D) $(\pm 9, 0)$

4. What are the foci of the hyperbola with the equation $\frac{y^2}{12} - \frac{x^2}{5} = 1$?

(F) $(0, \pm 5)$ (G) $(0, \pm 12)$ (H) $(0, \pm\sqrt{13})$ (I) $(0, \pm\sqrt{17})$

Short Response

5. What are the vertices, foci, and asymptotes of the hyperbola with the equation $4y^2 - 16x^2 = 64$?

Name ______________________ Class ____________ Date ____________

10-6 Think About a Plan

Translating Conic Sections

You designed an elliptical platform that is 12 ft across at its widest point. The choreographer of a play wants to place it on a diagram of her set so it is oriented horizontally with the center at (9, 7) from the front left corner of the stage. She also wants the front edge of the platform to be 3 ft from the front of the stage. Write an equation for your elliptical platform for her diagram.

Understanding the Problem

1. What is the width of the platform?

2. Where is the center of the platform on the diagram?

3. How far is the platform from the front of the stage?

4. What is the problem asking you to determine?

____

Planning the Solution

5. How can a sketch help you write the equation?

____

____.

6. Make a sketch of the stage.

7. What is the general form of the equation of a horizontal ellipse?

8. What information do you need to write the equation? ______________________

Getting an Answer

9. Write an equation for the elliptical platform.

Name ______________________ Class ____________ Date ____________

10-6 Practice

Form G

Translating Conic Sections

Write the standard-form equation of an ellipse with the given characteristics. Sketch the ellipse.

1. vertices (7, 3) and (−3, 3), focus (5, 3)

2. vertices (3, 6) and (3, −2), focus (3, 5)

3. vertices (11, −8) and (−19, −8), focus (5, −8)

4. vertices (2, 7) and (2, −1), focus $\left(2, 3 + \sqrt{7}\right)$

Identify the center, vertices, and foci of each hyperbola.

5. $\frac{(x-5)^2}{144} - \frac{(y-9)^2}{256} = 1$

6. $\frac{(y-9)^2}{49} - \frac{(x-3)^2}{4} = 1$

7. $\frac{(x-5)^2}{25} - \frac{(y-2)^2}{75} = 1$

Identify each conic section by writing the equation in standard form and sketching the graph. For a parabola, give the vertex. For a circle, give the center and the radius. For an ellipse or a hyperbola, give the center and the foci.

8. $3x^2 + 6x + 5y^2 - 20y - 13 = 0$

9. $x^2 - 9y^2 + 36y - 45 = 0$

10. $x^2 + 4y^2 + 8x - 48 = 0$

11. $x^2 + y^2 - 8x - 4y + 19 = 0$

12. $x^2 + y^2 + 6y - 27 = 0$

13. $x^2 - 10x - 4y^2 + 24y - 15 = 0$

10-6 Practice (continued) — Form G

Translating Conic Sections

14. Within a telescope, the path that light travels is 12 units closer to the focus of one reflector than the other. The foci are located at (0, 0) and (250, 0).
   a. What conic section models this problem?
   b. What part of the graph do the foci represent?
   c. What equation represents the path of the light?

15. **Writing** A vertical ellipse has center (0, −2), major axis length 5, and minor axis length 3. Describe how you can find the value of a. Then write the equation in standard form.

16. **Error Analysis** A student found that the equation of a hyperbola with center (−4, 5), vertex (−4, 7), and focus (−4, 8) was $\frac{(y-4)^2}{4} - \frac{(x+5)^2}{5} = 1$. Explain why the student is incorrect. Then find the correct answer.

Mental Math Use mental math to identify the center of each conic section.

17. $\frac{(x+1)^2}{16} + \frac{(y+3)^2}{4} = 1$

18. $\frac{(y+2)^2}{4} - \frac{(x-2)^2}{5} = 1$

19. $\frac{(x-2)^2}{5} + \frac{(y-5)^2}{6} = 1$

20. $\frac{(x-20)^2}{5} - \frac{(y+11)^2}{6} = 1$

21. **Reasoning** Explain how you can tell if an ellipse has been translated by looking at the standard form of the equation. Give an example.

The graph of each equation is to be translated 3 units right and 1 unit up. Write each new equation.

22. $(x+3)^2 + (y-5)^2 = 9$

23. $16x^2 - 64x - 9y^2 - 36y - 172 = 0$

Name ______________________ Class ____________ Date ____________

10-6 Standardized Test Prep

Translating Conic Sections

Multiple Choice

For Exercises 1–4, choose the correct letter.

1. A horizontal ellipse has the equation $\frac{(x-2)^2}{25} + \frac{(y-3)^2}{16} = 1$. Which is a vertex?

A $(-7, 3)$ B $(5, 4)$ C $(7, 3)$ D $(2, 3)$

2. A vertical ellipse has the equation $\frac{(x+8)^2}{81} + \frac{(y-7)^2}{36} = 1$. Which is a vertex?

F $(-8, 7)$ G $(8, 7)$ H $(7, 3)$ I $(-8, 13)$

3. What is the equation of a horizontal hyperbola with vertices $(8, -3)$ and $(2, -3)$ and focus $(10, -3)$?

A $\frac{(x-5)^2}{9} - \frac{(y+3)^2}{16} = 1$

B $\frac{(x-8)^2}{9} - \frac{(y+3)^2}{16} = 1$

C $\frac{(x-5)^2}{16} - \frac{(y+3)^2}{9} = 1$

D $\frac{(x+10)^2}{4} - \frac{(y-3)^2}{9} = 1$

4. What are the foci of the hyperbola with the equation $\frac{(y-7)^2}{81} - \frac{(x-2)^2}{144} = 1$?

F $(7, 2); (9, 14)$

G $(2, 16); (2, -2)$

H $(2, 22); (2, -8)$

I $(7, 22); (7, -8)$

Extended Response

5. Identify the conic section represented by $25x^2 + 50x - 9y^2 - 18y - 209 = 0$. Give the center and foci. Sketch the graph. Show your work.

Name _______________ Class _______ Date _______

11-1 Think About a Plan

Permutations and Combinations

Consumer Issues A consumer magazine rates televisions by identifying two levels of price, five levels of repair frequency, three levels of features, and two levels of picture quality. How many different ratings are possible?

Understanding the Problem

1. How many levels of price are possible?
2. How many levels of repair frequency are possible?
3. How many levels of features are possible?
4. How many levels of picture quality are possible?
5. What is the problem asking you to determine?

____

____

Planning the Solution

6. What is the Fundamental Counting Principle?

____

____.

7. How can the Fundamental Counting Principle help you solve the problem?

____

____

____

____.

Getting an Answer

8. Write an expression for the number of different ratings that are possible.
9. How many different ratings are possible?

Name ______________________ Class ____________ Date ____________

11-1 Practice

Form G

Permutations and Combinations

1. How many 2-letter pairs of 1 vowel and 1 consonant can you make from the English alphabet? Consider "y" to be a consonant.

2. An ice cream shop offers 33 flavors of ice cream and 7 toppings. How many different sundaes can the shop make using 1 flavor and 1 topping?

3. A contest winner gets to choose 1 of 8 possible vacations and bring 1 of 10 friends with her. How many different ways could the contest winner select her prize?

Evaluate each expression.

4. $8!$
5. $\frac{11!}{9!}$
6. $6!4!$
7. $3(5!)$
8. $\frac{9!}{2!6!}$
9. $3(7!)$
10. $\frac{10!}{5!}$
11. $\frac{3!8!}{5!}$

12. An art gallery plans to display 7 sculptures in a single row.
    a. How many different arrangements of the sculptures are possible?
    b. If one sculpture is taken out of the show, how many different arrangements are possible?

Evaluate each expression.

13. ${}_{12}P_{11}$
14. ${}_{12}P_{10}$
15. ${}_{12}P_{5}$
16. ${}_{12}P_{1}$
17. ${}_{5}P_{2}$
18. ${}_{7}P_{4}$
19. ${}_{8}P_{6}$
20. ${}_{6}P_{2}$

21. In how many ways can four distinct positions for a relay race be assigned from a team of nine runners?

Evaluate each expression.

22. ${}_{12}C_{11}$
23. ${}_{12}C_{10}$
24. ${}_{12}C_{5}$
25. ${}_{12}C_{1}$
26. ${}_{12}C_{12}$
27. ${}_{5}C_{4} + {}_{5}C_{3}$
28. $\frac{{}_{5}C_{3}}{{}_{5}C_{2}}$
29. $4({}_{7}C_{2})$

30. Thirty people apply for 10 job openings as welders. How many different groups of people can be hired?

Name ______________________ Class ____________ Date ____________

11-1 Practice (continued) Form G

Permutations and Combinations

For each situation, determine whether to use a permutation or a combination. Then solve the problem.

31. You draw the names of 5 raffle winners from a basket of 50 names. Each person wins the same prize. How many different groups of winners could you draw?

32. A paint store offers 15 different shades of blue. How many different ways could you purchase 3 shades of blue?

33. How many different 5-letter codes can you make from the letters in the word *cipher?*

Assume *a* and *b* are positive integers. Determine whether each statement is *true* or *false*. If it is true, explain why. If it is false, give a counterexample.

34. $a!b! = b!a!$

35. $(a^2)! = (a!)^2$

36. $a \cdot b! = (ab)!$

37. $(a + 0)! = a!$

38. $\frac{a!}{b!} = \left(\frac{a}{b}\right)!$

39. $a!(b! + c!) = a!b! + a!c!$

40. A restaurant offers a fixed-priced meal of 1 appetizer, 1 entrée, 2 sides, and 1 dessert. How many different meals could you choose from 4 appetizers, 5 entrees, 8 sides, and 3 desserts?

41. Writing Explain the difference between a permutation and a combination.

42. Reasoning Show that for $n = r$, the value of ${}_nC_r = 1$.

Name ______________________ Class ____________ Date ____________

11-1 Standardized Test Prep

Permutations and Combinations

Multiple Choice

For Exercises 1–5, choose the correct letter.

1. You choose 5 apples from a case of 24 apples. Which best represents the number of ways you can make your selection?

   (A) ${}_5C_{19}$ (B) ${}_{24}C_5$ (C) ${}_5P_{24}$ (D) ${}_{19}P_5$

2. Which is equivalent to ${}_7P_3$?

   (F) 28 (G) 35 (H) 210 (I) 840

3. A traveler can choose from three airlines, five hotels, and four rental car companies. How many arrangements of these services are possible?

   (A) 12 (B) 60 (C) 220 (D) 495

4. Which is equivalent to $a!(b!)$?

   (F) $(ab)!$ (G) $(ab!)!$ (H) $ba!$ (I) $b!(a!)$

5. Which is equivalent to ${}_9C_5$?

   (A) 126 (B) 3024 (C) 15,120 (D) 45,000

Short Response

6. You have a \$1 bill, a \$5 bill, a \$10 bill, a \$20 bill, a quarter, a dime, a nickel, and a penny. How many different total amounts can you make by choosing 6 bills and coins? Show your work.

Name ______________________ Class ______________ Date ______________

11-2 Think About a Plan

Probability

Lottery A lottery has 53 numbers from which five are drawn at random. Each number can only be drawn once. What is the probability of your lottery ticket matching all five numbers in any order?

Know

1. The lottery has [ ] possible numbers that can be drawn.

2. Each number can be drawn [ ] time(s).

3. A total of [ ] numbers will be drawn.

Need

4. To solve the problem I need to find:

____

____.

Plan

5. Because order does not matter, the size of the sample space is a [ ].

6. What is the sample space?

____

7. What is the size of the sample space?

8. How many of the events in the sample space represent your ticket?

9. What is the probability of your lottery ticket matching all five numbers in any order?

Name ______________________ Class ____________ Date ____________

11-2 Practice

Form G

Probability

1. A basketball player attempted 24 shots and made 13. Find the experimental probability that the player will make the next shot she attempts.

2. A baseball player attempted to steal a base 70 times and was successful 47 times. Find the experimental probability that the player will be successful on his next attempt to steal a base.

Graphing Calculator For Exercises 3–4, define a simulation by telling how you represent correct answers, incorrect answers, and the quiz. Use your simulation to find each experimental probability.

3. If you guess the answers at random, what is the probability of getting at least three correct answers on a four-question true-or-false quiz?

4. A five-question multiple-choice quiz has four choices for each answer. If you guess the answers at random, what is the probability of getting at least four correct answers?

A group of five cards are numbered 1–5. You choose one card at random. Find each theoretical probability.

5. *P*(card is a 2)

6. *P*(even number)

7. *P*(prime number)

8. *P*(less than 5)

A bucket contains 15 blue pens, 35 black pens, and 40 red pens. You pick one pen at random. Find each theoretical probability.

9. *P*(black pen)

10. *P*(blue pen or red pen)

11. *P*(not a blue pen)

12. *P*(black pen or not a red pen)

11-2 Practice (continued) Form G

Probability

13. There are 225 juniors and 255 seniors at your school. The school chooses 5 juniors and seniors as Student All-Stars. What is the theoretical probability that exactly 2 of the Student All-Stars will be juniors?

The rectangular yard shown below has a circular pool and a triangular garden. A ball from an adjacent golf course lands at a random point within the yard. Find each theoretical probability.

14. The ball lands in the pool.

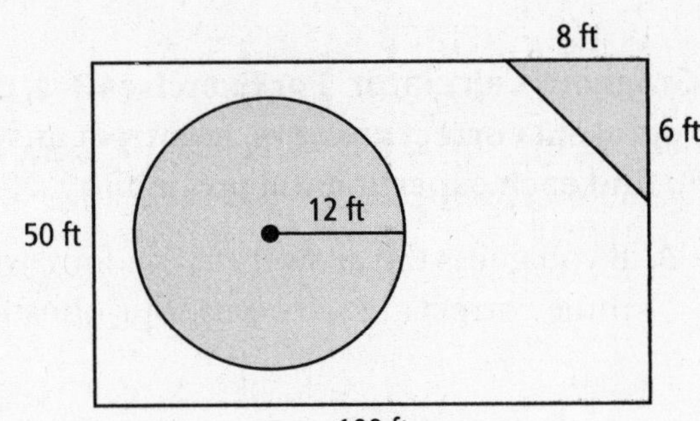

15. The ball lands in the garden

16. The ball lands in the garden or the pool.

17. The ball does not land in the pool.

Five people each flip a coin one time. Find each theoretical probability.

18. P(5 heads)

19. P(exactly 2 tails)

20. P(at least 3 heads)

21. P(less than 4 tails)

22. The spinner shown at the right has four equal-sized sections. Suppose you spin the spinner two times.

a. What is the sample space?

b. How many outcomes are there?

c. What is the theoretical probability of getting a sum of 4?

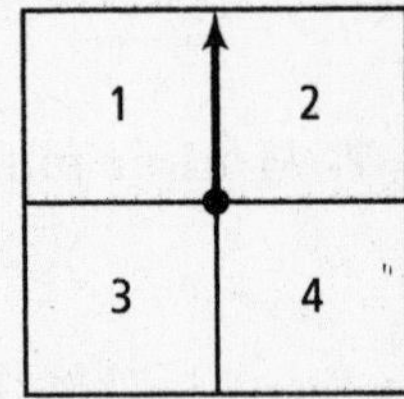

23. If x is a real number and $x = 0$, what is the probability that $\frac{1}{x}$ is undefined?

24. If x is a real number and $x \neq 0$, what is the probability that $\frac{1}{x}$ is undefined?

25. Of the 195 students in the senior class, 104 study Spanish and 86 study French, with 12 studying both Spanish and French. What is the theoretical probability that a student chosen at random is studying Spanish, but not French?

Name ____________________ Class ____________ Date ____________

11-2 Standardized Test Prep

Probability

Gridded Response

For Exercises 1–3, find each theoretical probability based on one roll of two number cubes. Enter each answer in the grid as a whole percent.

1. *P*(sum 9)

2. *P*(one even, one odd)

3. *P*(sum > 12)

For Exercises 4–5, find each theoretical probability based on one marble drawn at random from a bag of 14 red marbles, 10 pink marbles, 18 blue marbles, and 6 gold marbles. Enter each answer in the grid as a fraction in simplest form.

4. *P*(not pink)

5. *P*(blue or gold)

Answers

1. 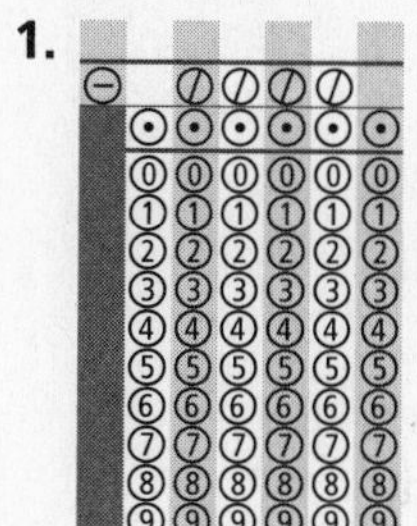

2. 

3. 

4. 

5.

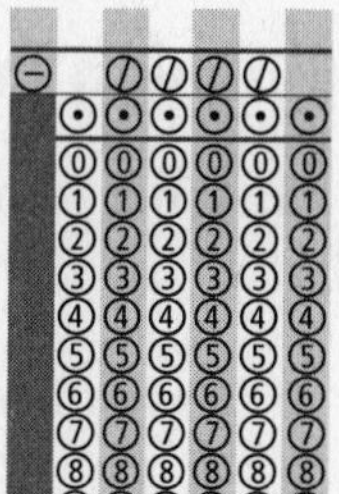

Name _______________ Class _______________ Date _______________

11-3 Think About a Plan

Probability of Multiple Events

Marbles A jar contains four blue marbles and two red marbles. Suppose you choose a marble at random, and do not replace it. Then you choose a second marble. Find the probability that you select a blue marble and then a red marble.

Understanding the Problem

1. How many marbles are blue?

2. How many marbles are red?

3. How many marbles are in the jar?

4. What is the problem asking you to determine?

____

____

Planning the Solution

5. What is the probability that you choose a blue marble from the jar?

6. Assuming you choose a blue marble and do not replace it, how many marbles of each color remain in the jar? What is the total number of marbles in the jar?

____

7. What is the probability that you now choose a red marble from the jar?

8. How can you find the probability that you select a blue marble and then a red marble? _______________

_______________.

Getting an Answer

9. What is the probability that you select a blue marble and then a red marble?

Name ______________________ Class ____________ Date ____________

11-3 Practice

Form G

Probability of Multiple Events

Classify each pair of events as *dependent* or *independent*.

1. A member of the junior class is selected; one of her pets is selected.

2. A member of the junior class is selected as junior class president; a freshman is selected as freshman class president.

3. An odd-numbered problem is assigned for homework; an even-numbered problem is picked for a test.

4. The sum of two rolls of a number cube is 6; the product of the same two rolls is 8.

***Q* and *R* are independent events. Find *P*(*Q* and *R*).**

5. $P(Q) = \frac{1}{8}, P(R) = \frac{2}{5}$

6. $P(Q) = 0.8, P(R) = 0.2$

7. $P(Q) = \frac{1}{4}, P(R) = \frac{1}{5}$

8. $P(Q) = \frac{3}{4}, P(R) = \frac{2}{3}$

9. Suppose you have seven CDs in a box. Four are rock, one is jazz, and two are country. Today you choose one CD without looking, play it, and put it back in the box. Tomorrow, you do the same thing. What is the probability that you choose a country CD both days?

You randomly select an integer from 1 to 100. State whether the events are mutually exclusive. Explain your reasoning.

10. The integer is less than 40; the integer is greater than 50.

11. The integer is odd; the integer is a multiple of 4.

12. The integer is less than 50; the integer is greater than 40.

***M* and *N* are mutually exclusive events. Find *P*(*M* or *N*).**

13. $P(M) = \frac{3}{4}, P(N) = \frac{1}{6}$

14. $P(M) = 10\%, P(N) = 45\%$

15. $P(M) = 20\%, P(N) = 18\%$

16. $P(M) = \frac{1}{10}, P(N) = \frac{3}{5}$

Name _______________ Class _______________ Date _______________

11-3 Practice (continued) Form G

Probability of Multiple Events

17. Exactly 62% of the students in your school are under 17 years old. In addition, 4% of the students are over 18. What is the probability that a student chosen at random is under 17 or over 18?

A fair number cube is tossed. Find each probability.

18. *P*(even or 3) **19.** *P*(less than 2 or even) **20.** *P*(prime or 4)

21. You randomly choose a natural number from 1 to 10. What is the probability that you choose a multiple of 2 or 3?

The graph at the right shows the types of bicycles in a bicycle rack. Find each probability.

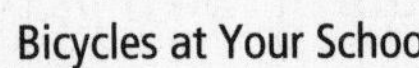

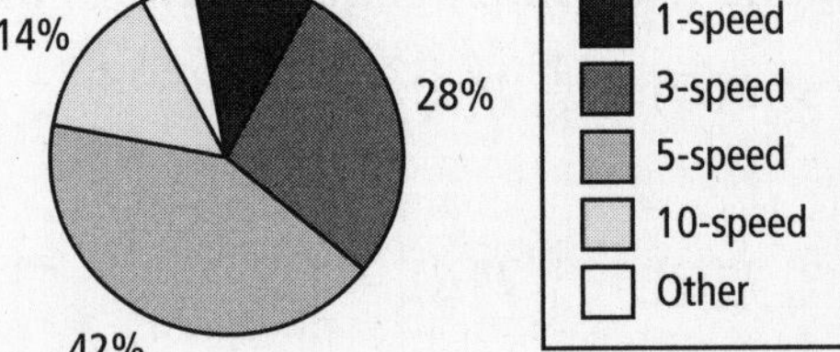

22. A bicycle is a 1-speed.

23. A bicycle is a 3-speed or a 5-speed.

24. A bicycle is not a 10-speed.

25. A bicycle is not a 1-, 3-, or 10-speed.

You have a drawer with five pairs of white socks, three pairs of black socks, and one pair of red socks. You choose one pair of socks at random each morning, starting on Monday. You do not put the socks you choose back in the drawer. Find the probability of each event.

26. You select black socks on Monday and white socks on Tuesday.

27. You select red socks on Monday and black socks on Tuesday.

28. You select white socks on Monday and Tuesday.

29. You select red socks on Monday.

30. Only 93% of the airplane parts being examined pass inspection. What is the probability that all of the next 5 parts examined will pass inspection?

Name ______________________ Class ____________ Date ____________

11-3 Standardized Test Prep

Probability of Multiple Events

Multiple Choice

For Exercises 1–4, choose the correct letter.

A store display shows two red shirts, one blue shirt, and three shirts with red and white stripes. The display also shows two pairs of blue jeans, one pair of white pants, and one pair of white shorts.

1. What is the probability of randomly selecting an item with white or red on it?

Ⓐ $\frac{1}{4}$ Ⓑ $\frac{3}{10}$ Ⓒ $\frac{1}{2}$ Ⓓ $\frac{7}{10}$

2. What is the probability of randomly selecting two items and getting a pair of blue jeans, putting them back in the display, and then randomly selecting a blue shirt?

Ⓕ $\frac{1}{50}$ Ⓖ $\frac{1}{45}$ Ⓗ $\frac{2}{10}$ Ⓘ $\frac{3}{10}$

3. What is the probability of randomly selecting a complete outfit (one shirt and one pair of jeans, pants, or shorts) on two picks?

Ⓐ $\frac{1}{24}$ Ⓑ $\frac{1}{5}$ Ⓒ $\frac{6}{25}$ Ⓓ $\frac{4}{15}$

4. What is the probability of selecting an item with red or blue on it?

Ⓕ $\frac{3}{20}$ Ⓖ $\frac{3}{10}$ Ⓗ $\frac{3}{5}$ Ⓘ $\frac{4}{5}$

Short Response

5. There is a 50% chance of thunderstorms on Monday, a 50% chance on Tuesday, and a 50% chance on Wednesday. Assume these are independent events. What is the probability that there will be thunderstorms on Monday, Tuesday, and Wednesday? Show your work.

Name ______________________ Class ____________ Date ____________

11-4 Think About a Plan

Conditional Probability

Transportation You can take Bus 65 or Bus 79. You take the first bus that arrives. The probability that Bus 65 arrives first is 75%. There is a 40% chance that Bus 65 picks up passengers along the way. There is a 60% chance that Bus 79 picks up passengers. Your bus picked up passengers. What is the probability that it was Bus 65?

Understanding the Problem

1. What is the probability that Bus 65 arrives first?

2. What is the probability that Bus 65 picks up passengers?

3. What is the probability that Bus 79 picks up passengers?

4. What is the problem asking you to determine?

   ____

Planning the Solution

5. Let B65 = Bus 65 arrived first, B79 = Bus 79 arrived first, P = passengers, NP = no passengers. What conditional probability are you looking for?

6. How can a tree diagram help you solve the problem?

   ____

   ____.

7. Write an equation you can use to find the probability that your bus was Bus 65.

Getting an Answer

8. Make a tree diagram for this problem.

9. Which two branches of the diagram show a bus picking up passengers?

10. What is the probability your bus was Bus 65?

Name ______________________ Class __________ Date __________

11-4 Practice
Conditional Probability

Form G

Use the table at the right to find each probability.

Education and Salary of Employees

	Under $20,000	$20,000 to $30,000	Over $30,000
Less than high school	69	36	2
High school	112	98	14
Some college	102	193	143
College degree	13	178	245

1. *P*(has less than high school education)
2. *P*(earns over $30,000 and has less than high school education)
3. *P*(earns over $30,000 | has only high school education)
4. *P*(has high school education or less | earns over $30,000)

Use the table below to find each probability. The table gives information about students at one school.

Favorite Leisure Activities

	Sports	Hiking	Reading	Phoning	Shopping	Other
Female	39	48	85	62	71	29
Male	67	58	76	54	68	39

5. *P*(sports | female)
6. *P*(female | sports)
7. *P*(reading | male)
8. *P*(male | reading)
9. *P*(hiking | female)
10. *P*(hiking | male)
11. *P*(male | shopping)
12. *P*(female | shopping)
13. The senior class is 55% female, and 32% of the class are females who play a competitive sport. What is the probability that a student plays a competitive sport, given that the student is female?
14. A softball game has an 80% chance of being cancelled if it rains and a 30% chance of being cancelled if there is fog when there is no rain. There is a 70% chance of fog with no rain and a 30% chance of rain.
    a. Make a tree diagram based on the information above.
    b. Find the probability that there will be fog and the game will be cancelled.
    c. Find the probability that there will be rain and the game will be played.
    d. Find the probability that the game will be cancelled.

Name _______________ Class _______________ Date _______________

11-4 Practice (continued) Form G

Conditional Probability

15. The population of a high school is 51% male. 45% of the males and 49% of the females attend concerts.

a. Make a tree diagram based on the information above.

b. Find the probability that a student is male and attends concerts.

c. Find the probability that a student is female and does not attend concerts.

d. Find the probability that a student attends concerts.

16. Reasoning A student says that if $P(A) = P(A \mid B)$, then A and B must be independent events. Is the student correct? Explain.

17. A school's colors are blue and gold. At a pep rally, 65% of the students are wearing both blue and gold, and 90% of the students are wearing blue.

a. What percent of students wearing blue are also wearing gold?

b. Writing Describe how a tree diagram could help you solve this problem.

You survey a group of juniors and seniors. The tree diagram relates student's class and whether a student is employed after school. Find each probability. Let J, S, E, and U represent junior, senior, employed, and unemployed, respectively.

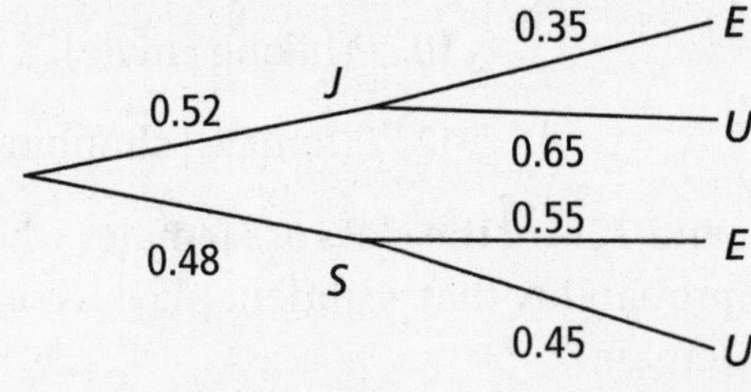

18. $P(\text{E})$

19. $P(\text{J and U})$

20. $P(\text{S} \mid \text{E})$

21. $P(\text{J} \mid \text{U})$

22. $P(\text{S} \mid \text{U})$

23. $P(\text{J} \mid \text{E})$

Name ______________________ Class ____________ Date ____________

11-4 Standardized Test Prep

Conditional Probability

Multiple Choice

For Exercises 1–2, choose the correct letter.

A local bookstore classifies its books by type of reader, type of book, and cost. Use the table at the right for Exercises 1–2.

		< \$10	> \$10
Child	Fiction	120	255
	Nonfiction	35	60
Adult	Fiction	200	110
	Nonfiction	75	150

1. What is the probability that a book selected at random is a child's book, given that it costs \$15?

(A) $\frac{315}{1005}$ (B) $\frac{470}{1005}$ (C) $\frac{315}{575}$ (D) $\frac{470}{575}$

2. What is the probability that a book selected at random is fiction, given that it costs \$6?

(F) $\frac{320}{1005}$ (G) $\frac{430}{1005}$ (H) $\frac{120}{430}$ (I) $\frac{320}{430}$

Extended Response

3. Of the photographs produced in one day at a photo shop, 25% are black-and-white, and the rest are in color. Portraits make up 65% of the black-and-white photos and 45% of the color photos. Let B, C, P, and N represent black-and-white, color, portrait, and not a portrait, respectively. Draw a tree diagram to represent this situation. What is the probability that a photo chosen at random is not a portrait? Show your work.

Name ______________________ Class ____________ Date ____________

11-5 Think About a Plan

Probability Models

Sports The Redskins' field goal kicker has made 16 out of 20 field goal attempts so far this season. So, the experimental probability that the kicker will make his next field goal kick is 80%. What is a simulation you could use to find, on average, how many field goals he will make next game if he has 3 attempts using this experimental probability?

Know

1. The probability that the kicker will make his next field goal attempt is ☐.

2. What is this probability written as a fraction in simplest form?

3. You are to assume that the kicker attempts ☐ field goals in his next game.

Need

4. How many equally likely outcomes should your probability model have? Explain.

____

____.

5. Which outcomes will indicate a successful field goal attempt? Explain.

____

____.

Plan

6. Describe a probability model you could use to simulate a field goal attempt by the kicker.

____

____

____.

7. How could you use your model to simulate the kicker's field goal attempts for the next game?

____.

8. Why is it important to repeat your simulation several times?

____.

Name ______________________ Class ____________ Date ____________

11-5 Practice

Form G

Probability Models

For Exercises 1 and 2, determine whether the strategies described result in a fair decision. Explain.

1. There are 16 players on a soccer team. The coach wants to choose 3 players at random to demonstrate a kicking drill. She makes a list of the number of goals scored by each player in the past 6 games. Then she chooses the top 3 scorers.

2. There are 84 people in the audience of a theater. The manager wants to choose 5 audience members at random to receive snack coupons. He places all of the ticket stubs in a box and picks 5 of them without looking. Then he calls out the ticket stub numbers to the audience so that they can check whether their tickets have the winning numbers.

For Exercises 3 and 4, use the lines from a random number table below.

79440	14939	47279	82830	23248	02248	73301
56409	99079	03881	90839	44182	09130	08834

3. A teacher wants to select 4 of the 28 students in her class at random to present their projects on Monday. She assigns a two-digit number from 01 to 28 to each student. What are the numbers of the students who will give their reports on Monday?

4. A restaurant owner wants to place survey cards on 4 of the 15 tables in his restaurant at random. He assigns a two-digit number from 01 to 15 to each table. What are the numbers of the tables that will have survey cards?

5. A juice company is having a promotion in which one of the letters J, U, I, C, E is printed on the inside of each of their bottle's lids. Customers win a free bottle of juice if they collect all 5 letters. Each lid is printed with exactly one letter, and the letters are equally and randomly distributed. Describe a simulation you can use to predict the number of bottles a customer would expect to buy to collect all 5 letters.

6. A cereal company is giving away 2 different CDs in its cereal boxes. Each box contains exactly one CD, and the CDs are equally and randomly distributed. Describe a simulation you can use to predict the number of boxes of cereal you would expect to buy to get both CDs.

Name ______________________ Class ____________ Date ____________

11-5 Practice (continued) *Form G*

Probability Models

7. The contingency table below shows the number of algebra students who used quiz software to study before a test and the number of students who received an *A* or *B* on the test.

	Quiz software	No quiz software	Totals
Received A or B	8	9	17
Received less than B	5	4	9
Totals	13	13	26

a. What is the probability that a student received an A or a B given that he or she used the quiz software?

b. What is the probability that a student received an A or a B given that he or she did not use the quiz software?

c. A school decides to purchase the quiz software for all of its algebra students. Is this a good decision? Explain.

8. There are 25 cats at an animal shelter. The shelter manager wants to randomly select 5 of the cats to take to a pet store for an adoption day. How can the shelter manager choose the 5 cats fairly? Explain.

9. A weather reporter states that there is a 50% chance of rain on each of the next 3 days. Based on this forecast, describe a simulation you could use to determine, on average, the number of days in the next 3 days that it will rain.

10. Writing Based on a simulation, a classmate concludes that he would have to buy on average 4 packs of trading cards to get all 6 different cards sold in the packs. If your classmate buys 4 packs of trading cards, is he guaranteed to get all 6 different cards? Explain.

Name ______________________ Class ____________ Date ____________

11-5 Standardized Test Prep
Probability Models

Multiple Choice

For Exercises 1–3, choose the correct letter.

1. There are 20 contestants in a talent contest. The contest organizer wants to choose 4 contestants at random to appear in the first round. Which strategy would result in the fairest decision?

(A) The organizer chooses the first 4 contestants to sign up for the contest.

(B) The organizer lists the contestants' names in alphabetical order and chooses the first 4 names.

(C) The organizer writes each contestant's name on a slip of paper and then arranges the names from shortest to longest. Then she chooses the 4 shortest names.

(D) The organizer assigns each contestant a number and spins a spinner numbered 1 to 20. She picks the contestants with the first 4 different numbers that she spins.

2. The head of an astronaut-training program wants to choose 3 of the 32 trainees at random to take a zero-gravity flight. He assigns a two-digit number from 01 to 32 to each trainee. Based on the line of the random number table below, what are the numbers of the trainees who will take the flight?

79577 01104 76390 49032 91662 36151 59491 03051 45469 24460

(F) 01, 03, 10 (G) 03, 05, 15 (H) 04, 11, 32 (I) 05, 07, 09

3. A company is testing the effectiveness of a new lotion to fight acne. In the test, 60 volunteers use the new lotion, and 60 volunteers do not use any lotion. Based on the contingency table, what is the approximate probability that a volunteer showed improvement, given that he or she used the lotion?

	Showed improvement	No improvement	Totals
Used lotion	32	28	60
Did not use lotion	12	48	60
Totals	44	76	120

(A) 27% (B) 37% (C) 53% (D) 73%

Short Response

4. Refer back to Exercise 3. The company decides to sell the lotion as an effective way to treat acne. Based on the results of the test, did the company make a good decision? Explain.

Name ______________________ Class ______________ Date ____________

11-6 Think About a Plan

Analyzing Data

Meteorology On May 3, 1999, 59 tornadoes hit Oklahoma in the largest tornado outbreak ever recorded in the state. Sixteen of these were classified as strong (F2 or F3) or violent (F4 or F5).

a. Make a box-and-whisker plot of the data for length of path.

b. Identify the outliers. Remove them from the data set and make a revised box-and-whisker plot.

c. Writing How does the removal of the outliers affect the box-and-whisker plot? How does it affect the median of the data set?

Major Tornadoes in Oklahoma, May 3, 1999

Length of path (miles)	Intensity
6	F3
9	F3
4	F2
37	F5
7	F2
12	F3
8	F2
7	F2
15	F4
39	F4
1	F2
22	F3
15	F3
8	F2
13	F3
2	F2

1. Arrange the data in increasing order.

____

2. Minimum value = ☐ Q_1 = ☐

Maximum value = ☐ Q_2 = ☐

Q_3 = ☐

3. Use your previous answers to make a box-and-whisker plot of the data for length of path.

4. How can you identify the outliers in the data set?

____

______________________________.

5. What are the outliers in the data set? ______________________________

6. Remove the outliers from the data set and make a revised box-and-whisker plot.

7. How does the removal of the outliers affect the box-and-whisker plot?

____

______________________________.

8. How does the removal of the outliers affect the median of the data set?

______________________________.

Name ____________________ Class ____________ Date ____________

11-6 Practice — Form G

Analyzing Data

Find the mean, median, and mode of each set of values.

1. Customers per day: 98 87 79 82 101 99 97 97 102 91 93

2.

Weight (g)	2.3	2.4	2.5	2.6	2.8	2.9
Frequency	1	4	1	1	1	2

3.

Length (m)	12	13	14	15	16	17	18
Frequency	2	5	3	7	4	9	1

Identify the outlier of each set of values.

4. 32 35 3 36 37 35 38 40 42 34

5. 153 156 176 156 165 110 159 169 172

6. The table shows the average monthly rainfall for two cities. How can you compare the rainfall amounts?

	J	F	M	A	M	J	J	A	S	O	N	D
City A	3.2	3.1	4.5	5.0	4.1	2.9	1.8	0.8	2.2	2.3	3.1	3.0
City B	4.2	4.0	4.7	4.8	4.5	4.3	4.0	3.9	4.3	4.4	4.6	4.5

7. The list gives the average temperatures in January for several cities in the mid-South. Make a box-and-whisker plot of the data.
   49.1 50.8 42.9 44.0 44.2 51.4 45.7
   39.9 50.8 46.7 52.4 50.4

Make a box-and-whisker plot for each set of values.

8. 2 8 3 7 3 6 4 9 10 15 21 29 32 30 5 7 32 4 11 13 11 14 10 12 13 15

9. 1054 1165 1287 1385 1456 1398 1298 1109 1067 1384 1499 1032 1222 1045

11-6 Practice (continued) Form G

Analyzing Data

Find the values at the 20th and 80th percentiles for each set of values.

10. 188 168 174 198 186 170 180 182 186 176

11. 376 324 346 348 350 352 356 368 345 360

Identify the outlier in each data set. Then find the mean, median, and mode of the data set when the outlier is included and when it is not.

12. 23 76 79 76 77 74 75

13. 43 46 49 50 52 54 78 47

14. The table shows the number of shaved-ice servings sold during the first week of July.

Date	7/1	7/2	7/3	7/4	7/5	7/6	7/7
Number Sold	65	70	67	98	72	67	64

a. Make a box-and-whisker plot of the data for the number of shaved-ice servings sold.

b. Find any outliers. Remove them from the data set and make a revised box-and-whisker plot.

c. Writing How does removing the outliers affect the box-and-whisker plot? How does it affect the measures of central tendency?

For Exercises 15–18, use the set of values below.

1 2 2 2 2 2 2 2 3 3 3 3 3 4 4 4 5 25 26 27

15. At what percentile is 1?

16. At what percentile is 25?

17. Find the mean, median, and mode of the data set.

18. Writing Suppose these values represent years of experience of the accountants at an accounting firm. Which measure(s) of central tendency best describe(s) the experience of the firm's accountants? Explain.

Name ____________________ Class ____________ Date ____________

11-6 Standardized Test Prep

Analyzing Data

Multiple Choice

For Exercises 1–5, choose the correct letter. Use the data set below.

Day	9/1	9/2	9/3	9/4	9/5	9/6	9/7	9/8	9/9	9/10	9/11	9/12
Deliveries	14	15	19	15	15	16	19	20	21	29	16	17

1. What is the mean of the data set?

Ⓐ 12 Ⓑ 15 Ⓒ 16.5 Ⓓ 18

2. How many modes does the data set have?

Ⓕ 0 Ⓖ 1 Ⓗ 2 Ⓘ 3

3. What is the interquartile range of the data?

Ⓐ 1.5 Ⓑ 3 Ⓒ 4.5 Ⓓ 15

4. What is the median value of the data set *without the outlier?*

Ⓕ 16 Ⓖ 17 Ⓗ 19 Ⓘ 29

5. What value is at the 50th percentile?

Ⓐ 16 Ⓑ 17 Ⓒ 19 Ⓓ 20

Short Response

6. Make a box-and-whisker plot of the data set. Label the median, minimum, maximum, first quartile, and third quartile.

Name ______________________ Class ____________ Date ____________

11-7 Think About a Plan

Standard Deviation

Energy The data for daily energy usage of a small town during ten days in January is shown.

83.8 MWh	87.1 MWh	92.5 MWh	80.6 MWh	82.4 MWh
77.6 MWh	78.9 MWh	78.2 MWh	81.8 MWh	80.1 MWh

a. Find the mean and the standard deviation of the data.

b. How many values in the data set fall within one standard deviation of the mean? Within two standard deviations? Within three standard deviations?

Know

1. The data values are: ______________________

2. The mean of a set of data is [ ].

3. The standard deviation of a set of n data values is [ ].

Need

4. To solve the problem I need to find:

____

______________________.

Plan

5. The mean of the data is [ ]. The standard deviation of the data is [ ].

6. Plot the data values on a number line. Mark off intervals of the standard deviation on either side of the mean.

7. How many values in the data set fall within one standard deviation of the mean? Within two standard deviations? Within three standard deviations?

Name ______________________ Class ____________ Date ____________

11-7 Practice

Form G

Standard Deviation

Find the mean, variance, and standard deviation for each data set.

1. 232 254 264 274 287 298 312 342 398

2. 26 27 28 28 28 29 30 30 32 35 35 36

3. 2.2 2.2 2.3 2.4 2.4 2.4 2.5 2.5 2.5 2.6

4. 75 73 77 79 79 74 81 74 70 68 70 72

Graphing Calculator Find the mean and the standard deviation.

5. price of XYZ Company stock for the first 12 weeks of 2006

5.34	5.40	5.41	5.42	5.50	5.55
5.55	5.57	5.70	5.65	5.66	5.68

6. price of XYZ Company stock for the first 12 weeks of 2009

6.00	5.95	5.92	5.80	5.81	5.75
5.75	5.75	5.64	5.52	5.40	5.03

Determine the whole number of standard deviations that includes all data values.

7. The hours students in your study group study is 66.1 min; the standard deviation is 2.9 min.

62 63 65 64 64 68 68 69 72 66

8. The mean weight of your pets is 18.25 lb; the standard deviation is 30.1 lb.

0.25 0.25 6 8 10 85

9. Use the data for average daily water usage of a family during the past 10 months. Find the mean and the standard deviation of the data. How many items in the data set fall within one standard deviation of the mean? Within two standard deviations?

124 gal	113 gal	152 gal	545 gal	150 gal
490 gal	442 gal	207 gal	124 gal	147 gal

10. Reasoning In Lesson 11-5 an outlier is defined as a value "substantially different from the rest of the data in a set." How could you use the concept of standard deviation to rewrite this definition?

Name ______________________ Class ____________ Date ____________

11-7 Practice (continued)

Form G

Standard Deviation

Find the standard deviation for each data set. Use the standard deviations to compare each pair of data sets.

11. prices of the first 10 cars sold at Joe's Used Car Lot in 1998:
$900 $1300 $1200 $850 $800 $1250 $795 $950 $1020 $975

prices of the first 10 cars sold at Joe's Used Car Lot in 2008:
$2500 $2700 $3600 $5000 $1900 $6175 $4000 $7200 $9250 $3000

12. times of boys in 100-m dash state high-school finals in 1998:
10.43 10.48 10.49 10.51 10.61 10.63 10.66 10.92

times of boys in 100-m dash state high-school finals in 2008:
10.32 10.38 10.39 10.48 10.70 10.74 10.83 10.90

Use the chart at the right for Exercises 13–17.

Fundraising at Smithburg High School

Club	2006–2007	2007–2008
Adventure	$500	$600
Car	$250	$250
Chess	$100	$120
Drama	$1500	$1400
Ecology	$475	$300
Film	$150	$250
Service	$2200	$4500
Spirit	$1000	$1500

13. Find the mean amount of money raised for each year.

14. Find the standard deviation for each year.

15. Writing Use the standard deviation for each year to describe how school fundraising varied from 2006–2007 to 2007–2008.

16. For 2007–2008, the amounts raised by which clubs are not within one standard deviation of the mean?

17. Error Analysis A student says that the amounts raised in 2006–2007 by the Drama Club, Service Club, and Spirit Club are not within one standard deviation of the mean. Do you agree? Explain.

18. a. Make a table showing the heights of ten books in your home.
b. Find the mean and standard deviation of the data.

Name ______________________ Class ____________ Date ____________

11-7 Standardized Test Prep

Standard Deviation

Multiple Choice

For Exercises 1–4, choose the correct letter.

1. Of the 25 students who take a standardized test, the minimum score is 98 and the maximum score is 472. The mean score is 216, and the standard deviation is 52. What is the number of standard deviations that includes all the data values?

   (A) 3 (B) 5 (C) 8 (D) 9

2. What is the standard deviation of the data set below?
   87 21 90 43 54 23 123 110 90 44 50

   (F) 33.1 (G) 47.0 (H) 66.8 (I) 89.0

3. A data set has a mean of 255 and a standard deviation of 12. All the data values are within two standard deviations of the mean. Which could be the maximum value of the data?

   (A) 232 (B) 244 (C) 268 (D) 280

4. The scores on a math test are:
   67 69 71 75 78 78 83 85 85 85 85 86 87 89 92 95 98 98 98 100.
   Within how many standard deviations of the mean is a score of 100?

   (F) 2 (G) 3 (H) 10 (I) 15

Short Response

5. The ages of students in a club are:
   13 17 18 15 16 14 15 18 17 16 15 16 13.
   Calculate the mean and standard deviation. What is the number of standard deviations that includes all the data values? Show your work.

Name ______________________ Class ____________ Date ____________

11-8 Think About a Plan

Samples and Surveys

Entertainment A magazine publisher mails a survey to every tenth person on a subscriber list. The survey asks for three favorite leisure activities. What sampling method is the survey using? Identify any bias in the sampling method.

Know

1. The company sending out the survey is a ______________________.

2. The surveys are mailed to ______________________

______________________.

3. The survey asks for ______________________.

Need

4. To solve the problem I need to find:

____

______________________.

Plan

5. What sampling method is the survey using? ______________________

6. Do the people who receive the survey represent the general population? Explain.

____

______________________.

7. Do the people who return the survey represent the general population? Explain.

____

______________________.

8. Is there any bias in the sampling method? Explain.

____

____

____

______________________.

Name ______________________ Class ____________ Date ____________

11-8 Practice

Form G

Samples and Surveys

Identify the sampling method. Then identify any bias in each method.

1. A teacher committee wants to find how much time students spend reading each week. They ask students as they enter the library.

2. The students planning the junior class party want to know what kinds of pizza to buy. They ask the pizza restaurant what kinds sell the most.

3. The county road department wants to know which roads cause the most concern among the residents of the county. They ask the local restaurants to hand out survey forms for customers to return by mail.

Identify the type of study method described in each situation, and explain whether the sample statistics should be used to make a general conclusion about the population.

4. A company that manufactures light bulbs selects 3 bulbs manufactured each day at random. Then these bulbs are tested to see how many hours they last.

5. A food product company is researching a new artificial sweetener. The company asks 100 people at a retirement home to rate the taste of a drink on a scale from 1 to 10. Half of the people are given tea sweetened with sugar, and half are given tea sweetened with the artificial sweetener. Then the results from the two groups are averaged.

6. A high-school principal wants to determine what classes students at the school would like to see added next year. He selects every 10th student listed in the school's database and asks each of them to list the 3 classes they would most like to see added to the school's class list.

7. **a.** What sampling method could you use to find the percent of people in your community who support tougher penalties for running red lights?
   b. What is an example of a survey question that is likely to yield unbiased information?

Name ______________________ Class ______________ Date ______________

11-8 Practice (continued) *Form G*

Samples and Surveys

8. A state's Department of Transportation wants to determine whether the drivers of semi-trailer trucks on an interstate highway would like to have a separate lane for large trucks.

a. What sampling method could the department use to find the percent of the semi-trailer truck drivers who would like a separate lane?

b. What is an example of a survey question that is likely to yield no bias?

A committee surveys public response to a plan to add bicycle lanes to downtown city streets. Describe a sampling method that can be used for each population.

9. bicyclists

10. car drivers

11. downtown business owners

12. a. Write a survey question to find out the number of students in your class who plan to travel out of state after graduation.

b. Describe the sampling method you would use.

c. Conduct your survey.

13. A television show's website asks every 20th person who visits the site to name their favorite TV star.

a. What sampling method is the survey using?

b. Describe any bias in the sampling method.

14. Biologists test 10 fish selected at random from each tank at a fish hatchery. The sample statistics show that 32% of the fish have a certain chemical present in their bodies and 68% do not have the chemical.

a. What is the population?

b. What is the sample?

c. What general conclusion can be made about the population?

15. Reasoning Explain why the results of a survey could be biased even if the survey sample is selected from the population at random.

Name ______________________ Class ____________ Date ____________

11-8 Standardized Test Prep

Samples and Surveys

Multiple Choice

For Exercises 1–4, choose the correct letter.

1. The School Dance Committee conducts a survey to find what type of music students would like to hear at the next dance. Which sampling method is *least* likely to result in a biased sample?

(A) Call 20% of the people in the senior class directory.

(B) Interview every 10th student as they enter the school.

(C) Ask every 5th person leaving a school orchestra concert.

(D) Set up a jazz website where students can list their 3 favorite songs.

2. A news reporter wants to determine what types of movies are most popular in her city. She surveys the first 20 people leaving a movie theater at 8:00 P.M. on a Friday. Which best describes the sampling method used in this situation?

(F) convenience sample

(G) self-selected sample

(H) random sample

(I) systematic sample

3. A veterinarian monitors a litter of 8 kittens and records their ages in days when they first open their eyes. Which type of study method was used in this situation?

(A) controlled experiment

(B) observational study

(C) random sample

(D) survey

4. A high-school principal wants to determine how students feel about a new gym that has been proposed for the school. Which survey question is most likely to yield information that has no bias?

(F) Do you think that the school should build a new gym?

(G) Do you think that building a new gym will be a waste of money?

(H) Shouldn't the school build a new gym to promote healthy exercise?

(I) Should the school build a new gym when the science lab is outdated?

5. The manager of an athletic store selects every tenth name on a list of the players in a city baseball league for middle school students. He asks each selected player what brand of glove he or she uses while playing baseball. Assuming that the sample accurately reflects the population, what is the population in this situation?

(A) all baseball players in the city

(B) all customers of the athletic store

(C) all baseball players in the league

(D) all middle school students in the city

Short Response

6. Describe a sampling method you could use to find the type of music that is most popular among students at your school. Tell why the sample is unlikely to have a bias.

Name ______________________ Class ____________ Date ____________

11-9 Think About a Plan

Binomial Distributions

Weather A scientist hopes to launch a weather balloon on one of the next three mornings. For each morning, there is a 40% chance of suitable weather. What is the probability that there will be at least one morning with suitable weather?

Understanding the Problem

1. What is the probability that a morning will have suitable weather?

2. What is the probability that a morning will have unsuitable weather?

3. How many chances does the scientist have to launch the balloon?

4. What is the problem asking you to determine?

____

____

Planning the Solution

5. What binomial can help you find the binomial distribution for this problem?

6. Expand your binomial.

7. What should you substitute for the variables in your binomial expansion?

____

8. Which terms of your binomial expansion do you need to solve the problem?

Explain.______________________________________

____

____.

Getting an Answer

9. Use your binomial expansion to find the probability that there will be at least one morning with suitable weather.

Name ______________________ Class ____________ Date ____________

11-9 Practice

Form G

Binomial Distributions

Find the probability of x successes in n trials for the given probability of success p on each trial.

1. $x = 5, n = 5, p = 0.4$
2. $x = 2, n = 8, p = 0.9$
3. $x = 3, n = 10, p = 0.25$
4. $x = 1, n = 3, p = 0.2$
5. A light fixture contains 6 light bulbs. With normal use, each bulb has an 85% chance of lasting for 4 months. What is the probability that all 6 bulbs will last for 4 months?

Expand each binomial.

6. $(2a + 4b)^3$
7. $(m + 3n)^4$
8. $(2c - d)^5$
9. $(5s + t)^4$

Find the indicated term of each binomial expansion.

10. third term of $(2a - b)^8$
11. fifth term of $(r + 3s)^5$
12. fourth term of $(-2x + 3y)^6$
13. first term of $(8g + 6h)^3$

Use the binomial expansion of $(p + q)^n$ to calculate each binomial distribution.

14. $n = 5, p = 0.6$
15. $n = 3, p = 0.7$
16. The probability that the weather will be acceptable for a launch of a satellite over the next 3 days is 70% each day. What is the probability that the weather will be acceptable at least 1 of the next 3 days?
17. A poll shows that 60% of a school district's home owners favor an increase in property tax to fund a new high school. What is the probability that exactly 4 of 5 people chosen at random favor a tax increase?

Name ______________________ Class __________ Date __________

11-9 Practice (continued)

Form G

Binomial Distributions

There is a 60% probability of rain each of the next 5 days. Find each probability. Round to the nearest whole percent.

18. It will rain on at least 3 of the next 5 days.

19. It will rain on at least 1 of the next 5 days.

20. It will rain on at least 1 of the next 4 days.

21. It will rain on at least 1 of the next 2 days.

22. **Open-Ended** Describe a situation with a 20% probability of success in each of 4 trials. Graph the binomial distribution.

23. The probability that an egg from one farm is small is 10%. What is the probability that exactly 1 egg in a sample of 4 eggs is too small?

In one neighborhood the probability of a power outage during a rainstorm is 4%. Find each probability.

24. P(at least 1 power outage in the next 5 rainstorms)

25. P(at least 2 power outages in the next 10 rainstorms)

26. P(at least 1 power outage in the next 20 rainstorms)

27. **Writing** Explain the relationship between the expansion of $(x + y)^{12}$ and the 12th row of Pascal's triangle.

28. A newspaper carrier can throw the paper and have it land on a customer's porch 85% of the time. Use the Binomial Theorem to calculate each probability for the deliverer's first 3 throws of the morning.
    a. The carrier does not land any papers on a porch.
    b. The carrier lands only 1 paper on a porch.
    c. The carrier lands exactly 2 papers on a porch.
    d. The carrier lands all 3 papers on a porch.

29. **Reasoning** The probability that a baby born in Scotland has red hair is 13%. A certain Scottish hospital has an average of 20 babies born per week. At the beginning of the week, the hospital has 3 "It's a Redhead!" stickers available to put on the babies' cribs. Does this seem to be an adequate amount? Justify your answer.

Name ______________________ Class ____________ Date ____________

11-9 Standardized Test Prep

Binomial Distributions

Multiple Choice

For Exercises 1–5, choose the correct letter.

1. The probability that a newborn baby at a certain hospital is male is 50%. What is the probability that exactly 2 of 3 babies born in the hospital on any day are male?

(A) 37.5% (B) 50% (C) 66.7% (D) 75%

2. The probability that a newborn baby at the hospital is female is 50%. What is the probability that at least 2 babies of 3 children born on a certain day are female?

(F) 33.3% (G) 37.5% (H) 50% (I) 66.7%

3. What is the fifth term of the expansion of $(2x - y)^8$?

(A) $-1792x^5y^3$ (B) $-448x^3y^5$ (C) $256x^4y^4$ (D) $1120x^4y^4$

4. A poll shows that 30% of voters favor an earlier curfew. Find the probability that all of five voters chosen at random favor an earlier curfew.

(F) 0.24% (G) 1.5% (H) 4.1% (I) 16.7%

5. The probability that a machine part is defective is 10%. Find the probability that no more than 2 out of 12 parts tested are defective.

(A) 28% (B) 66% (C) 89% (D) 98%

Short Response

6. A scientist runs an experiment 4 times. Each run has a 65% chance of success. Calculate and graph the distribution of binomial probabilities for the experiment.

Name ____________________ Class ____________ Date ____________

11-10 Think About a Plan

Normal Distributions

Agriculture To win a prize, a tomato must be greater than 4 in. in diameter. The diameters of a crop of tomatoes grown in a special soil are normally distributed, with a mean of 3.2 in. and a standard deviation of 0.4 in. What is the probability that a tomato grown in the special soil will be a winner?

Know

1. A tomato must have a diameter greater than ☐ to win a prize.

2. The mean diameter of the crop of tomatoes is ☐ .

3. The standard deviation of the diameters of the crop of tomatoes is ☐ .

Need

4. To solve the problem I need to find:

____

____.

Plan

5. Draw a normal curve. Label the mean and intervals that are multiples of the standard deviation from the mean.

6. What is the percent of the crop with diameters that are greater than the mean?

7. What is the percent of the crop with diameters that are greater than the mean and less than 4 in.? How do you know? ____________________

____.

8. How can you find the percent of the crop with diameters greater than 4 in.?

____

____.

9. What is the probability that a tomato grown in the special soil will be a winner?

Name ______________________ Class ____________ Date ____________

11-10 Practice — Normal Distributions

Form G

The actual weights of bags of pet food are normally distributed about the mean. Use the graph at the right for Exercises 1–4.

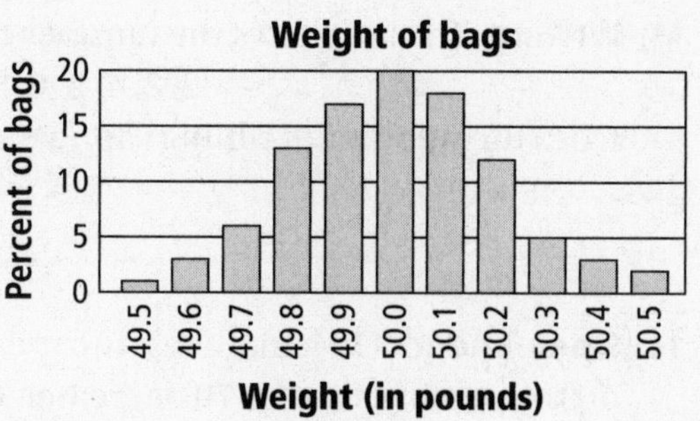

1. About what percent of bags of pet food weigh 49.9 lb–50.1 lb?

2. About what percent of bags weigh less than 49.8 lb?

3. In a group of 250 bags, how many would you expect to weigh more than 50.4 lb?

4. The mean of the data is 50, and the standard deviation is 0.2. Approximately what percent of bags are within one standard deviation of the mean weight?

Sketch a normal curve for each distribution. Label the *x*-axis values at one, two, and three standard deviations from the mean.

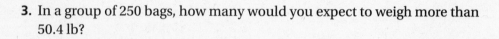

5. mean = 95; standard deviation = 12

6. mean = 100; standard deviation = 15

7. mean = 60; standard deviation = 6

8. mean = 23.8; standard deviation = 5.2

A set of data has a normal distribution with a mean of 5.1 and a standard deviation of 0.9. Find the percent of data within each interval.

9. from 4.2 to 5.1

10. from 6.0 to 6.9

11. greater than 6.9

12. The number of miles on a car when a certain part fails is normally distributed, with a mean of 60,000 and a standard deviation of 5000.
    a. Sketch the normal curve for the distribution. Label the *x*-axis values at one, two, and three standard deviations from the mean.
    b. What is the probability that the part will NOT fail between 55,000 and 65,000 miles?

Name ______________________ Class ____________ Date ____________

11-10 Practice (continued) — Form G
Normal Distributions

13. Writing The list shows the number of siblings for each person in a class:

2, 2, 4, 2, 0, 2, 5, 2, 2, 1, 0, 2

Does the number of siblings appear close to being distributed normally? Explain.

14. Open-Ended On a math test the mean score is 82 with a standard deviation of 3. A passing score is 70 or greater. Choose a passing score that you would consider to be an outlier. Justify your choice.

15. A college only accepts students who score in the top 16% on the entrance exam. The exam scores are normally distributed, with a mean of 25 and a standard deviation of 3.8. To the nearest whole number, what is the least score you could earn and still be accepted to the college?

A normal distribution has a mean of 50 and a standard deviation of 6. Find the probability that a value selected at random is in the given interval.

16. from 44 to 50

17. from 38 to 56

18. from 50 to 62

19. at least 50

20. at most 56

21. at least 38

22. The table at the right shows the heights of sunflowers planted at the same time in a garden.

a. Draw a histogram to represent the data.

b. Does the histogram approximate a normal curve? Explain.

Height (in.)	Frequency
56	3
57	2
58	2
59	6
60	3
61	4
62	5
63	5
64	3

23. Reasoning In a set of data, the value 591 is 2 standard deviations from the mean and the value 462 is 1 standard deviation from the mean. Name two possible values for the mean. Justify your answers.

Name ______________________ Class ____________ Date ____________

11-10 Standardized Test Prep

Normal Distributions

Multiple Choice

For Exercises 1–5, choose the correct letter.

1. The mean number of pairs of shoes sold daily by a shoe store is 36, with a standard deviation of 3. On what percent of days would you expect the store to sell from 33 to 42 pairs of shoes?

(A) 13.5% (B) 50% (C) 68% (D) 81.5%

2. What is the standard deviation for the normal distribution shown at the right?

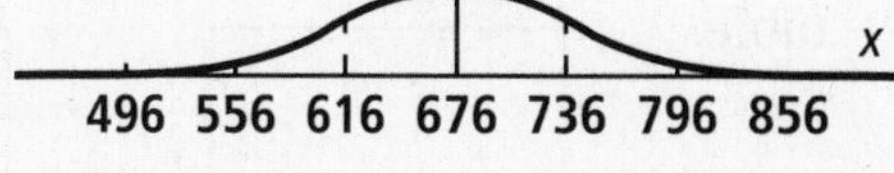

(F) 60 (H) 120

(G) 360 (I) 676

3. A normal distribution has a mean of 700 and a standard deviation of 35. What is the probability that a value selected at random is at most 630?

(A) 0.0235 (B) 0.025 (C) 0.700 (D) 0.975

4. Scores on an exam are distributed normally with a mean of 76 and a standard deviation of 10. Out of 230 tests, about how many students score above 96?

(F) 2 (G) 3 (H) 6 (I) 8

5. A hardware store sells bags of mixed nails. The number of nails of a given length is distributed normally with a mean length of 5 in. and a standard deviation of 0.03 in. About how many nails in a bag of 120 are between 4.97 in. and 5.03 in. long?

(A) 34 (B) 41 (C) 68 (D) 82

Short Response

6. The heights of the girls in a school choir are distributed normally, with a mean of 64 and a standard deviation of 1.75. If 38 girls are between 60.5 in. and 67.5 in. tall, how many girls are in the choir? Show your work.

Name ____________________ Class ____________ Date ____________

12-1 Think About a Plan

Adding and Subtracting Matrices

Data Analysis Refer to the table.

a. Find the total number of people participating in each activity.

b. Find the difference between the numbers of males and females in each activity.

c. Reasoning In part (b), does the order of the matrices matter? Explain.

U.S. Participation in Selected Leisure Activities (millions)

Activity	Male	Female
Movies	59.2	65.4
Exercise Programs	54.3	59.0
Sports Events	40.5	31.1
Home Improvement	45.4	41.8

SOURCE: U.S. National Endowment for the Arts

1. Write matrices to show the information from the table.

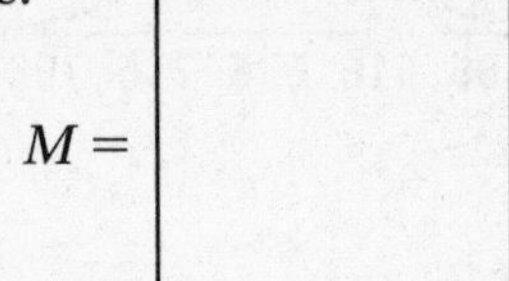

$M =$

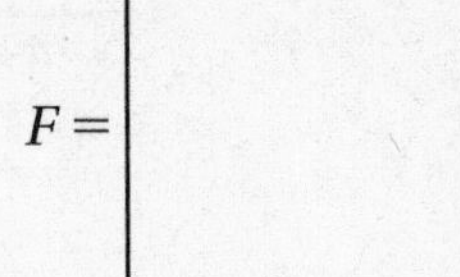

$F =$

2. Write a matrix equation to find the number of people, in millions, participating in each activity. $T =$

3. Solve the matrix equation. How many million people participate in each activity?

$T =$

Movies ______ Exercise Programs ______

Sports Events ______ Home Improvement ______

4. Write a matrix equation to find the difference, in millions, between the number of males and females in each activity. $T =$

5. Solve the matrix equation. What is the difference, in millions, between the number of males and females in each activity?

$T =$

Movies ______ Exercise Programs ______

Sports Events ______ Home Improvement ______

6. Does the order of the matrices matter? Explain. ____________________

____

____

____________________.

Name ______________________ Class ____________ Date ____________

12-1 Practice — Form G

Adding and Subtracting Matrices

Find each sum or difference.

1. $\begin{bmatrix} 3 & 2 \\ 8 & -1 \end{bmatrix} + \begin{bmatrix} -2 & 2 \\ 4 & 5 \end{bmatrix}$

2. $\begin{bmatrix} 3 & -4 \\ 1 & 2 \\ -7 & 1 \end{bmatrix} - \begin{bmatrix} 0 & 5 \\ -3 & 2 \\ -2 & 4 \end{bmatrix}$

3. $\begin{bmatrix} 6 & 3 \\ 9 & -1 \\ 2 & 4 \\ -3 & 0 \end{bmatrix} + \begin{bmatrix} 0 & -1 \\ 1 & 0 \\ 3 & 2 \\ 1 & 0 \end{bmatrix}$

4. $\begin{bmatrix} 0.5 & -0.1 \\ 1.2 & 2.3 \end{bmatrix} - \begin{bmatrix} 0.2 & 0.1 \\ 0.4 & -1.4 \end{bmatrix}$

Solve each matrix equation.

5. $X - \begin{bmatrix} 3 & 4 \\ 4 & 2 \\ 1 & 9 \end{bmatrix} = \begin{bmatrix} 5 & 7 \\ 9 & 12 \\ 3 & 2 \end{bmatrix}$

6. $X + \begin{bmatrix} 20 & -9 & -3 \\ 19 & -2 & -5 \\ -1 & 0 & -8 \end{bmatrix} = \begin{bmatrix} -7 & 92 & -5 \\ 0 & 91 & -6 \\ -9 & -1 & 12 \end{bmatrix}$

7. $\begin{bmatrix} -2 & -3 \\ 2 & 2 \end{bmatrix} = X - \begin{bmatrix} 1 & -1 \\ -2 & 2 \end{bmatrix}$

8. $\begin{bmatrix} 2 & 2 & 0 \\ 1 & -1 & -1 \end{bmatrix} = \begin{bmatrix} 2 & -2 & 3 \\ -3 & -3 & 4 \end{bmatrix} - X$

Find each sum.

9. $\begin{bmatrix} 5 & -2 & 1 \\ 0 & -3 & 4 \end{bmatrix} + \begin{bmatrix} -5 & 2 & -1 \\ 0 & 3 & -4 \end{bmatrix}$

10. $\begin{bmatrix} 0 & 0 \\ 0 & 0 \end{bmatrix} + \begin{bmatrix} -8 & 8 \\ 9 & -9 \end{bmatrix}$

Find the value of each variable.

11. $\begin{bmatrix} 8 & 6 \\ -2 & 0 \end{bmatrix} = \begin{bmatrix} 3a - 1 & 2a \\ 5b + 3 & a + 3b \end{bmatrix}$

12. $\begin{bmatrix} 4 & -3 \\ 7 & 1 \end{bmatrix} - \begin{bmatrix} 2 & 0 \\ 3 & -2 \end{bmatrix} = \begin{bmatrix} p & q \\ 4 & r \end{bmatrix}$

Find each matrix sum or difference if possible. If not possible, explain.

$P = \begin{bmatrix} 0 & 2 & 4 \\ 9 & 8 & 2 \end{bmatrix}$ $\quad Q = \begin{bmatrix} -2 & -4 & 1 \\ 9 & 7 & 0 \end{bmatrix}$ $\quad R = \begin{bmatrix} 4 & -1 & 0 \\ 2 & 3 & 5 \\ 0 & -6 & 1 \end{bmatrix}$ $\quad S = \begin{bmatrix} 0 & -6 & 7 \\ 3 & 8 & 2 \\ 0 & -1 & 5 \end{bmatrix}$

13. $P + Q$

14. $S - R$

15. $Q + R$

16. $Q - P$

Name ______________________ Class __________ Date __________

12-1 Practice (continued) — Form G

Adding and Subtracting Matrices

17. The table shows the number of males and females in four clubs at a high school for two school years.

Club Membership

	1961–1962		2009–2010	
	Males	Females	Males	Females
Beta	37	23	56	58
Spanish	0	93	76	82
Chess	87	0	102	34
Library	6	18	27	29

a. Write four 4×1 matrices, *A, B, C,* and *D,* to represent the male and female club membership for 1961–1962 and 2009–2010.

b. Write and solve a matrix equation to find matrix *X*, the total number of members in each club for 1961–1962.

c. Did the total number of female club members increase or decrease between the two school years? By what amount?

18. Reasoning Let $A = \begin{bmatrix} a_{11} & a_{12} \\ a_{21} & a_{22} \end{bmatrix}$, $B = \begin{bmatrix} b_{11} & b_{12} \\ b_{21} & b_{22} \end{bmatrix}$, and $A + B = \begin{bmatrix} 0 & 0 \\ 0 & 0 \end{bmatrix}$.

If $a_{11} \cdot b_{11} = -16$ and $a_{11} > 0$, what is the value of b_{11}?

19. The table shows the time each member of two relay teams took to complete her leg of a relay race. Team II won the race by 2 s. How many seconds did Trina take to run her leg of the race?

Relay Race Results

	Team I		Team II	
Leg	Name	Time (s)	Name	Time (s)
1	Ali	22	Lea	23
2	Bryn	25	Niki	22
3	Mai	23	Trina	■
4	Tara	21	Sara	20

Writing Determine whether the two matrices in each pair are equal. Explain.

20. $\begin{bmatrix} 2 \\ \sqrt{9} \\ 16 \end{bmatrix}$; $\begin{bmatrix} \frac{4}{2} & 3 & 4^2 \end{bmatrix}$

21. $\begin{bmatrix} 2(3) & 3(1.5) \\ 7 & \frac{10}{2} \end{bmatrix}$; $\begin{bmatrix} 6 & 4.5 \\ 7 & 5 \end{bmatrix}$

Name ____________________ Class __________ Date __________

12-1 Standardized Test Prep

Adding and Subtracting Matrices

Multiple Choice

For Exercises 1–4, choose the correct letter.

1. What matrix is equal to the difference $\begin{bmatrix} 5 & 9 & -3 \\ 6 & -2 & 1 \end{bmatrix} - \begin{bmatrix} 6 & 4 & 2 \\ 0 & 3 & 5 \end{bmatrix}$?

Ⓐ $\begin{bmatrix} -1 & -5 & -5 \\ -6 & -5 & -4 \end{bmatrix}$ Ⓑ $\begin{bmatrix} 1 & -5 & 5 \\ -6 & 5 & 4 \end{bmatrix}$ Ⓒ $\begin{bmatrix} -1 & 5 & -5 \\ 6 & -5 & -4 \end{bmatrix}$ Ⓓ $\begin{bmatrix} 1 & 5 & 5 \\ 6 & 5 & 4 \end{bmatrix}$

2. Which matrix is equivalent to X in the equation $\begin{bmatrix} 4 & 0 \\ 1 & -2 \end{bmatrix} + X = \begin{bmatrix} -2 & 0 \\ 1 & 4 \end{bmatrix}$?

Ⓕ $\begin{bmatrix} -6 & 0 \\ 0 & 6 \end{bmatrix}$ Ⓖ $\begin{bmatrix} 2 & 0 \\ 0 & 2 \end{bmatrix}$ Ⓗ $\begin{bmatrix} 2 & 0 \\ 2 & 2 \end{bmatrix}$ Ⓘ $\begin{bmatrix} 6 & 0 \\ 0 & -6 \end{bmatrix}$

3. Which matrix is equivalent to P in the equation $\begin{bmatrix} 7 & 8 \\ 9 & 10 \\ 11 & 12 \end{bmatrix} - P = \begin{bmatrix} 0 & 0 \\ 0 & 0 \\ 0 & 0 \end{bmatrix}$?

Ⓐ $\begin{bmatrix} 0 & 0 \\ 0 & 0 \\ 0 & 0 \end{bmatrix}$ Ⓑ $\begin{bmatrix} -1 & -1 \\ -1 & -1 \\ -1 & -1 \end{bmatrix}$ Ⓒ $\begin{bmatrix} -7 & -8 \\ -9 & -10 \\ -11 & -12 \end{bmatrix}$ Ⓓ $\begin{bmatrix} 7 & 8 \\ 9 & 10 \\ 11 & 12 \end{bmatrix}$

4. Let $R + S = \begin{bmatrix} 0 & 0 & 0 & 0 \\ 0 & 0 & 0 & 0 \end{bmatrix}$. If $R = \begin{bmatrix} -3 & 2 & 9 \\ 7 & 6 & -4 \end{bmatrix}$, which matrix is equivalent to S?

Ⓕ $\begin{bmatrix} -3 & 2 & 9 \\ 7 & 6 & -4 \end{bmatrix}$ Ⓖ $\begin{bmatrix} -1 & -1 & -1 \\ -1 & -1 & -1 \end{bmatrix}$ Ⓗ $\begin{bmatrix} 3 & -2 & -9 \\ -7 & -6 & 4 \end{bmatrix}$ Ⓓ $\begin{bmatrix} 0 & 0 & 0 \\ 0 & 0 & 0 \end{bmatrix}$

Short Response

5. If $\begin{bmatrix} 8 & 2x - 1 \\ 2y + 1 & 3 \end{bmatrix} = \begin{bmatrix} 8 & -7 \\ y & -x \end{bmatrix}$, what values of x and y make the equation true? Show your work.

Name ______________________ Class ______________ Date ____________

12-2 Think About a Plan

Matrix Multiplication

Sport Two teams are competing in a track meet. Points for individual events are awarded as follows: 5 points for first place, 3 points for second place, and 1 point for third place. Points for team relays are awarded as follows: 5 points for first place and no points for second place.

a. Use matrix operations to determine the score in the track meet.

b. Who would win if the scoring were changed to 5 points for first place, 2 points for second place, and 1 point for third place in each individual event with relay scoring remaining 5 points for first place?

Team	Individual Events			Relays	
	First	Second	Third	First	Second
West River	8	5	2	8	5
River's Edge	6	9	12	6	9

Know

1. What is the given information? ____

____.

Need

2. To solve the problem I need to: ____

____.

Plan

3. Write the number of wins as a 2×5 matrix and the original and alternate point values as 5×1 matrices.

4. Use matrix multiplication to find the original total team scores and the alternate total team scores for the track meet.

5. What was the score in the track meet? ______________________________________

6. Who would win if the scoring were changed? ____________________________________

Name ______________________ Class ____________ Date ____________

12-2 Practice — Form G

Matrix Multiplication

Use matrices *A*, *B*, *C*, and *D*. Find each product, sum, or difference.

$A = \begin{bmatrix} 1 & -1 \\ 3 & -2 \end{bmatrix}$ $B = \begin{bmatrix} 0 & 2 \\ -2 & 1 \\ -1 & 0 \end{bmatrix}$ $C = \begin{bmatrix} 3 & -3 & -1 \\ 2 & -2 & 4 \end{bmatrix}$ $D = \begin{bmatrix} 1 & 0 \\ 0 & 1 \end{bmatrix}$

1. $2D$

2. $0.2B$

3. $\frac{1}{4}C$

4. DC

5. BD

6. $2A + 4D$

7. $5D - A$

8. $3D + A$

9. $3C - 2DC$

Solve each matrix equation. Check your answers.

10. $2\begin{bmatrix} 0 & 1 \\ 3 & -4 \end{bmatrix} - 3X = \begin{bmatrix} 9 & -6 \\ 1 & -2 \end{bmatrix}$

11. $\frac{1}{2}X + \begin{bmatrix} 5 & -1 \\ 0 & \frac{2}{3} \end{bmatrix} = 2\begin{bmatrix} 3 & 0 \\ 1 & 2 \end{bmatrix}$

Find each product.

12. $\begin{bmatrix} 2 & -1 \\ 5 & 3 \end{bmatrix}\begin{bmatrix} 0 & 4 \\ -3 & 1 \end{bmatrix}$

13. $\begin{bmatrix} 0 & 4 \\ -3 & 1 \end{bmatrix}\begin{bmatrix} 2 & -1 \\ 5 & 3 \end{bmatrix}$

14. $\begin{bmatrix} 2 & -1 & 6 \end{bmatrix}\begin{bmatrix} 2 \\ -1 \\ 6 \end{bmatrix}$

15. $\begin{bmatrix} 2 & -1 & 6 \end{bmatrix}\begin{bmatrix} 0 & 2 \\ 0 & -1 \\ 0 & 6 \end{bmatrix}$

16. $\begin{bmatrix} 2 & -1 & 6 \end{bmatrix}\begin{bmatrix} 2 & 0 \\ -1 & 0 \\ 6 & 0 \end{bmatrix}$

17. $\begin{bmatrix} 0 & 0 & 0 \\ 2 & -1 & 6 \end{bmatrix}\begin{bmatrix} 2 & 0 \\ -1 & 0 \\ 6 & 0 \end{bmatrix}$

18. $\begin{bmatrix} -5 & 0 \\ 0 & -4 \end{bmatrix}\begin{bmatrix} -5 & 0 \\ 0 & -4 \end{bmatrix}$

19. $\begin{bmatrix} 4 & 3 \\ 9 & 7 \end{bmatrix}\begin{bmatrix} 6 & 3 \\ 9 & 4 \end{bmatrix}$

20. $\begin{bmatrix} 3 & 1 \\ -2 & 4 \\ -1 & 0 \end{bmatrix}\begin{bmatrix} -1 & 0 \\ 0 & -1 \end{bmatrix}$

21. $\begin{bmatrix} 0 & 4 & 1 \\ 2 & -2 & -1 \end{bmatrix}\begin{bmatrix} 1 \\ 6 \\ 3 \end{bmatrix}$

Name ______________________ Class ____________ Date ____________

12-2 Practice (continued) — Form G

Matrix Multiplication

22. A carpenter builds three boxes. One box uses 12 nails. The second box uses 6 nails and 6 screws. The third box uses 8 screws and 2 hinges. Nails cost $.04 each, screws cost $.06 each, and hinges cost $.12 each.

a. Write a matrix to show the number of each type of hardware in each box.

b. Write a matrix to show the cost of each type of hardware.

c. Find the matrix showing the cost of hardware for each box.

Determine whether the product exists.

$P = \begin{bmatrix} 4 & -5 \\ 0 & 1 \end{bmatrix}$ $Q = \begin{bmatrix} 5 \\ 9 \end{bmatrix}$ $R = \begin{bmatrix} -3 & 2 \end{bmatrix}$ $S = \begin{bmatrix} 0 & -1 \\ 4 & 6 \end{bmatrix}$

23. SP **24.** QS **25.** PR **26.** QR

27. A rugby game consists of two 40-min halves. In rugby, a try (T) is 5 points, a conversion kick (C) is 2 points, a penalty kick (PK) is 3 points, and a drop goal (DG) is 3 points.

a. Use matrix operations to determine the score in a game between the Austin Huns and the Dallas Harlequins.

Austin Huns vs. Dallas Harlequins

	First Half				Second Half			
Team	T	C	PK	DG	T	C	PK	DG
Austin	2	2	1	0	2	0	2	0
Dallas	1	0	3	0	2	1	0	1

b. Many years ago, a try was worth only 4 points and a conversion was worth 3 points. If the second half were scored by the old rules, which team would win the game?

28. Reasoning Real-number multiplication is commutative. Is the same true for matrix multiplication? Explain your reasoning.

29. Error Analysis A student says $\begin{bmatrix} 1 & 1 \\ 1 & 1 \end{bmatrix}$ is the multiplicative identity for a 2×2 matrix. Do you agree? If not, what is the correct matrix?

Name ______________________ Class ____________ Date ____________

12-2 Standardized Test Prep

Matrix Multiplication

Multiple Choice

For Exercises 1–3, choose the correct letter.

1. Which matrix is equivalent to $-2\begin{bmatrix} 1 & 5 & -3 \\ 0 & 2 & 4 \\ 7 & -2 & 0 \end{bmatrix}$?

(A) $\begin{bmatrix} -2 & -10 & 6 \\ 0 & -4 & -8 \\ -14 & 4 & 0 \end{bmatrix}$

(B) $\begin{bmatrix} 1 & 5 & -3 \\ 0 & -4 & -8 \\ 7 & -2 & 0 \end{bmatrix}$

(C) $\begin{bmatrix} -2 & -10 & 6 \\ 0 & 2 & 4 \\ 7 & -2 & 0 \end{bmatrix}$

(D) $\begin{bmatrix} -1 & 3 & -5 \\ -2 & 0 & 2 \\ 5 & -4 & -2 \end{bmatrix}$

2. What is the product $\begin{bmatrix} 6 & -1 \\ 3 & 9 \end{bmatrix}\begin{bmatrix} 3 \\ -6 \end{bmatrix}$?

(F) $\begin{bmatrix} 18 & -3 \\ -18 & -54 \end{bmatrix}$

(G) $\begin{bmatrix} 24 & -45 \end{bmatrix}$

(H) $\begin{bmatrix} 24 \\ -45 \end{bmatrix}$

(I) $\begin{bmatrix} 15 & 36 \\ -30 & -72 \end{bmatrix}$

3. Which matrix is the solution of $\begin{bmatrix} 1 & -1 & 2 \\ 2 & 0 & -1 \end{bmatrix} - 2X = \begin{bmatrix} 4 & 5 & 6 \\ 6 & 5 & 4 \end{bmatrix}$?

(A) $\begin{bmatrix} 3 & 6 & 4 \\ 4 & 5 & 5 \end{bmatrix}$

(B) $\begin{bmatrix} -6 & -12 & -8 \\ -8 & -10 & -10 \end{bmatrix}$

(C) $\begin{bmatrix} \frac{3}{2} & 3 & 2 \\ 2 & \frac{5}{2} & \frac{5}{2} \end{bmatrix}$

(D) $\begin{bmatrix} -\frac{3}{2} & -3 & -2 \\ -2 & -\frac{5}{2} & -\frac{5}{2} \end{bmatrix}$

Extended Response

4. The table shows the number of tiles used in a house. Blue tiles cost \$1.20 each, white cost \$1.50 each, and green cost \$.80 each. Write and solve a matrix equation to find the total cost of the tile. Show your work.

Tiles Used

	Blue	White	Green
Bath #1	20	50	10
Bath #2	15	30	5
Kitchen	25	100	50

Name ______________________ Class ____________ Date ____________

12-3 Think About a Plan

Determinants and Inverses

Geometry Find the area of the figure to the right.

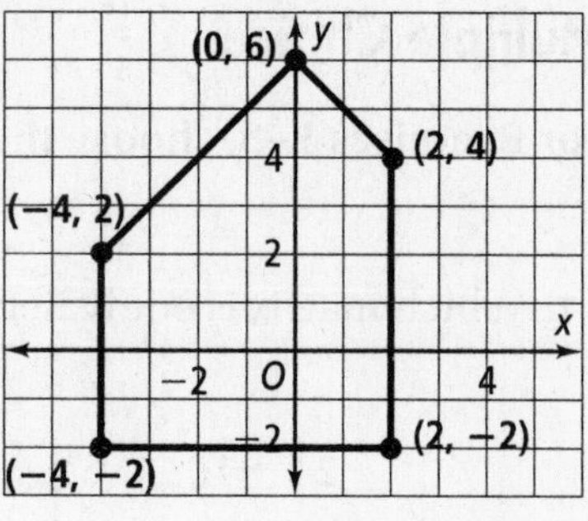

Understanding the Problem

1. You know how to find the area of what shape using matrices?

2. Can you divide the figure into these shapes? Explain.

____

____

____.

3. What is the problem asking you to find?

____

____

Planning the Solution

4. Divide the figure into these shapes. List the vertices of the shapes.

____

____.

5. Write an expression to find the area of the figure.

Getting an Answer

6. Simplify your expression to find the area of the figure.

7. Is your answer reasonable? Explain.

____

____.

Name ______________________ Class ____________ Date ____________

12-3 Practice

Form G

Determinants and Inverses

Determine whether the matrices are multiplicative inverses.

1. $\begin{bmatrix} 2 & 1 \\ 5 & 3 \end{bmatrix}, \begin{bmatrix} 3 & -1 \\ -5 & 2 \end{bmatrix}$

2. $\begin{bmatrix} 4 & 9 \\ 2 & 6 \end{bmatrix}, \begin{bmatrix} 1 & -\frac{3}{2} \\ -\frac{1}{3} & \frac{2}{3} \end{bmatrix}$

3. $\begin{bmatrix} 1 & 2 \\ 3 & 4 \end{bmatrix}, \begin{bmatrix} -2 & 1 \\ \frac{3}{2} & -\frac{1}{2} \end{bmatrix}$

4. $\begin{bmatrix} 2 & 1 & 1 \\ 1 & 1 & 2 \\ 1 & 2 & 1 \end{bmatrix}, \begin{bmatrix} \frac{3}{2} & -\frac{1}{2} & -\frac{1}{2} \\ -\frac{1}{2} & -\frac{1}{2} & \frac{3}{2} \\ -\frac{1}{2} & \frac{3}{2} & -\frac{1}{2} \end{bmatrix}$

5. $\begin{bmatrix} 2 & 3 & 1 \\ -1 & 3 & -2 \\ 1 & 2 & 0 \end{bmatrix}, \begin{bmatrix} -\frac{4}{3} & -\frac{2}{3} & 3 \\ \frac{2}{3} & \frac{1}{3} & -1 \\ \frac{5}{3} & \frac{1}{3} & -3 \end{bmatrix}$

Evaluate the determinant of each matrix.

6. $\begin{bmatrix} -3 & 4 \\ 1 & -1 \end{bmatrix}$

7. $\begin{bmatrix} 3 & 9 \\ 3 & 2 \end{bmatrix}$

8. $\begin{bmatrix} 1 & -4 \\ 2 & 6 \end{bmatrix}$

9. $\begin{bmatrix} 4 & -3 \\ 1 & -8 \end{bmatrix}$

10. $\begin{bmatrix} 5 & 4 \\ 4 & 5 \end{bmatrix}$

11. $\begin{bmatrix} 1 & -12 \\ 3 & 0 \end{bmatrix}$

12. $\begin{bmatrix} 1 & 2 & -2 \\ 0 & 3 & 2 \\ 1 & -1 & 3 \end{bmatrix}$

13. $\begin{bmatrix} 0 & 2 & 3 \\ 4 & 1 & -2 \\ -2 & 3 & 1 \end{bmatrix}$

14. $\begin{bmatrix} 8 & -1 & 0 \\ 0 & 0 & 2 \\ 9 & 12 & -4 \end{bmatrix}$

Graphing Calculator Evaluate the determinant of each 3×3 matrix.

15. $\begin{bmatrix} 0 & 0 & 1 \\ 0 & 1 & 0 \\ 1 & 0 & 0 \end{bmatrix}$

16. $\begin{bmatrix} 5 & 6 & 7 \\ -2 & 9 & 10 \\ 8 & -1 & 4 \end{bmatrix}$

17. $\begin{bmatrix} 5.4 & 2.6 & 1.9 \\ -5.5 & 5.1 & 8.2 \\ 4.8 & -8.2 & 2.7 \end{bmatrix}$

18. The area between the North Carolina cities of Raleigh, Durham, and Chapel Hill is called the Research Triangle. Use the map to determine the approximate area of the Research Triangle. The coordinates are given in miles.

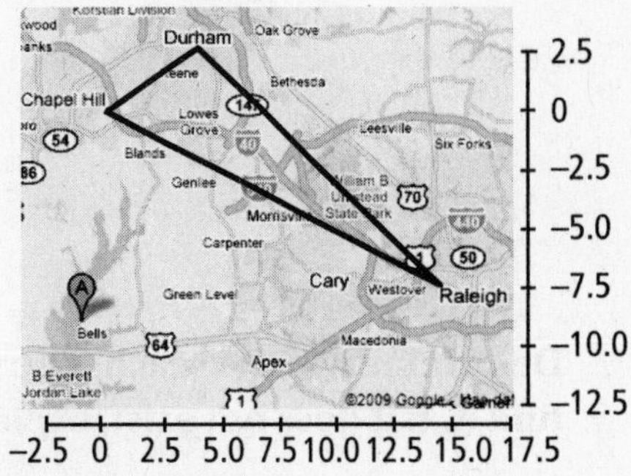

SOURCE: Google Maps

Name ______________________ Class ____________ Date ____________

12-3 Practice (continued)

Form G

Determinants and Inverses

Determine whether each matrix has an inverse. If an inverse matrix exists, find it.

19. $\begin{bmatrix} 3 & 4 \\ -3 & 4 \end{bmatrix}$

20. $\begin{bmatrix} 3 & 4 \\ 3 & 4 \end{bmatrix}$

21. $\begin{bmatrix} 4 & 3 \\ 3 & 2 \end{bmatrix}$

22. $\begin{bmatrix} 30 & -4 \\ -25 & 3 \end{bmatrix}$

23. $\begin{bmatrix} 5 & 0 \\ -5 & 1 \end{bmatrix}$

24. $\begin{bmatrix} -12 & 4 \\ -9 & 3 \end{bmatrix}$

25. Use the coding matrix $\begin{bmatrix} 3 & 6 \\ 9 & 12 \end{bmatrix}$ to encode the serial number 45-8-62-4-31-10.

Evaluate the determinant of each matrix.

26. $\begin{bmatrix} 7 & 3 \\ -6 & 4 \end{bmatrix}$

27. $\begin{bmatrix} -5 & 3 \\ 3 & 8 \end{bmatrix}$

28. $\begin{bmatrix} -2 & -2 \\ -2 & -4 \end{bmatrix}$

29. $\begin{bmatrix} 3 & -2 & 5 \\ 1 & 0 & -4 \\ -4 & 3 & 9 \end{bmatrix}$

30. $\begin{bmatrix} 4 & 4 & 4 \\ 3 & 3 & 3 \\ 1 & -1 & 3 \end{bmatrix}$

31. $\begin{bmatrix} 7 & 4 & -3 \\ 6 & 10 & -1 \\ 8 & 0 & 8 \end{bmatrix}$

32. Writing Describe how to use matrices to find the area of a polygon.

33. Find the area of the figure at the right.

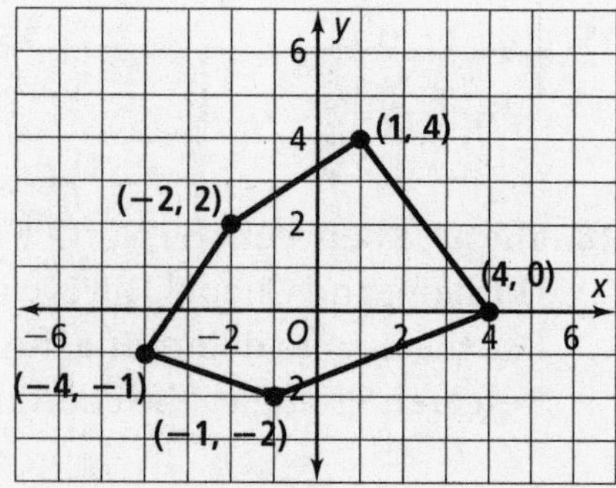

Determine whether each matrix has an inverse. If an inverse matrix exists, find it. If it does not exist, explain why not.

34. $\begin{bmatrix} 1 & 3 \\ 0 & 4 \end{bmatrix}$

35. $\begin{bmatrix} 0 & 2 \\ -1 & -1 \end{bmatrix}$

36. $\begin{bmatrix} 0 & 1 & 1 \\ 1 & 0 & 1 \\ 1 & 1 & 1 \end{bmatrix}$

Name _______________________ Class ____________ Date ____________

12-3 Standardized Test Prep

Determinants and Inverses

Gridded Response

Solve each exercise and enter your answer in the grid provided.

1. What is the determinant of $\begin{bmatrix} 4 & -2 \\ 5 & -3 \end{bmatrix}$?

2. If $A = \begin{bmatrix} 2 & 1 \\ -9 & 3 \end{bmatrix}$ and the inverse of A is $x \cdot \begin{bmatrix} 3 & -1 \\ 9 & 2 \end{bmatrix}$ what is the value of x?

3. If $\begin{bmatrix} 6 & 2 \\ 4 & 1 \end{bmatrix}$ and $A^{-1} = \begin{bmatrix} x & 1 \\ 2 & -3 \end{bmatrix}$ what is the value of x?

4. What is the determinant of $\begin{bmatrix} 1 & 0 & 2 \\ -1 & 2 & 3 \\ 0 & 3 & 2 \end{bmatrix}$?

5. What is the area of a triangle with vertices at $(-5, 0)$, $(3, -1)$, and $(2, 6)$?

Answers

1.

2.

3.

4.

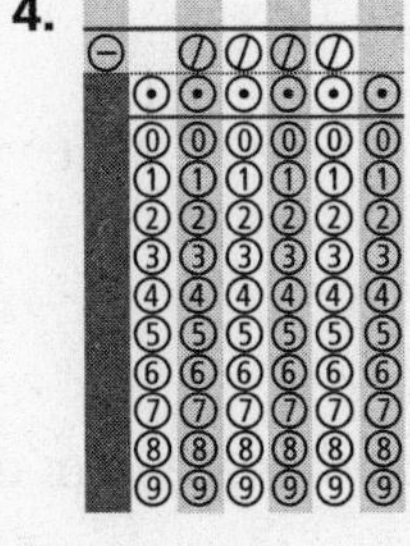

5.

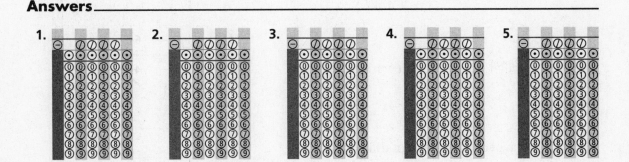

Name _______________ Class _______________ Date _______________

12-4 Think About a Plan

Inverse Matrices and Systems

Nutrition Suppose you are making a trail mix for your friends and want to fill three 1-lb bags. Almonds cost \$2.25/lb, peanuts cost \$1.30/lb, and raisins cost \$.90/lb. You want each bag to contain twice as much nuts as raisins by weight. If you spent \$4.45, how much of each ingredient did you buy?

Know

1. I need [ ] of ingredients that cost a total of [ ].

2. _______________.

3. _______________.

Need

4. To solve the problem I need to: _______________.

Plan

5. Let $x =$ the number of pounds of almonds, $y =$ the number of pounds peanuts, and $z =$ the number of pounds of raisins. Write a system of equations to solve the problem.

6. Write the system as a matrix equation.

7. Use a calculator. Solve for the variable matrix.

8. How much of each ingredient did you buy?

____

9. How can you check your solution? Does your solution check?

____

_______________.

Name ____________________ Class __________ Date __________

12-4 Practice — Form G

Inverse Matrices and Systems

Solve each matrix equation. If an equation cannot be solved, explain why.

1. $\begin{bmatrix} 0.25 & -0.75 \\ 3.5 & 2.25 \end{bmatrix} X = \begin{bmatrix} 1.5 \\ -3.75 \end{bmatrix}$

2. $\begin{bmatrix} 3 & -9 \\ 1 & -6 \end{bmatrix} X = \begin{bmatrix} 12 \\ 0 \end{bmatrix}$

3. $\begin{bmatrix} 3 & -6 \\ -1 & 2 \end{bmatrix} X = \begin{bmatrix} 4 \\ 9 \end{bmatrix}$

4. $\begin{bmatrix} 1 & 0 & -1 \\ 3 & 2 & 1 \\ -1 & 2 & 2 \end{bmatrix} X = \begin{bmatrix} 2 \\ 2 \\ -2 \end{bmatrix}$

Write each system as a matrix equation. Identify the coefficient matrix, the variable matrix, and the constant matrix.

5. $\begin{cases} 6x + 9y = 36 \\ 4x + 13y = 2 \end{cases}$

6. $\begin{cases} 3x - 4y = -9 \\ 7y = 24 \end{cases}$

7. $\begin{cases} 3a = 5 \\ b = 12 + a \end{cases}$

8. $\begin{cases} 4x - z = 9 \\ 12x + 2y = 17 \\ x - y + 12z = 3 \end{cases}$

Solve each system of equations using a matrix equation. Check your answers.

9. $\begin{cases} x + 3y = 5 \\ x + 4y = 6 \end{cases}$

10. $\begin{cases} 2x + 3y = 12 \\ x + 2y = 7 \end{cases}$

11. $\begin{cases} x - 3y = -1 \\ -6x + 19y = 6 \end{cases}$

12. $\begin{cases} 4x - 3y = 55 \\ x + y = 5 \end{cases}$

13. $\begin{cases} 6x + 7y = -12 \\ 3x - 4y = -6 \end{cases}$

14. $\begin{cases} 3x - y = 6 \\ -2x + 3y = 10 \end{cases}$

15. $\begin{cases} -3x + 4y - z = -5 \\ x - y - z = -8 \\ 2x + y + 2z = 9 \end{cases}$

16. $\begin{cases} x + y + z = 31 \\ x - y + z = 1 \\ x - 2y + 2z = 7 \end{cases}$

17. $\begin{cases} x + 2y - z = 8 \\ -2x + 3z = -4 \\ y + z = 3 \end{cases}$

18. $\begin{cases} 3x - 2y + 4z = -10 \\ y - 3z = 1 \\ 2x + z = -3 \end{cases}$

12-4 Practice (continued) Form G

Inverse Matrices and Systems

19. An apartment building has 50 units. All have one or two bedrooms. One-bedroom units rent for \$425/mo. Two-bedroom units rent for \$550/mo. When all units are occupied, the total monthly rent collected is \$25,000. How many units of each type are in the building?

20. The difference between twice Bill's age and Carlos's age is 26. The sum of Anna's age, three times Bill's age, and Carlos's age is 92. The total of the three ages is 52.

a. Write a matrix equation to represent this situation.

b. How old is each person?

Solve each system.

21. $\begin{cases} x + 2y - 3z = 18 \\ -3x - z = -20 \\ y + 3z = -13 \end{cases}$

22. $\begin{cases} x + y + 3z = 9 \\ 2y - 5z = -21 \\ 2x - 5y = 21 \end{cases}$

23. $\begin{cases} w + 2x - 3y + z = -2 \\ 2w - x - y + 3z = 3 \\ -w + 3x + y - z = 0 \\ 3w - x - 2y + 2z = -1 \end{cases}$

24. $\begin{cases} 2w + 3x - y + z = -11 \\ w + x + y + z = 0 \\ -3w - 2x - y - z = -3 \\ -2w + x + 3y + 2z = -5 \end{cases}$

Solve each matrix equation. If the coefficient matrix has no inverse, write *no unique solution.*

25. $\begin{bmatrix} 12 & -3 \\ 16 & 4 \end{bmatrix}\begin{bmatrix} x \\ y \end{bmatrix} = \begin{bmatrix} 144 \\ -64 \end{bmatrix}$

26. $\begin{bmatrix} 3 & 1 \\ 12 & 4 \end{bmatrix}\begin{bmatrix} x \\ y \end{bmatrix} = \begin{bmatrix} 9 \\ 10 \end{bmatrix}$

Determine whether each system has a unique solution.

27. $\begin{cases} 4d + 2e = 4 \\ d + 3e = 6 \end{cases}$

28. $\begin{cases} 3x - 2y = 43 \\ 9x - 6y = 40 \end{cases}$

29. $\begin{cases} -y - z = 3 \\ x + 2y + 3z = 1 \\ 4x - 5y - 6z = -50 \end{cases}$

30. Reasoning Explain how you could use a matrix equation to show that the lines represented by $y = -3x + 4$ and $y = -4x - 8$ intersect.

Name ______________________ Class ____________ Date ____________

12-4 Standardized Test Prep

Inverse Matrices and Systems

Multiple Choice

For Exercises 1–4, choose the correct letter.

1. Which matrix equation represents the system $\begin{cases} 2x - y = 11 \\ x + 3y = 2 \end{cases}$?

(A) $\begin{bmatrix} x \\ y \end{bmatrix}\begin{bmatrix} 2 & -1 \\ 1 & 3 \end{bmatrix} = \begin{bmatrix} 11 \\ 2 \end{bmatrix}$

(B) $\begin{bmatrix} 2 & -1 & 11 \\ 1 & 3 & 2 \end{bmatrix} = \begin{bmatrix} x \\ y \end{bmatrix}$

(C) $\begin{bmatrix} 2 & -1 \\ 1 & 3 \end{bmatrix}\begin{bmatrix} x \\ y \end{bmatrix} = \begin{bmatrix} 11 \\ 2 \end{bmatrix}$

(D) $\begin{bmatrix} 2 & -1 \\ 1 & 3 \end{bmatrix} = \begin{bmatrix} x \\ y \end{bmatrix}\begin{bmatrix} 11 \\ 2 \end{bmatrix}$

2. Let $\begin{bmatrix} 3 & 5 \\ -4 & -1 \end{bmatrix}\begin{bmatrix} x \\ y \end{bmatrix} = \begin{bmatrix} -4 \\ -6 \end{bmatrix}$. What values of x and y make the equation true?

(F) $(-12, -1)$ (G) $(-4, -6)$ (H) $(-3, -20)$ (I) $(2, -2)$

3. Which system has a unique solution?

(A) $\begin{cases} 3x - 2y = 43 \\ 9x - 6y = 40 \end{cases}$

(B) $\begin{cases} 6x + 8y = 16 \\ -3x - 4y = 12 \end{cases}$

(C) $\begin{cases} 2x - 5y = 6 \\ 4x + 7y = 12 \end{cases}$

(D) $\begin{cases} 4x + 2y = 10 \\ 8x + 4y = 18 \end{cases}$

4. Let $\begin{bmatrix} 5 & 1 \\ 2 & -1 \end{bmatrix}X = \begin{bmatrix} 0 \\ -14 \end{bmatrix}$. What value of X makes the equation true?

(F) $\begin{bmatrix} -2 \\ 10 \end{bmatrix}$ (G) $\begin{bmatrix} -6 \\ -15 \end{bmatrix}$ (H) $\begin{bmatrix} 0 \\ 14 \end{bmatrix}$ (I) $\begin{bmatrix} -5 \\ 2 \end{bmatrix}$

Short Response

5. The Spirit Club sold buttons for $1, hats for $4, and t-shirts for $8. They sold 3 times as many buttons as hats. Together, the number of hats and t-shirts sold was equal to the number of buttons sold. They earned a total of $460. Write and solve a matrix equation to find how many buttons, hats, and t-shirts the club sold.

Name ______________________ Class __________ Date __________

12-5 Think About a Plan

Geometric Transformations

Animation In an upcoming cartoon, the hero is a gymnast. In one scene he swings around a high bar, making two complete revolutions around the bar. What rotation matrices are needed so eight frames of the movie would show the illustrated motion, one frame after the other?

Frame 1

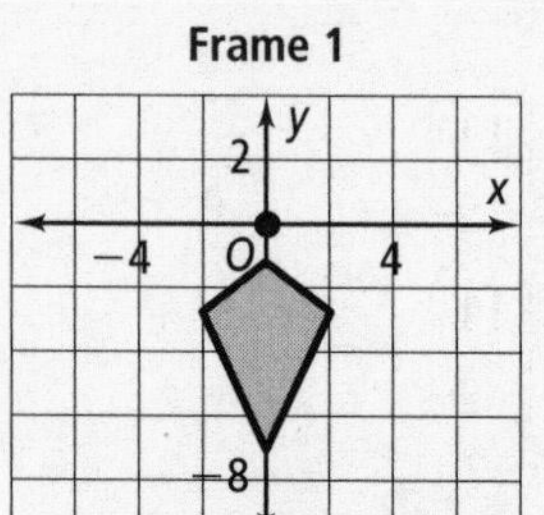

Frame 2

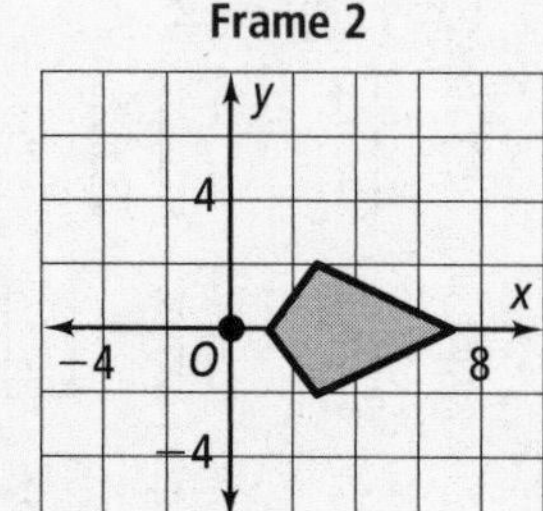

Frame 3

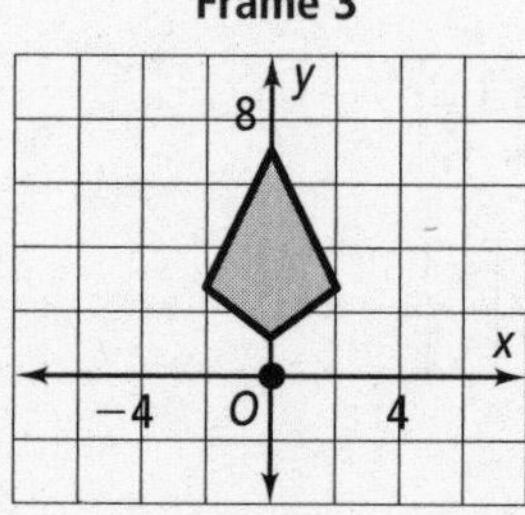

Frame 4

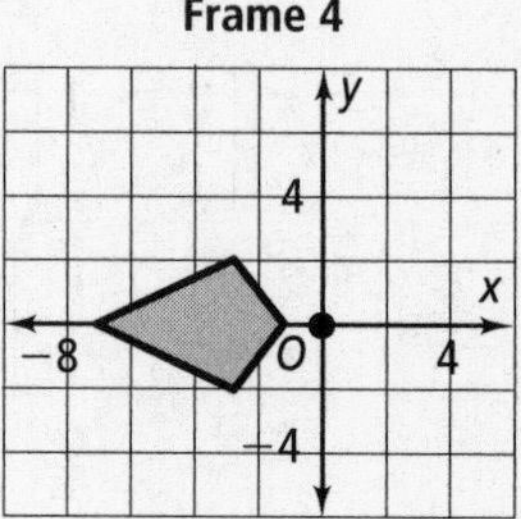

Understanding the Problem

1. Describe the rotation that occurs from one frame to the next. ______________________

2. What is the problem asking you to determine?

____

____

____.

Planning the Solution

3. Describe how the first four frames relate to the next four frames in the scene.

____

____

4. How many rotation matrices do you need? Explain.

____

____

____.

Getting an Answer

5. What rotation matrices are needed so eight frames of the movie would show the illustrated motion, one frame after the other?

Name ______________________ Class ____________ Date ____________

12-5 Practice

Form G

Geometric Transformations

Use matrix addition to find the coordinates of each image after a translation 2 units right and 4 units down. If possible, graph each pair of figures on the same coordinate plane.

1. $A(2, 4), B(4, 5), C(1, 6)$

2. $D(-5, 2), E(-6, 1), F(-3, 0)$

3. $K(1, 1), L(4, 1), M(5, -1)$

4. $G(-3, -2), H(-1, 0), J(-1, -2)$

Find the coordinates of each image after the given dilation.

5. $\begin{bmatrix} 2 & -3 & 6 & 4 \\ 0 & 1 & 1 & -4 \end{bmatrix}, 2$

6. $\begin{bmatrix} -3 & 4 & 4 \\ 0 & 2 & -2 \end{bmatrix}, 1.1$

Graph each figure and its image after the given rotation.

7. $\begin{bmatrix} 2 & 1 & 6 & -4 \\ 0 & -3 & 5 & -2 \end{bmatrix}$; 180°

8. $\begin{bmatrix} 0 & -1 & 2 \\ 1 & -3 & 0 \end{bmatrix}$, 90°

Find the coordinates of each image after the given rotation.

9. $\begin{bmatrix} -3 & -1 & 0 & 2 & 4 \\ 3 & 2 & 1 & 0 & -4 \end{bmatrix}$; 270°

10. $\begin{bmatrix} 5 & 2 & 9 & 8 & 6 \\ 1 & -2 & 3 & 5 & -4 \end{bmatrix}$; 360°

Graph each figure and its image after reflection in the given line.

11. $\begin{bmatrix} -2 & -3 & -1 \\ 3 & -3 & -2 \end{bmatrix}$; *y*-axis

12. $\begin{bmatrix} -2 & -2 & -4 & -5 & -5 \\ 5 & 1 & 2 & 1 & 3 \end{bmatrix}$; $y = x$

Name ______________________ Class ____________ Date ____________

12-5 Practice (continued)

Form G

Geometric Transformations

Find the coordinates of each image after reflection in the given line.

13. $\begin{bmatrix} 9 & 3 & -2 & 4 \\ 5 & 1 & 0 & 6 \end{bmatrix}$; $y = -x$

14. $\begin{bmatrix} 2 & -3 & -2 & 6 & 9 \\ 2 & 4 & -2 & -1 & 1 \end{bmatrix}$; x-axis

Geometry Each matrix represents the vertices of a polygon. Translate each figure 6 units right and 2 units up. Express your answer as a matrix.

15. $\begin{bmatrix} 2 & 3 & 3 & 2 & 1 & 1 \\ -2 & -3 & -4 & -5 & -4 & -3 \end{bmatrix}$

16. $\begin{bmatrix} 2 & 3 & 1 \\ 3 & 5 & 7 \end{bmatrix}$

For Exercises 17–20, use $\triangle ABC$. Write the coordinates of each image in matrix form.

17. a dilation of 1.5

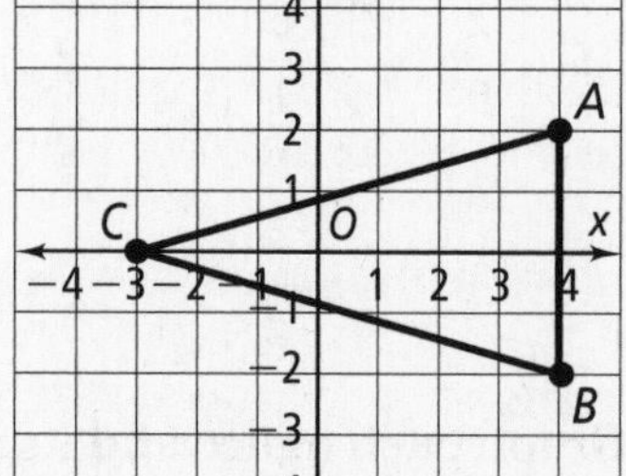

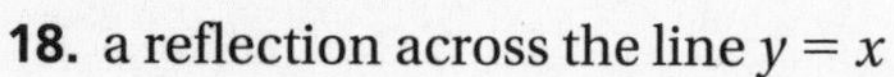

18. a reflection across the line $y = x$

19. a rotation of 270°

20. a translation 2 units right and 6 units down

Each pair of matrices represents the coordinates of the vertices of the preimage and image of a polygon. Describe the transformation.

21. $\begin{bmatrix} -1 & 2 & 4 & 5 \\ -4 & 4 & 5 & 2 \end{bmatrix}, \begin{bmatrix} -4 & -1 & 1 & 2 \\ -5 & 3 & 4 & 1 \end{bmatrix}$

22. $\begin{bmatrix} 4 & 12 & 20 & 16 \\ 8 & 4 & 0 & 12 \end{bmatrix}, \begin{bmatrix} 1 & 3 & 5 & 4 \\ 2 & 1 & 0 & 3 \end{bmatrix}$

23. Writing The matrices $\begin{bmatrix} -4 & -1 & -3 \\ 4 & 5 & 2 \end{bmatrix}$ and $\begin{bmatrix} 4 & 5 & 2 \\ -4 & -1 & -3 \end{bmatrix}$ represent the coordinates of the vertices of a triangle before and after a reflection in the line $y = x$. Describe the relationship between the coordinates of the corresponding vertices.

Name _______________ Class _______________ Date _______________

12-5 Standardized Test Prep

Geometric Transformations

Multiple Choice

For Exercises 1–3, choose the correct letter.

1. A triangle has vertices $A(4, 6)$, $B(1, -5)$, and $C(-3, 1)$. What are the vertices of the image of the triangle after a rotation of 90°?

   (A) $A'(-6, 4), B'(5, 1), C'(-1, -3)$
   (B) $A'(-4, 6), B'(-1, -5), C'(3, 1)$
   (C) $A'(6, 4), B'(-5, 1), C'(1, -3)$
   (D) $A'(-6, -4), B'(5, -1), C'(-1, 3)$

2. The matrix $\begin{bmatrix} -5 & -3 & 0 & 1 \\ 5 & 6 & 7 & 9 \end{bmatrix}$ represents the vertices of a polygon. Which matrix represents the vertices of the image of the polygon after a dilation of 3?

   (F) $\begin{bmatrix} -5 & -3 & 0 & 1 \\ 8 & 9 & 10 & 12 \end{bmatrix}$
   (G) $\begin{bmatrix} -15 & -9 & 0 & 3 \\ 15 & 18 & 21 & 27 \end{bmatrix}$
   (H) $\begin{bmatrix} -2 & 0 & 3 & 4 \\ 5 & 6 & 7 & 9 \end{bmatrix}$
   (I) $\begin{bmatrix} -15 & -9 & 0 & 3 \\ 5 & 6 & 7 & 9 \end{bmatrix}$

3. The matrix $\begin{bmatrix} -2 & 0 & 1 & 3 & 6 \\ 3 & 4 & 5 & 4 & 2 \end{bmatrix}$ represents the vertices of a polygon. Which matrix represents the vertices of the image of the polygon after a translation 1 unit left and 2 units up?

   (A) $\begin{bmatrix} 0 & 2 & 3 & 5 & 8 \\ 2 & 3 & 4 & 3 & 1 \end{bmatrix}$
   (B) $\begin{bmatrix} -1 & 1 & 2 & 4 & 7 \\ 5 & 6 & 7 & 6 & 4 \end{bmatrix}$
   (C) $\begin{bmatrix} -3 & -1 & 0 & 2 & 5 \\ 5 & 6 & 7 & 6 & 4 \end{bmatrix}$
   (D) $\begin{bmatrix} -3 & 0 & 1 & 3 & 6 \\ 5 & 4 & 5 & 4 & 2 \end{bmatrix}$

Short Response

4. The matrix $\begin{bmatrix} -4 & -6 & -3 & -1 \\ -1 & -2 & -5 & -8 \end{bmatrix}$ represents the vertices of polygon $ABCD$. List the coordinates of the vertices of $A'B'C'D'$ after a reflection across the y-axis. Show your work.

Name ______________________ Class ____________ Date ____________

12-6 Think About a Plan

Vectors

Aviation A twin-engine airplane has a speed of 300 mi/h in still air. Suppose the airplane heads south and encounters a wind blowing 50 mi/h due east. What is the resultant speed of the airplane?

Know

1. The airplane is traveling [ ] at a speed of [ ].

2. The wind is blowing [ ] at a speed of [ ].

Need

3. To solve the problem I need to find: ______________________________
____.

Plan

4. Sketch the speed of the airplane and the speed of the wind as vectors. Then use the tip-to-tail method to sketch **a** + **w**.

5. What is the component form of the vector for the speed of the airplane? **a** =

6. What is the component form of the vector for the speed of the wind? **w** =

7. Express **a** + **w** in component form. **a** + **w** =

8. What equation can you use to find the magnitude of **a** + **w**? |**a** + **w**| =

9. What is the resultant speed of the airplane? ______________________________

Name ______________________ Class ____________ Date ____________

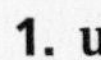

12-6 Practice

Form G

Vectors

Referring to the graph, what are the component forms of the following vectors?

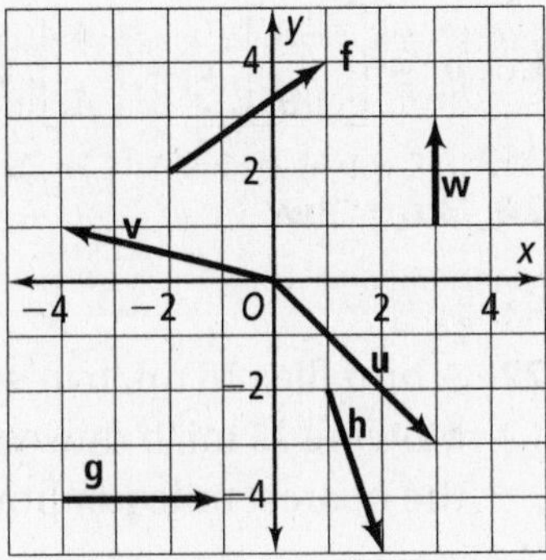

1. **u**

2. **v**

3. **w**

4. **f**

5. **g**

6. **h**

Transform each vector as described. Write the resultant vector in component form.

7. $\langle 2, -8\rangle$; rotate 270°

8. $\langle 6, 4\rangle$; rotate 90°

9. $\langle -9, -3\rangle$; reflect across y-axis

10. $\langle -3, 7\rangle$; reflect across x-axis

11. $\langle 0, 16\rangle$; reflect across $y = -x$

12. $\langle 5, 2\rangle$; reflect across $y = x$

Let u = $\langle 3, -4\rangle$, v = $\langle -7, 8\rangle$, and w = $\langle 5, 5\rangle$. Find the component forms of the following vectors.

13. **u** + **w**

14. **w** + **v**

15. **v** − **w**

16. −2**v**

17. 3**u**

18. $\frac{3}{5}$**w**

Determine whether the vectors in each pair are normal.

19. $\langle 12, -4\rangle$ and $\langle 3, 9\rangle$

20. $\langle 7, 11\rangle$ and $\langle 11, 7\rangle$

21. $\begin{bmatrix} 3 \\ 2 \end{bmatrix}$ and $\begin{bmatrix} -9 \\ 6 \end{bmatrix}$

22. $\begin{bmatrix} 1 \\ -1 \end{bmatrix}$ and $\begin{bmatrix} -1 \\ -1 \end{bmatrix}$

23. The speed of a swimmer in still water is 1.5 mi/h. The swimmer swims due west in a current flowing due north at 2.5 mi/h.

a. Use the tip-to-tail method to draw a vector representing the speed and direction of the swimmer.

b. Write a formula to find the swimmer's speed.

c. What is the swimmer's approximate speed, rounded to the nearest tenth?

12-6 Practice (continued) Form G

Vectors

Let $\mathbf{u} = \begin{bmatrix} -5 \\ 9 \end{bmatrix}$, $\mathbf{v} = \begin{bmatrix} 4 \\ 4 \end{bmatrix}$, and $\mathbf{w} = \begin{bmatrix} -2 \\ 6 \end{bmatrix}$. Find the following vectors.

24. $3\mathbf{u} + 2\mathbf{w}$

25. $-\mathbf{v} + 3\mathbf{w}$

26. $\mathbf{w} - \frac{3}{2}\mathbf{v} - 2\mathbf{u}$

27. A bird flies 16 mi/h in still air. Suppose the bird flies due south with a wind blowing 15 mi/h due east. What is the resultant speed of the bird rounded to the nearest mile per hour?

28. A model rocket lands 245 ft west and 162 ft south of the point from which it was launched. How far did the rocket fly? Round your answer to the nearest foot.

29. Consider a polygon with vertices at $A(-3, 5)$, $B(2, 3)$, $C(4, -4)$, and $D(-6, -3)$. Express the sides of the polygon as vectors $\overrightarrow{AB}$, $\overrightarrow{BC}$, $\overrightarrow{CD}$ and $\overrightarrow{DA}$.

Let $\mathbf{a} = \langle 7, 5 \rangle$, $\mathbf{b} = \langle 4, -1 \rangle$, and $\mathbf{c} = \langle 0, -3 \rangle$. Solve each of the following for the unknown vector v.

30. $\mathbf{b} - \mathbf{v} = \mathbf{c}$

31. $\mathbf{v} + \mathbf{a} = \mathbf{b}$

32. $\mathbf{a} + \mathbf{b} = \mathbf{v} - \mathbf{c}$

33. $\mathbf{a} - \mathbf{v} + \mathbf{b} - \mathbf{c} = \langle 1, 1 \rangle$

34. A train leaves Dawson station and travels 360 mi due north. Then it turns and travels 120 mi due west to reach New Port. If the train travels 75 mi/h on a straight route directly back to Dawson, how long will the return trip take? Round your answer to the nearest hour.

35. Reasoning Identify the additive identity vector **v**, if it exists. Explain your reasoning.

Let $\mathbf{u} = \begin{bmatrix} -2 \\ 2 \end{bmatrix}$ and $\mathbf{v} = \begin{bmatrix} 3 \\ -1 \end{bmatrix}$. Graph the following vectors.

36. $3\mathbf{u}$

37. $-\mathbf{v}$

38. $-\frac{1}{2}\mathbf{u}$

Name ______________________ Class ____________ Date ____________

12-6 Standardized Test Prep

Vectors

Multiple Choice

For Exercises 1–5, choose the correct letter.

1. Let $\mathbf{u} = \langle 4, -7 \rangle$ and $\mathbf{v} = \langle -1, 3 \rangle$. What is $|\mathbf{u} + \mathbf{v}|$?

 A -5 B -1 C 1 D 5

2. What is the component form of vector **v**?

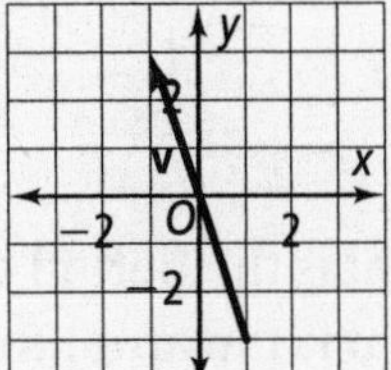

 F $\langle -2, 6 \rangle$ H $\langle -1, 3 \rangle$

 G $\langle 0, 0 \rangle$ I $\langle 1, -3 \rangle$

3. Which represents the vector $\mathbf{u} = \langle 16, -9 \rangle$ rotated 180°?

 A $\begin{bmatrix} -9 \\ -16 \end{bmatrix}$ B $\begin{bmatrix} -9 \\ 16 \end{bmatrix}$ C $\begin{bmatrix} -16 \\ 9 \end{bmatrix}$ D $\begin{bmatrix} 16 \\ 9 \end{bmatrix}$

4. Let $\mathbf{u} = \begin{bmatrix} 5 \\ 8 \end{bmatrix}$ and $\mathbf{v} = \begin{bmatrix} -2 \\ -4 \end{bmatrix}$. What is the vector $-2\mathbf{u} - \frac{5}{2}\mathbf{v}$?

 F $\begin{bmatrix} -15 \\ -26 \end{bmatrix}$ G $\begin{bmatrix} -5 \\ -6 \end{bmatrix}$ H $\begin{bmatrix} 0 \\ 8 \end{bmatrix}$ I $\begin{bmatrix} 10 \\ 4 \end{bmatrix}$

5. Which represents the vector $\mathbf{w} = \begin{bmatrix} 8 \\ 14 \end{bmatrix}$ reflected across $y = x$?

 A $\begin{bmatrix} -14 \\ 8 \end{bmatrix}$ B $\begin{bmatrix} 14 \\ 8 \end{bmatrix}$ C $\begin{bmatrix} -8 \\ 14 \end{bmatrix}$ D $\begin{bmatrix} -8 \\ -14 \end{bmatrix}$

Short Response

6. Let $\mathbf{p} = \langle 6, -1 \rangle$ and $\mathbf{q} = \langle 3, 5 \rangle$. Are **p** and **q** normal? Show your work.

Name ____________________ Class ____________ Date ____________

13-1 Think About a Plan

Exploring Periodic Data

Health An electrocardiogram (EKG or ECG) measures the electrical activity of a person's heart in millivolts over time.

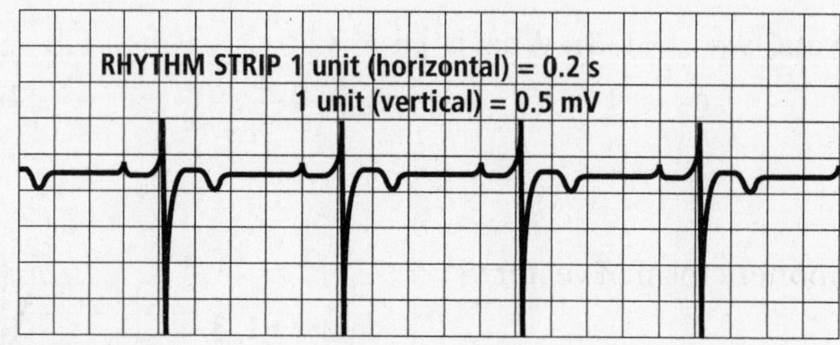

a. What is the period of the EKG shown above?

b. What is the amplitude of the EKG?

Know

1. One horizontal unit on the graph represents [ ].

2. One vertical unit on the graph represents [ ].

3. ____________________

Need

4. To solve the problem, I need to find ____________________.

Plan

5. One cycle of the function has a length of [ ].

6. What is the period of the function?

7. What is the definition of amplitude?

8. The amplitude of the function is [ ].

Name ______________________ Class ____________ Date ____________

13-1 Practice

Form G

Exploring Periodic Data

Name one cycle in two different ways. Then determine the period of the function.

1. 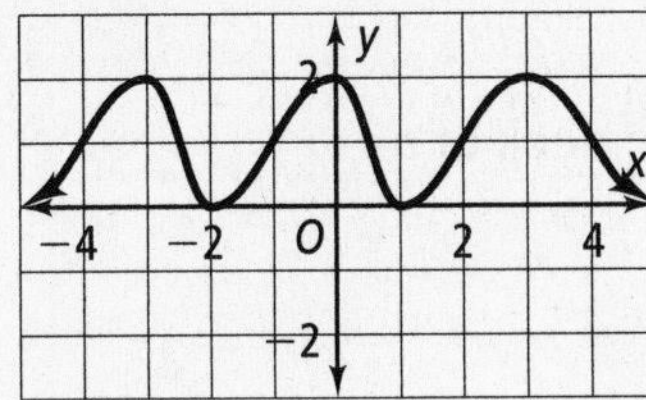

2. 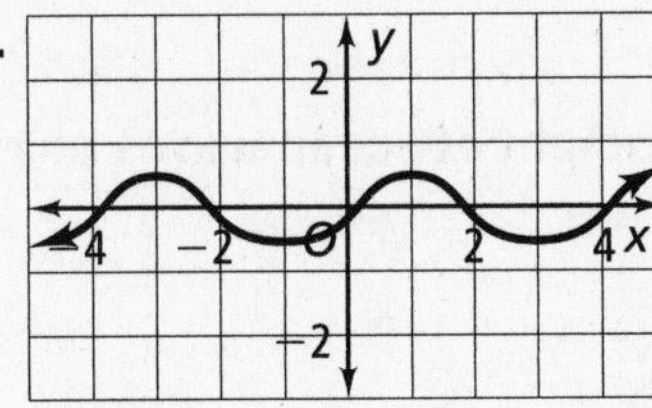

3. 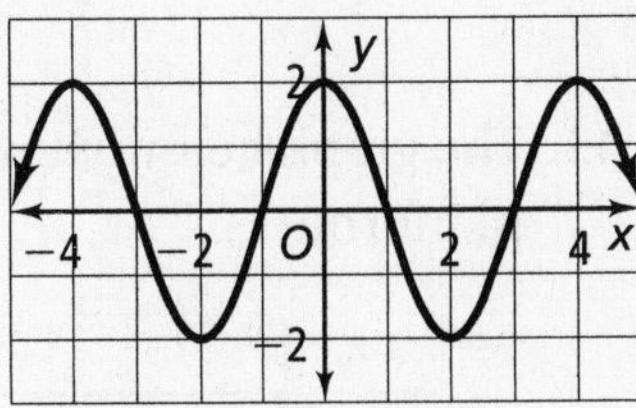

Determine whether each function *is* or *is not* periodic. If it is, find the period.

4. 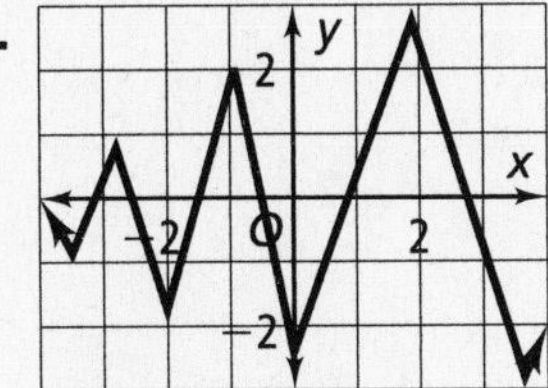

5. 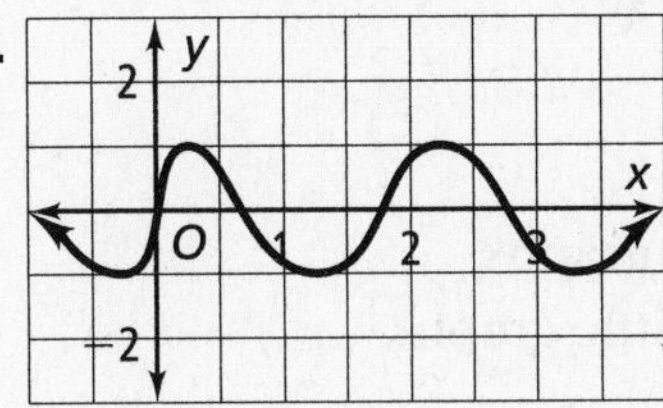

6. 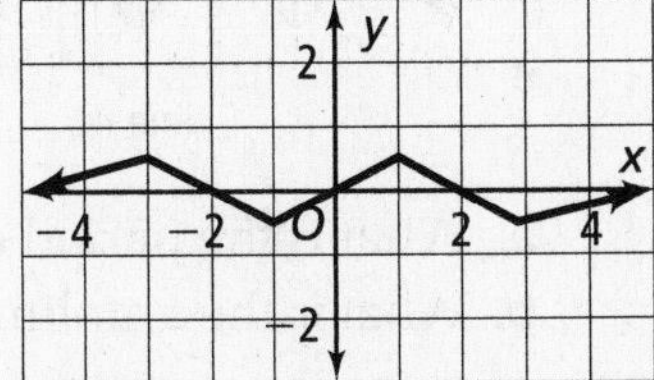

Find the amplitude of each periodic function.

7. 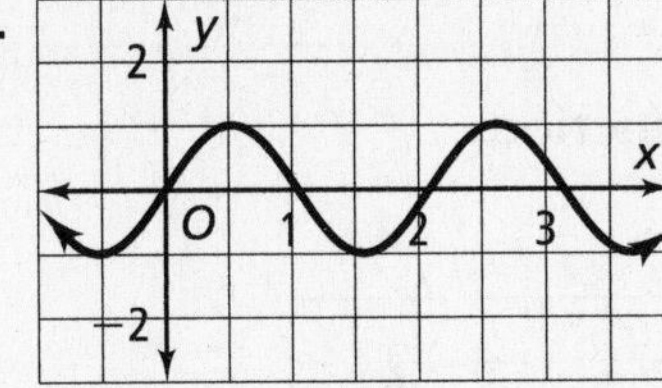

8. 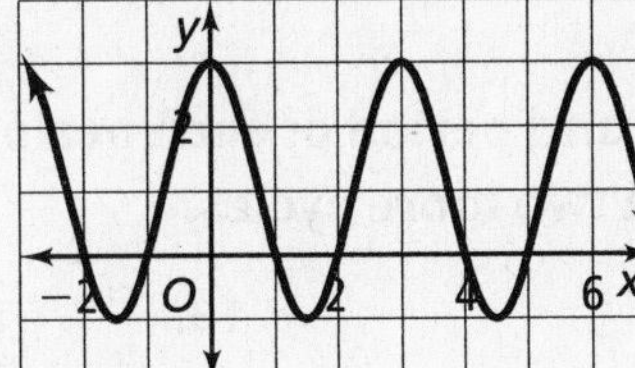

9. 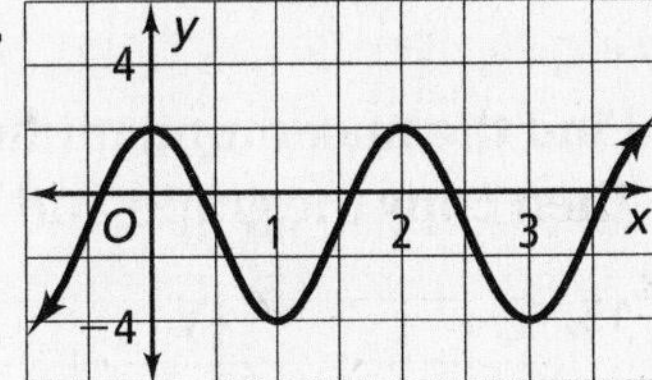

Sketch the graph of a sound wave with the given period and amplitude.

10. period 0.03, amplitude 2

11. period 0.006, amplitude 3

13-1 Practice (continued) — Form G

Exploring Periodic Data

12. Open-Ended Describe a situation that you could represent with a periodic function.

13. The graph below shows the height of ocean waves below the deck of a platform.

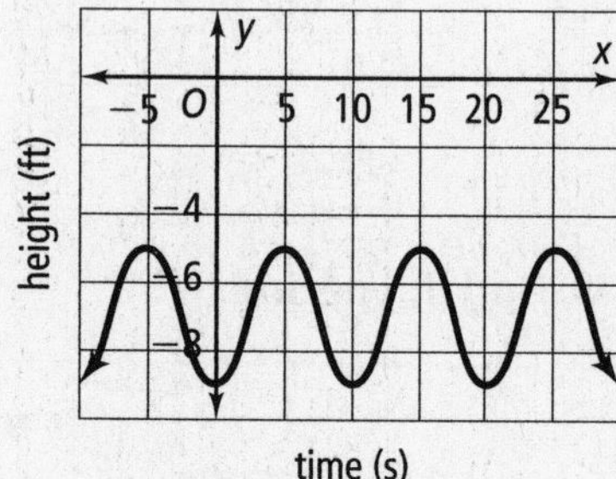

a. What is the period of the graph?

b. What is the amplitude of the graph?

14. Open-Ended Sketch a graph of a periodic function that has a period of 8 and an amplitude of $3\frac{1}{2}$.

Find the maximum, minimum, and period of each periodic function. Then copy the graph and sketch two more cycles.

15.

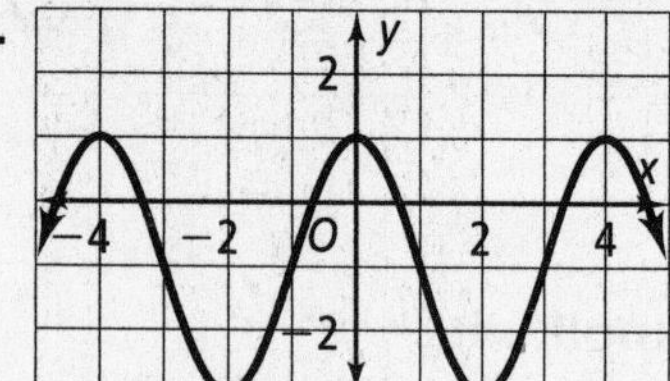

16.

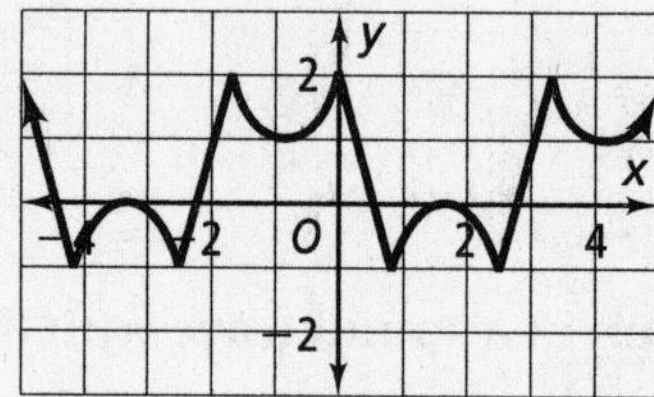

Name ______________________ Class ____________ Date ____________

13-1 Standardized Test Prep

Exploring Periodic Data

Multiple Choice

For Exercises 1–3, choose the correct letter.

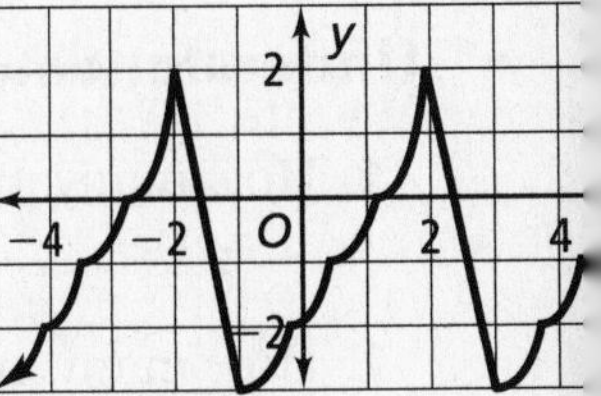

1. Which pair of coordinates names one complete cycle of the periodic function?

   A $(-5, -3)$ to $(-2, 2)$ C $(-2, 2)$ to $(-1, -3)$

   B $(-5, -3)$ to $(5, 0)$ D $(-1, -3)$ to $(3, -3)$

2. Which graph is NOT the graph of a periodic function?

   F 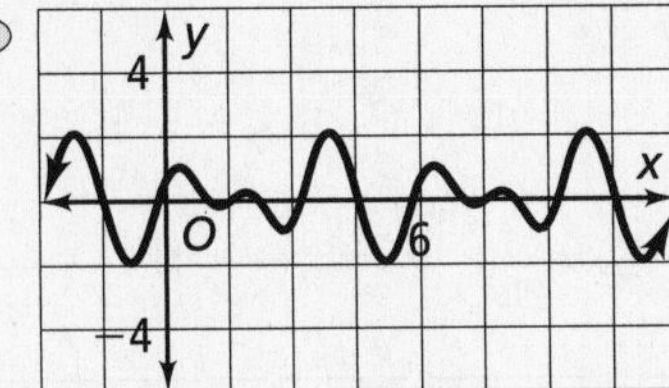

   H 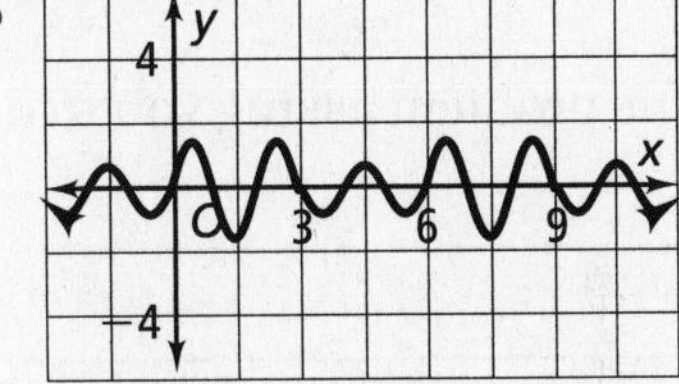

   G 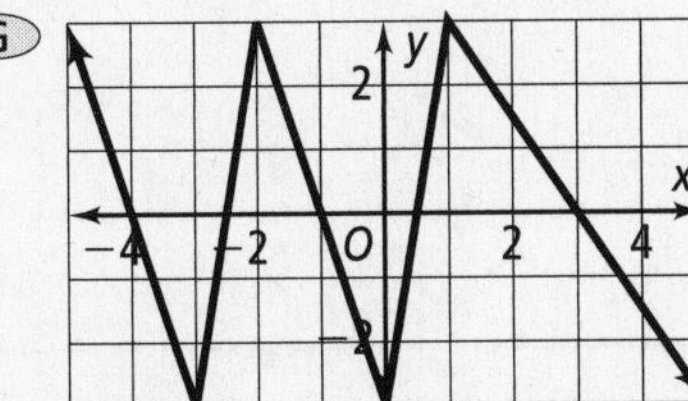

   I 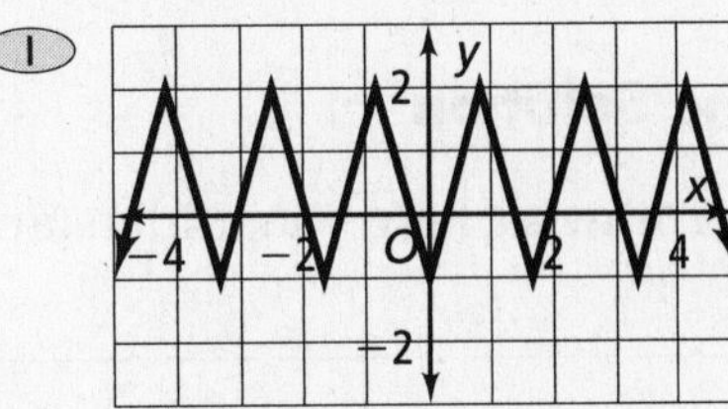

3. A periodic function has a period of 12 s. How many cycles does it go through in 40 s?

   A $3\frac{1}{3}$ cycles   B $\frac{3}{10}$ cycle   C 28 cycles   D 480 cycles

Short Response

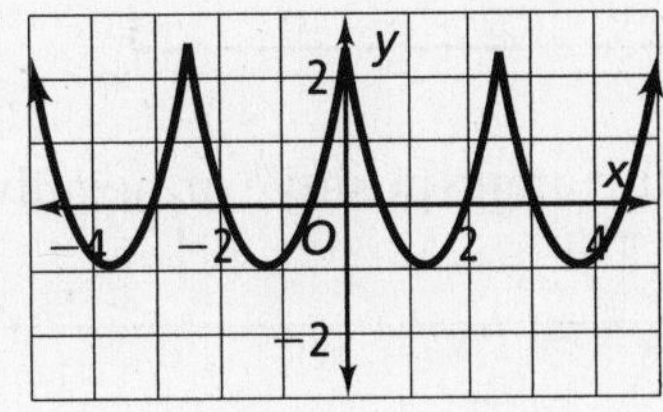

4. The graph at the right represents a periodic function.
   a. What is the period of the function?
   b. What is the amplitude of the function?

Name ______________________ Class ____________ Date ____________

13-2 Think About a Plan

Angles and the Unit Circle

Time The time is 2:46 P.M. What is the measure of the angle that the minute hand swept through since 2:00 P.M.?

Understanding the Problem

1. How many minutes have passed since 2:00 P.M.?

2. How many minutes does a full-circle sweep of the minute hand represent?

3. How many degrees are in a circle?

4. What is the problem asking you to determine?

____

____.

Planning the Solution

5. How can a drawing help you understand the problem?

____

____.

6. Make a drawing that represents the clock and the starting and ending position of the minute hand.

7. Write a proportion that you can use to determine the measure of the angle that the minute hand swept through since 2:00 P.M.

8. Is the angle positive or negative? Explain.

____

____.

Getting an Answer

9. Solve your proportion to find the measure of the angle.

Name ____________________ Class ____________ Date ____________

13-2 Practice

Form G

Angles and the Unit Circle

Find the measure of each angle in standard position.

1.

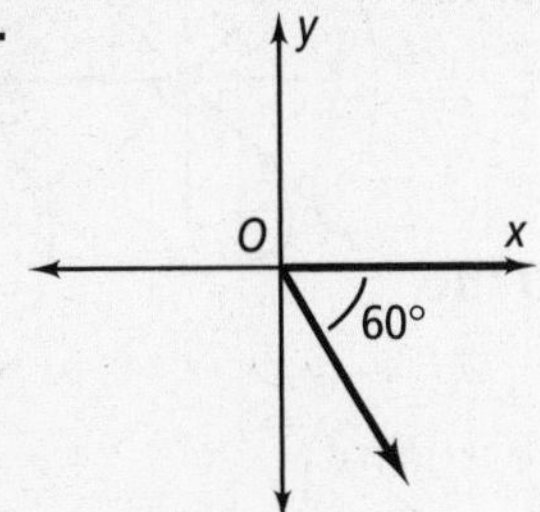

2.

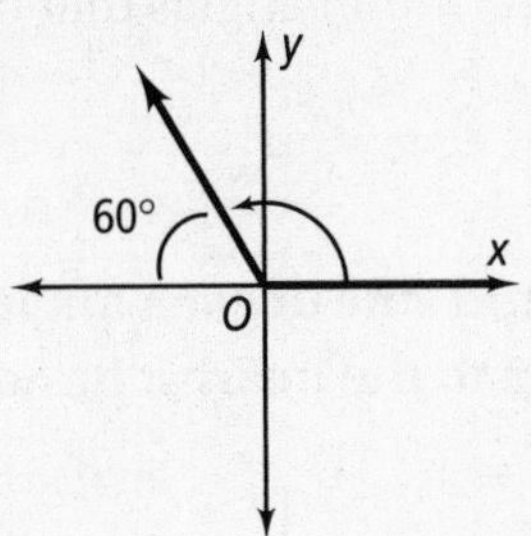

3.

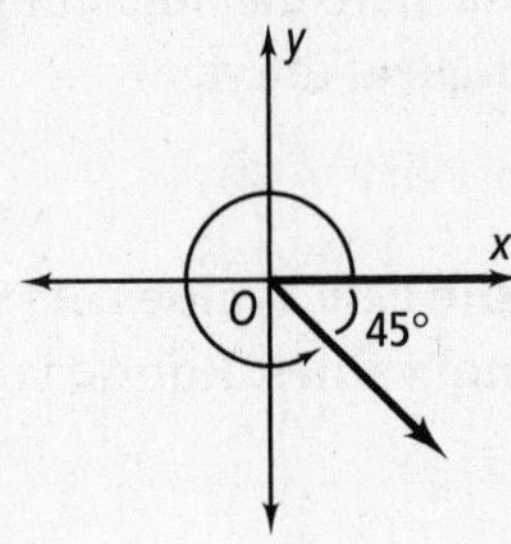

Sketch each angle in standard position.

4. 100° **5.** 210° **6.** −45° **7.** −90°

8. −330° **9.** −180° **10.** −145° **11.** 60°

Find the measure of an angle between 0° and 360° coterminal with each given angle.

12. −100° **13.** −60° **14.** −225° **15.** −145° **16.** 372°

17. −15° **18.** 482° **19.** 484° **20.** −20° **21.** 421°

22. 409° **23.** −38° **24.** 376° **25.** −210° **26.** 387°

27. 390° **28.** 660° **29.** 440° **30.** −170° **31.** 370°

32. −700° **33.** 458° **34.** 480° **35.** 406° **36.** −120°

37. 460° **38.** −222° **39.** −330° **40.** −127° **41.** 377°

Name ______________________ Class ____________ Date ____________

13-2 Practice (continued)

Form G

Angles and the Unit Circle

42. The spokes shown on the bicycle wheel at the right form an angle. Estimate the measures of two coterminal angles that coincide with the angle at the right.

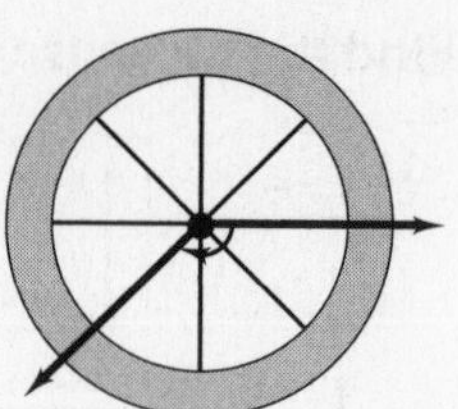

Find the exact values of the cosine and sine of each angle. Then find the decimal values. Round your answers to the nearest hundredth.

43.

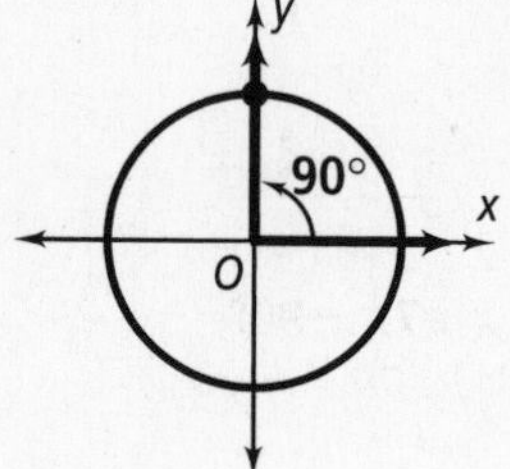

44.

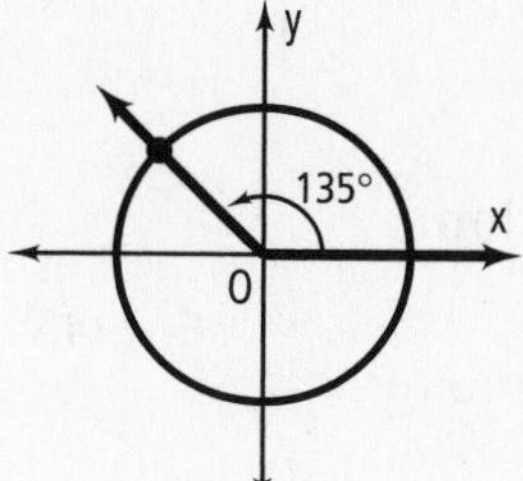

45.

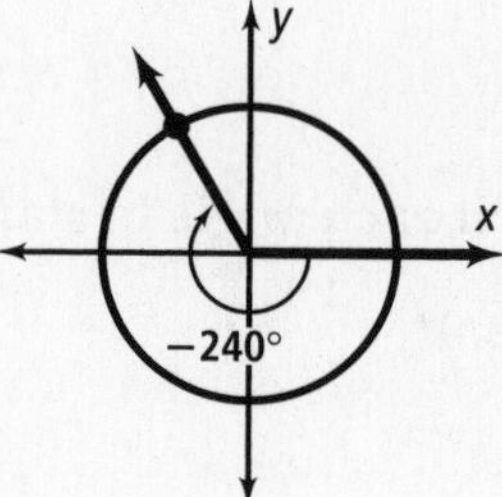

46. 45°

47. −150°

48. 720°

Graphing Calculator For each angle θ, find the values of $\cos\theta$ and $\sin\theta$. Round your answers to the nearest hundredth.

49. 225°

50. −225°

51. −45°

52. 330°

53. −330°

54. 150°

Open-Ended Find a positive and a negative coterminal angle for the given angle.

55. 50°

56. −130°

57. −680°

58. 395°

59. −38°

60. −434°

61. a. Suppose you know the terminal side of angle θ lies in Quadrant II. What is the sign of $\cos\theta$? $\sin\theta$?

b. Writing Describe the reasoning you followed to answer part (a).

Name ______________________________ Class ______________ Date ____________

13-2 Standardized Test Prep

Angles and the Unit Circle

Multiple Choice

For Exercises 1–4, choose the correct letter.

1. Which angle, in standard position, is coterminal with an angle in standard position measuring 152°?

(A) 28° (B) 62° (C) −152° (D) −208°

2. Which could be the measure of an angle θ where $\sin\theta$ is $-\frac{\sqrt{3}}{2}$?

(F) −330° (G) 240° (H) 60° (I) 150°

3. An angle in standard position intersects the unit circle at (0, −1). Which could be the measure of the angle?

(A) 90° (B) −270° (C) −450° (D) 540°

4. What are the coordinates of the point where the terminal side of a 135° angle intersects the unit circle?

(F) $\left(-\frac{\sqrt{2}}{2}, \frac{\sqrt{2}}{2}\right)$ (G) $\left(\frac{\sqrt{2}}{2}, -\frac{\sqrt{2}}{2}\right)$ (H) $\left(\frac{\sqrt{2}}{2}, \frac{\sqrt{2}}{2}\right)$ (I) $\left(-\frac{\sqrt{2}}{2}, -\frac{\sqrt{2}}{2}\right)$

Short Response

5. What is the exact value of sin (300°)? Show your work.

Name ______________________ Class ____________ Date ____________

13-3 Think About a Plan

Radian Measure

Transportation Suppose the radius of a bicycle wheel is 13 in. (measured to the outside of the tire). Find the number of radians through which a point on the tire turns when the bicycle has moved forward a distance of 12 ft.

Know

1. The radius of the tire is [ ].

2. The bicycle moves forward a distance of [ ].

3. The formula for the circumference of a circle is [ ].

Need

4. To solve the problem I need to find ____

____.

Plan

5. The circumference of the tire is [ ].

6. The distance the bicycle travels forward is [ ] in.

7. The number of radians a point on the tire turns in one complete rotation is [ ].

8. What proportion can you use to find the radians through which a point on the tire turns when the bicycle has moved forward a distance of 12 ft?

9. Solve your proportion to find the radians through which a point on the tire turns when the bicycle has moved forward a distance of 12 ft.

13-3 Practice

Form G

Radian Measure

Write each measure in radians. Express your answer in terms of π and as a decimal rounded to the nearest hundredth.

1. 45°

2. 90°

3. 30°

4. −150°

5. 180°

6. −240°

7. 270°

8. 300°

Write each measure in degrees. Round your answer to the nearest degree, if necessary.

9. $\frac{\pi}{6}$ radians

10. $-\frac{7\pi}{6}$ radians

11. $\frac{7\pi}{4}$ radians

12. −4 radians

13. 1.8 radians

14. 0.45 radians

The measure θ of an angle in standard position is given. Find the exact values of $\cos\theta$ and $\sin\theta$ for each angle measure.

15. $\frac{\pi}{6}$

16. $\frac{\pi}{3}$

17. $-\frac{3\pi}{4}$

18. $\frac{7\pi}{4}$

19. $\frac{11\pi}{6}$

20. $-\frac{2\pi}{3}$

Use each circle to find the length of the indicated arc. Round your answer to the nearest tenth.

21.

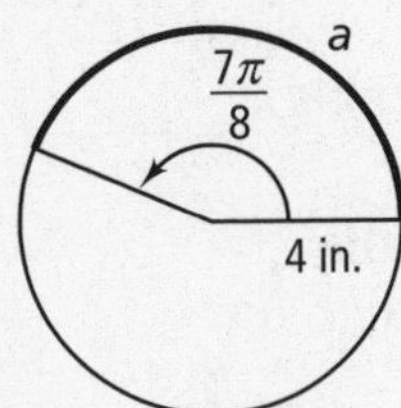

22.

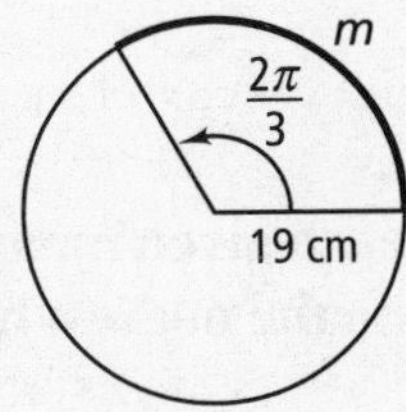

23.

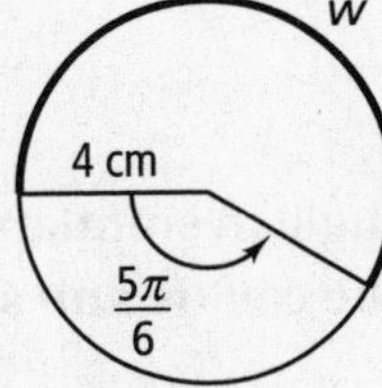

24.

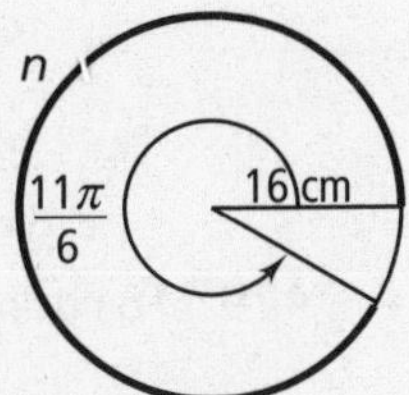

25.

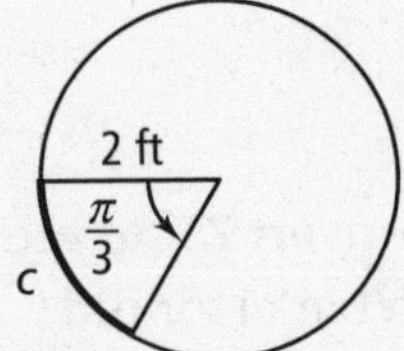

26.

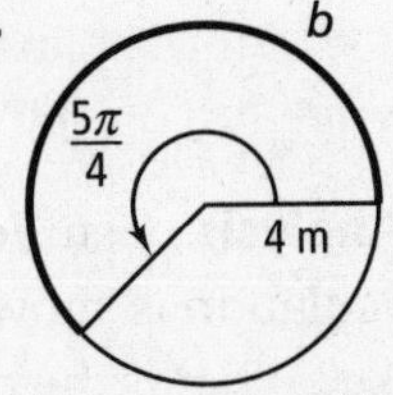

Name ______________________ Class ____________ Date ____________

13-3 Practice (continued) Form G

Radian Measure

27. The minute hand of a clock is 8 in. long.

a. What distance does the tip of the minute hand travel in 10 min?

b. What distance does the tip of the minute hand travel in 40.5 min?

c. What distance does the tip of the minute hand travel in 3.25 h?

d. Reasoning After approximately how many hours has the tip of the minute hand traveled 100 ft?

28. A 0.8 m pendulum swings through an angle of 86°. What distance does the tip of the pendulum travel?

29. A scientist studies two islands shown at the right. The distance from the center of the Earth to the equator is about 3960 mi.

a. What is the measure in radians of the central angle that intercepts the arc along the equator between the islands?

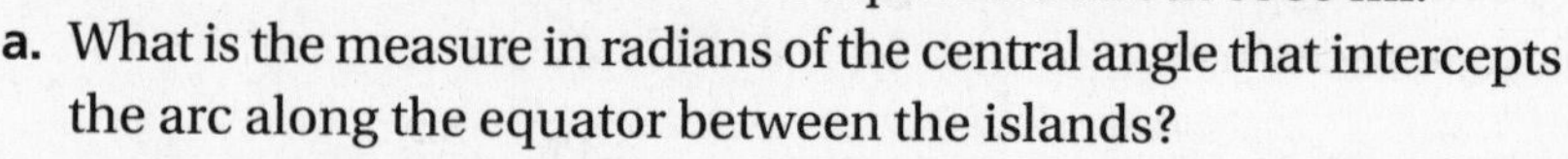

b. About how far apart are the two islands?

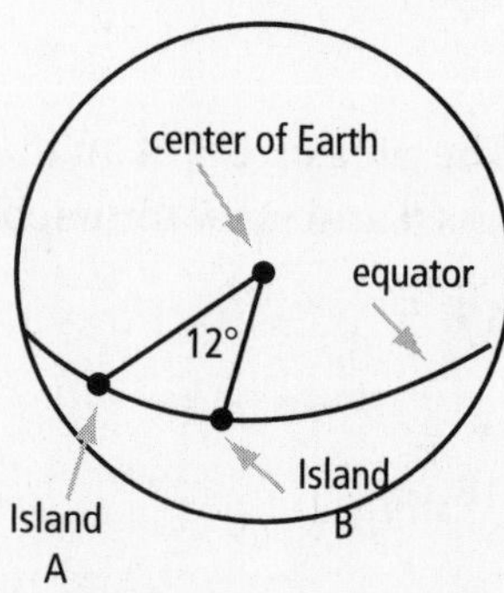

Determine the quadrant or axis where the terminal side of each angle lies.

30. $\frac{\pi}{5}$

31. $-\frac{5\pi}{2}$

32. $\frac{5\pi}{3}$

33. $\frac{8\pi}{7}$

Draw an angle in standard position with each given measure. Then find the values of the cosine and sine of the angle to the nearest hundredth.

34. $\frac{5\pi}{4}$

35. -3π

36. $\frac{2\pi}{9}$

37. Error Analysis A student wanted to convert 75° to radians. His calculation is shown at the right. What error did he make? What is the correct conversion?

$$\frac{(75 \times 180)}{\pi} \approx 4297.18 \text{ radians}$$

Name ____________ Class ____________ Date ____________

13-3 Standardized Test Prep

Radian Measure

Multiple Choice

For Exercises 1–4, choose the correct letter.

1. Which angle measure is equivalent to $\frac{4\pi}{3}$ radians?

   (A) 60° (B) 120° (C) 135° (D) 240°

2. If $\sin \theta = \frac{\sqrt{3}}{2}$, which could be the value of θ?

   (F) $\frac{2\pi}{3}$ radians (G) $\frac{3\pi}{4}$ radians (H) $\frac{4\pi}{3}$ radians (I) $\frac{3\pi}{2}$ radians

3. In a circle with a 12 mm radius, a central angle measuring $\frac{7\pi}{6}$ radians intercepts an arc. What is the length of the arc?

   (A) $\frac{2\pi}{7}$ mm (B) $\frac{72\pi}{7}$ mm (C) 12π mm (D) 14π mm

4. Circle X has a central angle of $\frac{3\pi}{8}$ radians intercepting an arc 3π ft long. Circle Y has a central angle of $\frac{3\pi}{4}$ radians intercepting an arc 3π ft long. Which best describes the radii of circle X and circle Y?

   (F) The radius of circle X is half as long as the radius of circle Y.

   (G) The radius of circle X is twice as long as the radius of circle Y.

   (H) The radius of circle X is the same length as the radius of circle Y.

   (I) The radius of circle X is more than twice as long as the radius of circle Y.

Short Response

5. Describe the relationship between the total number of radians in a circle and the circumference of the circle.

Name ________________ Class ________ Date ________

13-4 Think About a Plan

The Sine Function

Music The sound wave for a certain pitch fork can be modeled by the function $y = \sin 1320\pi\theta$. Sketch a graph of the sine curve.

Understanding the Problem

1. What is the function that models the sound wave?

2. What is the standard form of a sine function?

3. What is the problem asking you to determine?

____

____

Planning the Solution

4. How can you find the period and amplitude from the function rule?

____

____

5. What are the period and amplitude of the function?

6. How many cycles of the graph are between 0 and 2π?

Getting an Answer

7. Sketch a graph of the function $y = \sin 1320\pi\theta$. Adjust the scale of the axes to make the function easier to draw.

Name ______________________ Class ____________ Date ____________

13-4 Standardized Test Prep

The Sine Function

Multiple Choice

For Exercises 1–5, choose the correct letter.

1. Which expressions have the same value?

I. $\sin(-30°)$ II. $\sin 390°$ III. $\sin 30°$

(A) I and II (B) I and III (C) II and III (D) I, II, and III

2. What is the period of the function $y = -\frac{2}{5}\sin 6\pi\theta$?

(F) $\frac{1}{3}$ (G) $\frac{2}{5}$ (H) $\frac{1}{3}\pi$ (I) 6π

3. Which function has an amplitude of 3 and a period of 3π?

(A) $y = \frac{2}{3}\sin 3\theta$ (B) $y = \frac{3}{2}\sin\frac{2}{3}\theta$ (C) $y = 3\sin 3\pi\theta$ (D) $y = 3\sin\frac{2}{3}\theta$

4. What is the amplitude and period of the sine curve shown at the right?

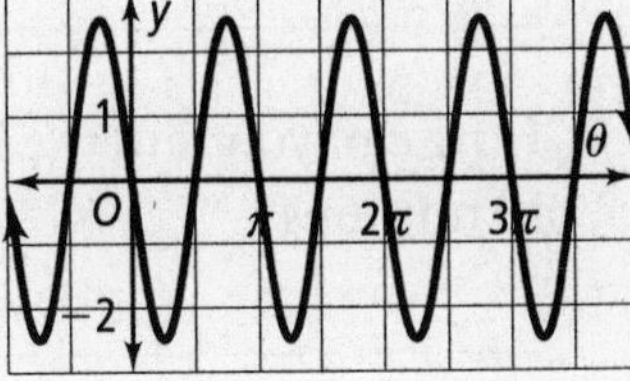

(F) amplitude −2.5, period 4π

(G) amplitude 2.5, period $\frac{3}{2}\pi$

(H) amplitude −2.5, period π

(I) amplitude 2.5, period π

5. Which function represents the sine curve shown at the right?

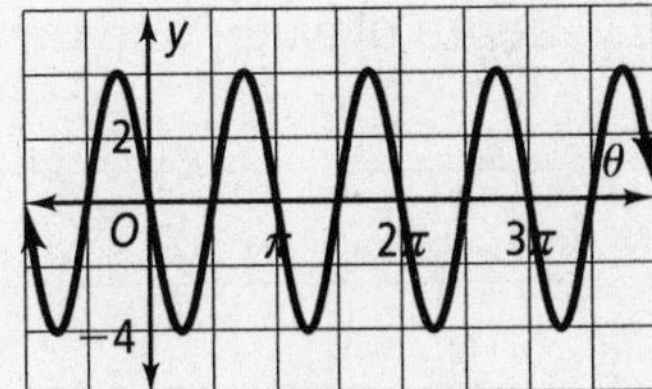

(A) $y = -4\sin 2\theta$

(B) $y = 4\sin\pi\theta$

(C) $y = -4\sin\theta$

(D) $y = 4\sin 2\pi\theta$

Extended Response

6. The function $y = \frac{2}{3}\sin\frac{7\pi}{9}\theta$ represents a sine curve. Find the amplitude of the sine curve and its period in radians. Show your work.

Name ______________________ Class ____________ Date ____________

13-5 Think About a Plan

The Cosine Function

Tides The table at the right shows the times for high tide and low tide of one day. The markings on the side of a local pier showed a high tide of 7 ft and a low tide of 4 ft on the previous day.

Tide Table	
High Tide	4:03 A.M.
Low Tide	10:14 A.M.
High Tide	4:25 P.M.
Low Tide	10:36 P.M.

a. What is the average depth of water at the pier? What is the amplitude of the variation from the average depth?

b. How long is one cycle of the tide?

c. Write a cosine function that models the relationship between the depth of water and the time of day. Use $y = 0$ to represent the average depth of water. Use $t = 0$ to represent the time 4:03 A.M.

d. Reasoning Suppose your boat needs at least 5 ft of water to approach or leave the pier. Between what times could you come and go?

1. What is the average depth of water at the pier?

2. How can you find the amplitude of the variation from the average depth? What is the amplitude?

 ____

3. How can you find the length of one cycle of the tide? What is the cycle length in minutes?

 ____

 ____.

4. How can you find a cosine function that models the relationship between the depth of water and the time of day? Write the cosine function.

 ____

 ____

5. How can you use a graph to find the times of day when the water depth is at least 5 ft?

 ____

 ____

 ____.

6. Over what domain should you graph the cosine function to represent the entire day? ______________________

7. Between what times could you come and go? ______________________

Name ______________________ Class ____________ Date ____________

13-5 Practice

Form G

The Cosine Function

Find the period and amplitude of each cosine function. Determine the values of θ for $0 \le \theta < 2\pi$ that the maximum value(s), minimum value(s), and zeros occur.

1. 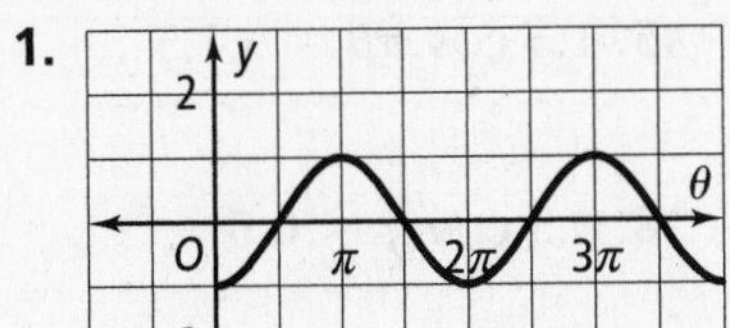

2. 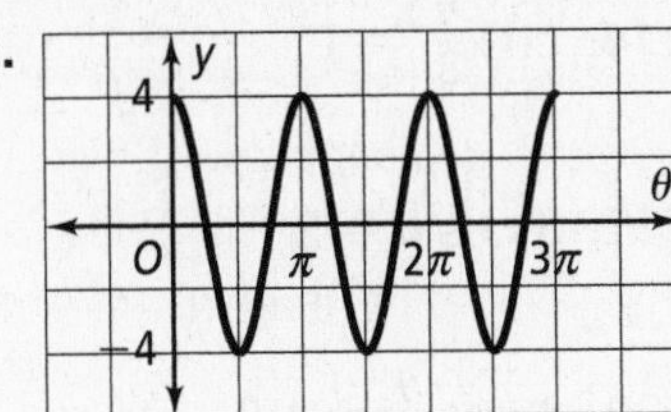

3. 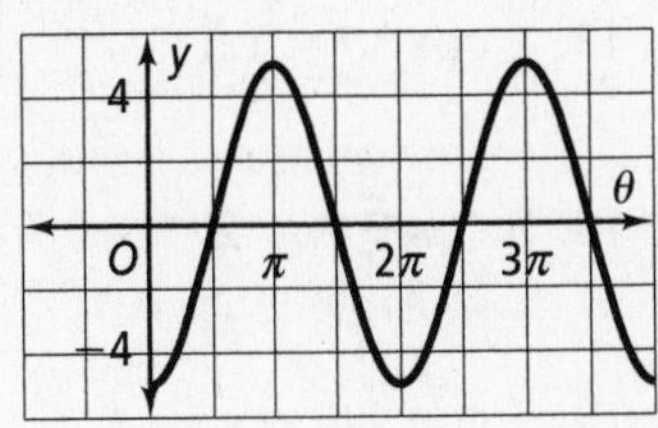

Sketch the graph of each function in the interval from 0 to 2π.

4. $y = \cos \theta$

5. $y = -5 \cos \theta$

6. $y = \cos \frac{\theta}{2}$

7. $y = -3 \cos \frac{\pi}{2}\theta$

Write a cosine function for each description. Assume that $a > 0$.

8. amplitude 2π, period 1

9. amplitude $\frac{1}{2}$, period π

Write an equation of a cosine function for each graph.

10. 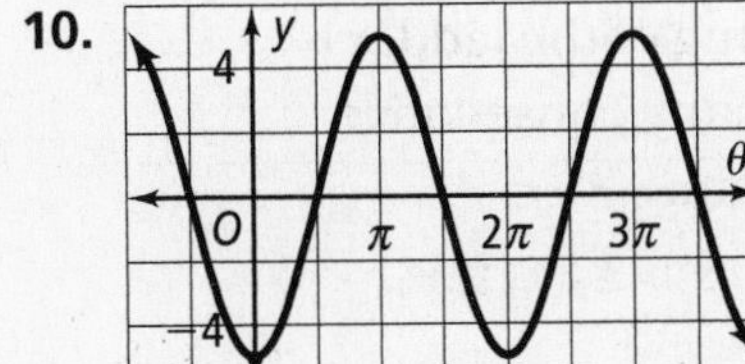

11. y 4 θ O π 2π 3π −4

12. 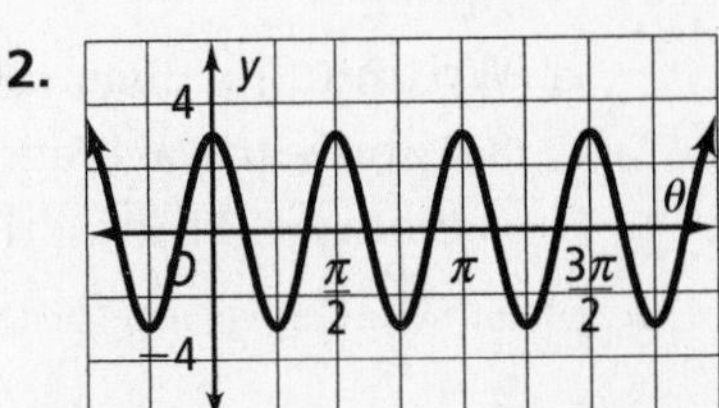

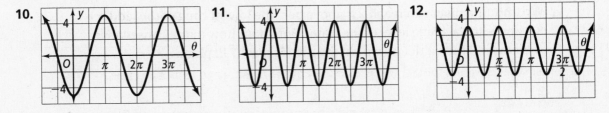

Name ______________________ Class ____________ Date ____________

13-5 Practice (continued)

Form G

The Cosine Function

Solve each equation in the interval from 0 to 2π. Round your answer to the nearest hundredth.

13. $2\cos 3\theta = 1.5$

14. $\cos\frac{\theta}{3} = 1$

15. $1.5\cos \pi\theta = -1.5$

16. $3\cos\frac{\pi}{5}\theta = 2$

17. $3\cos\theta = 2$

18. $0.5\cos\frac{\theta}{2} = 0.5$

19. $4\cos\frac{\pi}{4}\theta = -2$

20. $3\cos\frac{\theta}{4} = 1.5$

21. $3\cos\theta = -3$

22. $\sin\theta = -0.4$

23. $5\sin\frac{1}{2}\theta = 2$

24. $\sin\frac{\pi}{3}\theta = \frac{2}{3}$

Identify the period, range, and amplitude of each function.

25. $y = -\cos\theta$

26. $y = \cos 2\pi\theta$

27. $y = -2\cos 2\theta$

28. $y = 3\cos 4\theta$

29. $y = 3\cos 8\theta$

30. $y = -4\cos\pi\theta$

31. **Reasoning** Let the variable n represent a solution of $y = a\sin b\theta$ in the interval from 0 to 2π. Write a solution in terms of n for the equation in the interval from 2π to 4π.

32. A carousel horse can move up to 8 in. above or below its starting position. The equation $y = 8\cos 2\theta$ describes the horse's vertical movement as the carousel revolves.
    a. Graph the equation.
    b. If the horse starts at its maximum height, how many times does it reach its minimum height in one full revolution of the carousel?

33. A helicopter lowers a rope ladder to a scuba diver floating on the ocean surface. The waves crest at 4 ft above the lowest level of the water every 8 s.
    a. Write a cosine equation to describe the height of the diver as a function of time t.
    b. **Writing** The diver can reach 2 ft above her. The lowest rung of the ladder is 3 ft above the average level of the water. For about how many consecutive seconds will the ladder be within the diver's reach? Explain.

13-5 Standardized Test Prep

The Cosine Function

Multiple Choice

For Exercises 1–5, choose the correct letter.

1. Which is equivalent to $-\cos(\theta + 2\pi)$?

   (A) $\cos\theta$ (B) $-\cos\pi\theta$ (C) $\cos(\theta + \pi)$ (D) $\cos(\theta + 2\pi)$

2. Which function has the same period as $f(x) = 2\cos 3\pi\theta$?

   (F) $f(x) = 2\cos\theta$ (G) $f(x) = \cos 3\theta$ (H) $f(x) = 2\cos\pi\theta$ (I) $f(x) = \cos 3\pi\theta$

3. Which graph represents $y = -3\cos 2\pi\theta$?

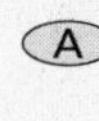
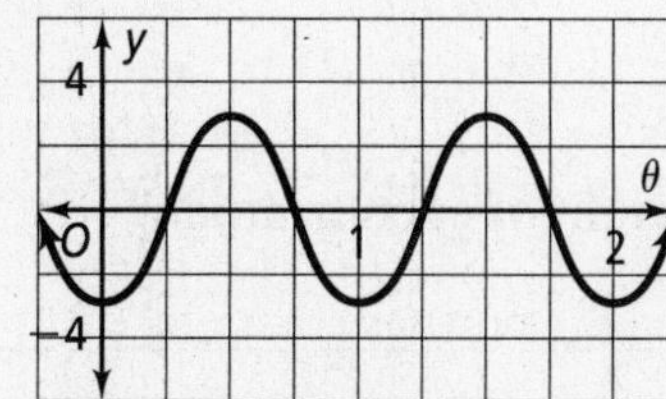

(C)

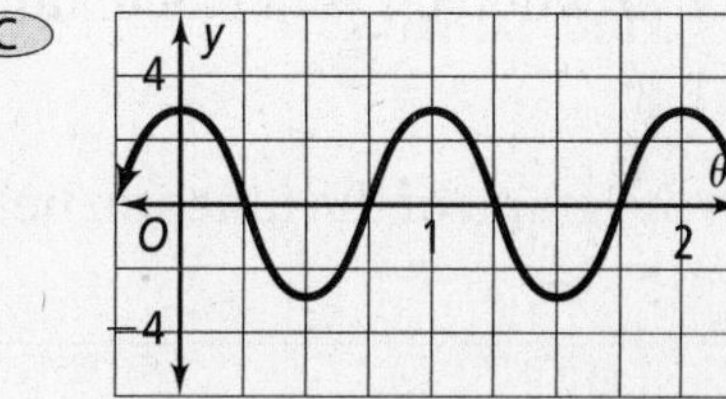

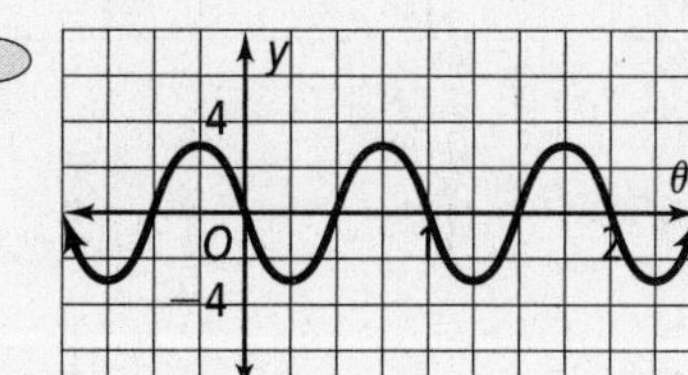

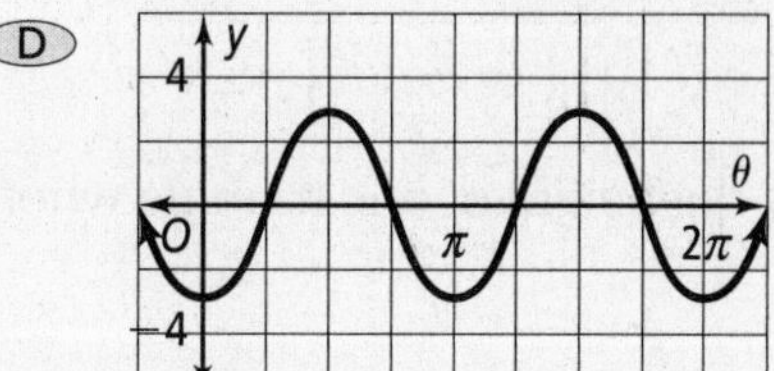

4. Which equation has the greatest number of solutions for $0 \le \theta \le 2\pi$?

   (F) $\cos\theta = 1$ (G) $2\cos\theta = 1$ (H) $\cos 2\theta = 1$ (I) $-\cos 2\theta = 1$

5. Which approximate value of θ is a solution of $-4\cos 2\theta = 3$ for $0 \le \theta \le 2\pi$?

   (A) 1.2 (B) 1.6 (C) 2.4 (D) 3.1

Short Response

6. Solve $-\cos 2\theta = 0$ for $0 \le \theta \le 2\pi$.

Name ______________________ Class ____________ Date ____________

13-6 Think About a Plan

The Tangent Function

Construction An architect is designing a hexagonal gazebo. The floor is a hexagon made up of six isosceles triangles. The function $y = 4 \tan \theta$ models the height of one triangle, where θ is the measure of one of the base angles and the base of the triangle is 8 ft long.

a. Graph the function. Find the height of one triangle when $\theta = 60°$.
b. Find the area of one triangle in square feet when $\theta = 60°$.
c. Find the area of the gazebo floor in square feet when the triangles forming the hexagon are equilateral.

1. Make a sketch of one triangle in the hexagonal floor.

2. Graph the function on your calculator.

3. How can the graph of the function help you find the height of each triangle?

____

____.

4. What is the height of one triangle when $\theta = 60°$?

5. What is the formula for the area of a triangle?

6. What is the area of one triangle in square feet when $\theta = 60°$?

7. What is θ when the triangle is equilateral? Explain.

____.

8. How many triangles make up the hexagonal floor?

9. What is the area of the gazebo floor in square feet when the triangles forming the hexagon are equilateral?

Name ______________________ Class ____________ Date ____________

13-6 Practice

Form G

The Tangent Function

Find each value without using a calculator.

1. $\tan \frac{\pi}{4}$

2. $\tan 3\pi$

3. $\tan\left(-\frac{\pi}{4}\right)$

4. $\tan\left(-\frac{3\pi}{2}\right)$

Graphing Calculator **Graph each function on the interval $0 \leq x \leq 2\pi$ and $-200 \leq y \leq 200$. Evaluate each function at $x = \frac{\pi}{4}, \frac{\pi}{2}$, and $\frac{3\pi}{4}$. Round to the nearest tenth, if necessary.**

5. $y = 200 \tan x$

6. $y = -75 \tan\left(\frac{1}{4}x\right)$

7. $y = -50 \tan x$

Each graphing calculator screen shows the interval 0 to 2π. What is the period of each graph?

8. 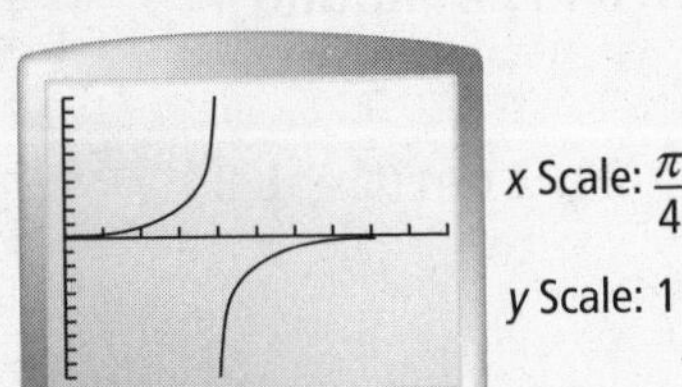

x Scale: $\frac{\pi}{4}$

y Scale: 1

9. 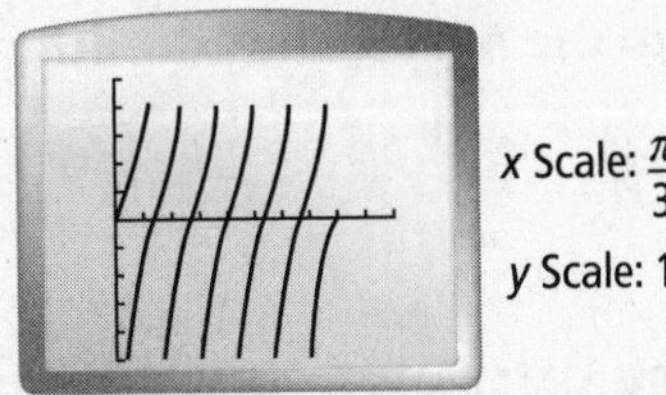

x Scale: $\frac{\pi}{3}$

y Scale: 1

Identify the period and determine where two asymptotes occur for each function.

10. $y = 2 \tan \frac{\theta}{2}$

11. $y = -\tan \frac{\pi}{2}\theta$

12. $y = 4 \tan 2\theta$

Sketch the graph of each tangent curve in the interval from 0 to 2π.

13. $y = -2 \tan \theta$

14. $y = -0.5 \tan 2\theta$

Name ______________________ Class ____________ Date ____________

13-6 Practice (continued)

Form G

The Tangent Function

15. Graphing Calculator A banner hangs from the ceiling of a school gym as shown at the right. The function $y = 15 \tan \theta$ models the perpendicular distance from the ceiling to the tip of the banner. The base of the banner is 30 ft wide.

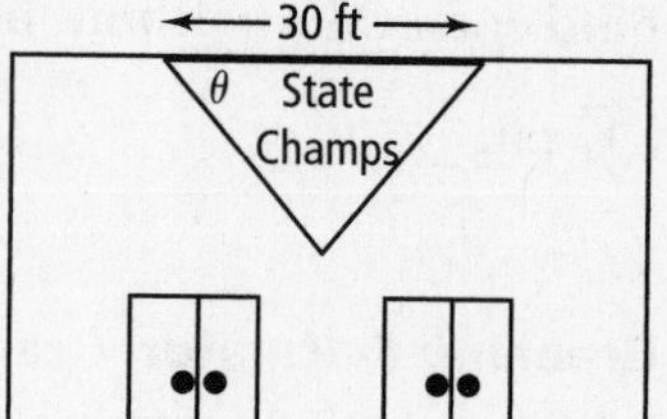

a. Graph the function on a graphing calculator.

b. How far down from the ceiling does the banner hang when $\theta = 30°$?

c. How far down from the ceiling does the banner hang when $\theta = 35°$?

Identify the period for each tangent function. Then graph each function in the interval from -2π to 2π.

16. $y = \tan \frac{1}{4}\theta$

17. $y = \tan(0.75\theta)$

Graphing Calculator Solve each equation in the interval from 0 to 2π. Round your answers to the nearest hundredth.

18. $\tan \theta = \frac{1}{2}$

19. $\tan \theta = -1$

20. $3 \tan \theta = 1$

21. a. Graphing Calculator Graph the functions $y = \tan x$, $y = 5 \tan x$, and $y = 25 \tan x$ on the same set of axes on the interval $-2\pi \leq x \leq 2\pi$ and $-4 \leq y \leq 4$.

b. Writing Describe the relationship between the values of y for each function for a given x-value.

c. Reasoning Without using a calculator, predict the value of $y = 125 \tan x$ for $x = 4$.

22. a. Open-Ended Write a tangent function that has an asymptote through $\theta = \pi$.

b. Graph the function on the interval -2π to 2π.

Use the function $y = 150 \tan x$ on the interval $0° \leq x \leq 141°$. Complete each ordered pair. Round your answers to the nearest whole number.

23. $(45°, \blacksquare)$

24. $(\blacksquare°, -150)$

25. $(141°, \blacksquare)$

26. $(\blacksquare°, 8594)$

Name ______________________ Class ____________ Date ____________

13-7 Practice

Form G

Translating Sine and Cosine Functions

Determine the value of h in each translation. Describe each phase shift (use a phrase like *3 units to the left*).

1. $g(x) = f(x + 2)$
2. $g(x) = f(x - 1)$
3. $h(t) = f(t + 1.5)$
4. $f(x) = g(x - 1)$
5. $y = \cos\left(x - \frac{\pi}{2}\right)$
6. $y = \cos(x + \pi)$

Use the function $f(x)$ at the right. Graph each translation.

7. $f(x) - 5$
8. $f(x + 3)$

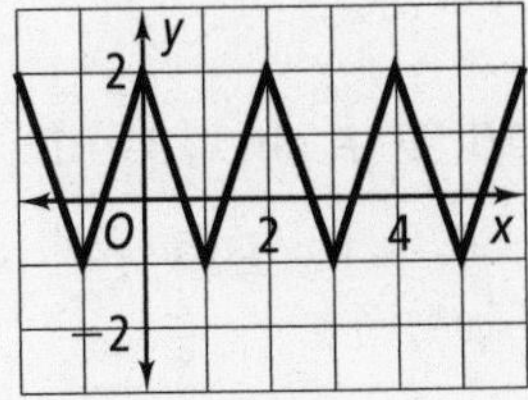

Graph each translation of $y = \cos x$ in the interval from 0 to 2π.

9. $y = \cos(x + 4)$
10. $y = \cos x + 3$
11. $y = \cos\left(x + \frac{\pi}{6}\right)$

Describe any phase shift and vertical shift in the graph.

12. $y = 3\cos x + 2$
13. $y = 2\cos(x - 1) + 3$
14. $y = \sin\left(x + \frac{3\pi}{2}\right) - 1$

Graph each function in the interval from 0 to 2π.

15. $y = 3\sin\left(x - \frac{\pi}{4}\right) + 2$
16. $y = \cos\left(x + \frac{\pi}{2}\right) - 1$
17. $y = \sin(x - \pi) + 2$
18. $y = \cos\frac{1}{2}x + 1$
19. $y = \sin 2\left(x - \frac{\pi}{3}\right)$
20. $y = -\cos 2\left(x + \frac{\pi}{4}\right)$

13-7 Practice (continued)

Form G

Translating Sine and Cosine Functions

Write an equation for each translation.

21. $y = \sin x$, 2 units down

22. $y = \cos x$, π units to the left

23. $y = \cos x$, $\frac{\pi}{4}$ units up

24. $y = \sin x$, 3.2 units to the right

25. $y = \sin x$; 3 units to the left, 1 unit down

26. $y = \cos x$; $\frac{\pi}{2}$ units to the right, 2 units up

27. The table below shows the temperatures at a weather station on several days of the year.

Day of the Year	15	48	73	104	136	169	196	228	257	290	323	352
Temp. (°F)	76	73	75	79	82	87	90	89	88	87	83	79

a. Plot the data

b. Write a cosine model for the data

Write a cosine function for each graph. Then write a sine function for each graph.

28.

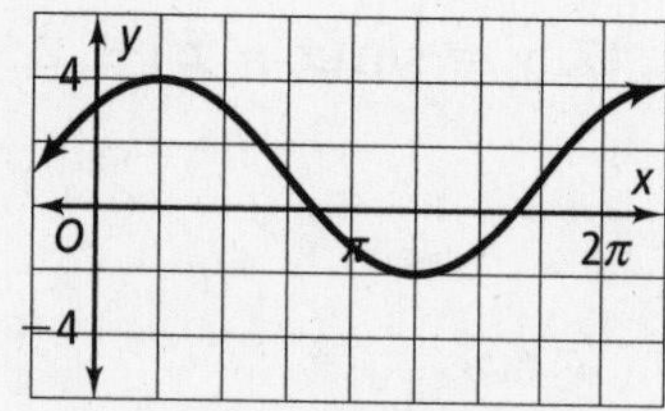

29.

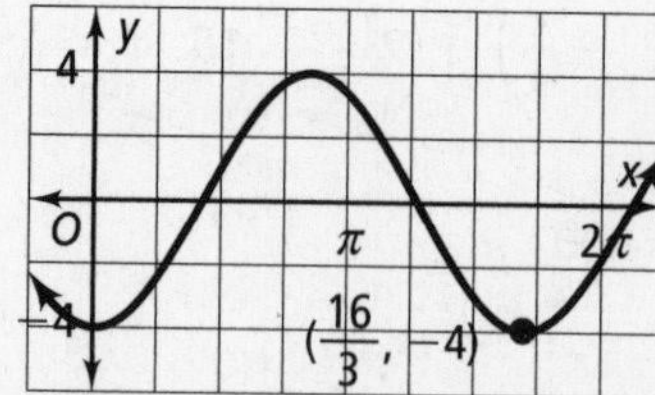

30. a. Write a sine function to model the weather station data in Exercise 27.

b. Writing How do the cosine and sine models differ?

c. Estimation Use your sine model to estimate the temperature at the weather station on December 31 (day 365).

Name ______________________ Class ____________ Date ____________

13-7 Standardized Test Prep

Translating Sine and Cosine Functions

Multiple Choice

For Exercises 1–4, choose the correct letter.

1. Which function is a phase shift of $y = \cos\theta$ by 3 units to the right?

(A) $y = 3\cos\theta$ (B) $y = \cos\theta - 3$ (C) $y = \cos(\theta - 3)$ (D) $y = \cos 3\theta$

2. Which function is a translation of $y = \sin\theta$ by 3 units up?

(F) $y = 3\sin\theta$ (G) $y = \sin(\theta + 3)$ (H) $y = \sin\theta + 3$ (I) $y = \sin 3\theta$

3. Which function is a translation of $y = \cos\theta$ by $\frac{\pi}{4}$ units down and π units to the left?

(A) $y = -\frac{\pi}{4}\cos\pi\theta$

(B) $y = \cos\left(\theta - \frac{\pi}{4}\right) + \pi$

(C) $y = \cos(\theta + \pi) - \frac{\pi}{4}$

(D) $y = \pi\cos\left(-\frac{\pi}{4}\theta\right)$

4. Which best describes the function $y = \sin 2\left(x - \frac{2\pi}{3}\right)$?

(F) a translation of $y = \sin 2x$ $\frac{2\pi}{3}$ units to the left

(G) a translation of $y = \sin 2x$ $\frac{2\pi}{3}$ units to the right

(H) a translation of $y = \sin x$ $\frac{2\pi}{3}$ units to the left and 2 units up

(I) a translation of $y = \sin x$ $\frac{2\pi}{3}$ units to the right and 2 units up

Short Response

5. Write a function that is a transformation of $y = \cos\theta$ so that its amplitude is 9 and its minimum value is 3. Show your work.

Name ______________________ Class ____________ Date ____________

13-8 Think About a Plan

Reciprocal Trigonometric Functions

Indirect Measurement The function $y = 60\sec\theta$ models the length y in feet of a fire ladder as a function of the measure of the angle θ formed by the ladder and the horizontal when the hinge of the ladder is 60 ft from the building.

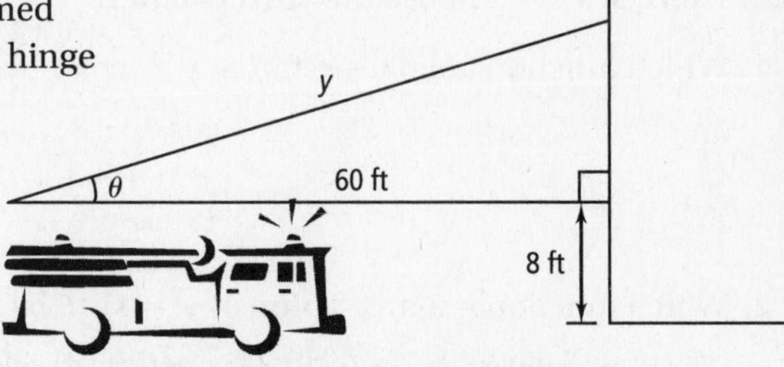

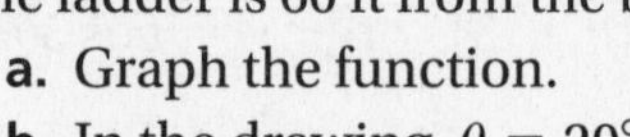

a. Graph the function.

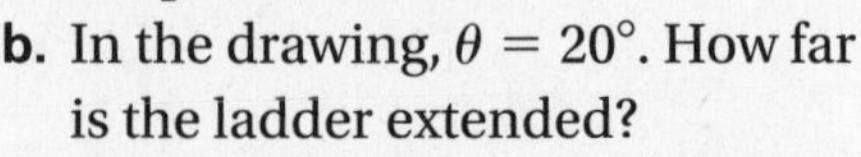

b. In the drawing, $\theta = 20°$. How far is the ladder extended?

c. How far is the ladder extended when it forms an angle of 30°?

d. Suppose the ladder is extended to its full length of 80 ft. What angle does it form with the horizontal? How far up a building can the ladder reach when fully extended? (*Hint:* Use the information in the drawing.)

1. What is a reasonable domain and range for the function?

____

2. Graph the function on your graphing calculator. Sketch the graph.

3. How can the graph help you find the length of the ladder?

____

____.

4. How far is the ladder extended when it forms an angle of 20°? When it forms an angle of 30°? ______________________________

5. Write an equation you can solve to find the angle the ladder forms with the horizontal when it is fully extended to 80 ft.

6. How can you use your graphing calculator to solve your equation? What is the solution?

____

____

7. How can you find the length of the vertical leg of the right triangle in the drawing?

____

8. How far up a building can the ladder reach when fully extended?

Name ____________________ Class ____________ Date ____________

13-8 Practice

Form G

Reciprocal Trigonometric Functions

Find each value without using a calculator. If the expression is undefined, write *undefined*.

1. $\csc(-\pi)$

2. $\cot\frac{2\pi}{3}$

3. $\sec\left(-\frac{11\pi}{6}\right)$

4. $\csc\frac{3\pi}{4}$

5. $\cot\left(-\frac{\pi}{2}\right)$

6. $\csc 3\pi$

7. $\sec\frac{\pi}{3}$

8. $\cot\left(-\frac{\pi}{6}\right)$

Graphing Calculator **Use a calculator to find each value. Round your answers to the nearest thousandth.**

9. $\cot 42^\circ$

10. $\csc\frac{\pi}{6}$

11. $\csc(-2)$

12. $\sec\pi$

13. $\cot(-4)$

14. $\sec(-35^\circ)$

15. $\cot\frac{\pi}{3}$

16. $\sec 1.5$

Graph each function in the interval from 0 to 2π.

17. $y = \cot 2\theta$

18. $y = -\csc 3\theta$

19. $y = \sec\theta + 2$

Graphing Calculator **Use the graph of the appropriate reciprocal trigonometric function to find each value. Round to four decimal places.**

20. $\cot 30^\circ$

21. $\csc 180^\circ$

22. $\cot 70^\circ$

23. $\sec 100^\circ$

24. $\sec 50^\circ$

25. $\csc 100^\circ$

26. $\cot 0^\circ$

27. $\sec 125^\circ$

28. A sparrow perches on the ledge of a building. It is 122 ft above the ground. It looks down at a squirrel along a line of sight that makes an angle of θ with the building. The distance in feet of an object on the ground from the sparrow is modeled by the function $d = 122\sec\theta$. How far away are squirrels sighted at angles of 35° and 50°?

13-8 Practice (continued) — Form G

Reciprocal Trigonometric Functions

Graphing Calculator Graph each function in the interval from 0 to 2π. Describe any phase shift and vertical shift in the graph.

29. $y = -\cot\frac{1}{2}\theta$

30. $y = \sec\left(\theta - \frac{\pi}{2}\right)$

31. $y = \csc 2\theta + 1$

32. $y = \cot(\theta + \pi)$

33. $y = \sec\frac{1}{4}\theta$

34. $y = \csc\theta - 1$

35. **a.** Graph $y = -\sin x$ and $y = -\csc x$ on the same axes in the interval from 0 to 2π.

b. State the domain, range, and period of each function.

c. For which values of x does $-\sin x = -\csc x$?

d. **Compare and Contrast** Compare the two graphs in part (a). How are they alike? How are they different?

e. **Reasoning** Is the value of $-\csc x$ positive when $-\sin x$ is positive and negative when $-\sin x$ is negative? Justify your answer.

36. A fire truck is parked on the shoulder of a freeway next to a long wall. The red light on the top of the truck rotates through one complete revolution every 2 s. The function $y = 10\sec\pi t$ models the length of the beam in feet to a point on the wall in terms of time t.

a. Graph the function.

b. Find the length at time 1.75 s.

c. Find the length at time 2 s.

Name ______________________ Class __________ Date __________

13-8 Standardized Test Prep

Reciprocal Trigonometric Functions

Gridded Response

Solve each exercise and enter your answer in the grid provided.

For Exercises 1–2, let $\cos\theta = \frac{5}{13}$ and $\sin\theta > 0$. Enter each answer as a fraction.

1. What is $\cot\theta$?

2. What is $\csc\theta$?

For Exercises 3–5, let $\tan\theta = \frac{12}{5}$ and $-\frac{\pi}{2} \le \theta < \frac{\pi}{2}$. Enter each answer as a decimal rounded to the nearest hundredth.

3. What is $\cot\theta + \cos\theta$?

4. What is $(\sin\theta)(\cot\theta)$?

5. What is $\sec\theta + \tan\theta$?

Answers

1. 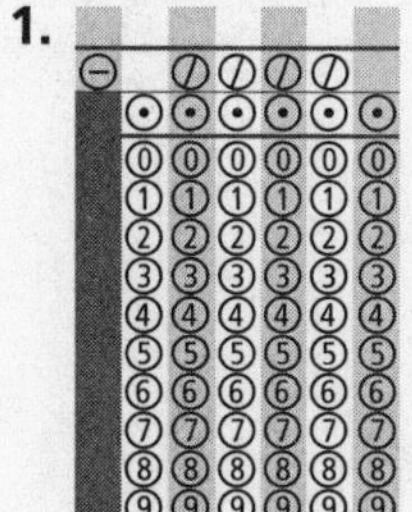

2. 

3. 

4. 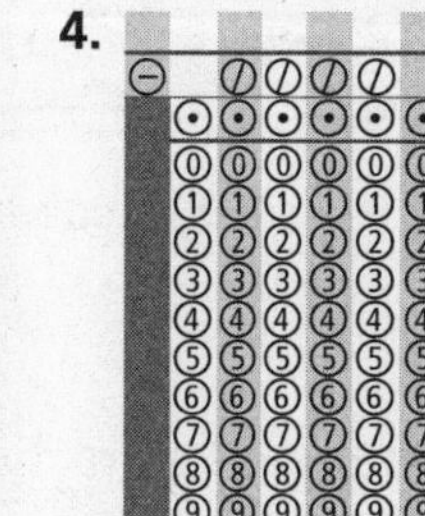

5. 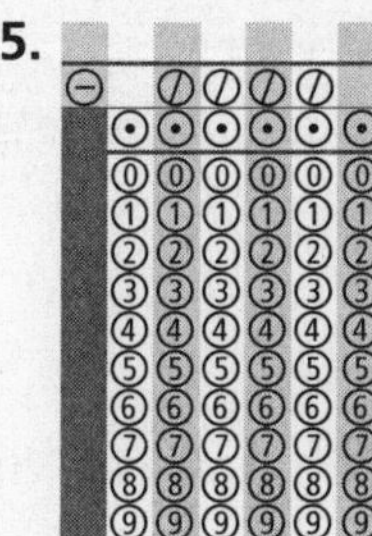

Name ______________________ Class ____________ Date ____________

14-1 Think About a Plan

Trigonometric Identities

Simplify the trigonometric expression. $\dfrac{\csc \theta}{\sin \theta + \cos \theta \cot \theta}$

Know

1. $\csc \theta =$ ☐ $\cot \theta =$ ☐

2. The Pythagorean identity involving the sine and cosine functions is

☐.

Need

3. To solve the problem I need to:

____

____.

Plan

4. Write each function in the expression in terms of sines and cosines.

$$\frac{\csc \theta}{\sin \theta + \cos \theta \cot \theta} = \frac{\square}{\sin \theta + \cos \theta \left(\square\right)}$$

5. How can you eliminate the fractions in the numerator and denominator?

____.

6. Simplify the trigonometric expression.

$$\frac{\csc \theta}{\sin \theta + \cos \theta \cot \theta} =$$

Name ______________________ Class __________ Date __________

14-1 Practice

Form G

Trigonometric Identities

Verify each identity. Give the domain of validity for each identity.

1. $\sin\theta \sec\theta \cot\theta = 1$

2. $\csc\theta = \cot\theta \sec\theta$

3. $\dfrac{\sin\theta}{\csc\theta} = \sin^2\theta$

4. $\cos\theta \csc\theta \tan\theta = 1$

5. $\sin\theta \tan\theta + \cos\theta = \sec\theta$

6. $\dfrac{\csc\theta}{\cot\theta} = \sec\theta$

7. $\sec\theta = \tan\theta \csc\theta$

8. $\tan\theta + \cot\theta = \sec\theta \csc\theta$

9. $\tan^2\theta + 1 = \sec^2\theta$

10. $\cos\theta \cot\theta + \sin\theta = \csc\theta$

11. $\dfrac{\sec\theta}{\csc\theta} = \tan\theta$

12. $\sec\theta \cot\theta = \csc\theta$

13. $\sec^2\theta - \tan^2\theta = 1$

14. $\sec\theta = \csc\theta \tan\theta$

15. $\dfrac{\sin\theta + \cos\theta}{\sin\theta} = 1 + \cot\theta$

16. $\cos\theta(\sec\theta - \cos\theta) = \sin^2\theta$

17. $\cot\theta \sec\theta = \csc\theta$

18. $(1 - \sin\theta)(1 + \sin\theta) = \cos^2\theta$

Simplify each trigonometric expression.

19. $1 - \sec^2\theta$

20. $\dfrac{\sec\theta}{\tan\theta}$

Name ______________________ Class ____________ Date ____________

14-1 Practice (continued)

Form G

Trigonometric Identities

Simplify each trigonometric expression.

21. $\csc\theta\tan\theta$

22. $\sec\theta\cos^2\theta$

23. $\csc^2\theta - \cot^2\theta$

24. $1 - \sin^2\theta$

25. $\tan\theta\cot\theta$

26. $\cos\theta\cot\theta + \sin\theta$

27. $\cos\theta\tan\theta$

28. $\dfrac{\sin\theta\cot\theta}{\cos\theta}$

29. $\sec\theta\tan\theta\csc\theta$

30. $\sec\theta\cot\theta$

31. $\dfrac{\sin\theta}{\csc\theta} + \dfrac{\cos\theta}{\sec\theta}$

32. $\dfrac{\tan\theta\csc\theta}{\sec\theta}$

33. $\cot^2\theta - \csc^2\theta$

34. $\dfrac{\cot\theta}{\csc\theta}$

Express the first trigonometric function in terms of the second.

35. $\csc\theta$, $\sin\theta$

36. $\cot\theta$, $\tan\theta$

37. $\sec\theta$, $\cos\theta$

38. $\cos\theta$, $\sin\theta$

39. Writing Which side of the equation below should you transform to verify the identity? Explain. $\dfrac{\cos^2\theta + \tan^2\theta - 1}{\sin^2\theta} = \tan^2\theta$

Name ______________________ Class ______________ Date ______________

14-1 Standardized Test Prep

Trigonometric Identities

Multiple Choice

For Exercises 1–5, choose the correct letter.

1. The expression $\csc\theta \sin\theta + \cot^2\theta$ is equivalent to which of the following?

   (A) $\sin^2\theta$ (B) $\cot^2\theta$ (C) $\csc^2\theta$ (D) $\cos^2\theta$

2. How can you express $(1 + \sin\theta)(\sec\theta - \tan\theta)$ in terms of $\cos\theta$?

   (F) $\frac{1}{\cos\theta}$ (G) $\cos^2\theta$ (H) $1 - \cos^2\theta$ (I) $\cos\theta$

3. Which of the following expressions are equivalent?

   I. $\frac{\cos^2\theta}{\cot^2\theta}$ **II.** $\sin^2\theta$ **III.** $1 - \cos^2\theta$

   (A) I and II only (C) II and III only

   (B) I and III only (D) I, II, and III

4. Which equation is not true?

   (F) $\tan\theta = \frac{\cos\theta}{\sin\theta}$ (H) $\sin^2\theta = 1 - \cos^2\theta$

   (G) $\csc\theta = \frac{1}{\sin\theta}$ (I) $\csc^2\theta = \cot^2\theta + 1$

5. Which of the following is the expression $\sin\theta\cos\theta(\tan\theta + \cot\theta)$ in simplified form?

   (A) $\cos\theta$ (B) 1 (C) $\tan\theta$ (D) $\sin^2\theta$

Short Response

6. Show that $\frac{\csc^2\theta - \cot^2\theta}{1 - \sin^2\theta} = \sec^2\theta$ is an identity.

Name ____________________ Class ____________ Date ____________

14-2 Think About a Plan

Solving Trigonometric Equations Using Inverses

Electricity The function $I = 40 \sin 60\pi t$ models the current I in amps that an electric generator is producing after t seconds. When is the first time that the current will reach 20 amps? -20 amps?

Understanding the Problem

1. How many amps does the generator produce after t seconds?

2. Write the current function using an inverse trigonometric function.

3. What is the problem asking you to determine?

   ____

   ____.

Planning the Solution

4. Write an equation that you can use to determine when the generator first produces 20 amps.

5. Write an equation that you can use to determine when the generator first produces -20 amps.

Getting an Answer

6. Solve your equations to find the first time that the current will reach 20 amps and the first time that the current will reach -20 amps.

Name ______________________ Class ____________ Date ____________

14-2 Practice

Form G

Solving Trigonometric Equations Using Inverses

Use a unit circle, a 45°-45°-90° triangle, and an inverse function to find the degree measure of each angle.

1. angle whose sine is $\frac{\sqrt{2}}{2}$

2. angle whose tangent is 1

3. angle whose cosine is $-\frac{\sqrt{2}}{2}$

4. angle whose sine is 1

Use a calculator and inverse functions to find the radian measures of all angles having the given trigonometric values.

5. angles whose tangent is 2.5

6. angles whose sine is 0.75

7. angles whose cosine is -0.24

8. angles whose cosine is 0.45

9. angles whose sine is -1.1

10. angles whose tangent is (-3)

Solve each equation for θ with $0 \leq \theta < 2\pi$.

11. $2 \tan \theta + 2 = 0$

12. $2 \cos \theta = 1$

13. $2 \cos \theta + \sqrt{3} = 0$

14. $\sqrt{3} \cot \theta - 1 = 0$

15. $4 \sin \theta - 3 = 0$

16. $4 \sin \theta + 3 = 0$

17. $(2 \cos \theta + \sqrt{3})(2 \cos \theta + 1) = 0$

18. $\sqrt{3} \tan \theta - 2 \sin \theta \tan \theta = 0$

19. $2 \cos^2 \theta + \cos \theta = 0$

20. $5 \cos \theta - 3 = 0$

21. $\tan \theta - 2 \cos \theta \tan \theta = 0$

22. $\tan \theta (\tan \theta + 1) = 0$

23. $(\cos \theta - 1)(2 \cos \theta - 1) = 0$

24. $\tan^2 \theta - \tan \theta = 0$

25. If a model rocket is fired into the air with an initial velocity v at an angle of elevation θ, then the height h in feet of the projectile at time t in seconds is given by $h = -16t^2 + vt \sin \theta$.

a. Find the angle of elevation θ, to the nearest tenth of a degree, if a rocket launched at 1500 ft/s takes 2 s to reach a height of 750 ft.

b. Find the angle of elevation θ, to the nearest tenth of a degree, if a rocket launched at 1500 ft/s takes 3 s to reach a height of 750 ft.

14-2 Practice (continued) — Form G

Solving Trigonometric Equations Using Inverses

Each diagram shows one solution to the equation below it. Find the complete solution of each equation.

26. 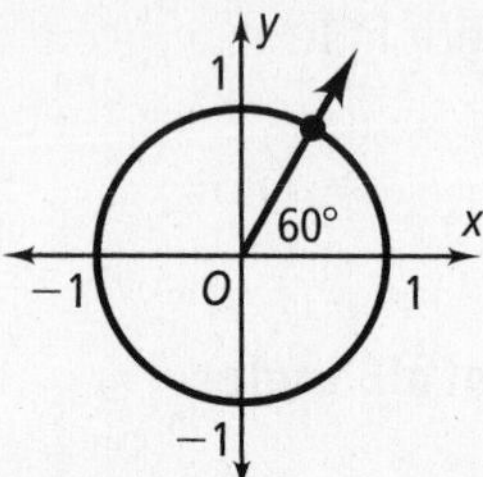

$\sin\theta = \sqrt{3} - \sin\theta$

27. 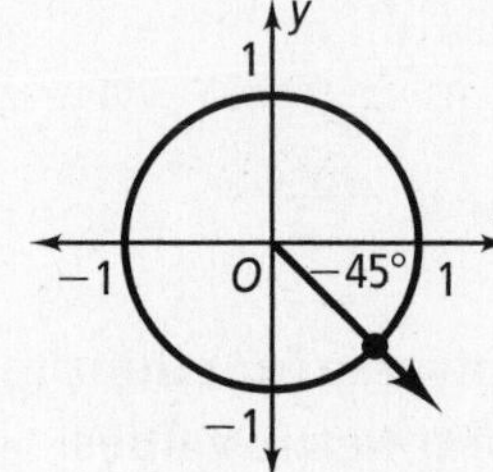

$4\tan\theta + 1 = 3\tan\theta$

28. 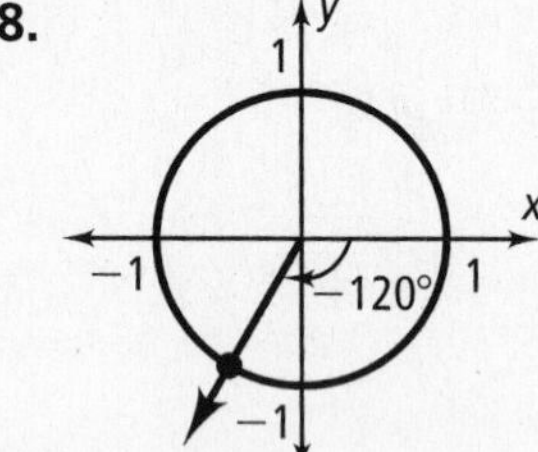

$9\cos\theta + 1 = 7\cos\theta$

29. 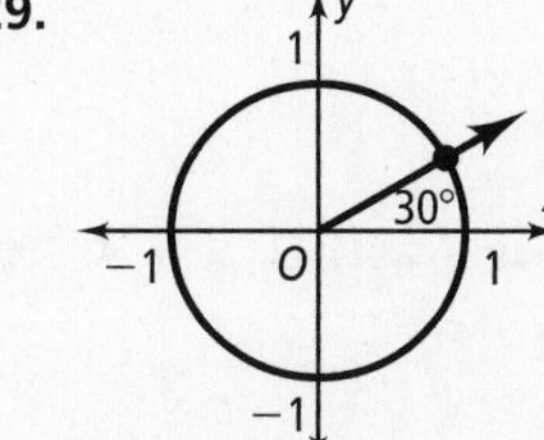

$8\cos\theta + 3\sqrt{3} = 7\sqrt{3}$

30. Reasoning Write a trigonometric equation that has solutions of $\frac{\pi}{12}$, $\frac{5\pi}{12}$, and $\frac{3\pi}{4}$ in the domain $[0, 2\pi)$.

31. Error Analysis A student solved the equation $2\cos\theta = \sqrt{2}$ for $0 \leq \theta < 2\pi$ and got $\theta = \frac{\pi}{4}$. What was her error?

Find the x-intercepts of the graph of each function.

32. $y = 2\cos^4\theta - 1$

33. $y = 2\sin\theta - 1$

34. $y = \sin^2\theta - \cos\theta$

35. $y = \tan^4\theta - 2$

Name ______________________ Class ____________ Date ____________

14-2 Standardized Test Prep

Solving Trigonometric Equations Using Inverses

Multiple Choice

For Exercises 1–5, choose the correct letter.

1. What is $\sin^{-1}\frac{\sqrt{2}}{2}$, in degrees?

(A) 0° (B) 30° (C) 45° (D) 90°

2. What are the radian measures of all angles whose sine is $\frac{1}{2}$?

(F) $\frac{\pi}{2} + 2\pi n$ and $\frac{3\pi}{2} + 2\pi n$

(G) $\frac{\pi}{3} + 2\pi n$ and $\frac{4\pi}{3} + 2\pi n$

(H) $\frac{\pi}{6} + 2\pi n$ and $\frac{5\pi}{6} + 2\pi n$

(I) $\frac{\pi}{6} + 2\pi n$ and $\frac{7\pi}{6} + 2\pi n$

3. What values for θ satisfy the equation $3\tan\theta + 4 = 0$ for $0 \leq \theta < 2\pi$?

(A) 2.21 and 5.36

(B) 0.93 and 4.07

(C) –0.93 and –4.07

(D) –2.21 and –5.36

4. What values for θ satisfy the equation $2\cos\theta - \sqrt{3} = 0$ for $0 \leq \theta < 2\pi$?

(F) $\frac{\pi}{6}, \frac{5\pi}{6}$ (G) $\frac{\pi}{6}, \frac{11\pi}{6}$ (H) $\frac{\pi}{3}, \frac{2\pi}{3}$ (I) $\frac{\pi}{3}, \frac{5\pi}{3}$

5. In which quadrants are the solutions to $2\sin\theta - 1 = 0$?

(A) Quadrants I and II

(B) Quadrants I and III

(C) Quadrants II and III

(D) Quadrants II and IV

Short Response

6. Solve $2\cos^2\theta + 2\cos\theta = 0$ for $0 \leq \theta < 2\pi$. Show your work.

Name ______________________ Class ____________ Date ____________

14-3 Think About a Plan

Right Triangles and Trigonometric Ratios

A 150-ft redwood tree casts a shadow. Express the length x of the shadow as a function of the angle of elevation of the sun θ. Then find x when $\theta = 35^\circ$ and $\theta = 70^\circ$.

Understanding the Problem

1. How tall is the tree?

2. How long is the shadow?

3. What is the problem asking you to determine?

____

____.

Planning the Solution

4. How can a drawing help you solve the problem?

____

____.

5. Make a drawing of the tree, its shadow, and the sun. Label the height of the tree, the length x of the shadow, and the angle of elevation of the sun θ.

6. Use a trigonometric ratio to relate the height of the tree, x, and θ.

Getting an Answer

7. Express the length x of the shadow as a function of the angle of elevation of the sun θ.

8. What is x when $\theta = 35^\circ$? What is x when $\theta = 70^\circ$?

Name ______________________ Class ____________ Date ____________

14-3 Practice
Form G

Right Triangles and Trigonometric Ratios

Find the values of the six trigonometric functions for the angle in standard position determined by each point.

1. $(-3, 4)$

2. $(12, -5)$

3. $(-2, -1)$

4. $(\sqrt{5}, 2)$

5. A hiker is standing on one bank of a river. A tree stands on the opposite bank, which is 750 ft away. A line from the top of the tree to the ground at the hiker's feet makes an angle of 12° with the ground. How tall is the tree?

6. In $\triangle ABC$, find each value as a fraction and as a decimal. Round to the nearest hundredth.

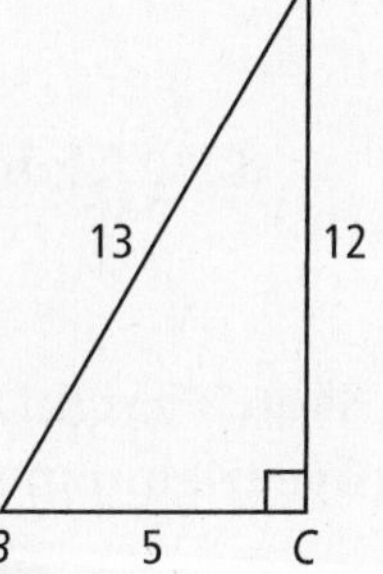

a. $\cos A$ 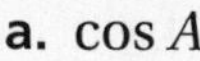

b. $\csc A$

c. $\tan B$

d. $\sec B$ 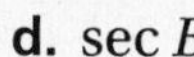

e. $\cot A$

f. $\csc B$

7. In $\triangle ABC$, $\angle C$ is a right angle and $\tan A = \frac{2}{3}$. Draw a diagram and find each value in fraction form and in decimal form. Round your answer to the nearest tenth, if necessary.

a. $\cos A$

b. $\tan B$

c. $\sin A$

d. $\cot B$

e. $\sec A$

f. $\csc B$

Find each length x. Round to the nearest tenth.

8.

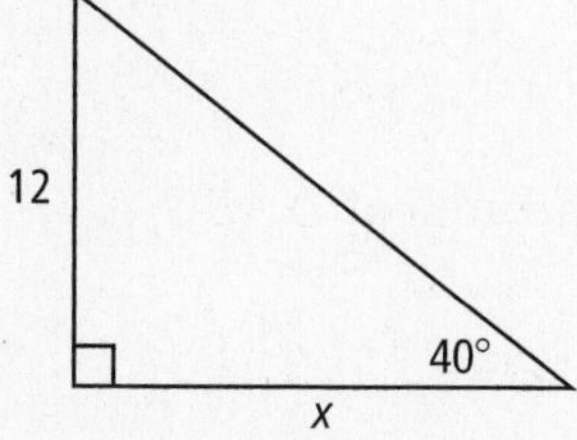

9.

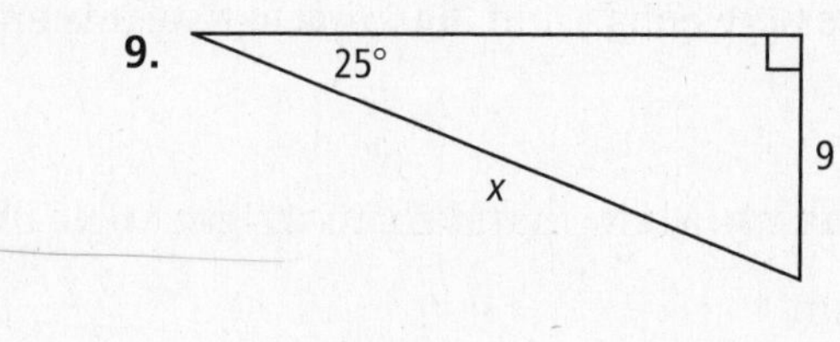

Name ______________________ Class ____________ Date ____________

14-3 Practice (continued) — Form G

Right Triangles and Trigonometric Ratios

10. A kite string makes a 62° angle with the horizontal, and 300 ft of string is let out. The string is held 6 ft off the ground. How high is the kite?

In $\triangle DEF$, $\angle D$ is a right angle. Find the remaining sides and angles. Round answers to the nearest tenth.

11. $f = 8, e = 15$

12. $f = 1, e = 2$

13. $f = 2, e = 1$

14. $f = 1, d = 500$

15. $d = 21, e = 8$

16. $e = 5, f = 1$

17. You are designing several access ramps. What angle would each ramp make with the ground, to the nearest 0.1°?

a. 20 ft long, rises 16 in.

b. 8 ft long, rises 8 in.

c. 12 ft long, rises 6 in.

d. 30 ft long, rises 32 in.

e. 4 ft long, rises 6 in.

f. 6 ft long, rises 14 in.

Sketch a right triangle with θ as the measure of one acute angle. Find the other five trigonometric ratios of θ.

18. $\cos\theta = \frac{4}{11}$

19. $\sin\theta = \frac{7}{12}$

20. $\csc\theta = \frac{14}{6}$

21. $\cos\theta = \frac{9}{16}$

22. $\sin\theta = 0.45$

23. $\sec\theta = 7.6$

24. Open-Ended If $\cos\theta = \frac{1}{2}$, describe a method you could use to find all the angles between 0° and 360° that satisfy this equation.

25. Reasoning Show that if $\angle C$ is a right angle in $\triangle ABC$, then the area of $\triangle ABC$ is $\frac{bc}{2}\sin A$.

Name ______________________ Class ____________ Date ____________

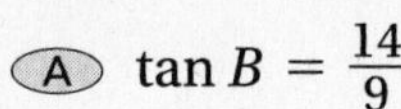

14-3 Standardized Test Prep

Right Triangles and Trigonometric Ratios

Multiple Choice

For Exercises 1–4, choose the correct letter.

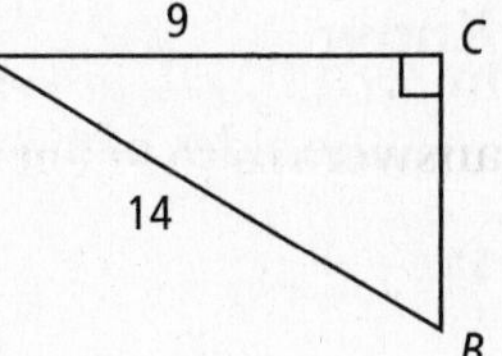

1. Which equation could be used to find the measure of one acute angle in the right triangle at the right?

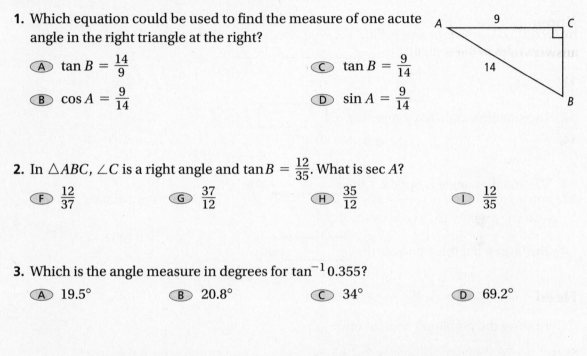

(A) $\tan B = \frac{14}{9}$ (C) $\tan B = \frac{9}{14}$

(B) $\cos A = \frac{9}{14}$ (D) $\sin A = \frac{9}{14}$

2. In $\triangle ABC$, $\angle C$ is a right angle and $\tan B = \frac{12}{35}$. What is $\sec A$?

(F) $\frac{12}{37}$ (G) $\frac{37}{12}$ (H) $\frac{35}{12}$ (I) $\frac{12}{35}$

3. Which is the angle measure in degrees for $\tan^{-1} 0.355$?

(A) 19.5° (B) 20.8° (C) 34° (D) 69.2°

4. A kite is on a 300-ft string. The angle of elevation from the ground to the kite is 39°. Which is the best estimate of the height of the kite above the ground?

(F) 629 ft (G) 243 ft (H) 189 ft (I) 233 ft

Extended Response

5. What are the measures of the acute angles of a right triangle, to the nearest tenth, if the legs are 48 in. and 55 in.? Show your work.

Name ______________________ Class ____________ Date ____________

14-4 Think About a Plan

Area and the Law of Sines

Geometry The sides of a triangle are 15 in., 17 in., and 16 in. The smallest angle has a measure of 54°. Find the measure of the largest angle. Round to the nearest degree.

Know

1. The sides of the triangle are ______________________.

2. The smallest angle has a measure of [ ].

3. The smallest angle is opposite the [ ] side.

4. The largest angle is opposite the [ ] side.

Need

5. To solve the problem I need to find:

____

____.

Plan

6. What equation can you use to find the measure of the largest angle?

7. Solve your equation for the measure of the largest angle.

8. What is the measure of the largest angle?

Name ______________________ Class ____________ Date ____________

14-4 Practice

Form G

Area and the Law of Sines

Find the area of each triangle. Round your answers to the nearest tenth.

1. 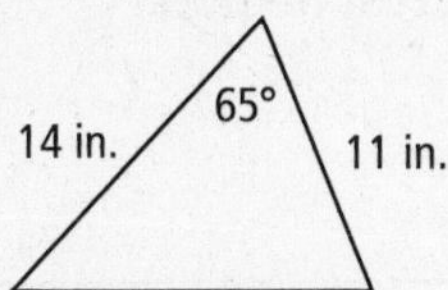

2. 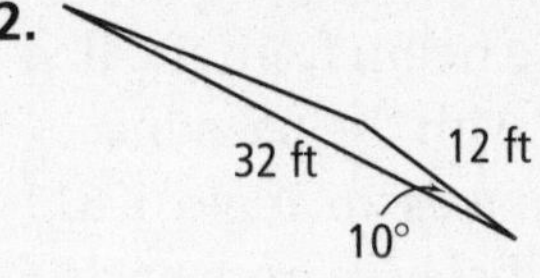

3. 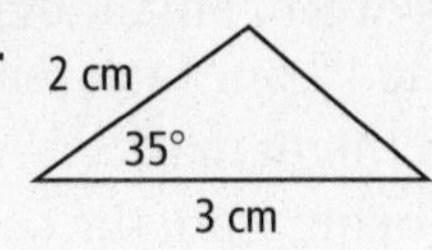

4. A triangle has sides of lengths 15 in. and 22 in., and the measure of the angle between them is 95°. Find the area of the triangle.

Use the Law of Sines. Find the measure x to the nearest tenth.

5. 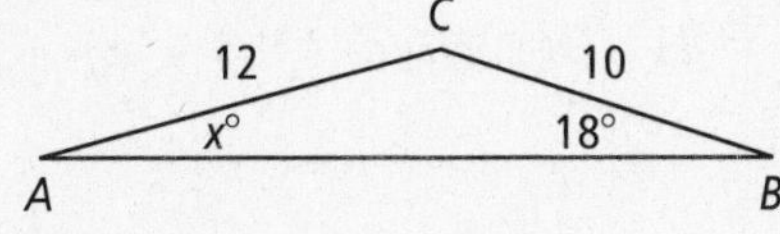

6. 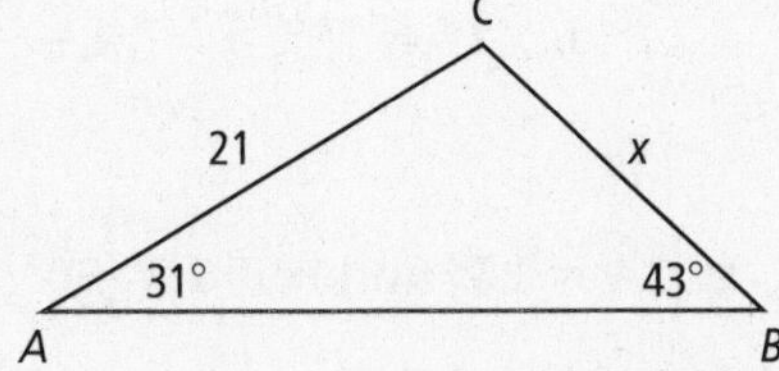

7. 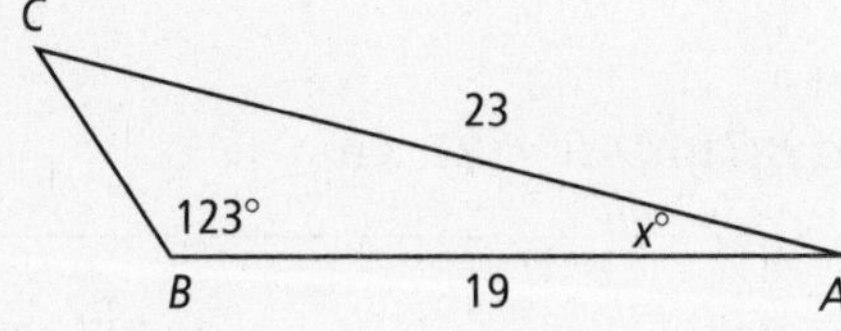

8. 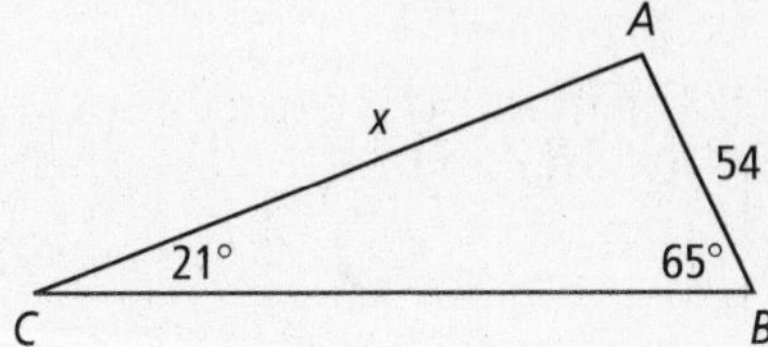

9. In $\triangle GHJ$, $m\angle J = 39°$, $h = 36$ cm, and $j = 42$ cm. Find $m\angle H$.

10. In $\triangle MNP$, $m\angle P = 33°$, $m = 54$ ft, and $p = 63$ ft. Find $m\angle M$.

11. A hot-air balloon is observed from two points, A and B, on the ground 800 ft apart as shown in the diagram. The angle of elevation of the balloon is 65° from point A and 37° from point B. Find the distance from point A to the balloon.

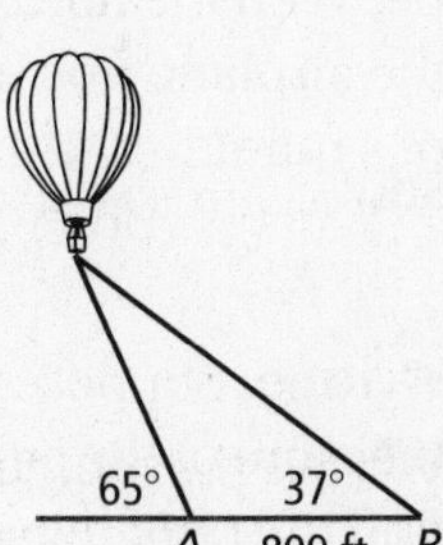

Find the remaining sides and angles of $\triangle PQR$. Round your answers to the nearest tenth.

12. $m\angle Q = 64°$, $m\angle R = 64°$, and $r = 8$

13. $m\angle Q = 64°$, $q = 22$, and $r = 14$

14-4 Practice (continued) Form G

Area and the Law of Sines

14. Two searchlights on the shore of a lake are located 3020 yd apart as shown in the diagram. A ship in distress is spotted from each searchlight. The beam from the first searchlight makes an angle of 38° with the baseline. The beam from the second light makes an angle of 57° with the baseline. Find the ship's distance from each searchlight.

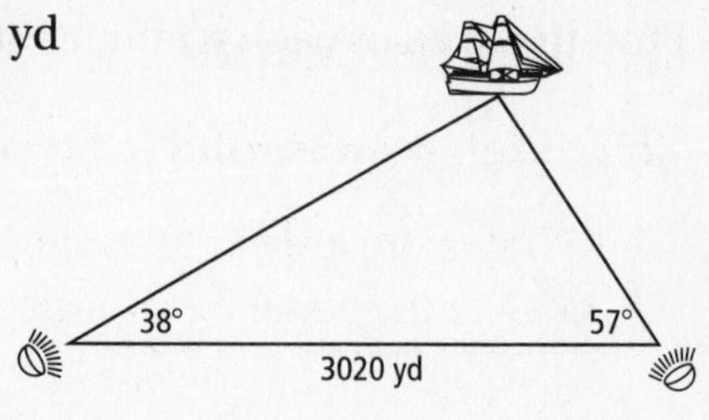

Find the area of $\triangle ABC$. Round your answer to the nearest tenth.

15. $m\angle B = 28°, m\angle C = 70°, a = 9.8$

16. $m\angle A = 42°, a = 4.17, c = 5.02$

17. $m\angle A = 17°, m\angle C = 75°, b = 18.1$

18. $m\angle C = 81°, b = 6.7, c = 9.3$

In $\triangle ABC$, $m\angle A = 25°$ and $m\angle B = 50°$. Find each value to the nearest tenth.

19. Find AC for $BC = 6.2$ in.

20. Find BC for $AC = 14.9$ cm.

21. Find AC for $AB = 53.7$ ft.

22. Find BC for $AB = 27.3$ m.

23. An airplane is flying between two airports that are 35 mi apart. The radar in one airport registers a 27° angle between the horizontal and the airplane. The radar system in the other airport registers a 69° angle between the horizontal and the airplane. How far is the airplane from each airport to the nearest tenth of a mile?

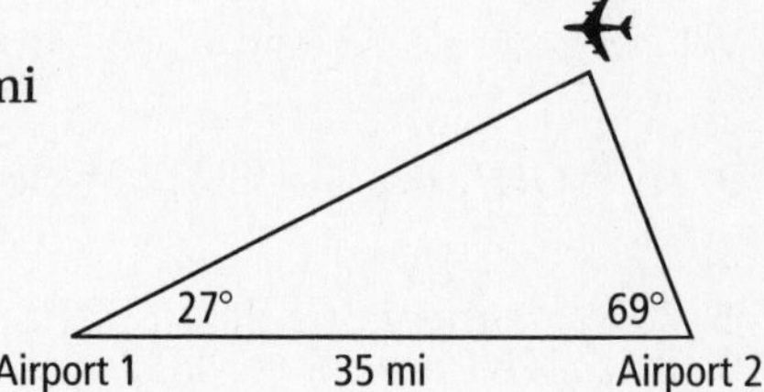

24. Writing Suppose you know the measures of two sides of a triangle and the measure of the angle between the two sides. Can you use the Law of Sines to find the remaining side and angle measures? Explain.

25. Reasoning How can you find the measures of the angles of $\triangle ABC$ if you know the measures of its sides and its area?

Name ______________________ Class ____________ Date ____________

14-4 Standardized Test Prep

Area and the Law of Sines

Gridded Response

Solve each exercise and enter your answer in the grid provided.

1. What is the area of the triangle at the right? Round your answer to the nearest tenth of a meter.

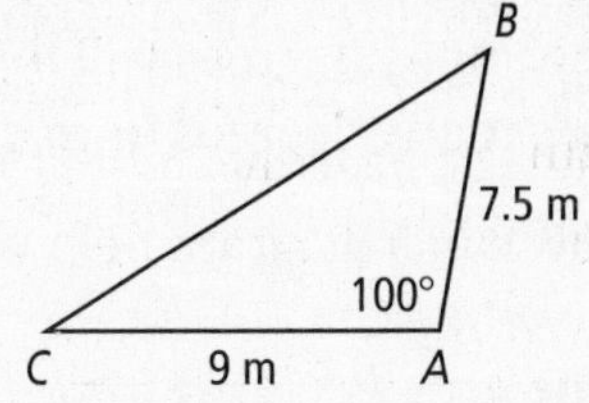

2. A triangle has side lengths 202 ft and 201.5 ft, and the measure of the angle between them is 82.5°. What is the area of the triangle? Round your answer to the nearest square foot.

3. In $\triangle ABC$, $m\angle A = 38°$, $m\angle C = 32°$, and $BC = 40$ cm. What is the length of AC? Round your answer to the nearest tenth of a centimeter.

For Exercises 4 and 5, use $\triangle XYZ$, where $x = 10$, $z = 6$, and $m\angle X = 115°$.

4. What is $m\angle Y$? Round your answer to the nearest tenth.

5. What is the value of sin Z? Round your answer to the nearest thousandth.

Answers

1. 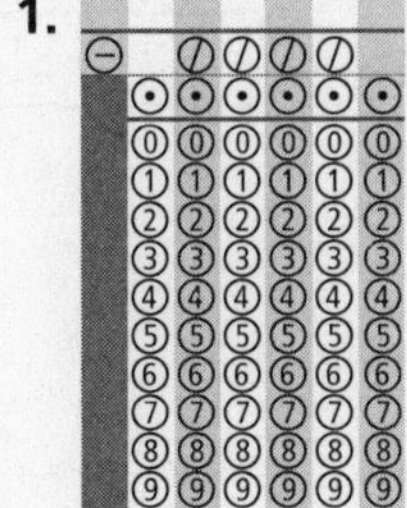

2. 

3. 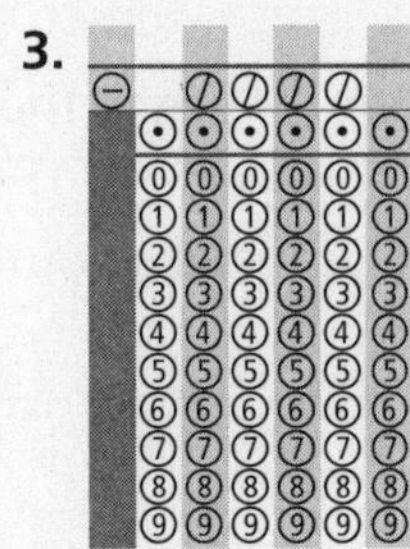

4. 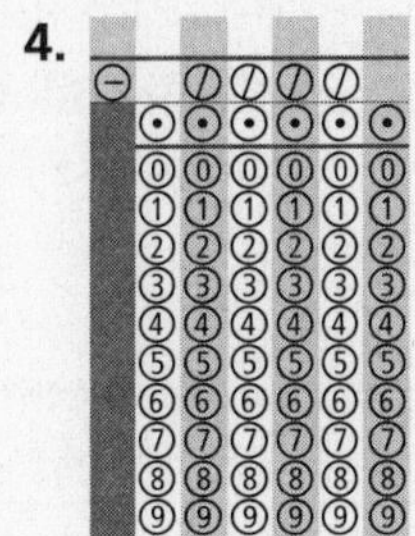

5. 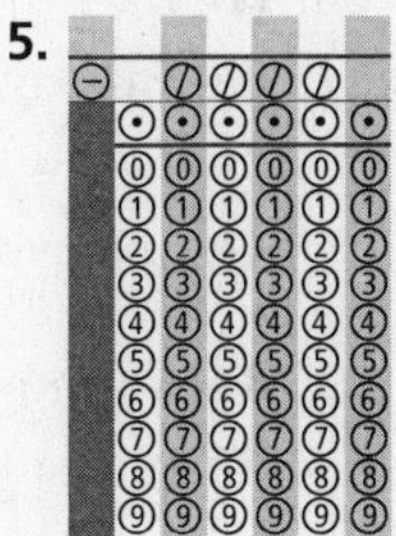

Name ______________________ Class ____________ Date ____________

14-5 Think About a Plan

The Law of Cosines

Navigation A pilot is flying from city A to city B, which is 85 mi due north. After flying 20 mi, the pilot must change course and fly 10° east of north to avoid a cloud bank.

a. If the pilot remains on this course for 20 mi, how far will the plane be from city B?

b. How many degrees will the pilot have to turn to the left to fly directly to city B? How many degrees from due north is this course?

1. How can a diagram help you solve this problem?

____

____.

2. Fill in the missing information in the diagram.

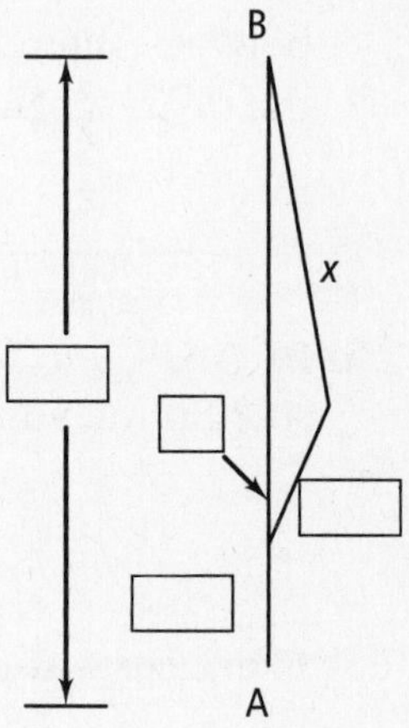

B

x

A

3. How can you find the length of the other unknown side of the triangle?

____.

4. How can the Law of Cosines help you find the length x?

____

____.

5. Find x, the distance the plane is from city B. [ ]

6. How can you find the number of degrees the pilot will have to turn to the left to fly directly to city B?

____

____

____

____.

7. How many degrees will the pilot have to turn to the left to fly directly to city B? [ ]

8. How can you find the number of degrees this course is from due north?

____

____.

9. How many degrees from due north is this course? [ ]

Name ____________________ Class ____________ Date ____________

14-5 Practice

Form G

The Law of Cosines

Use the Law of Cosines. Find length x to the nearest tenth.

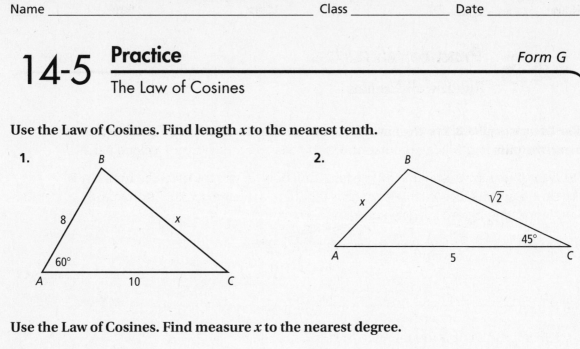

1.

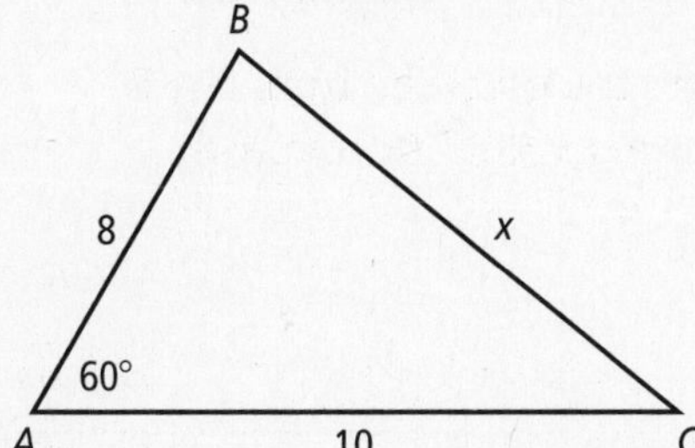

2.

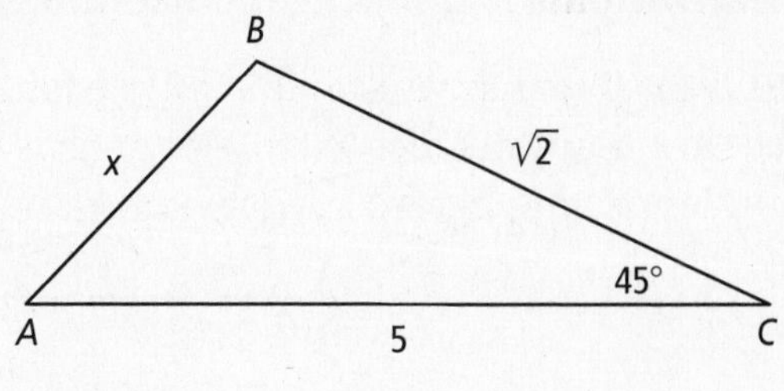

Use the Law of Cosines. Find measure x to the nearest degree.

3.

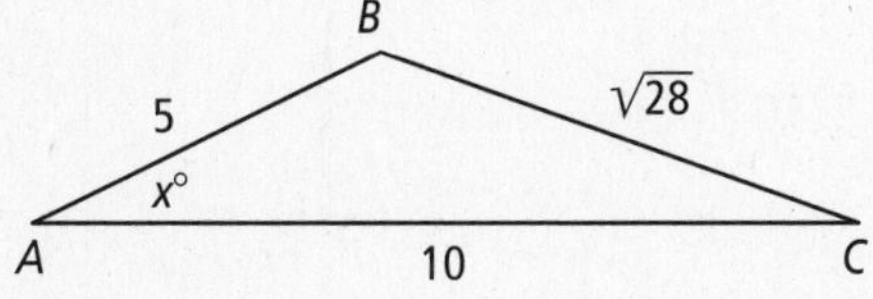

4.

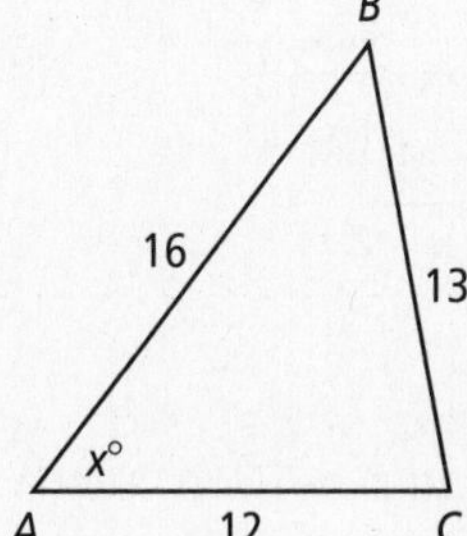

5. In $\triangle XYZ$, $x = 4$ cm, $y = 7$ cm, and $z = 10$ cm. Find $m\angle X$.

6. In $\triangle FGH$, $f = 32$ in., $g = 79$ in., and $h = 86$ in. Find $m\angle G$.

7. In $\triangle ABC$, $a = 3$ ft, $b = 2.9$ ft, and $c = 4.6$ ft. Find $m\angle C$.

8. In $\triangle FGH$, $f = 34$ m, $g = 18.9$ m, and $h = 21.5$ m. Find $m\angle G$.

9. In $\triangle ABC$, $a = 14$ yd, $b = 16$ yd, and $c = 18$ yd. Find $m\angle C$.

Name ______________________ Class ____________ Date ____________

14-5 Practice (continued) — Form G

The Law of Cosines

For Exercises 10–13, use the Law of Cosines and the Law of Sines. Find x to the nearest tenth.

10.

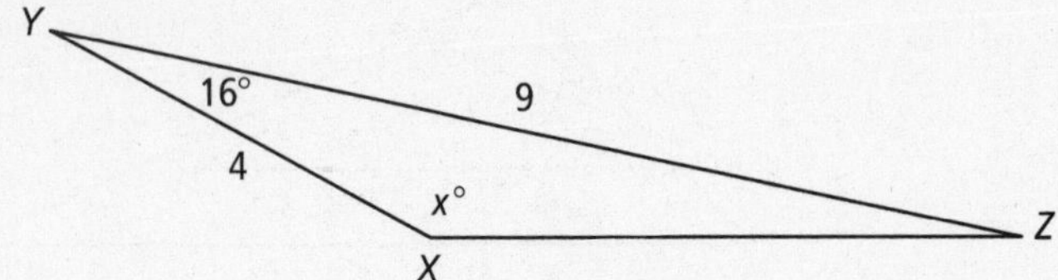

11.

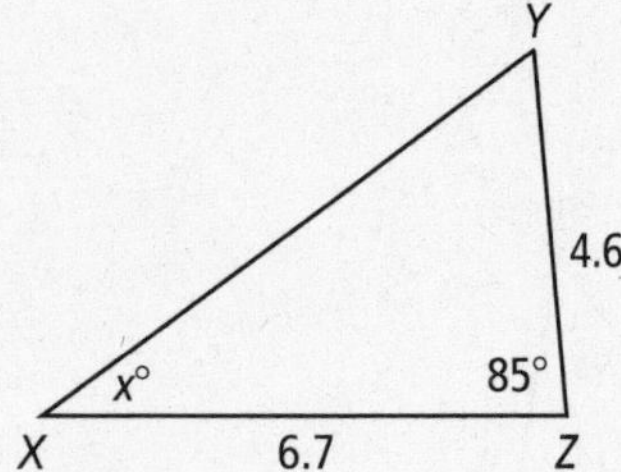

12. In $\triangle ABC$, $b = 8$ cm, $c = 7$ cm, and $m\angle A = 149°$. Find $m\angle C$.

13. In $\triangle FGH$, $f = 7$ yd, $g = 22$ yd, and $m\angle H = 85°$. Find $m\angle F$.

14. The sides of a triangular lot are 158 ft, 173 ft, and 191 ft. Find the measure of the angle opposite the longest side to the nearest tenth of a degree.

15. A car travels 50 mi due west from point A. At point B, the car turns and travels at an angle of 35° north of due east. The car travels in this direction for 40 mi, to point C. How far is point C from point A?

16. a. In $\triangle ABC$, $m\angle A = 84.1°$, $b = 4.8$, and $c = 7.2$. Use the Law of Cosines to find a and then use the Law of Sines to find the measure of angles B and C. Round to the nearest tenth.

b. Error Analysis Your classmate says that this triangle does not exist. You say that it does. Who is correct? Explain.

Name ________________ Class ________ Date ________

14-5 Standardized Test Prep

The Law of Cosines

Multiple Choice

For Exercises 1–5, choose the correct letter.

1. What is length x to the nearest tenth?

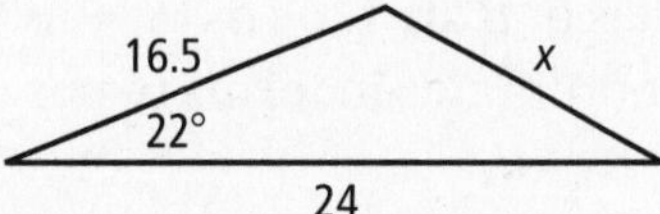

Ⓐ 10.7 Ⓒ 39.8

Ⓑ 21.9 Ⓓ 113.9

2. What is measure x to the nearest tenth?

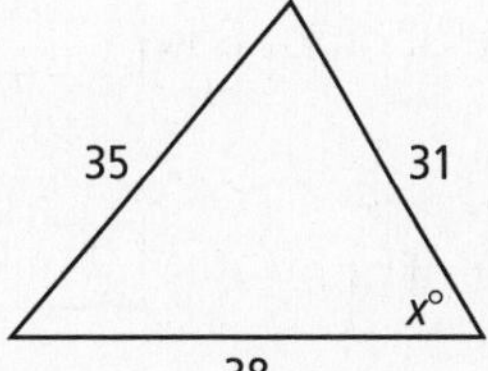

Ⓕ 7.7° Ⓗ 59.9°

Ⓖ 50.1° Ⓘ 70.0°

3. What is length x to the nearest tenth?

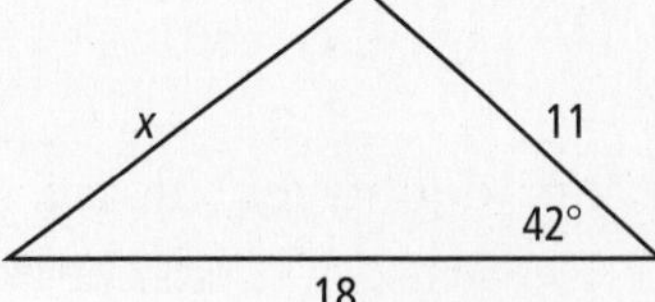

Ⓐ 27.2 Ⓒ 13.4

Ⓑ 17.3 Ⓓ 12.3

4. What is measure x to the nearest tenth?

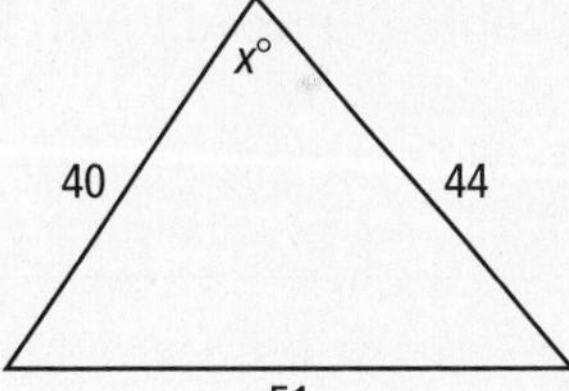

Ⓕ 36.5° Ⓗ 56.3°

Ⓖ 49.1° Ⓘ 74.6°

5. In $\triangle ABC$, $a = 20$, $b = 12$, and $c = 30$. What is the area of $\triangle ABC$ to the nearest tenth?

Ⓐ 75.5 units^2 Ⓑ 80.5 units^2 Ⓒ 85 units^2 Ⓓ 95 units^2

Short Response

6. Find the remaining side and angles in the triangle.

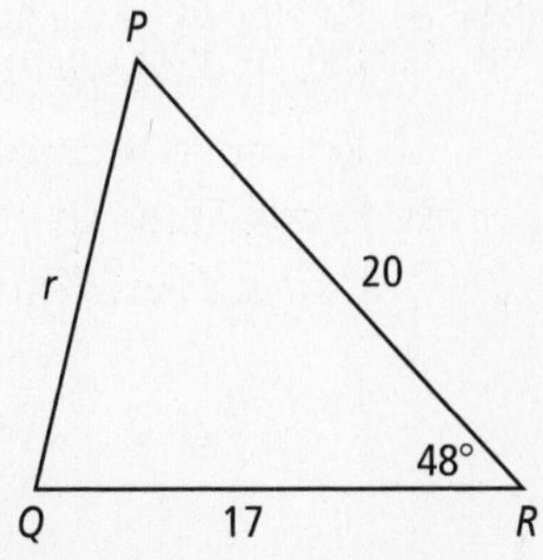

Name ____________________ Class __________ Date __________

14-6 Think About a Plan

Angle Identities

Gears The diagram at the right shows a gear whose radius is 10 cm. Point A represents a 60° counterclockwise rotation of point $P(10, 0)$. Point B represents a θ-degree rotation of point A. The coordinates of B are $(10 \cos(\theta + 60°), 10 \sin(\theta + 60°))$. Write these coordinates in terms of $\cos\theta$ and $\sin\theta$.

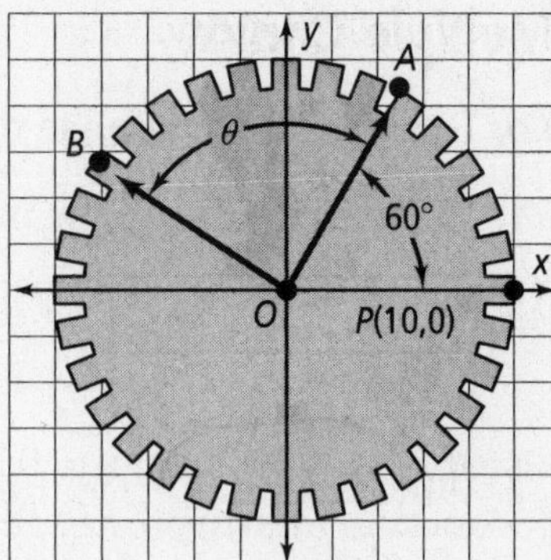

Know

1. The x-coordinate of point B is ______.

2. The y-coordinate of point B is ______.

3. The angle sum identity for cosine is ______.

4. The angle sum identity for sine is ______.

Need

5. To solve the problem, I need to:

____

______________________________.

Plan

6. What should you substitute for A and B in the angle sum identities? ______

7. Write the x-coordinate in terms of $\cos\theta$ and $\sin\theta$. ______

8. Write the y-coordinate in terms of $\cos\theta$ and $\sin\theta$. ______

Name ______________________ Class ____________ Date ____________

14-6 Practice

Form G

Angle Identities

Verify each identity.

1. $\cot\left(\theta - \frac{\pi}{2}\right) = -\tan\theta$

2. $\sin\left(\theta - \frac{\pi}{2}\right) = -\cos\theta$

3. $\cos\left(\theta - \frac{\pi}{2}\right) = \sin\theta$

4. $\sec\left(\theta - \frac{\pi}{2}\right) = \csc\theta$

Use the definitions of the trigonometric ratios for a right triangle to derive a cofunction identity for each expression.

5. $\cot(90^\circ - A)$

6. $\cos(90^\circ - A)$

Solve each trigonometric equation for θ with $0 \leq \theta < 2\pi$.

7. $2\sin\left(\frac{\pi}{2} - \theta\right)\tan\theta = 1$

8. $\cos\left(\frac{\pi}{2} - \theta\right)\tan\theta - \sec(-\theta) = 1$

9. $\sin^2\theta + \cos^2\theta = \tan\theta$

10. $2\sin^2\theta = \sin(-\theta)$

11. $\sqrt{3}\cos\left(\frac{\pi}{2} - \theta\right) = \cos(-\theta)$

12. $\cot\left(\frac{\pi}{2} - \theta\right) = \sin\theta$

13. $\csc\left(\frac{\pi}{2} - \theta\right) = \tan\theta$

14. $2\cos\left(\frac{\pi}{2} - \theta\right) = \tan(-\theta)$

15. $\csc^2\theta - \cot^2\theta = 2\cos\theta$

16. $\sin\left(\theta - \frac{\pi}{2}\right)\cos\theta = 0$

Mental Math Find the value of each trigonometric expression.

17. $\sin 10^\circ \cos 80^\circ + \cos 10^\circ \sin 80^\circ$

18. $\cos 110^\circ \cos 70^\circ - \sin 110^\circ \sin 70^\circ$

19. $\sin 310^\circ \cos 130^\circ - \cos 310^\circ \sin 130^\circ$

20. $\cos 95^\circ \cos 50^\circ + \sin 95^\circ \sin 50^\circ$

Name ______________________ Class ____________ Date ____________

14-6 Practice (continued) Form G

Angle Identities

Find each exact value. Use a sum or difference identity.

21. $\sin 240°$

22. $\tan(-300°)$

23. $\sin(-105°)$

24. $\cos 15°$

25. $\sin 15°$

26. $\sin 135°$

27. $\cos 225°$

28. $\tan 225°$

29. $\tan 240°$

30. $\cos 390°$

31. $\sin(-300°)$

32. $\tan(-75°)$

Verify each identity.

33. $\frac{1 - \cos\theta}{\sin\theta} = \frac{\sin\theta}{1 + \cos\theta}$

34. $\frac{1 + \tan\theta}{1 + \cot\theta} = \frac{\sin\theta}{\cos\theta}$

35. Which of the following is equivalent to $\sin\theta + \cot\theta\cos\theta$?

(A) $2\sin\theta$

(B) $\frac{1}{\sin\theta}$

(C) $\cos^2\theta$

(D) $\frac{\sin\theta + \cos\theta}{\sin^2\theta}$

36. Error Analysis A student found the exact value of cos 30° using the fact that $30° = 90° - 60°$ and got $\frac{1}{2}$. What was his error?

37. Reasoning Explain how you can use the identity for $\cos(A - B)$ to simplify $\cos(-\theta)$.

Name ______________________ Class ____________ Date ____________

14-6 Standardized Test Prep

Angle Identities

Multiple Choice

For Exercises 1–5, choose the correct letter.

1. Which of the following expressions are equivalent?

I. $\sin(-\theta)$ **II.** $-\sin\theta$ **III.** $-\sin(\pi - \theta)$

(A) I and II only (B) I and III only (C) II and III only (D) I, II, and III

2. Which of the following is a solution to $\tan(\theta + \pi) + 2\sin(\theta + \pi) = 0$?

(F) 0 (G) $\frac{\pi}{2}$ (H) $\frac{2\pi}{3}$ (I) $\frac{7\pi}{4}$

3. Which expression is equivalent to $\tan 75°$?

(A) $\frac{\tan 135° + \tan 60°}{1 - \tan 135° \tan 60°}$

(B) $\frac{\tan 30° - \tan 45°}{1 + \tan 30° \tan 45°}$

(C) $\frac{\tan 30° + \tan 45°}{1 - \tan 30° \tan 45°}$

(D) $\frac{\tan 60° - \tan 135°}{1 - \tan 60° \tan 135°}$

4. Which is the exact value of $\cos(-105°)$?

(F) $\frac{\sqrt{2} - \sqrt{6}}{4}$ (G) –1.05 (H) $\frac{-\sqrt{2} + \sqrt{6}}{4}$ (I) 1.05

5. Which of the following expressions are equivalent?

I. $\sin 2\theta \cos\theta + \cos 2\theta \sin\theta$ **II.** $\cos 3\theta$ **III.** $\sin 3\theta$

(A) I and II only (B) I and III only (C) II and III only (D) I, II, and III

Short Response

6. What is the solution to $\sin\left(\theta + \frac{\pi}{4}\right) + \sin\left(\theta - \frac{\pi}{4}\right) = 0$ for $0 \le \theta < 2\pi$? Show your work.

Name ______________________ Class ____________ Date ____________

14-7 Think About a Plan

Double-Angle and Half-Angle Identities

$\triangle RST$ has a right angle at T. Use identities to show that the equation is true.

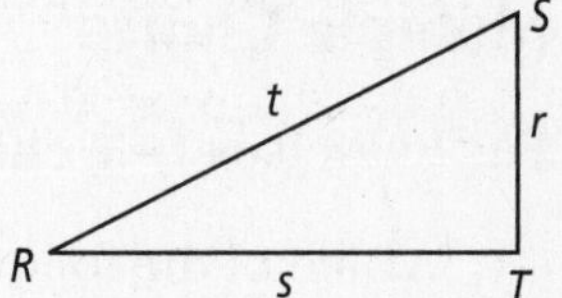

$$\tan \frac{R}{2} = \frac{r}{t + s}$$

1. The half-angle identity for the tangent function is [ ]

2. Write $\tan \frac{R}{2}$ using the half-angle identity. $\tan \frac{R}{2} =$ [ ]

3. You can multiply the numerator and denominator by an expression so that the numerator is a Pythagorean identity. What is that expression?

4. Rewrite $\tan \frac{R}{2}$ by multiplying the numerator and denominator by your expression.

$\tan \frac{R}{2} =$ [ ]

5. Eliminate the square root. $\tan \frac{R}{2} =$ [ ]

6. How can you replace the trigonometric functions of R by side lengths?

____.

7. Substitute for the trigonometric functions and simplify your expression for $\tan \frac{R}{2}$.

$\tan \frac{R}{2} =$ [ ]

Name ______________________ Class ____________ Date ____________

14-7 Practice

Form G

Double-Angle and Half-Angle Identities

Use an angle sum identity to derive each double-angle identity.

1. $\cos 2\theta = \cos^2\theta - \sin^2\theta$

2. $\cos 2\theta = 2\cos^2\theta - 1$

3. $\cos 2\theta = 1 - 2\sin^2\theta$

4. $\sin 2\theta = 2\sin\theta\cos\theta$

Use a double-angle identity to find the exact value of each expression.

5. $\sin 120^\circ$

6. $\tan 600^\circ$

7. $\sin 660^\circ$

8. $\cos 660^\circ$

9. $\tan 90^\circ$

10. $\cos 90^\circ$

11. $\tan 660^\circ$

12. $\sin 240^\circ$

13. $\tan 120^\circ$

Use a half-angle identity to find the exact value of each expression.

14. $\cos 15^\circ$

15. $\cos 7.5^\circ$

16. $\tan 7.5^\circ$

17. $\sin 7.5^\circ$

18. $\cos 45^\circ$

19. $\tan 22.5^\circ$

20. $\cos 22.5^\circ$

21. $\sin 90^\circ$

22. $\cos 90^\circ$

Given $\sin\theta = \frac{7}{25}$ and $90^\circ < \theta < 180^\circ$, find the exact value of each expression.

23. $\cos\frac{\theta}{2}$

24. $\sin\frac{\theta}{2}$

25. $\tan\frac{\theta}{2}$

26. $\sec\frac{\theta}{2}$

27. $\csc\frac{\theta}{2}$

28. $\cot\frac{\theta}{2}$

Name ______________________________ Class ____________ Date ____________

14-7 Practice (continued) Form G

Double-Angle and Half-Angle Identities

Given $\cos\theta = -\frac{8}{17}$ and $180° < \theta < 270°$, find the exact value of each expression.

29. $\sin\frac{\theta}{2}$

30. $\cos\frac{\theta}{2}$

31. $\cot\frac{\theta}{2}$

32. $\tan\frac{\theta}{2}$

33. $\csc\frac{\theta}{2}$

34. $\sec\frac{\theta}{2}$

Verify each identity.

35. $\cos^2\theta = \frac{1 + \cos 2\theta}{2}$

36. $\cot\theta = \frac{\sin 2\theta}{1 - \cos 2\theta}$

37. $\tan\theta + \cot\theta = 2\csc 2\theta$

38. $\frac{\cos 2\theta}{\sin\theta\cos\theta} = \cot\theta - \tan\theta$

39. What is the exact value of $\cos 2\theta$ if $\sin\theta = \frac{-\sqrt{5}}{3}$ and $180° < \theta < 270°$?

(A) $\frac{-\sqrt{6}}{6}$ (B) $\frac{-\sqrt{30}}{6}$ (C) $\frac{-4\sqrt{5}}{9}$ (D) $\frac{-1}{9}$

40. A scanner takes thermal images from altitudes of 300 to 12,000 m. The width W of the swath covered by the image is given by $W = 2H'\tan\theta$, where H' is the height and θ is half the scanner's field of view. Verify that $\frac{2H'\sin 2\theta}{1 + \cos 2\theta} = 2H'\tan\theta$.

Name ______________________ Class ____________ Date ____________

14-7 Standardized Test Prep

Double-Angle and Half-Angle Identities

Multiple Choice

For Exercises 1–5, choose the correct letter.

1. What is the exact value of the expression tan 105°?

(A) $\sqrt{3} + 2$ (B) $\frac{\sqrt{3}}{2}$ (C) $-\sqrt{3} - 2$ (D) $-\frac{\sqrt{3}}{2}$

2. What is the exact value of the expression cos 67.5°?

(F) $\sqrt{1 - \sqrt{2}}$ (G) $\frac{\sqrt{2 - \sqrt{2}}}{2}$ (H) $\sqrt{1 + \sqrt{2}}$ (I) $\frac{\sqrt{2 + \sqrt{2}}}{2}$

3. If θ is in Quadrant II and $\tan\theta = -\sqrt{3}$, what is an exact value of $\tan 2\theta$?

(A) $-\frac{1}{2}$ (B) $\frac{1}{2}$ (C) $-\sqrt{3}$ (D) $\sqrt{3}$

4. If θ is in Quadrant IV and $\cos\theta = \frac{1}{3}$, what is the exact value of $\cos\frac{\theta}{2}$?

(F) $-\frac{\sqrt{2}}{2}$ (G) $\frac{1}{2}$ (H) $-\frac{\sqrt{3}}{6}$ (I) $-\frac{\sqrt{6}}{3}$

5. What is the exact value of the expression sin 112.5°?

(A) $\frac{\sqrt{\sqrt{2} + 2}}{2}$ (B) $\sqrt{2} + 1$ (C) $\frac{\sqrt{\sqrt{2} - 2}}{2}$ (D) $\sqrt{2} - 1$

Short Response

6. Verify the identity $\frac{\sin 2\theta}{1 - \cos 2\theta} = \cot\theta$.